SIR RICHARD GRENVILLE
OF THE *REVENGE*
AN ELIZABETHAN HERO

D1493417

Sir Richard Granville, killed
in a sea-fight near the Azores.
1591

SIR RICHARD GRENVILLE.

SIR RICHARD GRENVILLE
OF THE *REVENGE*
AN ELIZABETHAN HERO

BY

A. L. ROWSE
FELLOW OF ALL SOULS COLLEGE, OXFORD

'That memorable fight of an English ship called
the Revenge . . . memorable (I say) even beyond
credit, and to the height of some heroical fable.'

BACON

65808

ERITH
PUBLIC LIBRARIES

JONATHAN CAPE
THIRTY BEDFORD SQUARE
LONDON

FIRST PUBLISHED JUNE 1937
SECOND IMPRESSION, SEPTEMBER 1937

Grenville, Sir Richard (b c. 1541 d 1591)
Seaman

JONATHAN CAPE LTD., 30 BEDFORD SQUARE, LONDON
AND 91 WELLINGTON STREET WEST, TORONTO

920
GRE

65808

46576
B

17 OCT 1960

BEXLEY LIBRARY
Acc. No.   Erith
45638   P.L.
17 oct 1960
942·055 GRE

PRINTED IN GREAT BRITAIN
BY BUTLER AND TANNER LTD., FROME AND LONDON
BOUND BY A. W. BAIN AND CO. LTD.
PAPER MADE BY JOHN DICKINSON AND CO. LTD.

TO

Q,

A GREAT CORNISHMAN,
MY FIRST AND CONSTANT ADMIRATION,
WITH AFFECTION

CONTENTS

ILLUSTRATIONS

The device on the binding is the Grenville crest

PREFACE

A curious fate has befallen the memory of Sir Richard Grenville. I suppose his is one of the best-known names, not only among Elizabethan west-countrymen, but of all the great fighting-men of that age, the heroic age in our history. He has become, partly no doubt owing to Ralegh's magnificent prose and Tennyson's ballad, but still more owing to some quality in the man and in his death, a mythical figure in the tradition of the English people. A household name; and yet, as is the way with mythical figures, very little has been known about his life, except for his manner of leaving it, the famous last fight of the *Revenge* in the Azores, and not even for certain about that. Perhaps this book may in part dispel the myth and make him more real as a man.

But it is no accident that so little should have been known about his life hitherto. For an extraordinary series of mischances has destroyed, so far as one can gather, all the original documents of a personal and family character, which should have remained in private hands. No doubt the end of the male-line of Grenvilles in the eighteenth century, and the division of the inheritance, had its effect. Then the pulling down of the old house at Stowe by the Earl of Bath in 1679, and the destruction of the great new house he built, by the egregious Countess Granville in 1720, must have meant a great dispersion and destruction of documents. There is the curious story told by Baring-Gould in his *Hawker of Morwenstow,* how Hawker found a chest of letters remaining at Stowe farm and sent them up to Lord Carteret, but somehow they got lost: Canon Granville says that he consigned them to the flames as the best thing to do with old documents. I found myself on going to Bideford, where there should have been a great deal of Grenville material among the town muniments, that they had been destroyed by some miserable

9

town clerk in the last century. A warning to leave old houses and archives undisturbed!

The result is that to reconstruct the life of Grenville one is thrown back upon such printed sources as there are, and the documents in public archives, without the aid, the delicious aid, of private and familiar correspondence. I remember Sir John Squire, who once had the intention of writing the life of Grenville, telling me that it could not be done.

But in the course of several years of research, I have had the good fortune to make a number of new discoveries, some of them exciting, and all of them helping to round out and present at length a fairly full portrait of the man there was behind the myth. A charming diary of an Elizabethan Cornish gentleman, William Carnsew, lurking in a quiet corner of the Public Record Office, has yielded several personal glimpses of Grenville. The Patent Roll revealed a wholly unsuspected and most exciting story that must have gone out of mind with Grenville's own generation, of the man he killed in an affray in the streets of London, when still in his minority: his first appearance upon the public scene. I have at last tracked down the date of Grenville's birth, which is of the more value since those of so many other Elizabethan seamen, Drake among them, remain unknown. Further new material from English sources adds to our knowledge at a good many points.

The yield from the Spanish archives has been even more exciting. Hitherto we have had to depend for our knowledge of the action off Flores upon English sources, none of them first hand. It is not surprising that the action has always remained something of a mystery. But I have had the inestimable good fortune to track down in Spanish archives an actual first-hand account of the battle from on board one of the Spanish ships, an official account, objective, reliable, matter of fact. This will, I hope, go far to disperse the mystery that has always overhung that famous fight.

Other Spanish documents brought to light give us new information about Grenville's doings in the West Indies on his way out to the planting of the first English colony in America, the Virginia colony of 1585–6; and an account from the Spanish side of his capture of a rich Spanish prize off the Bermudas on his way home. We derive from this account of a captured Portuguese merchant a close-up of Grenville as captor: a great Elizabethan gentleman at sea, served upon silver, who ate to the sound of music, as Drake did upon his voyage round the world. Other documents again, Spanish and English, throw light upon Grenville's great project for a Pacific voyage, four years before Drake actually sailed upon his, and upon the curious state of relations, half rivalry, half mutual-exclusion, that existed between Grenville and Drake.

It is a pleasure to acknowledge so many kindnesses and so much help received on every hand. To the Dowager Lady Seaton, the representative of the Drakes, I am indebted for much kindness and help at Buckland Abbey, as also to Sir Hugh Stucley and Miss E. F. Stucley who helped me greatly at Bideford and at Stowe. From representatives of the Grenfells, Miss Maud Grenfell and Mrs. W. H. Buckler, I have had much kindness and encouragement. To Miss I. A. Wright, of Seville, I am most indebted for tracing and having transcribed a number of Spanish documents, and to Mrs. Charles Henderson for helping me with their translation.

I wish to thank Mr. R. Pearse Chope, whose articles in the *Transactions of the Devonshire Association* (1917) laid the foundation for subsequent study of Grenville, and Dr. J. A. Williamson, whose studies have carried our knowledge a stage further, both of whom have aided me much in discussion. Dr. V. T. Harlow drew my attention to a new and important aspect of Grenville's projected Pacific Voyage and helped me with valuable suggestions. I am much obliged to the Deputy Town Clerk of Plymouth who permitted me to research among the admirably-kept archives of the town; to the Rector of Kilkhampton, the Rev. R. Dew, who kindly searched his early Register for me; and to the Vicar of Buckland Monachorum who allowed me to see his parish register. My debt to the tolerant and helpful officials at the Record Office and at the British Museum is a very great one; in particular I should like to acknowledge the aid I have been given at every stage by Mr. J. R. Crompton of the Record Office. I have reason to be very grateful to the Bodleian and Codrington Libraries at Oxford, to the Institute of Historical Research in London and to Mr. J. Hirschfield who has helped me over the Court of Wards. To Miss N. McN. O'Farrell and Miss P. Schrader I am grateful for much help in transcribing documents and for many helpful suggestions.

I cannot sufficiently acknowledge what I owe to Professor J. E. Neale, who has read the whole of my manuscript with a kindly severity, saved me from several errors and indicated innumerable improvements. All I can say is that if he should read this book again, he will see something of what I owe to him. My greatest obligation is to my college, which has enabled me for some years now to pursue my researches into west-country history in the sixteenth century, of which the fruit is in part this book.

My best thanks are due to my friends Mr. K. B. McFarlane, Fellow of Magdalen, and Mr. G. F. Hudson, Fellow of All Souls, who have been so good as to read the proofs.

A. L. ROWSE

ALL SOULS COLLEGE,
    OXFORD

SIR RICHARD GRENVILLE
OF THE *REVENGE*
AN ELIZABETHAN HERO

CHAPTER I

THE GRENVILLES AND THEIR COUNTRY

*From the Conquest to the Restoration your Ancestors con-
stantly resided amongst their country men, except when the
public service called upon them to sacrifice their lives for it.*
GEORGE GRANVILLE (later Lord Lansdowne)
to the third Earl of Bath, 1710

IF you look at a map of the West Country, by which I mean
especially Devon and Cornwall, and notice where the peninsula
thickens out to its broadest between the Bristol and the English
Channel, along the northern strip of coast between Bude and
Bideford, that great high tableland that thrusts out into the sea,
you will find what was once the Grenville country. For a short
time, too, for some forty years in the middle of the sixteenth century, the Grenvilles possessed land in the south of the peninsula,
Buckland Abbey, and were very familiar with the country between Yelverton and the gates of Plymouth. But that was a
mere episode in the long story of their settlement on the northern
coast, going back perhaps to the Conquest and certainly to not
long after.

Their family life for centuries revolved round the twin centres
of Stowe, in the parish of Kilkhampton, across the Cornish
border, and the town of Bideford in Devon; the years, the ages
were filled with their comings and goings across the high ground
and the moors, along the lanes and in and out of the valleys,
between the one and the other. They are all gone now, as the
Godolphins have gone from their lonely deserted house with the
granite colonnade and the overgrown terraces, not far from the
Land's End, or their cousins the Eriseys from the charming
Caroline house near the Lizard, or the Killigrews from Arwen-

15

nack overlooking Falmouth Haven. Of the Grenvilles, even less remains. At Stowe there is only a farm-house, built on the site of the old stables, and the level spaces where their successive houses stood looking down upon the woods of Coombe, and beyond to the tower of Kilkhampton church upon the skyline, now silver in the sun, now grey with the shadows of clouds passing and re-passing; while at Bideford, men cannot tell you for sure where it was that the Grenvilles' town house stood upon the quay. Only the country remains, not so very different in its essential lines, having suffered less change than they.

To those who know it, it is a singularly impressive country, having more a character of its own than, if possible, any other tract in all the West Country. Some may think it a forbidding character, as certainly the coast is savage in the extreme. For forty miles those limestone and shale cliffs run, tortured into fantastic shapes, with horizontal reefs pushing jagged-edged out to sea, among which no boat could live with any sea running, the cliffs going up to six and seven hundred feet high, the full beat of the Atlantic upon them, and not a harbour from Padstow to Bideford, except that cleft in the coast at Boscastle, the tortuous snake-like entry, the jade-green waters. No wonder the old couplet goes:

'From Padstow Bar to Lundy Light
Is a sailor's grave, by day or night:'

– so many hundreds of good men have found it so.

The interior, when it is not too high and windswept (for much of it is a high tableland), is fertile and good corn-growing land, with much pasture. Stowe itself, though not far in from the coast, is well-placed upon just such a strip of good farming land, turning its back to the sea and high up on the edge of the deep valley of Coombe, which runs inwards from its mouth near Steeple Point almost to Kilkhampton. These deep clefts are very characteristic of the country; the high ground as it gets towards the sea is broken into a number of transverse valleys, each of them with its stream, a few narrow meadows rich with grass, and in spring exquisite with the first and fullest primroses and spring violets. There is Coombe, very narrow and steep, which from the time of the Grenvilles seems to have been wooded; then there are the valleys of Marsland Mouth and Welcombe; next, Speke's Mill Mouth, with its trout-stream and waterfall to the sea; and lastly, Hartland the most fertile and beautiful of them all, after which the coast from going due north breaks away to the east and changes in character. It becomes less severe; and so with the interior – as you move away from the high ground near the western coast, you get on to the downward slope of the tableland towards Woolfardisworthy and Bradworthy, the vale of the Torridge, and so on to Parkham and Abbotsham and into Bideford, country altogether more fertile, more gracious and homely.

The origin of the family is, as these things often are, clothed in obscurity. Not the less so, either, for the inflated and somewhat baroque story of their illustrious descent from the Norman Earls of Corbeil, which became current in the days of their triumph at the Restoration, served their advance in the peerage under Charles II, and consoled the last days of Denis Granville the Dean, in exile at St. Germains. Dr. J. H. Round concentrated all the resources of his scholarship upon what he described as 'the great Granville story.' [1] He maintains the view that the family derives not from that Richard de Grainville, the founder of Neath Abbey about 1129, whom they looked upon as the beginner of its fortunes in England, but from the more obscure Robert, who witnessed the Abbey's Foundation charter. But not all Dr. Round's erosive scholarship could deny that the Grenvilles were Normans, and that they came raiding out of Normandy very early on – earlier, for example, than the Courtenays or the Arundells – if not with the Conqueror himself. What we do know for certain is that as early as Henry II's reign, a Grenville held half a knight's fee in Bideford, and this is the real starting-point of our knowledge of them in the west. [2]

They then held of the honour of Gloucester ; and, according to Round, these Devonshire lands of that honour, Bideford, Littleham and Ash, had before been held by Mathilde, wife of the Conqueror, and before that by the Saxon Briktric. By the

---

[1] J. H. Round, *Family Origins* : 'The Granvilles and the Monks.'
[2] Granville, *History of the Granville Family*, 31.

twelfth year of Henry II, a Richard de Grenville is holding three knights' fees and a half in Devon and Cornwall – so, for the first time extending across the border into Cornwall. From that time onwards, for some five hundred years, there were Grenvilles settled here. At Stowe throughout the later Middle Ages they lived, in no spectacular fashion, cultivating their lands, adding acre to acre and field to field, serving the King in his wars, keeping the King's peace as justices for Devon and Cornwall, frequently being in the Commissions for both, sometimes breaking the peace themselves or resisting authority, for the most part quiet enough in the labour of their lives, begetting their children, providing for them, so that generation after generation, whatever else might befall, the family should go on.

They were not a very distinguished lot, nor was the family at all important outside the sphere of its immediate influence. The highest flight that they attained to, was to produce an Archbishop of York (William Grenville, Archbishop 1304–15). The Grenvilles were very much the ordinary run of country gentry of the fourteenth and fifteenth centuries, marrying into western families of similar position. They married Courtenays of Haccombe and of Powderham; Arundells of Lanherne and Trerice (those two lovely Tudor houses yet remaining, again not far from the sea on the north Cornish coast); Vyvyans and St. Aubyns; Devonshire Gilberts and Bonvilles. But other western families far surpassed them in wealth – the Courtenays, for instance, who coming out of France rather later, among the court-following of Eleanor of Aquitaine, married the Redvers heiress and later entered the ranks of the nobility as Earls of Devon; or the Cornish Arundells, who by a succession of provident marriages, became the first and wealthiest family in Cornwall.

The Grenvilles remained of no great possessions, though they retained their special relation to the town of Bideford, of which they were overlords. Here also they added to their possession of house-property, and the town's trade must have been a source of mobile wealth to them. In the fifteenth century, in the affairs of the country at large, they were content to be followers of the Earls of Devon and with them were adherents of the Lancas-

trian cause – as indeed most western families were. Thomas
Grenville and Richard Edgcumbe of Cotehele were involved
with the Courtenays in the conspiracy of Buckingham against
Richard III. The story of Edgcumbe's hiding in the woods of
Cotehele, down the steep sides of the gorge of the Tamar, until
he could get away to Brittany and Henry of Richmond, is well
known. The Courtenays also fled, and Thomas Grenville,
being then very young, lay low for a time.

When the Lancastrian cause won at Bosworth and Henry
VII became king, the prospects of these faithful west-country
followers improved accordingly. The Courtenays were restored to their wide lands and married into the Yorkist Royal
line: it proved, after a period of great splendour in the blaze of
royal favour, to be their undoing. Sir Richard Edgcumbe became Comptroller of the Royal Household and, an intimate
friend of Henry's, was rewarded with the large estates of the
Cornish Yorkist Sir Henry Bodrugan: the foundation of their
greatness to this day in the west. Thomas Grenville gained
nothing like so much. He was made an Esquire of the Body to
Henry VII, a position of personal attendance which was not
without its opportunities; a similar position held at about the
same time by David Cecil, Burghley's grandfather, made the
family fortunes of the Cecils.

Whether it was a reluctance to live away from the west, at
Court, or a premature appreciation of the joys of matrimony,
Thomas Grenville made no such career for himself. He lived on
in the west, twice married, begetting his children (no less than
ten of them lived to be provided for), serving as Sheriff for
Cornwall, coming up to the Court from time to time, once, we
know, on the occasion of the marriage of Prince Arthur with
Catherine of Aragon – a great event, harbinger of what later
troubles! It was then that he was made a Knight of the Bath.
But he soon returned to the west, where he died on March 18,
1513, and now lies buried in his fine tomb of white limestone
in the church of Bideford. He had bequeathed his 'body to be
buried in the church earth of Bideford, in the south-east part of
the chancel door, where my mind is if I live to make an altar
and a priest to sing there to pray for me and mine ancestors and

heirs for ever.' Alas, for man's hopes to put a stay to time passing!

There he is, looking down at us out of time, the first Grenville whom we seem to hear and recognise across the centuries as a person, for in those words we listen to his last wishes, face to face with death.

II

We are now well over the threshold of the sixteenth century – the formative period of modern England, in which English society came to be constituted upon the foundations we know. It was a time of the rise of the gentry as a class, of the lesser landed interest as a dominating factor in the national life. Two factors chiefly aided it. The value of land was increasing, as again in the eighteenth century; so that those whose wealth was in land and the cultivation of it for themselves, rather than in money or fixed rents and services, were on the upgrade of power.

A second factor which enormously strengthened the trend in favour of the landed classes was the Reformation, the dispersion of church lands. The steady rain of Church-property which fell upon the thirsty ground all through this century, in the end benefited most, not the nobility or the Crown, so much as the lesser landed gentry. Lands often slipped through the fingers of the greater courtiers; when it was not by extravagance or inadvertence there was the convenient process of attainder to help it: some of the greatest collections of monastic property were broken up in this way. But when an attractive manor, or some morsels of a small religious house came into the hands of a family living close to the soil itself, cultivating its own land, struggling to keep its head above water and to provide for its all too numerous progeny, property had a habit of remaining there. This meant a tremendous afforcement of power to the gentry as a class; for where in so many English villages before the Reformation there were no lords but the distant monks in their abbeys, the hours slipping lazily through their fingers over their prayers or their provender, now every village came to have its squire, greedy of power, having to make his way in the world, energetic, hard, pushing. The Grenvilles were carried up on this tide, like so many others, their cousins and friends; while the Courtenays and the Cornish Arundells went down.

But personal factors were at work in the process as well. Whatever the reason, and nothing is more mysterious in life than this, a new and active strain, of immense and passionate energy, came into the family in the sixteenth century. It may be that the two things, the historical circumstances and the psychological response, are functions of each other; for it is striking, how in history an upward-moving cause elicits ability and energy, while that on the downgrade is often accompanied by stupidity and listlessness. Perhaps the family generates energy as the opportunity is presented to it. Certain it is that the Grenvilles, a family hitherto of no particular consequence, suddenly throws up a number of remarkable and forceful characters, who over several generations push the family into a position of prominence, whence, after a time the energy lapses, and it sinks back again.

Amid the diversity of their characteristics, a certain dominant streak is observable: a harsh domineering note, proud in the extreme, unyielding, betraying signs of overstrain and un-balance, forceful, highly strung, bent on action, capable of the uttermost devotion; above all, exciting. It comes out, though not so harshly, in Sir Richard Grenville the elder, Marshal of Calais, more noticeably in the case of his aunt, Honor Gren-ville, Lady Lisle; it reaches its apex with the extraordinary character and career of Sir Richard Grenville of the *Revenge*; it is accentuated, but debased, in the person of the third Sir Richard, of the Civil War, whose character may be said to have gone to shipwreck on it.

Other characteristics there were too: a generous disregard of consequences in any course that they embarked upon, that was not incompatible with a practical hard-headed turn of mind in matters of business; above all, fidelity and loyalty. In four generations following each other, a Grenville died in the service of his country: Roger, our Sir Richard's father, drowned in the *Mary Rose* at Portsmouth in 1545; Sir Richard himself mortally wounded off Flores in the Azores in the last fight of the *Revenge*; his son John died upon Ralegh's famous expedition to Guiana in 1595;[1] his grandson Sir Bevil, that Bayard of the Royalist cause, killed at Lansdown in 1643. No wonder the old Cornish proverb which says, 'a Godolphin never wanted wit' goes on to add, 'nor a Grenville loyalty.'

III

Much then as our Richard owed to his family, which reached the apex of its achievement and fame with him, his career owed still more to his age and time. Indeed, the actual character of his career, the precise shape that it traced upon the map of our history, would be unthinkable outside the circumstances of the Elizabethan age.

It was the heroic age in our history, when the nation saw great opportunities of expansion and achievement opening before it. Young, fresh, vigorous, full of self-confidence and spirit, it knew how to take them. For these very opportunities at the same time imposed a test, a test of nerve, character, intelligence. There were the complex dangers of the Reformation, a movement full of eddies and shoals; there was the difficult rôle we had to play in Europe, not without subtlety, in an exposed and sometimes isolated position; there was finally the prolonged duel with Spain that lasted all the latter part of the Queen's reign. It was the fact that the opportunities given were so triumphantly taken, our difficulties surmounted in spite of the odds against us, that made the Elizabethan the heroic age in our history. It is an age to which in these less successful, more disillusioning times, we may well look back for inspiration and renewal.

The very opportunities that were afforded, to Drake, Hawkins, Cavendish at sea, to the Cecils in politics, to Byrd, Marlowe, Shakespeare no less in the realm of the arts or to Bacon in that of the intellect, to Ralegh and Grenville in the field of colonisation, gave the men of the time a supreme chance to realise themselves and all their potentialities.

It was in the realm of action, at its most heightened and intense moments, that the pure quality of the heroic emerges: that

---

[1] Not, as Granville says (p. 123), while serving under Drake in the West Indies.

sort of gesture by which a man goes down to posterity for something not only memorable in itself, but in which subsequent ages find significance, inspiration in its defiance, strength in its courage. It is some quality of the action in itself by which it survives, like Falkland's riding into the mêlée with 'Peace, Peace' upon his lips, or Nelson ignoring his superior's orders at Copenhagen, or walking the deck of the *Victory* at Trafalgar, blazing with medals.

Of such was Grenville's last action in the *Revenge*. There was never any fight more famous in a nation's history; never any that was more purely heroic in quality – that mixture of daredevilry, defiance of fate, supreme indifference to consequences, which men admire more than anything, because their own ordinary lives are at every point so circumscribed by circumstance, from which there is, save in such moments, no emancipation.

This book then has some contemporary significance. We shall trace a career not hitherto fully recorded, of which little indeed has been known, and of which now only the outline of its traces upon the track of time remains. Too little evidence remains for a portrait of the inner man; we can only build up our portrait of that from his external actions and achievements such as they are left. There are certain aspects of them, episodes in his life, that are wholly new and are here brought to light after the lapse of centuries. As regards the rest of his career, we shall trace in Grenville himself, and by reference to his family before and after, the emergence of those qualities, a creation out of diverse elements, from which the heroic at the moment of crisis sprang forth.

Nor ought we to leave altogether on one side the question of what this heroic spirit meant for that age, why it was that the Elizabethans surrounded its memory with fame. For there was a *raison d'être* in the legend which grew up about Grenville's name. The fame a man achieves is as much a function of his time as it is his own creation or desert. So active and restless a life, so heroic an end was what the Elizabethan admired and thought of for himself. He saw himself as the fighter and hero. Much as in our time Lawrence of Arabia – it is curious to think of Grenville as the Elizabethan Lawrence – expressed for so many Englishmen that latent desire for the romance of action which the conditions of contemporary life denied; though in the latter there is more in the nature of escape than the natural seeing of yourself in the mirror of a national hero.

This was the early Elizabethan Age, before disillusionment, the disenchantments of long war and weariness came down upon them. In the years spanned by Grenville's active life, the success of the voyages and the seamen opened up new worlds of mind for their contemporaries, for 'man's imagination is limited by the horizon of his experience.' [1] It was this enlargement of horizons, coinciding with the boundless confidence brought to the nation by its success upon the sea, that made the supreme triumph of the Elizabethan drama. The influence of all this, the voyages, the discoveries, the exploits and victories, upon the great literature of the time has, according to Professor Raleigh, 'been little recognised, because the reflection of contemporary events in thought and imagination is always indirect, difficult to outline, and utterly unlike common expectation.'

Yet the point can be made quite directly from Marlowe, who expressed all the spirit of this earlier time – the lust for discovery, for knowledge and power, a specific geographical excitement even, before disillusionment had come to the Elizabethans, that 'kind of weariness of institutions which pervades Shakespeare's later plays.' What is of extreme significance for us is that Marlowe was a member of Ralegh's circle no less than Grenville was, in close intellectual sympathy with Ralegh, a friend too of Harriot's. Should we not expect to find in Marlowe an expression of the common spirit in which Grenville shared?

After all, it was Grenville, not Ralegh, who led the Voyage to Virginia in 1585 which made so much impression in this immediate circle; and all Marlowe's journeying was done in those 'realms of gold,' his mind. Within the next two years Marlowe wrote his *Tamburlaine*, the real subject of which is the excitement, the lust for dominion and power which the new dis-

[1] Professor Sir Walter Raleigh, *English Voyages of the Sixteenth Century*, 152.

coveries and knowledge of the world were arousing in contemporary minds.

> Look here, my boys; see what a world of ground
> Lies westward from the midst of Cancer's line
> Unto the rising of this earthly globe,
> Whereas the sun, declining from our sight,
> Begins the day with our Antipodes!
> And shall I die, and this unconquered?
> Lo, here, my sons, are all the golden mines,
> Inestimable drugs and precious stones,
> More worth than Asia and the world beside;
> And from th' Antarctick Pole eastward behold
> As much more land, which never was descried,
> Wherein the rocks of pearl that shine as bright
> As all the lamps that beautify the sky!
> And shall I die, and this unconquered?
> Here, lovely boys; what death forbids my life,
> That let your lives command in spite of death.

It has a curious prophetic quality, when one thinks of the end of both Marlowe and Grenville within so short a time. There is no doubt of the sort of men Marlowe admired: the fighting men, the men of action, restless, for ever spurred on by passion and desire.

> Nature that framed us of four elements
> Warring within our breasts for regiment,
> Doth teach us all to have aspiring minds:
> Our souls, whose faculties can comprehend
> The wondrous architecture of the world,
> And measure every wandering planet's course,
> Still climbing after knowledge infinite,
> And always moving as the restless spheres,
> Will teach us to wear ourselves, and never rest . . .

There is the final expression of the character and spirit common to this circle, in which Grenville shared on the side of action, if not intellectually: the spirit with which they inspired the nation and for which the nation rewarded them by making it its own.

25

CHAPTER II

THE MARSHAL OF CALAIS: FROM
GRANDFATHER TO GRANDSON

Who seeks the way to win renown,
Or flies with wings of high desire;
Who seeks to wear the laurel crown,
Or hath the mind that would aspire:
Tell him his native soil eschew,
Tell him go range and seek anew.

SIR RICHARD GRENVILLE: *In Praise of Sea-faring
Men in Hopes of Good Fortune*

Two figures dominated the family history of the Grenvilles in the first half of the sixteenth century. These were Sir Richard Grenville the elder, Marshal of Calais, grandfather of our Sir Richard, who succeeded him as a minor owing to the early death of his father, Roger, the Marshal's son; and Honor Grenville, Lady Lisle, the Marshal's aunt, whose marriage to Arthur Plantagent, Lord Lisle, a natural son of Edward IV, and Lord Deputy of Calais, made her much the most exalted member of the family and brought the Grenvilles, so long as her good fortune held, into close contact with the court circle. It was a dazzling situation, not without its disappointments and its dangers.

It was to this marriage that Sir Richard owed his office as High Marshal of Calais, a military position of considerable importance at the one outpost remaining of all our former possessions upon French soil. The position of the Lord Deputy corresponded to that of a modern Viceroy or Governor-General; it was one of great state and responsibility, more especially the latter in these last years of English rule. So long as the Lisles

26

and their nephew Grenville remained at Calais – Lisle was Deputy from 1533 to 1540 – the effective centre of the family was there and Stowe remained deserted, waiting for its master to return.

Lady Lisle's good fortune did not hold for long; for after seven years in high office, a sudden blow descended upon her husband, as upon so many other persons in the storms of Henry VIII's later years. Lisle was summoned from Calais, and sent to the Tower, where he ended his days after two years of imprisonment. All his correspondence was impounded, and so we come by the *Lisle Papers*, which form a sort of *Paston Letters* for the reign of Henry VIII, in many ways more intimate and revealing than those. From it we derive a most detailed and attractive picture of the life of that society; what is more important for us, it portrays the characters of members of the family circle fully and personally, in a way not possible before, nor for very long after.

But, first, for the family succession at Stowe. Lady Lisle's father, and the Marshal's grandfather, was that Sir Thomas with whom we crossed the threshold of the sixteenth century, the first Grenville of whom we have a personal glimpse. He left behind him a mass of children; among others, two sons, Roger his heir and John who was destined for the Church. Of the daughters, Katherine married Sir John Arundell of Lanherne, a very successful match for her, the richest in the county. But we do not hear anything more of her in connection with the family at Stowe, and later there was not much love lost between the Grenvilles and the Arundells. Jane, the eldest daughter, married Sir John Arundell of Trerice, with whose family the Grenvilles remained on the friendliest terms. Unlike the people at Lanherne, who remained straightest and most unyielding of Catholics, the Trerice Arundells went hand-in-hand with the Grenvilles in sympathy with the Reformation and with the new trends in national policy. A third daughter, Agnes, married John Roscarrock. Later we shall find that there was great friendship between our Sir Richard, the younger, and his cousins at Roscarrock, where we find him frequently paying visits. Though the Roscarrocks have all gone now, something of their house remains, an oriel window high up under the roof, a little cramped Tudor courtyard, hidden behind the Georgian front of a farm-house, lying among the same wide placid fields, the sea-gulls coming in from the coast, and from above the house, the view away to Pentire Head and the mouth of Padstow haven.

Sir Thomas had willed his son John, 'if he be disposed to be a priest, to have the next avoidance of one of the benefices of Bideford or of Kilkhampton.' He was fortunately so disposed, and thus Kilkhampton came by its Rector (1524–80) who remained in possession throughout all the changes of the Reformation, under seven Bishops of Exeter, Catholic and Protestant, under Henry VIII, Edward VI, Mary and well into the reign of Elizabeth. While still a student at Oxford, he was presented to the family living; later on, in 1536, he was given that of Launcells, Morwenstow in 1541, and Week St. Mary in 1558. Altogether he must have had a comfortable time. A trusty servant of the great lady his sister, wrote to her when Latimer and Shaxton resigned their bishoprics: 'they be not of the wisest sort methinks, for few nowadays will leave and give over such promotions for keeping of opinion.' [1] That must have been much what John Grenville thought.

What he did with all his time we do not certainly know. Perhaps he gave himself up to the pleasures of avuncularity, for Richard Carew, that delightful antiquary, says: 'Sir John Chamond was uncle and great-uncle to at least 300, wherein yet his uncle and neighbour, Master Grenville, Parson of Kilkhampton, did exceed him.' [2] The Grenvilles were a prolific lot at this time, but on the whole not long-lived. The Rector's long span must have meant that he came at the end to represent the family's continuity more than any other of its numerous figures. Four generations of Grenvilles passed before him; he must have been a very familiar figure, part of the landscape at Kilkhampton, to his great-great-nephew, our Sir Richard. When he came at length to die, in 1580, most of the younger Sir Richard's career was over: it was only some eleven years away from that fatal day in the Azores.

[1] *L. and P.*, XIV, part 1, 220. [2] Carew, *Survey of Cornwall* (1811), 279.

Parson John's elder brother, Sir Roger, did not reign long at Stowe, only from 1513 to 1523 – so short a time, indeed, that one wonders how he came by the title 'the great housekeeper' with which his descendant endows him.[1] He seems to have spent all his time in the west, taking more than his share of local responsibilities, for he was three times Sheriff, in 1510, 1518, and 1522. Like his father he begot a large family of children. It must have been something of a strain to settle them all, and the marriages his children made were on a more homely level than those of the previous generation. Nobody repeated the perilous experiment in grandeur of their aunt, Lady Lisle. They married Cornish Eriseys, Bevils and Tremaynes, Devonshire Fitzes and Specotts. Sir Roger himself left home on one occasion for a celebrated, a too celebrated event, since we find his name among the Cornish gentlemen attending the King to the Field of the Cloth of Gold. That was in 1520. On 21 July, 1523, we find his son Richard, Sewer of the Chamber, named as Sheriff of Cornwall in place of his father, who had died in his year of office, evidently unexpectedly.[2] He was only forty-six. And Richard his son reigned in his stead.

Richard very early got down to the duties of his position. The fact that he held the office of Sewer of the Chamber meant that already as a young man he was acquainted with the Court; his subsequent career brought him still more closely into contact. But first he turned his attention to Cornwall. He was one of the Commissioners to collect the subsidy there, next year; he was Sheriff in 1526, and in 1529 was chosen knight of the shire. Along with Sir Piers Edgcumbe, he was returned to that great Parliament which carried through the breach with Rome and with it the Reformation in England. These were years of momentous consequence for the country: one after another the cables were cut which throughout the ages had held this country to the Catholic Church. The gentry of the shires and the burgesses from the towns were consenting parties to every step that was taken, from the abolition of appeals to Rome, to the Act of Supremacy by which the process was consummated. Grenville was in all this: he served throughout that Parliament and was in

---

[1] Granville, 71.   [2] *L. and P.*, part III, no. 3214.

agreement with what it did; he helped to destroy what it destroyed, the age-long independence of the Church, and to set up what it set up, the supremacy of the Tudor monarchy.

In the early years, he passed his time partly in the west, partly in attendance on Parliament. In 1522, there was an interesting struggle between the Arundells and him for nomination as Sheriff of Devon: it is the first evidence we have of the ill-feeling between them, which was to culminate so tragically in the next generation. We find Thomas Arundell, the clever and intriguing younger son of Sir John – he had been trained as a lawyer and later married the sister of Queen Katherine Howard – writing to Cromwell: 'Pray let not Sir Richard Grenville be Sheriff of Devonshire; for sith I cannot have it myself, I am so full of charity that I would be right glad that he should go without it.' [1] A regular Tudor sentiment, and one that is understandable at all times. However, Grenville had a powerful friend at Court in Sir Francis Bryan, one of the Boleyn circle; and these were the brief days of Anne Boleyn's ascendancy. Grenville was made Sheriff; and next year, at the splendid ceremonies with which Anne's coronation was celebrated (Anne going in procession to Westminster, already big with the child that was to be Elizabeth), Sir Richard was among the Knights who served the Queen's board in Westminster Hall.

On 24 March, 1533, Sir Richard's uncle, Lord Lisle, was appointed Lord Deputy of Calais. It was an event of great importance for the family; for, from now on for the next seven years, the life of the Grenvilles centres upon Calais, being drawn there like a magnet by the position of its most exalted members. It was not long before Sir Richard followed the Lisles. He had set his heart upon the second post at Calais, after the Lord Deputy, that of High Marshal. It was one that carried with it a considerable establishment, but the getting of it cost him a large expenditure of effort and money. He paid Sir Edward Ringely some £400 for the reversion to the office, but even then there were months of difficult negotiation before Grenville could enter upon it, the path being carefully smoothed by the all-powerful Cromwell.

[1] *L. and P.*, V, no. 1553.

At length Sir Richard arrived at Calais, and was welcomed by the Lisles with open arms. As the result of an excessively jubilant celebration of his accession to office Sir Richard was ill all the early part of the New Year. There were rumours at Court of his vacating the Marshalship, and to put a stop to them he wrote to the King explaining his indisposition, 'having drunk something that troubled his stomach in my Lord Deputy's company and other of the Council at a tavern soon after Christmas.' Perhaps it was too much to expect two such forceful personalities as Lady Lisle and her nephew to get on together; but certain it is that not long after his arrival, they were on bad terms. The native quarrelsomeness of the Grenville temperament asserted itself. Sir Richard wrote to Cromwell that he had expected to find kindness at Calais, but had encountered the contrary and 'do find most in the feminine person.' [1]

It is impossible not to sympathise with Lady Lisle, not so much because she was a woman, but because she was such a gallant, high-spirited one. One cannot but admire the vitality and vigour of her personality. Through all the lapse of time, she comes to us, as so rarely, a perfectly definite human person, so ready-hearted, so busy and generous about life's affairs, so human in her affections, her troubles and sorrows. There was a warmth about her nature that drew innumerable others to her, so much so that one can read her character in the many facets of their attitude to her. It is like seeing her image reflected in a gallery of mirrors. We are fortunate to have so much of this woman's life preserved to us; we know more about her and her ways of mind and heart than of any early Tudor character, save only the greatest. She was, more than most great ladies of her time, very devout; in fact, she was rather preyed upon by her churchmen. She had a large clientèle of them, from the humble parson of St. Keverne in remotest Cornwall, to the saintly Hugh Faringdon, last Abbot of Reading, and Bishop Gardiner, a foremost figure in the land.

She was very matriarchal, too, which was not to be wondered at, considering all the little Bassets she had been left with by Sir John, her first husband, and Lord Lisle's children by his first

[1] *L. and P.*. X, no. 755.

wife, too, in addition to the wide fringe of Grenvilles extending in every direction. To one of her daughters, Anne Basset, there befell a curious momentary fate: she might have been Queen of England. Lady Lisle had obtained for her daughter a place at Court as maid-of-honour to Jane Seymour, and there she remained under Katherine Howard. After the latter's fall, it was rumoured at Court that the King's favour had fallen upon Anne; the Imperial Ambassador wrote off to Charles V that the King 'is said to have a fancy for the daughter (by her first marriage) of the wife of Lord Lisle', and describing the great banquet that he gave, with twenty-six ladies at his table, of whom Anne was one. Somehow nothing came of it, but trouble for the Lisles instead.

Lady Lisle had indeed more than her share of troubles. Her marriage to Lisle remained fruitless in spite of the great love that was between them and their fervent hopes of an heir. Lisle had no son by his first marriage and this meant that his title would become extinct with him. As against this, they were very happy in the marriage of Lisle's daughter Frances to John, Lady Lisle's eldest son, the Basset heir. John died not long after his marriage, but he left a son called Arthur after Lord Lisle, a friend and contemporary of our Sir Richard the younger, and partner in some of his enterprises.

Difficulties, public as well as private, thickened round the Lisles. Calais stood exposed to all the winds of doctrine that blew, whether from France or the Netherlands, from Rome or the obscure recesses of Germany. The place was a prey to dreary preaching Protestants and to no less dreary, but fortunately not preaching Catholics. The Council which governed Calais could scarcely govern itself, for it was divided from top to bottom between those who favoured the old and those who leaned to the new. Even the Grenville interest was divided against itself, for while Lady Lisle was a devout Catholic, Sir Richard Grenville was an opportunist and supported the Reformers. As Lisle grew older, his grip upon the administration, never very firm, grew slacker; an easy-going, good-natured old person, it was evident that he was incompetent. His position was not helped at such a time, when the religious changes were going through in England, by his wife's demon-strative attachment to Catholic practices, upon which Cranmer once and again remonstrated with her.

Things came to a head early in 1540 with an affair which made Lisle's incompetence, in such a dangerous time, look more like treason. His chaplain had been to Rome, and there had got into communication with Henry's arch-enemy, Car-dinal Pole. Lisle's Yorkist blood told against him; at once Henry and Cromwell scented a conspiracy. Lisle was sum-moned to England and sent to the Tower, where he remained for the next two years, and after surviving the imminent threat of execution, died upon the rumour of his release. Lady Lisle remained for a time in confinement, and then was allowed to retire into the country, being driven to distraction, so Foxe the martyrologist informs us, by her troubles.[1] The circle at Calais was broken for ever. Silence draws down upon them and their doings. There are no more letters with their delicious revela-tions of all the to and fro of that busy generous household. Yet Lady Lisle lived on for many years, until in fact her infant grandson, Arthur Basset, attained his majority; and that is the last that we hear of her.

II

The downfall of the Lisles did not immediately affect Sir Richard's position at Calais. He remained on, performing his duties as High Marshal which there is every reason to suppose he had competently fulfilled. Moreover, he had been careful to keep on friendly terms with Cromwell; we hear of him send-ing a leash of falcons, or making other gifts to the Lord Privy Seal. Only once was there a serious brush between them, and that was over the marriage of Grenville's daughter Margaret.

Sir Richard Lee, who had risen from the ranks as one of Cromwell's agents to be Surveyor of Calais, wished to marry into the Grenville family. But he offered nothing like such a good jointure as Mr. Tregian, one of the wealthiest men in Cornwall, had offered with his son and heir. It was an awkward

---

[1] Foxe, *Book of Martyrs*, (ed. 1583), 1223.

predicament, for the Marshal was very anxious not to offend Cromwell, and yet these were not very good terms for a Grenville to marry a Lee upon. Sir Richard hesitated; he thought that the Surveyor was presuming. This drew a round declaration from Cromwell that the lady would be marrying into as good a house as her own. This, from such a quarter, was a strong recommendation; the marriage took place, and Sir Richard had to make the best of it. Tregian's son married instead, Katherine, eldest daughter of Sir John Arundell of Lanherne. The son of this marriage was Francis Tregian, the Catholic and recusant; and Grenville's grandson, our Sir Richard, was the instrument of the ruin of that family's fortunes. It is a curious tale which falls in due place.

In the last year of Lisle's administration Sir Richard obtained permission to come over to look to his affairs. It was a very important juncture: it was just at this time that the full tide of monastic lands began to flow into the market and had to be taken advantage of by the provident husbandman. Grenville had had an interview with the King, who asked about Calais and then rode hunting. But it was not until he arrived in the west and saw the opportunities afforded by the dissolution of the monasteries, that he made up his mind for himself. From Stowe, he addressed a long letter to Cromwell, a very significant historical document which reveals as hardly any other what was passing in the minds of so many of these country gentry confronted with a unique opportunity.[1]

When last he was with Cromwell, he wrote, he had said that he had no suit to the King for land or fee; but since then he has bethought him that if he has not some piece of the suppressed land, by purchase or gift, 'I should stand out of the case of few men of worship of this realm.' He is as glad as any man in the realm of the suppression of these orgulous persons and devourers of God's word and takers away of the glory of Christ, who, he reckons, were also takers away of the wealth of the realm and 'spys to the devilish Bishop of Rome.' Then follows the most revealing passage, one which might have been taken for their text by Henry and Cromwell in their dispersion of

[1] *L. and P.*, XIV, no. 1338.

church-property, so well does it express the social motive behind it. He says that he would gladly buy some of the suppressed lands in these parts, *that his heirs may be of the same mind for their own profit.* He suggests the priory of Launceston, valued at £14 per annum, and the Manor of Norton at £19. If the King would make him a gift up to the value of £8 per annum, he will give twenty years purchase for the rest.

It was a cool suggestion, but he did not obtain it. Only those who stood on terms of intimate favour with the King, such as Cromwell himself, or in the west, Lord Russell, got gifts of land. Others had to buy in the ordinary course of a competitive market. Launceston priory went in the end, not to Grenville, but to Sir Gawen Carew. But the letter is a superb piece of unconscious self-portraiture: the cool self-interest of it identified with the greater glory of Christ; the candid and correct assumption that the possession of church lands would commit later generations to the Suppression. No wonder that Catholics, and not they alone, have so hated the men of the Reformation. Sir Richard Grenville was no exception; everybody else of his class, or everybody who could, went and did likewise. He was rather nicer and more candid than most.

That summer Grenville and his wife spent in the West Country, from the end of July to mid-October. No doubt there was much business to be looked to, but it was also the season of harvest, of visiting, and as autumn came on, of much merrymaking. They went on a round of visits to their friends and kinsfolk, staying for a time with Lord Russell at Exeter, now the greatest man in the west. After this Grenville returned to Calais for the last year of his uncle's administration; he took his part in the elaborate ceremonies of welcome to Anne of Cleves who passed through Calais to a reluctant spouse awaiting her in England: her reception was the last official act of the Lisles. Upon their recall, Grenville remained on for seven months more, continuing to perform his duties as High Marshal until October 1540. The King, however, was determined to have a complete change in the administration, and on 3 October Sir Thomas Poynings was appointed Marshal in his place.[1] Sir

[1] *L. and P.*, XVI, no. 114.

Richard was written to by the Privy Council to come over, being assured that the King was 'his good Lord as at his coming hither (which he should accelerate) he should perceive.' Henry was as good as his word: Sir Richard was not implicated in the suspicions regarding Lisle, but it was the end of his career in office.

Some time before the Marshal's return, we do not know precisely when, his son and heir Roger married ; it may be that this was the purpose of Sir Richard's long stay in the West Country in 1539. Of Roger, our Sir Richard's father, we know nothing except when he married, the names of his children, and the manner of his end. His wife was Thomasine Cole of Slade, a Devonshire family with whom the Grenvilles had married in previous generations; and they seem to have had two sons, Charles and John, before the young Richard, who survived them, was born. On his return to England, Sir Richard bought the reversion to Buckland Abbey in Devonshire, for which on 24 May 1541, he paid the sum of £233 3s. 4d.[1] It seems likely that he bought the estate upon which to settle his heir; for, from the fact that his son's child, Charles, was buried at the parish church of Buckland Monachorum nearby on 28 August 1544,[2] we may surmise that the monastic house was being used as a residence and Roger Grenville's young family being brought up there.

Not much change in the buildings was effected at first, but later when the young Richard grew up and lived for some years here, he devoted himself to pulling down and reconstructing. The possession of Buckland gave the Grenvilles what they had never had before, a footing in South Devon. The Abbey lies some way up the charming and wooded valley of the Tavy, two or three miles from the junction of Tavy and Tamar. Considerably farther up lay, in those days, the great Abbey of Tavistock. Buckland lies in a wooded hollow, the great Roborough Down above it extending all along the ridge from Yelverton to Plymouth. The proximity to Plymouth must have itself been a considerable influence upon the young Richard as a lad, for some part of his early years was probably spent at Buckland, and much of his early manhood.

[1] *L. and P.*, XVI, no. 878 (69).   [2] Granville, 82.

But very little is known of his early years; in that respect he is like practically all the great figures of the Tudor Age: we do not know much of the childhood even of royal persons, of Elizabeth herself. As regards many of the sea-captains, we do not know the date of their birth. This has been the case hitherto with Grenville.[1] But a new document, the Inquisition taken after the death of old Sir Richard the Marshal, informs us that his grandson and heir was eight years old on 15 June 1550.[2] We may take it then that he was born on or about 15 June 1542; and some such date is borne out by the inscription on the portrait of him painted in 1571, stating that he was then 29.[3] Somewhere about the same time, within a year or two, there was born upon the barton of Crowndale, farther up the valley in the parish of Tavistock, Francis Drake, greatest of Elizabethan sea-captains and Grenville's great rival.

The Marshal, having now retired to Stowe, went on gathering desirable bits of church property: these years provided opportunities not to be missed. He bought the rectory and advowson of Morwenstow, that loneliest and remotest of all Cornish parishes in the north-eastern corner of the county, with its Norman church perched in the throat of a gully, and beyond, a four hundred feet drop to the sea. Four years later he carried through his largest transaction of this kind; along with Roger Blewett of Holcombe Regis, he bought for £1196 19s. the fat manor of Tynyell in Landulph parish, on the banks of the Tamar, which had belonged to St. German's priory, and a number of properties in Devonshire and other counties.[4]

Later he sold off much of this property. In 1547, for example, he broke up the manor of Tynyell, and sold the barton of Clifton in Landulph parish, with 100 acres of land and a fishery next the seashore there, to Thomas Arundell of Leigh and Thomasine his wife. What makes this transaction interesting is that this Thomasine was the young widow of Roger, Sir Richard's son, who after his death married Thomas Arundell; and it is probable that the young Richard was partly brought up as a child

[1] cf. the inadequate and unreliable article on Grenville in *Dict. Nat. Biog.*
[2] Inq. post-mortem, Chancery Series 11, vol. 90, no. 12.
[3] See later, p. 79.   [4] *L. and P.*, XXI, part 11, 200 (19), 712 (15).

with the Arundells at Clifton. What is more curious and exciting, is that this is the Cornish farm to which one of the last representatives of the Emperors at Constantinople, John Palæologus, came and settled down, who now lies buried here in the little church at Landulph by a quiet reach of the river.

Sir Richard, gathering years now, yet not old, settled well into the routine of his West-Country life once more: we find him in the commissions of the Peace for both Devon and Cornwall in 1543 and 1544, and in the latter year he became Sheriff of Cornwall for the third time. But he was not yet to rust in retirement. On the outbreak of the French war in 1543, the last and fiercest of Henry's reign, he was appointed with others a collector of the moneys levied for the defence of the country. The war – it was a peculiarly senseless one and waged for no particular object – waxed fiercer, more determined on both sides.

In 1546, when it became evident that it was to be a fight to a finish between the English and the French, the Emperor having withdrawn, orders were sent out for musters to be levied in the counties. Devonshire was to provide 500 men for the war in France and Cornwall 300. Sir Richard was appointed chief captain to lead the Devonshire contingent, and we find him paid conduct money for 200 soldiers, fife, drum and all, all the way from Calstock to Dover. One imagines the straggling little bands, brave in their new coats, marching up from the West Country to fight in the fields of France: it is a perennial theme in our history. What they did in the war we do not know, except that some of them died: there is so little record of the simple inarticulate men upon whom the blank burden of history falls. For Sir Richard, it was a renewal of his acquaintance with French soil, his last term abroad.

Already, in 1545, he had suffered a heavy blow in the loss of his son Roger. It was all the more bitter, because it happened by an accident which should have been avoidable, the capsizing of the *Mary Rose*. That summer the sea-warfare was at its height, and there was a tremendous struggle for the mastery of the Channel. The French gathered a great fleet together in the Norman harbours: never had they been so powerful at sea – this was the heyday of their maritime power. Along the English coast and into the west there was consternation; preparations for defence were hurriedly pushed forward. The English fleet was concentrated at Portsmouth; by 17 July, some eighty sail were there, 'forty of the ships large and beautiful,' waiting to be joined by sixty more from the west. The King himself went down, ageing and swollen, but indomitable as ever; what happened, happened under his eye.

On Sunday, 19 July, while Henry was at dinner on his flagship, the *Great Harry*, the French fleet suddenly appeared. It was a hot, windless day; the English ships could not get out to meet them and the French sent their galleys into the harbour. Henry hurriedly left his ship, and all day there was fighting in and around the harbour. The galleys were beaten off; but in the evening about five o'clock, after the fighting was over, the *Mary Rose*, the second largest of Henry's ships, suddenly heeled over and capsized. It was an accident like that which overtook the *Royal George* in the same spot some two hundred years later. It appears – so the Imperial Ambassador was told by a Fleming among the survivors – that after the firing and the heat, for the *Mary Rose* was a heavily armed ship, the lowest row of gunports was left open, and a sudden wind arising towards evening, she heeled over and foundered with all aboard, some five hundred men in all.[1] Only twenty or thirty of them were picked up and they 'servants, sailors and the like.' She was commanded by the Vice-Admiral, Sir George Carew; young Roger Grenville was her Captain; there must have been many western men among all those who were drowned.

Peace was made in 1546, leaving Boulogne in English hands, and more of a nuisance than it was worth, as certainly it could not be maintained in the weak grasp of Henry's successor, a child in his minority, under the government of the Protector Somerset. One of the worst legacies of the war, most important for the West Country, was the growth of piracy and disorder in the Channel. Private depredations on commerce went on all around these coasts to such an extent as to amount to open, if unacknowledged, warfare. In August 1548, the Council sent down a general Commission to the western counties permitting

[1] *L. and P.*, XX, part 1, 1263.

them to set forth ships to prey upon the French: license to take the law into their own hands, to wage private war. Sir Richard Grenville was appointed to the Commission for licences for Devonshire; his brother John joyfully seized the opportunity to fit out ships on his own and do a little privateering off the coast of France. But this was not the end of the trouble; in these years, adventuring, privateering, piracy, flourished together. This then was the atmosphere in which the grandson, young Richard, grew up: the school of Elizabethan seamanship.

Nor were conditions inland any less disturbed. Henry VIII's government had prevented unrest in a backward county like Cornwall, going through the disturbing process of the Reformation, from coming to a dangerous head. But there were disturbances, natural enough in so primitive and raw a population, very ignorant and all the more attached to its traditional Catholic rites. The Cornish were anxious to retain their holydays and feasts, which were far too numerous in the eyes of the rising class of gentry, bent on speeding up the pace of work under the stimulus of gain.

When Henry's rule gave way to the weak benevolence of the Protector Somerset, things grew to a storm. In the summer of 1548, the western parishes were in a flame, what with the Commission for the survey of church goods, and the Injunctions for the removal of images, the abolishing of the ancient ceremonies. There were tumultuous assemblies at Penryn and Helston; at the latter, William Body, Archdeacon of Cornwall, who had bought his archdeaconry from Thomas Winter, Wolsey's natural son, was murdered by a pious but infuriated mob. All this gave food for thought to the gentry who supported the new dispensation, as it certainly filled their hands with work. Sir Richard Grenville was appointed to head the special commission of Oyer and Terminer, which assembled at Launceston on 21 May to hear the indictment of some twenty-two prisoners, six having already been sent up to stand their trial in London.[1] Sir Martin Geoffrey, the priest who was the ring-leader, was hanged at Smithfield; at Launceston some seven or eight were condemned to the horrible penalties for high treason.

[1] F. Rose-Troup, *The Western Rebellion of 1549*, 84.

Next year, the whole of the west was in a blaze of rebellion. The occasion was the introduction of the new Prayer Book, with the service in English, in place of the old Latin mass: to the Cornish, who knew little or no English at this time, the new service was no better than the 'Christmas mumming' which they called it in the Articles containing their demands. This time it was a general movement: some thousands of men swarmed together with the instinctive stirring of a hive of bees; the gentry could make no head against them, could not even resist. Some of them may have been sympathetic, certainly the Arundells of Lanherne, who definitely leaned to the Catholic side: it was the turning-point in that family's long record of prosperity. Humphrey Arundell of Helland, their cousin, became the leader of the rebels.

They concentrated at Bodmin, whence they marched, joined by the Devonshire contingents, upon Exeter, which was besieged by this army of ten thousand men from the end of June to the beginning of August. Exeter held out, ever loyal to the Tudors – though even more to itself: for its citizens well knew the destruction of property which would ensue if the wild Cornishmen were once admitted within those walls to plunder the well-stocked shops, the wealthy merchants. Lord Russell was sent to their relief, with an army of German mercenaries and ordnance from the Tower; it was only after a series of hotly contested actions that he succeeded in raising the siege. Plymouth, which was not then fortified, had fallen to the rebels, except for its castle.

It must have been at the hands of a contingent *en route* for Plymouth that Sir Richard Grenville met with the misadventure so charmingly told by Carew. Sir Richard was then in the vicinity of Plymouth, and for safety threw himself into Trematon Castle, now only a girdle of grey walls upon a high knoll, looking down on one side upon Antony passage, and on the other through the leaves of the trees, across the broad water of the Hamoaze to Devonport. Carew relates:

'At the last Cornish commotion, Sir Richard Grenville the elder, with his Lady and followers, put themselves into this castle, and there for a while endured the Rebels' siege, encamped in three places against it, who wanting great ordinance, could have wrought the besieged small scathe, had his friends or enemies, kept faith and promise: but some of those within, slipping by night over the walls, with their bodies after their hearts, and those without mingling humble entreatings with rude menaces, he was hereby won, to issue forth at a postern gate for parley. The while a part of those rakehells, not knowing what honesty, and far less how much the word of a soldier imported, stepped between him and home, laid hold on his aged unwieldy body and threatened to leave it lifeless, if the enclosed did not leave their resistance. So prosecuting their first treachery against the Prince, with suitable actions towards his subjects, they seized the Castle and exercised the uttermost of their barbarous cruelties (death excepted) on the surprised prisoners. The seely gentlewomen, without regard of sex or shame, were stripped from their apparrel to their very smocks, and some of their fingers broken, to pluck away their rings, and Sir Richard himself made an exchange from Trematon Castle to that of Launceston, with the gaol to boot.' [1]

It was a humiliating experience for an old warrior. Here he remained, until in August, Humphrey Arundell returned defeated from the fierce battles that had raged round Exeter. There was some further resistance put up in the streets of Launceston; and Russell wrote to the Council that Arundell upon arriving there 'immediately began to practice with the townsmen and the keepers of Grenville and other gentlemen for the murder of them that night.' There is no other evidence to corroborate this, and it is inherently improbable. Arundell himself deposed, when in the Tower, that he had fled from the rebels, over-riding them through the night, 'and declared all the matter to Sir Richard Grenville and there was stayed.' He was sent up to London, along with Sir Thomas Pomeroy, John Winslade and other leaders, and there with them executed.

This rebellion, or the 'Commotion' as it was most often called in contemporary literature, was much the most important event

[1] Carew, 265.

in Cornish history of the sixteenth century. It was the last pathetic protest of the old Catholic medieval order. After its defeat, the west settled down under the new regime; and with the growth of hostility to Spain in western waters and with the struggle opening out for command of the seaways to the New World, the western sea-board was brought into the forefront of the long battle-line. With this movement, it swung forward into line with the rest of the nation, or rather, for the next fifty years, into the vanguard of it; from being Catholic and backward, it became aggressively Protestant ; at any rate, its leading families were and recruited the forward school of action in Elizabeth's reign.

These exciting events must have been not without some in-fluence upon the young Richard Grenville's mind. We do not know where he was at the time, but he may have been in Trematon Castle with his grandfather; almost certainly, if he were living then with his mother and his stepfather, Thomas Arundell of Leigh, at Clifton. For Clifton lies out on a low-lying neck of land, on the Tamar above Saltash, where the river loops round to Halton Quay; and it would be the natural thing for a family of gentry in time of 'Commotion' to seek refuge in Trematon, the nearest stronghold. We know from a Chancery case many years afterwards, when Richard Grenville had run his life's course and died a hero in a blaze of glory, that he had grown up with Alexander Arundell his half-brother, between whom throughout their lives 'divers enterprises of kindness and friendship did pass,' and that they frequently lent each other money, 'being so linked in true and firm love each to other that as the nearest in blood so in love none were more sure and steadfast.' [1]

Not long after the rising, on 15 March 1550, old Sir Richard died; and within a month after, his wife followed him. They were buried together at Kilkhampton, the one on 24 March, the other on 25 April 1550. [2] It may be, as the earliest and best biography of our Sir Richard suggests, with its aristocratic, eighteenth-century prejudice, that it was the vexation and hard-

---

[1] Chanc. Proc. Eliz. G 8/34, July 1595.
[2] Dew, *History of the Parish of Kilkhampton*, 70.

ships this distinguished old couple endured at the hands of the rebels, which brought them so soon afterwards to their grave.[1] We may take leave to suppose that it was due rather to old age.

From his will, we can see that the family property, under Sir Richard's hands, had grown considerably.[2] An entry in the books of the Court of Wards gives us for the first time a statement of the annual value of the estate: £237 3s. 9d.[3] This was no inconsiderable amount in those days: it was something approaching one-half the value of the Earl of Devonshire's large estates in the west. It meant that with the exception of the Arundells of Lanherne, the Grenvilles were about the richest of Cornish landowners. Most of his property, Sir Richard's will left to his wife, during the minority of his grandson. She was to have Buckland, which he names Buckland Grenville, for a long period of years; and it appears from the provision that she was to cut down as much timber as she pleased for 'the building of the mansion place,' that the work of turning the abbey into a house in which to dwell was either already started or in contemplation. Dame Maude was also to have Stowe, according to the will, during the minority. After various legacies, the residue of the property and the entailed estate were demised upon his grandson and heir, who was not yet eight years old. The ink was hardly dry upon the will before its elaborate provisions regarding Dame Maude lapsed with her death, and the young Richard succeeded, a minor.

Except for the medieval Archbishop, old Sir Richard was the most distinguished figure the family produced, until his grandson who out-distanced him. We have no such intimate a view into his mind and heart as we have of Lady Lisle, perhaps partly for the reason that he was a man, and she a woman. Carew summed up his life objectively enough: 'So did Sir Richard Grenville the elder interlace his home magistracy with

---

[1] *Biographia Britannica* (1757), IV, 2283: 'It was the vexation, hardships and fatigue, which this aged couple went through from the madness of this insolent rabble, that brought them both soon after to their end.'

[2] Inq. post-mortem, Chancery Series 11, vol. 90, no. 12; and Court of Wards, vol. 5, no. 109.

[3] Court of Wards, Misc. Books 154. For this reference I am indebted to Mr. J. Hirschfield.

martial employments abroad; whereof the King testified his good liking by his liberality.' But there was another side to him than this. At the gay court of Henry VIII, where the young peers the Earl of Surrey and Lord Vaux, and the brilliant Sir Thomas Wyatt and Sir Francis Bryan, friend of the Lisles, were writing in the dawn of that sweet new Italian style which was to lead on to the splendid day of Spenser and Marlowe and Shakespeare, Sir Richard had his part. There is very little of his writing left, only two poems of his preserved in the British Museum; [1] but they are sufficiently accomplished, and what is more they are personal in tone, true to the man he was. When others were singing, like Surrey, of his love:

> 'When raging love with extreme pain
> Most cruelly distrains my heart';

or with Wyatt, to his lute:

> 'My lute, awake! perform the last
> Labour that thou and I shall waste,
> And end that I have now begun';

Sir Richard Grenville, going abroad to seek his fortune, wrote a poem:

In Praise of Seafaring Men in Hopes of Good Fortune

> Who seeks the way to win renown,
>   Or flies with wings of high desire;
> Who seeks to wear the laurel crown,
>   Or hath the mind that would aspire:
> Tell him his native soil eschew,
> Tell him go range and seek anew.
>
> To pass the seas some think a toil,
>   Some think it strange abroad to roam,
> Some think it grief to leave their soil,
>   Their parents, kinsfolk and their home;
> Think so who list, I like it not,
> I must abroad to try my lot.

[1] Sloane MSS. 2497.

> Who list at home at cart to trudge,
> And cark and care for worldly trash,
> With buckled shoes let him go trudge,
> Instead of lance a whip to slash:
> A mind that base his kind will show
> Of carrion sweet to feed a crow.
>
> If Jason of that mind had been
> The Grecians when they came to Troy,
> Had never so the Trojans fought,
> Nor never put them to such annoy:
> Wherefore who list to live at home,
> To purchase fame I will go roam.

If it is a character of poetry to bring physical images to mind, then this is not mere versifying:

> Who list at home at cart to trudge . . .
> Instead of lance a whip to slash:

One seems almost to see the carter trudging by his horses, cracking his whip as he goes through the slush and mire of those vacant fields around the vanished house at Stowe.

But there was another theme which prompted him, tossed to and fro as he frequently was on the seas between this country and France, or journeying from the far west up to Court, from London to Calais and back again to the west:

Another of Sea Fardingers describing evil Fortunes

> What pen can well report the plight
> Of those that travel on the sea;
> To pass the weary winter's night
> With stormy clouds, wishing for day;
> With waves that toss them to and fro;
> Their poor estate is hard to show.
>
> We wander still from luff to lee
> And find no steadfast winds to blow;
> We still remain in jeopardy,
> Each perilous point is hard to show;
> In time we hope to find redress
> That long have lived in heaviness . . .

When frets and states have had their fill,
   The gentle calm the coast will clear,
The haughty hearts shall have their will,
   That long hath wept with mourning cheer;
And leave the seas with their annoy,
At home at ease to live in joy.

Such was the voice of the old, the passing age: something of
geniality, of a care-free spirit, went with it. A new generation
sprang up, a new age: one more strenuous, even to the point of
communicating a certain strain to its choicest spirits, less given
to happy ease and enjoyment.

CHAPTER III

EARLY ADVENTURES: HUNGARY AND IRELAND

Travel, in the younger sort, is a part of education.

BACON: *Essays*

SUCH were the years in which the young Sir Richard grew up; such was his environment. Hardly anything is known of him directly and personally in these years; but then that is a difficulty common in writing the life of any Elizabethan. In his case, one or two facts emerge regarding his wardship, which give us a starting-point.

On old Sir Richard's death, his widow at once preferred a suit to the Court of Wards for the wardship of her grandson.[1] This was according to custom; the heirs to estates of any extent, who succeeded as minors, became wards of the Crown which enjoyed the profits of their estates until they reached their majority. It was the custom to sell these wardships, with the right of marrying the heir, to suitable purchasers: a regular source of revenue for the Crown. We learn that upon Dame Maude's death within a month of her husband, the wardship of the young heir was granted to Nicholas Wadham, esquire, 'who gave up his interest to Sir Hugh Paulet, Knight.' Paulet was granted custody of him on 21 November 1550, with the usual right of marriage of the ward, and an annuity for his maintenance out of the Grenville lands at Bideford, Buckland and Stowe.[2] It must have seemed a suitable appointment, for Paulet was an old companion-in-arms of his grandfather in the

[1] Court of Wards, Misc. Books 154.
[2] Cal. Pat. Rolls Edward VI, III, no. 210.

French war, and had been Knight Marshal of the army under
Russell which beat down the Rising of 1549.

But Paulet's wardship can have had little influence upon the
ward – he was so much abroad, for some years as Governor of
Jersey, and then fighting in France on the Huguenot side under
Ambrose, Earl of Warwick. Indeed, there is no evidence of any
kind of Sir Hugh's exerting himself in relation to his charge; and
it was quite usual in cases like this for arrangements to be made
for the ward to be brought up with his relatives, in this case his
mother. As we shall see from Grenville's first appearance in
person upon the public scene, we derive the impression of a
young heir left to grow up as he chose, wayward and wilful.
This strain runs throughout his life; and no doubt it was an
essential characteristic of his heredity. It was left to experience
of the world, that harsh task-master, to discipline him; and
even to the end, though it is evident that he made efforts to
bring himself under control, the process was not complete.
Something of this, however, may have been due to the special
position that he would occupy in his stepfather's household, the
only remaining child of his mother's first marriage and the heir
to large estates. For, as we have seen, it is probable that he grew
up with the Arundells at Clifton, though he may have spent
some periods at Stowe and Buckland.

Thomas Arundell, his stepfather, was of the younger branch
of the Arundells of Trerice, a family with seafaring traditions.
Clifton was not far from Buckland; in fact down the Tamar and
round the next point, the high bluff above the junction of the
two rivers, and up the Tavy; or across the river at Weirquay,
and then by the road through Bere Alston to Buckland, over the
neck of the pretty wooded peninsula between Tavy and Tamar.
It was only a matter of a few miles; but the river, which
dominates all this country and hugs Clifton on two sides, with
the boats going down to Saltash and Plymouth, must have
played some part in his boyhood.

While Grenville was growing up here, the young Francis
Drake, an exile from home, was learning that mastery in hand-
ling a boat which singled him out among all the great sea-
captains of the age, upon the dull waters of the Medway, where

his father read prayers on board the ships in the river. At the same time, William and John Hawkins, by several years senior to Drake and Grenville, were getting their experience of ocean-going trade along the new routes to Bombay and Guinea from Plymouth where their father, a Tavistock man too by origin, had become the principal citizen of the town and amassed considerable property there.[1]

But these were not born in the same station of life as Grenville; they came from the middle-classes, Drake of yeoman stock and the Hawkins' merchants, while Grenville belonged to the old county gentry and was very conscious of it. All the country-side round was filled with his relatives and friends: lower down the river there were the Edgcumbes, young Peter Edgcumbe the heir, his contemporary and friend growing up in the newly built house in that magnificent situation overlooking the Hamoaze, which the Duke of Medina Sidonia – so the West Country said – singled out for his own before the Armada sailed. At Collacombe, above Tavistock, there were the Tremaynes, his cousins – Edmund Tremayne was destined to become his brother-in-law: a numerous tribe. Old Thomas Tremayne had married Philippa, daughter of Sir Thomas Grenville, and by her had sixteen children. The most distinguished of them was Edmund, who later rose high in the favour of Queen Elizabeth, became Clerk of the Privy Council and a person of considerable importance in the Government. His brothers Nicholas and Andrew, who were nearer Grenville's own age, went abroad to fight in the wars about the same time as he did; and never came back. The same was true of Philip Budockshide (or Butshed) of Butshed, an ancient barton on the Devonshire side of the Tamar, by the creek going up to Tamerton Foliot. Farther afield were the Champernownes, to whom Grenville was related, and with them to the Raleghs and Gilberts: all of them, like him later, concerned in the wars abroad where they served their apprenticeship in the art of fighting.

Some such outlet for their high spirits and hot blood was indeed necessary, not only personally, but politically. In Mary's reign there were two occasions of trouble in the west,

---

[1] cf. Bracken, *History of Plymouth*, c. VIII.

the circumstances of which are very revealing of the new currents flowing. The trouble arose over her marriage with Philip of Spain. As long as Mary was content to reign as Queen of England, either single or married to an Englishman, her rule was not unpopular. But when it became clear that her mind was set on the marriage with Philip, things began to go wrong. Intrigues and conspiracies thickened around her, special precautions had to be taken against demonstrations of anti-foreign feeling in the west when Philip landed. The West Country would have welcomed a marriage with Courtenay; and when they realised that there was no hope of this, Sir Peter and Sir Gawen Carew slipped away to Devon to raise the country. At the crucial moment Courtenay's nerve failed him. In Exeter it was rumoured that the Earl was on the way, that he was even now at Mohun's Ottery with the Carews. The latter fortified their house and put it in a state to stand a siege – it was in an impregnable position. With Courtenay's failure to appear their hopes of support collapsed; the Chichesters and Champernownes washed their hands of the affair; but fellow-feeling among the Devonshire gentry was sufficient to allow the Carews to get away to France in a bark brought round to Weymouth by Walter Ralegh, the father of Sir Walter.[1]

This was in January and February of 1554. Wyatt's Rebellion, the most dangerous of the reign, was crushed; Mary married her Philip; the Earl of Devonshire was given prolonged leave of absence and went abroad, where he died at Padua, unmarried and without an heir, the last of the elder branch of the Courtenays. Within two years there was another conspiracy against Mary's rule. Here again the westerners were involved, particularly the sea-board families, the Horseys of Dorset, the Tremaynes and Killigrews of Devon and Cornwall. They had joined the Carews in France, where Havre de Grace and the Normandy ports were centres of émigré activities against Mary's government. The Killigrews' ships kept the various parties in touch with each other and with what was happening in England, and this they combined with depredations upon Spanish shipping in and out of the Channel.[2]

[1] S.P. Dom. Mary, 11, 12–16; 111, 5.   [2] ibid. 9, nos. 24–26.

It is this aspect of their activities that is so significant for the future. The importance for Spain of the alliance with England was that it ensured the protection of the sea-route between Spain and the Netherlands. Its consequence was such an increase in Spanish power that the French were driven to aid and abet all the enemies of Mary's rule. The Carews, Tremaynes and the rest were welcomed and encouraged by the French King. Here is a main link in the chain of events which brought about a complete change-over in the sea-politics of the Channel, from the Channel warfare with France which was characteristic of the Middle Ages and lasted up to Mary's reign, to the opening out of the struggle with Spain which developed as Elizabeth's reign progressed. There were other factors at work besides the growth of Spain's power, notably the weakening of French naval power consequent upon the internal divisions of the religious wars. But the process of changing over from one to the other was not complete until well on in the reign of Elizabeth. In that process Grenville was to play a part no less than other seamen of the time, and to be no less affected by it.

So the years of childhood and youth passed, with their influences such as can only now be surmised. We can be sure only of the routine of the seasons; inland, seed-time and harvest, spring and autumn ploughing, on the coast, fair summer seas and winter gales bringing in the wreckage. We are to imagine him growing up, at work and at play, running and riding about the country-side, bird-nesting, hawking, hunting, all the familiar occupations of an Elizabethan boy brought up in the country. In addition, there must have been lessons, not only in reading and writing, conning one of those text-books so popular with Tudor schoolmasters, Lily's *Grammar* or Record's *Arithmetic* – but also in fencing, the use of sword and rapier, in the art of fighting, occupations which were to lead him so soon into trouble and only cease to excite him with his death.

Of his education in the strict sense we know hardly anything specific. His earliest biographer says sedately, 'We have no distinct account of the place or manner of his breeding, which, however, we have not the least cause to doubt, was in every respect suitable to his family and fortune, both being as fair as

any gentleman could boast in the west of England.' [1] We have
no evidence that he attended school; probably he was taught by
a tutor at home. He does not appear to have been at either
University; neither his interests nor his talents would lead him
in that direction. Moreover the times were disturbed, and the
universities greatly affected, by the religious changes; students
were falling off at Oxford in these years. By the time Grenville
reached the age to go to the university, Mary's reign and the
Catholic revival in England were flickering to their end.

But it was usual for some coping-stone, either at the university or at an Inn of Court, to be placed upon the education of a
young gentleman of family. And in the Michaelmas term of
1559, Grenville was admitted as a student to the Inner Temple.[2]
Amid so much that is dark, it may be that one can detect the
influence of his sojourn there upon the later man. It was not a
question of shining as a lawyer; the sons of the gentry were sent
there rather for a general training in business and to equip them
with a sufficient knowledge of law and procedure to manage
their own affairs. And this Grenville gained: he emerged with
a distinct competence for affairs, clearness in stating his case
and an ability to present it himself – a plausibility even not
wholly to be dissociated from an early training at the law –
which we shall observe at work in later transactions. A good
man of business, he was in time to be used on committees of the
House of Commons, trusted by other people to manage their
affairs and by the government with much of the business of his
county.

For the rest, he must have lived the life of a young man about
town, as it was lived by numbers of other young men of his
class and time, by his west-country cousins Gilbert and Ralegh
for example. We know nothing of it, though it can be easily
imagined. For the country in general and London in particular,
it was a new dispensation. Elizabeth was Queen. A new spirit
reigned in Whitehall. No longer the fires burned at Smithfield;
no longer the lugubrious processions that marked the last years
of the catholic Queen, disappointed, prematurely ageing, ill,

[1] *Biographia Britannica*, IV, 2283.
[2] *Students admitted to the Inner Temple, 1547–1660.*

without earthly hope. A new spirit reigned, one of gaiety, bravery, even of dare-devilry when one thinks of the risks Elizabeth was prepared to take, with King Philip and his Ambassador, with France, Scotland, for the future of her people, a nation renewed and vigorous.

Of the vigour and high spirit there can be no doubt. And of its overflow in Grenville's case we have evidence from what is at once the most surprising and least unexpected discovery among the original documents remaining. Surprising, for the story seems to have gone completely out of mind with Grenville himself and perhaps a generation or two of the family after him. There is no printed reference to it; nothing remains in letters, correspondence, or documents relating to him; no one for centuries would seem to have known the dark Elizabethan story which lies behind the entry of a Pardon in the Patent Roll of the fifth year of Elizabeth, 1563.[1] Yet what it reveals of Grenville is so true to what we know of him later, so corroborates the fragmentary glimpses which are all we have hitherto had of him, that it may be said in a sense to be not unexpected.

The story that the Patent Roll reveals is by no means uncommon; it is that of a typical Elizabethan affray such as Christopher Marlowe was frequently engaged in, of some such affair as that in which he met his end. It appears that between the hours of three and four in the afternoon, on 19 November 1562, there was an affray in the open street somewhere in the parish of St. Clement Danes. We do not know where; one imagines one of the narrow lanes running down to the river from the Strand, where the great houses of the nobility stood, Arundel House, Durham House, Essex House – or it may have been in the Strand itself. What makes it remarkable were the combatants: for on one side were Sir Edward Unton, Fulke Greville, and Robert Bannester, with Thomas Allen yeoman, and the servants of Sir Edward and Fulke Greville; on the other were Richard Grenville and Nicholas Specott, with Lewis Lloyd and Edward Horseman, yeomen, their attendants. Unton belonged to the Oxfordshire family of that name, the brother of Sir Henry Unton who was afterwards Ambassador

[1] Pat. Rolls Eliz. 989.

to France. Fulke Greville was the father of Sir Philip Sidney's friend, the poet; Bannester was a Londoner, but a gentleman. Grenville was accompanied by his cousin, a Devonshire Specott.

Suddenly, according to the account on the Patent Roll, 'they ran together in an affray, and when they were all fighting together, Grenville ran through Bannester with his sword, giving him a mortal wound, six inches in depth and one and a half in breadth, of which he died within an hour afterwards.' Thereupon the said Richard Grenville and Nicholas Specott fled, so that their goods and chattels lay under sentence of outlawry. This was found by inquest held upon the body of Bannester on 21 November, before Thomas Wente, Coroner of the Household, and Robert Cooke, Coroner of Middlesex. The Patent Roll then recites the pardon to Richard Grenville, late of London, alias of Stowe in Cornwall, of his felony and relieves him of all forfeitures, outlawries, etc., incurred thereby.

Thus far the Patent Roll; there is no more. We do not know what lay behind it, nor whether Grenville knew the man whom he had killed. He was young at the time, not having yet attained his majority. It may be that the fact that he was a minor contributed to the ease of his pardon. Certainly he was let off lightly. There is an entry in the King's Bench Controlment Roll for Middlesex of his and his fellows' indictment on the morrow of Holy Trinity, which would seem to imply that they cooled their heels in prison for a time, if they were not bailed out earlier; then follows the note of pardon in the margin.[1] To the Elizabethans, human life was rated more cheaply; and it may be that one of the reasons for the silence of our records concerning this event in Grenville's life, why it had lapsed out of all memory was just that it was considered unimportant. Every gentleman had his duels; at a time when it was the regular thing for a gentleman to wear a sword and rapier, many a quarrel that might have left no mark, ended fatally. Did not Ben Jonson kill his man in Moorfields, or Marlowe's friend Thomas Watson, the poet, kill William Bradley in Hog Lane?[2] It was not to be expected that the young bloods of

[1] K.B. 29/196.   [2] Eccles, *Christopher Marlowe in London*.

Elizabethan society were any less high-spirited than the poets.

That such an incident was not taken too seriously by Elizabethans may be witnessed by the fact that a short time after, in January of the New Year 1563, he was returned while still a minor, if it is he, as Member of Parliament.[1] There is a possibility that it may have been another Richard Grenville, a cousin of Penheale. But the fact of being a minor was no bar apparently to election, for his cousin Arthur Basset who had not yet attained his majority, was returned at the same time. The chances are that it is our Richard who was returned this year as one of the members for the borough of Dunheved (i.e. Launceston).

Parliament had been called to help in financing the French war, but from the first it displayed much more interest in the question of the succession. The Queen had been ill that autumn with small-pox, and for a few days her life had been despaired of. It called very vividly to men's minds the dangers of a disputed succession; and Parliament met in an atmosphere of fervent devotion to the Queen, combined with a determination to see her well and safely married. In this last resolve they met more than their match in Elizabeth, and after a few months of petitions and speeches and mutual sparring they were sent away unsatisfied.

Since this would be Grenville's first Parliament, we are to suppose him for the first time witnessing the splendid ceremonial that attended the opening: the Queen coming in state to Westminster, riding on horseback in crimson velvet and ermine, glittering with jewels, Lord Robert Dudley riding behind her, leading the spare horse.[2] So she proceeded to the Abbey to hear a sermon, and afterwards into the Parliament Chamber, the sword and cap of maintenance borne before her. Among the large west-country contingent to witness these and other ceremonies at the prorogation of Parliament were many relatives and friends of Grenville, Bassets, Edgcumbes, Champernownes, Killigrews.

[1] *Official Return of Members of Parliament*, 1, p. 403.
[2] D'Ewes, *Journal of the Lords and Commons* (1693), 59.

Within a month or two of the prorogation, Grenville attained his majority; and on 28 June 1563, he obtained license to enter upon his estates, with the usual grant of all the issues therefrom, from the date when he reached the age of twenty-one.[1] About the same date, his cousin Arthur Basset attained his majority.[2] Accession to his estates, and to a position of responsibility as active head of the family, may have had some influence in steadying him, as it certainly gave him more to occupy his energies. We find him later in the same year alienating lands in the parish of Landulph, to his stepfather Thomas Arundell and his mother.[3] In the next year, 12 September 1565, he makes a more substantial grant to them, the manor of Tynyell with its appurtenances in Cargreen and Landulph, also parcel of the monastic property bought by his grandfather.[4] Old Sir Richard had previously granted the barton of Clifton with a hundred acres of land to Arundell and his wife; so that these subsequent grants served to round off the Clifton property handsomely, and make all within that little peninsula of the Tamar a substantial domain. It was off the main track of the Grenville properties, so that the young heir can have had no strong inducement to hold on to it; in all probability he was carrying out the policy with regard to the estates indicated by his grandfather. In the same year he made another grant of lands, this time at Buckland Monachorum and Buckland Grenville (i.e. Buckland Abbey) to Nicholas Specott, his companion in the adventure of two years before.[5]

What these arrangements indicate is Grenville's settling down, if the phrase may be used for one of his restless activity, into family life. It was natural enough that upon succeeding to his inheritance he should be employed in putting things in order, selling off outlying land and putting the proceeds to use nearer home. One or two of these documents describe him simply as of Stowe; and by the time he had reached his majority he was probably residing there, if he had not been before, setting up his own household in the house of his fathers, directing

---

[1] Pat. Rolls 5 Eliz. 28 June.
[2] ibid. 10 March.
[3] ibid., 6 Eliz., 29 December.
[4] ibid., 7 Eliz. 12 September.
[5] Pat. Rolls 7 Eliz. 30 April.

repairs, laying out his crops, gathering in his harvests. For what lies behind these indications – there is now no doubt – is his marriage, which must have taken place upon reaching his majority. Hitherto it has remained obscure when Grenville married; but the entry of the burial of a son, Roger, in the parish Register at Kilkhampton on 10 December 1565,[1] gives us a limiting date: Grenville could not have been married later than early 1565, and it may have been earlier than that. It is a touching thought that he should have called his first son after his father, whom he can hardly have known; he was so young, a child of three only, when his father was drowned. This earlier date for Grenville's marriage is corroborated by the fact that Bernard, his second son and heir, who succeeded him, was born in 1567.[2]

Grenville married Mary St. Leger, the eldest daughter of Sir John St. Leger of Annery, near Bideford. His succession to Stowe threw him naturally into closer association with his North Devon neighbours; and Annery is a charming place upon a hill a mile or two up the Torridge from Bideford, looking down upon the walls and battlements of Wear Giffard beside the river. The St. Legers were a branch of the great Kentish family who had a long-standing connection with Ireland, dating from the great Lord-Deputy, Sir Anthony St. Leger, who was the chief architect of Henry VIII's rule there. His son was Sir Warham St. Leger with whom Grenville was to be closely associated in Munster, induced to take a hand in Irish affairs by his marriage; and Sir John St. Leger, his wife's father, was Sir Warham's cousin. This marriage in the end brought into the family an intolerable deal of quarterings, including some royal descents and a remote connection through the Ormondes with Queen Elizabeth.[3]

Hardly anything is known of Grenville's wife; partly, it may be, because of the destruction of all his private letters and documents, but partly, it is to be feared, because the lady was a dull soul and there is nothing much to be known. There was a soft

[1] Vivian, *Visitations of Cornwall*, 192.
[2] Inq. post-mortem, Chancery Series 11, vol. 233, no. 119.
[3] Granville, 88–9.

spot in the St. Legers of Annery: one cannot help feeling that the
quiet contentment, the placidity of Sir Bernard, after the excitements and ardours of his father, came from the mother. Sir
John St. Leger, by his marriage with an Ormonde heiress, had
come into possession of a large inheritance which he entirely
wasted; so that his son John, succeeding to little enough and
becoming a hopeless drunkard like his father, fell to Grenville's
responsibility. He died unmarried, leaving his four sisters as
co-heiresses to nothing much: Grenville's wife, Frances who
married a Stukely, Margaret, wife of Richard Bellew of Alver-
discott, and Eulalia, wife of Edmund Tremayne of Collacombe.

Such was the family circle. There is no evidence, either one
way or the other, as to any gallantry towards women in Grenville's nature. Marrying and carrying on the family was to a
man like him part of the natural order. Marriage was a business, and this alliance a suitable one. It was one with any other
propertied arrangements incumbent upon the young head of a
house entering upon his responsibilities. The Elizabethan attitude on this subject was a robuster one than ours. In this he was
like what we know of all the great sea-captains of the age. They
do not appear to have wasted much time or thought upon sex;
they were men of action. This is as true of Drake and Hawkins
as it is of Grenville. Nor did the family commitments retain him
at home when he wished to go abroad to see service in the wars
or undertake some enterprise at sea. Within a year or two of
marriage, the summer after his infant son's death, 1566, he went
abroad with a band of his Devonshire cousins to the war in Hungary. Three years later we find him engaged in Ireland, a new
field of enterprise, this time taking wife and children with him.

Meanwhile the merchants and sea-going folk, taking advantage of the changed circumstances with Mary's death and Elizabeth's accession, were pressing forward along the outer sea-
routes, impelled by the passion to share the lucrative profits of
the Portuguese and the Spaniards in the African and American
trades. The French had already shown the way to these intruders into the Spanish monopoly of the southern hemisphere.
At Plymouth in these years, Hawkins was fitting out those slaving voyages which were to make his name and fortune, and to

59

have such consequences for the future of the New World.[1] Similarly Drake in these years was undergoing his apprenticeship in a harder school. According to Camden, his father

'by reason of his poverty . . . put his son to the master of a bark, his neighbour, who held him hard to his business in the bark, with which he used to coast along the shore, and sometimes to carry merchandise into Zealand and France. The youth, being painful and diligent, so pleased the old man by his industry, that, being a bachelor, at his death he bequeathed the bark unto him by will and testament.' [2]

It may have been in this bark that Drake made his suspected early voyages to the West Indies in 1565 and 1566, before throwing in his lot with Hawkins for the third great enterprise which ended so disastrously at San Juan de Ulloa and gave so many western seamen an undying determination to be revenged upon the Spaniards.

Grenville's attention was not as yet drawn to the sea. These were men of a humbler station of life, whose fortunes were for the most part yet to be made. It was natural that he should follow the habit of his class and look to a military career, and, in the peaceful conditions established by Elizabeth's rule, by service abroad. Already a number of his west-country cousins, a few years older than himself, had had their baptism of fire, in Scotland or in France. Some of them had already, in the ardour of their youth, achieved the reward of fame with their lives. There were Nicholas and Andrew Tremayne, the brothers who had gone abroad with Sir Peter Carew under Mary. With Elizabeth's accession they returned and entered her service. Andrew led a brilliant cavalry charge against the French at Leith in 1560; while Nicholas, who was a special favourite of the Queen's, was employed in carrying dispatches to and from France. When Elizabeth intervened on the side of the Protestants in the first French War of Religion, the brothers served in the forces under Ambrose Dudley, Earl of Warwick. Here they were both killed in the flower of their youth, in the defence of Havre against the

---

[1] Williamson: *Sir John Hawkins*, IV–V.
[2] Camden, *History of the Reign of Elizabeth* (1675), 248.

French; Nicholas on 26 May and Andrew on 18 July. What made the story of the Tremaynes so affecting, and in its day famous, was the perfect love that reigned between them; they were twins, and inseparable.

It may easily be conceived how such events stirred the minds of the younger men of the time, and among them Grenville. The Tremaynes were Grenvilles on their mother's side. But there were others abroad, too; there was his cousin Humphrey Gilbert, who like his half-brother Ralegh after him, was getting his first experience of war in France (how it runs through the ages!), where he had been wounded at the siege of Havre on 26 September 1563. Now, peace having been made, he was at home again, in 1566, on his way to Ireland, the second great theatre of war for Elizabethans.

Peace, of a sort, reigned in France from the Peace of Amboise in 1564 to 1567, when the Second Religious War broke out; so that in the interim, these young gallants who wanted to prove themselves in the profession of war, had to look to another field for the exercise of their valour. Quite another part of Europe attracted their attention. In this year the uneasy peace between the Emperor Maximilian II and the Ottoman Empire broke down, and the armies began to march once more over the disputed plains of Hungary. A great sensation was made in Europe by the renewed march of the Turks towards Vienna, and by the preparations being made for his thirteenth campaign by the great Sultan, Solyman the Magnificent. The news determined Grenville and a whole group of his friends; for what strikes one in Camden's account of their going abroad to the wars is that they were obviously a band of friends and relatives, all west-countrymen.

'But others of the English nation,' he says by way of pointing the contrast with the Earl of Arundel who left the realm that year for foreign travel, ostensibly by reason of the gout, but really out of pique with Elizabeth – 'who, according to their innate fortitude thought themselves born to arms, not to idleness, when gentlemen out of all parts of Europe were excited upon the fame of the Turks, went into Hungary. Amongst whom those of the better note were Sir John Smith, cousin-

german to King Edward the Sixth, being son to the sister of
Jane Seymour, the King's mother, Henry Champernowne,
Philip Budockshide, Richard Grenville, William Gorges,
Thomas Cotton and others.'[1]

These young men can hardly have been in time for the opening of the great campaign by the Sultan, who, leaving Constantinople on 1 May marched rapidly by Sofia and Nish to
Belgrade and then sat down with his army of a hundred thousand men before the strongly-fortified town of Szigeth. In the
middle of the siege, the Sultan died; but his death was kept
secret until the town fell. After this, the war lost something of
its concentration of purpose and degenerated into desultory
fighting and raiding across the plains of Hungary; but it went
on for a year or more. It must have been an exotic scene for
these young west-countrymen, all contracted by family ties to
within a few miles of Devonshire countryside. Smith was a
nephew of Protector Somerset and the Seymours were connected
by marriage with the Champernownes. Henry Champernowne,
four years senior to Grenville, was the son of John Champernowne of Modbury and the nephew of Sir Arthur of Dartington.
Grenville himself was related to the Champernownes through
his mother, whose brother had married a sister of Sir Arthur
Champernowne. Yet another sister of the last had married
Roger Budockshide, and their only son was this Philip now
abroad on campaign with his cousins. It was this Philip too who
played such a delightful game of bluff with a large fleet of
Flemish hulks in Plymouth Sound in the critical year 1569 when
war threatened with Spain. William Gorges, of a Somersetshire
family, married Philip Budockshide's eldest sister and afterwards
succeeded to the property.[2]

Within a year of their return from the Hungarian war, Champernowne and Budockshide went abroad again to the renewed
war in France, taking with them yet another young west-country cousin who was destined to leave a greater mark on history

[1] Camden, 82.
[2] R. P. Chope: 'New Light on Sir Richard Grenville,' in *Trans. Devon
Assoc.* (1917), 211–12.

than any of them: Walter Ralegh. It was his first acquaintance with war. Camden relates how in the year 1569, the Protestant cause in France being 'now in a distressed and almost desperate condition,' Queen Elizabeth sent them supplies of money and

'permitted Henry Champernowne (whose cousin-german Gawen had married the Earl of Montgomery's daughter) to carry into France a troup of a hundred volunteer gentlemen on horseback, who had in his colours this motto, *Finem det mihi Virtus*, that is, let Virtue give me my end. Amongst these volunteer gentlemen were Philip Budockshide, Francis Berkely, and Walter Ralegh, a very young man, who now first began to be of any note.' [1]

From this expedition, Champernowne and Budockshide came home no more to Devonshire; they died in the next year, it is not known how. A year or two more, in 1573, the father died, last of the Budockshides, and the Gorges family reigned in their stead. In the next generation they placed a lovely painted altar-tomb of slate over them all in the little church of St. Budeaux on the hill outside Plymouth overlooking the Tamar – the church in which Drake married Mary Newman of Saltash.

By the summer of 1567 peace negotiations were on foot between the Emperor and the new Sultan, who was weary of the Hungarian war and anxious to press forward the attack on Venice and to expand Turkish sea-power in the Mediterranean. In February 1568, peace was signed and there was no longer any point in the little band of west-countrymen remaining in Hungary. We do not know how they acquitted themselves: the only reference that has come down to us is to Grenville; for his contemporary, Richard Carew, in the *Survey of Cornwall* mentions his 'following the wars under the Emperor Maximilian against the great Turk, for which his name is recorded by sundry foreign writers.' [2] Who these writers were has never been specified; it is likely enough that this episode was remembered more on account of his subsequent fame than because of any signal achievement by it. It may be noted here that the later tradition

[1] Camden, 137.   [2] Carew, 176.

that Grenville fought at the battle of Lepanto is unlikely in itself
and is probably explained by his taking part in the fighting
against the Turks in Hungary, which, to the mind of later centuries, coloured as it was by the fame of his sea-exploits, would
tend to become confused with the great naval battle of Lepanto.
But by that time – it was fought in October 1571 – Grenville
had subscribed the oath according to the Act of Uniformity and
was a Member of the Parliament of that year.

That Grenville was at home again in 1568 we know from his
granting to John Halse of Efford in that year, 'all these lands in
East Buckland, sometime the property of my grandfather.' [1]
The property had come into the hands of the Grenvilles by the
marriage of his great-grandfather, Sir Roger, to the co-heiress
of Richard Whitley of Efford. [2] The real interest of this grant,
however, is not genealogical, but in what it suggests of the next
phase in Grenville's career, which was connected with Ireland;
here we find him selling off still more of the Buckland property,
without doubt to raise money for his next venture.

Ireland was an obvious field for Elizabethan adventurers. It
was their earlier America – or at least so they hoped; but in fact,
for one who made his fortune out of it, many more lost theirs;
for one or two who gained an estate, hundreds found a grave.
The country was in great disorder; in these years more than
usually so. It was not so much that Ireland had not been effec-
tively brought under the Reformation system, which was con-
temporaneously making the fortunes of England; but that its
whole social system, based upon the clans and customary rights,
with an altogether more primitive mode of life and outlook,
Celtic and pre-medieval in character, was breaking up under
the pressure of the new social forces of the age, and among them,
that of the integrated power-state which the English had
achieved as the result of Renaissance and Reformation. [3] Over
large areas of Ireland civilised order was in dissolution, contested by contrary systems of society, while the lot of the people
went from bad to worse, lapsing from misery into savagery. The
English were not strong enough to tackle the gigantic problem

[1] Granville, 86.   [2] Court of Wards 15/1. Pleadings.
[3] Mathew, *Celtic Peoples and Renaissance Europe.*

as a whole, and impose a solution which would have been in the best interests of the country.

Sir Henry Sidney, the Lord Deputy of Ireland, on returning to his charge in 1568, made a tour throughout the whole of the south and wrote a long and terrible account of its misery and devastation to the Queen. Of Munster he wrote:

'as touching the estate of the whole country, for so much as I saw of it, having travelled from Youghal to Cork, from Cork to Kinsale, and from thence to the uttermost bounds of it towards Limerick: like as I never was in a more pleasant country in all my life, so never saw I a more waste and desolate land, no, not in the confines of other countries where actual war hath continually been kept by the greatest princes of Christendom; and never heard I such lamentable cries and doleful complaints made by that small remain of poor people which yet are left.' [1]

He goes on in a well-known passage to describe the scenes of desolation he saw and to indict the Earl of Desmond,

'who enjoyeth under his rule, or rather tyranny, the third part of this great country, which I assure your Majesty, I know to be greater than Yorkshire. In all which his limits neither is your name reverenced, or your laws obeyed. Neither dare my Sheriff execute any part of his office therein.'

Sidney's remedy for this disorder was the introduction of a local system of government after the English model. 'But surely it will never be thoroughly well, till the same be made shire ground, and your Highness' writ current there as in your other countries.' He was in favour of Munster being erected into a Presidency on its own and given in charge to Sir Warham St. Leger as President.

St. Leger had had many years experience of Irish affairs. His relations with Desmond, the chief native ruler in Munster, were not unfriendly; Desmond had mortgaged to him several estates in Cork for certain large sums which he had received from him. These lands included the castle-abbey of Traghton, the castle of

[1] *Sidney Letters and Memorials* (ed. Collins) I, 24.

E

Carrigaline on the shores of Cork harbour, the whole district of Kerrycurrihy. Old Irish maps show the Kerrycurrihy country as lying to the west of Cork harbour, the best and most fertile park and ploughland. St. Leger no doubt was glad to bring Grenville, a relative by marriage and a man of property, into partnership with him in the occupation and cultivation of these lands. Grenville, on his return from Hungary in 1568, was free for another sphere of enterprise in which to invest money and energy: we hear later of a 'tall ship' of his in Cork harbour and he certainly took across with him a number of followers with the idea of settling them.

This fell in with the ideas of the Lord Deputy for introducing English administration into Munster, and Grenville was appointed Sheriff of Cork, we learn, during royal pleasure.[1] But St. Leger failed to be appointed President of Munster. He had a powerful enemy at Court in the Earl of Ormonde, a great favourite with the Queen; and he was thought by the English government too sympathetic to Desmond for Munster to be trusted to his hands. This had a paralysing effect upon St. Leger's and Grenville's efforts to administer and settle the country, just at the moment of greatest danger.

For James Fitzmaurice of Desmond, cousin of the Earl and the militant leader of his people, was just at this moment planning a large outbreak in the west with the connivance of Spain. Munster had been reduced to order by the visit of the Lord Deputy in 1568, and by the presence of St. Leger and Grenville. What added to James Fitzmaurice's determination to attack them was the fact that he had claims upon the country of Kerrycurrihy himself. The imprisonment of Desmond in London disturbed the whole province and gave Fitzmaurice the chance he was waiting for, to exert his own leadership. He saw his opportunity of linking up his Geraldine forces with the restive MacCarthies of the extreme western fastnesses and with the Butlers, who were in revolt against the decision to give Sir Peter Carew the barony of Idrone, in Leinster.

It was an extremely dangerous situation. The revolt might easily spread over the whole south of Ireland. The Lord Deputy

[1] *Biographia Britannica*, IV, 2284.

was out of the country; so also were Ormonde and Desmond, the two most powerful nobles whose presence might quell the gathering storm. St. Leger was in England about the Presidency, trying to get the powers which, if granted in time, would have forestalled the trouble. The Government, too late, appointed a Lord President, but not St. Leger; they nominated another Devonshire man, Sir John Pollard, to the office.

Grenville was left, virtually alone and without resources, to face this threatening situation. He decided to cross over to England himself to aid St. Leger's representations at Court, to press upon the dilatory government the urgency of the position and demand immediate reinforcements. Lady St. Leger and Mrs. Grenville with her children were left behind in Cork. He can hardly have known how near the Irish were to breaking out, though he realised the danger. He left Cork on 15 June, and the very day after he sailed Fitzmaurice and MacCarthy More, the head of the MacCarthies, broke out into the plains and descended upon Kerrycurrihy.

The first news we have of them is from Andrew Skiddy, a loyal citizen of Cork with whom Grenville was on friendly terms, who wrote to the Lord Deputy on 17 June, that the rebels were even now spoiling all the inhabitants of Kerrycurrihy and laying siege to the abbey of Traghton; 'they have continued in camp all this last night . . . the abbey is seven miles hence.' [1] The same day the Mayor of Cork reported that Fitzmaurice and MacCarthy More had with them 'a great host of horsemen, kerne, and gallowglass to the number of two thousand'; that they were bent on spoiling the whole of the country in the occupation of St. Leger and Grenville; that they were cutting off such citizens of Cork as were without the walls and threatening Kinsale as well as Cork; and desiring corn to be sent them from Waterford to provision the city against siege.[2]

Lady St. Leger and Mrs. Grenville shut themselves up in the city, drawing in what outposts they could; but the descent had been so sudden, they were evidently taken by surprise and without preparations. Next day, Lady St. Leger wrote to the Lord Deputy of the rapid progress the rebels were making:

[1] S.P. Ireland, 28, no. 35.   [2] ibid. no. 36.

'On Wednesday last the Sheriff went into England; on the morrow after, James Fitzmaurice with four thousand people, was in Kerrycurrihy by seven of the clock. Warning we had none, so that our houses were not so well furnished as they ought to have been. So, my Lord, they have taken Traghton and all that I had there and killed all my men. All this they did on Friday. My men kept the house until they had gotten pick-axes and then they undermined the house and came in. The first man they killed was John Enchedon and all that was in the house. Then the next morning, being Saturday, they came to the castle of Carrigaline. In the meantime I caused them to come away, for they had neither meat nor drink, nor powder for to keep it one day. The enemies were informed by the tenants what victual and provision was in the castle; they understanding their want, were determined to tarry the famishing of them. So that Saturday morning before James's coming there I sent a boat for them and had not time to carry away my stuff. So, my good Lord, the best and the greatest store of my stuff is gone, and all our horses that we and the Sheriff had. James hath confessed and showed your Lordship's letters that you sent to the Sheriff. Good my Lord, take pity on me; they say plainly that they will never leave the town of Cork till they have me and the Sheriff's wife.' [1]

Lady St. Leger's letter gives the impression of a high-spirited and courageous woman, capable of taking the initiative in her husband's absence. She certainly needed to be, in the frontier conditions prevailing west of Cork, and particularly at a moment like this with James Fitzmaurice and his hordes clamouring at the gates for her and Mrs. Grenville's surrender – a surrender which the citizens began to consider as hope of succour was delayed. What would have happened to them if they had fallen into the hands of the natives, we may imagine from what happened to the various ladies who fell into Shane O'Neill's hands later on.

A fuller report of Jasper Horsey's informs us that within Traghton Abbey there were six English arquebusiers with John

[1] S.P. Ireland, no. 37.

Enchedon and sixteen kerne, all of whom were slain. Fitzmaurice had shown intercepted letters from the Lord Deputy to
Grenville ordering the apprehension and detention of Lords
Roche and Barry, so that they were making no resistance to the
rebels. Horsey reported that in the far west the galleys were
being manned to spoil along the coast; 'and here is a tall ship of
Sir Warham St. Leger and of Mr. Grenville's, very well
appointed and all unrigged, and no more keeping her than four
men, who is daily threatened to be burned by James Fitzmaurice and his wicked company.' He adds that if he could get
mariners enough to sail her and victual to feed them, he would
gladly go and meet the western galleys.[1]

While Cork held out, the newly-appointed President of Munster was detained by contrary winds and an attack of gout, at
Ilfracombe. St. Leger, consumed with anxiety and impatience,
bombarded Cecil with letters from his Southwark house; he
wrote that it would be better for the Queen to spend £40,000
than that Cork should be lost. Towards the middle of July,
Fitzmaurice addressed a demand to the Mayor and citizens 'to
abolish out of the city that old heresy newly raised and invented,
and namely Barnaby Daly and all therein that be Huguenots
both men and women and Grenville's wife and children,' and
that they should restore Catholicism.[2] It is evident that the
Rising was nationalist in character, a revolt of the native Irish
against both Protestantism and the English.

But relief was now at hand. It must have been the result of
Grenville's importunity that within a fortnight of his leaving
Cork, the Council sent orders down to the south-western
counties to levy soldiers immediately for service in Ireland.
Before the end of the month, a relief force of some four hundred
men had arrived,[3] and the Lord Deputy was on the way with
six hundred more from Dublin. Lady St. Leger was fully re-
lieved at Cork; Carrigaline Castle re-taken and garrisoned; the
local chiefs submitted after some wasting of the country;
Ormonde arrived and restored order in Leinster. Hard on the
heels of the Lord Deputy, there followed the young Humphrey

[1] S.P. Ireland, no. 38.   [2] ibid. 29, no. 8.
[3] S.P. Dom. Eliz. 54, nos. 1–3.

Gilbert, to whom was entrusted the task of pacifying Munster. It was in this campaign that he first won fame; his progress through the province was characterised by extraordinary dash and a foolhardy bravery which paralysed his opponents. James Fitzmaurice was driven once more into the wilds of the forest of Aherlow in the far west.[1]

Grenville returned with St. Leger to take part in the subjugation of the rebels and remained there for another year engaged in the heartrending task of erecting order out of the chaos of Munster. The Lord Deputy wrote a handsome testimony to their part in staying the insurrection from engulfing the whole of the south of Ireland. MacCarthy More, he wrote to Cecil, had the intention of making himself 'King of the south part of this Realm; and I find good proof by letters from her Majesty's good subjects of those parts, that Sir Warham hath been the greatest stay, without whom and Grenville, they suppose the most of the Irishry had revolted.' [2]

But neither did this move the Government in St. Leger's favour; in justifiable resentment, he withdrew to England where he spent the next ten years. Grenville had embarked upon the Irish enterprise under St. Leger's ægis; he was a young man and St. Leger fifteen years his senior. He now withdrew with St. Leger. It had been an unfortunate venture; everything he had put into it, he had lost; the country he had hoped to cultivate, lay waste; nothing of it all remained save his claims upon the land. Before the year 1569 was out, or at latest, early in 1570, he brought his family back to Stowe. He did not see Ireland again for twenty years.

[1] Bagwell, c. XXVI.   [2] *Sidney Letters and Memorials*, I, 39.

CHAPTER IV

THE WESTERN SEA-BOARD

DURING this time in which Grenville was occupied in Ireland, momentous things were happening on the western sea-board and to the minds of the western seamen. And not their minds only; there was the actual disaster that overtook the third and most important of Hawkins' slaving voyages at San Juan de Ulloa and brought him struggling home across the Atlantic through the winter of 1568, to arrive in Mount's Bay in the *Minion* with a handful of starving sailors.

Hawkins had set out on 2 October 1567 from Plymouth with a little fleet of four trading vessels and two old Queen's ships, the *Jesus of Lübeck* and the *Minion*; there sailed with him, his kinsman the young Francis Drake. They made a good voyage along the coast of Guinea collecting slaves, and with the new year crossed over to the Caribbean to dispose of them. Here they had good trade, especially, after some forcible persuasion, at Rio de la Hacha, 'from whence come all the pearls.' They were about to leave the Caribbean by the Florida channel when they were driven back by storms to the coast of Mexico and were forced to enter the harbour of San Juan de Ulloa to refit. Here the plate fleet from Spain, bringing Don Martin Enriquez, the new Viceroy of Mexico, bore down upon them. They could have resisted and prevented him from entering the harbour; but that would have been an overt act of war and Hawkins' whole case was that his was peaceable and lawful trading. He took the risk; and the Spaniards made a surprise attack upon the English. A regular, or rather irregular, action developed in which Hawkins lost most of his men and ships; only the *Minion* and the *Judith* succeeded in making good their escape, the latter under Drake parting company in the night and making straight for home – 'which bark,' as Hawkins wrote with severity afterwards, 'the same night forsook us in our great misery.'

It was a turning-point in the relations between England and Spain, which had hitherto, in spite of Elizabeth's Protestantism, been those of amity. The disastrous consequences for Spain of a breakdown of the friendship with England were to be forcibly brought home to Philip before the old year was out. The breakdown, when it came, was the result of several factors operating together. There was Philip's decision to send his ablest and most ruthless soldier, Alva, with the pick of the Spanish veterans from Italy, to crush the Protestant resistance in the Netherlands. This, England could never afford to allow; a great power dominant in the Netherlands, particularly Catholic Spain, would have been a threat to her national security. It was vital to keep the resistance in the Netherlands alive by some means or other. Happily it was the good fortune of the western ports to provide the means.

In the autumn of 1568 Philip had raised a large loan from the Italian bankers for the payment of Alva's troops, restive for lack of pay; and at the end of November he despatched it up the Channel, a large mass of treasure, in a fleet of small ships, unarmed merchantmen and pinnaces. He was evidently re-lying on the English alliance—or assuming the same state of affairs to prevail as when he had been King in England; for the Channel was swarming with the privateers which the re-sumption of the wars in France had brought out, most of them Huguenot, belonging to the port of Rochelle, flying under the flag of the Prince of Condé or William of Orange, but many of them English and west-countrymen. The autumn storms and the ubiquitous privateers, drove Philip's treasure-ships to take refuge in English ports; one with fifty-nine chests of specie, fled into Southampton to avoid her pursuers, others with still more aboard were driven in to shelter at Saltash and at Fowey.

Already as the year wore on and there was no news of Haw-kins, his friends and backers in the voyage began to be anxious. On 3 December his brother William heard a report that he had been killed by the Spaniards and at once wrote to Cecil suggesting reprisals on the Spanish treasure-ships. Perhaps Cecil did not need the hint; the general posture of affairs was so critical, with Mary Queen of Scots now on his hands, and a threat of a most formidable combination of the northern Catholic Lords with the aristocratic conservatives headed by Norfolk and Arundel. He acted with decision and at once wrote to Sir Arthur Champernowne to put through the delicate operation.

What precisely Elizabeth meant by her action, whether to annex the treasure or no, was a matter for much discussion and diplomatic finessing over the next few months; but one cannot have much doubt what Champernowne understood it to be from the first, if one attends to his own words:

'I have so devised,' he wrote, 'that neither these of Saltash, nor the others of Fowey shall depart, having in such sort persuaded with them for their abode there until the departure of the French fleet which lay in wait for them, that they seemed to take my said persuasions in good part, although the favour which I show to Monsieur Chatelier might give them some occasion to suspect my dealings . . . The whole treasure in both places is such that it is supposed to be worth £40,000 sterling, and therefore most fit for her majesty, and not to be enterprised of any subject . . . Wherefore if it shall seem good to your Honour that I with others shall give the attempt for the recovery of it to her majesty's use, which cannot be without blood, I will not only take it in hand to be brought to good effect, but also receive the blame thereof unto myself to the end so great a commodity should redound to her grace, hoping that after bitter storms of her displeasure showed at the beginning to colour the fact, I shall find the calm of her favour in such sort as I am most willing to hazard myself to serve her majesty.' [1]

Of such were the servants of Elizabeth made; it was the same terms on which Drake later roamed the seas. The goodly, not to say godly, enterprise went through and Philip's treasure, for lack of which the troops in the Netherlands turned mutinous, found its way to the Tower of London. It was as pretty a piece of Machiavellianism as had been seen out of Italy; but it kept

[1] S.P. Dom. Eliz. 49, no. 1.

Alva employed on the other side of the water when he might
have been aiding the Rising of the Northern Earls and it greatly
hindered the forward advance of Catholicism at a moment of
great danger.

These years from 1569 to 1571 were perhaps the most critical
in all Elizabeth's reign. The Armada year was more spectacular, but it is doubtful if it offered such a combination of
dangers as the earlier crisis. For at this time there were wide-
spread and powerful forces in opposition to the Queen and
Cecil, which might have formed an overmastering combination
with foreign powers; whereas by 1588 the country was ready to
face the great challenge from Spain unitedly. These forces were
the Catholic opposition now raising its head after ten years of
Elizabeth's rule, and the feudal aristocracy which hated Cecil's
government. What made the situation dangerous was that the
conservative lords were at times a majority of the Council and
only the Queen's unwavering support brought Cecil safely
through. Their leaders were the Duke of Norfolk and the in-
sufferably aristocratic Earl of Arundel, the twelfth of his line.
Norfolk's first wife was his daughter and heiress, and the plan
was now to marry Norfolk to Mary as a step to the English
throne. The crisis lasted for two years during which intrigue
and counter-intrigue went on. The rising of the Northern Earls
in the autumn of 1569 and Pius V's excommunication of Elizabeth in February 1570 were but incidents in it. Norfolk and
Arundel were in and out of the Tower or in confinement in their
town houses; sometimes Cecil's power seemed to fail and he had
to buy over the Duke to divide his opponents. Finally the
threads of the conspiracy, as brought together by Ridolfi, an
Italian agent in England, were unravelled and evidence
obtained by which the Duke was brought to the block.

Such was the excitement in 1569 that orders went forth for
musters to be taken throughout the country and for the coasts
to be put in a state of defence. In Cornwall the Catholic Sir
John Arundell of Lanherne appeared in his place along with
Sir William Godolphin at the head of the Commission for
mustering the county – men, horses, armour and weapons.

Grenville was absent in Ireland; and in his place in the Returns from the parishes, we find Diggory Tremayne as the chief person at Kilkhampton, returning 'one light gelding able and meet for a light horseman with harness and weapons requisite for the same.' [1]

Next year the Government made up its mind to impose the Oath subscribing to the Act of Uniformity, as the test of loyalty to the Elizabethan Establishment, upon all Justices of the Peace throughout the country. It had come to the parting of the ways; hitherto there had been a rough toleration extended to Catholics under Elizabeth's government. From now on, since the Pope had thrown down his challenge to her title, Catholics were to be confronted with the direct choice; either to conform to the established forms in religion and go forward in agreement with Elizabeth's regime, or to be dropped from all place and responsibility under it and to tread the path that led to isolation, fines, imprisonment and, not impossibly, death.

In Cornwall, the first victim of the new test was Sir John Arundell. At December Quarter Sessions 1559, the Cornish Justices met at Bodmin to make their subscription to the Oath. Sir John did not appear, although, as his fellow-justices wrote to the Council, 'at our last assembly Sir John Arundell did then forbear to subscribe, but (as we thought) not with other purpose than the accomplishment of his duty at this day of our new assembly, which was by him specially appointed and he is now absent for what cause we are ignorant.' Apparently Sir John had had difficulties with his conscience in the interval; nor did he subscribe, when several months later at the April Quarter Sessions at Helston, Sir William Godolphin, who had previously been absent upon his government of the Scilly Isles, gave in his adhesion. The Justices, thereupon, according to the tenor of the council's letters, required a recognisance from Arundell to appear before the Council when required. On 28 April 1570, at Bodmin, Grenville subscribed the Oath; its tenor was to observe the Act for Uniformity of common prayer and service in church and the administration of the sacraments. He promised that his family should repair to the parish church for divine

[1] S.P. Dom. Eliz., 52, no. 3.

75

service and receive the sacraments 'from time to time according to the tenor of the act of Parliament' – in its way, a nice epitome of the Elizabethan settlement.[1]

Next year, the crisis still continuing, though tension was somewhat relaxed, Elizabeth summoned a Parliament, the third of her reign. She had had such a disillusioning experience with her previous Parliament, perpetually pestering her on the subject of marriage and the succession—a question which she was by no means so sure of solving by marriage as they were – that she told the French Ambassador that three Parliaments were enough for any reign and she would have no more of them. But the alarms of the past two years had cost money and she wanted legislation passed in reply to the Bulls of the Pope; so that when the time came, she was as gracious as ever to her faithful Commons. Parliament was summoned for 2 April 1571, and Grenville was returned to it as Knight of the shire for Cornwall.[2] Among the west-country contingent that went up to Westminster were his father-in-law, Sir John St. Leger, who sat, with Peter Edgcumbe, as Knight of the shire for Devon. His cousin George Grenville was returned for one of the Launceston seats; Henry and John Killigrew were there, and Sir Humphrey Gilbert, fresh from his triumphs in Ireland, for which he had been knighted by the Lord Deputy. He and John Hawkins were members for Plymouth.

Grenville was at once brought into the committee-work of the House, a circumstance which lends additional support to the view that this was not his first Parliament. It seems possible that he was a member, if D'Ewes's name Greithfield is a misprint for Greenfield, of the important Committee of supply which was set up at the beginning of the Parliament 'to consider of the proportion, and time of yielding some relief unto her Majesty.'[3] But he was indubitably member of a small, though important committee, to which was committed the second of the several bills brought forward for ecclesiastical reform. We read that on Saturday 28 April,

[1] S.P. Dom. Eliz., 67, no. 9.
[2] Browne Willis, *Notitia Parliamentaria*, 79.
[3] D'Ewes, *Journal*, 159.

'the second Bill for Religion was read the second time, and committed unto the Lord President of the Marches of Wales, Sir Thomas Smith, Sir Thomas Scott, Mr. Attorney of the Wards, Mr. Norton, Mr. Greenfield, Mr. Grimston, Mr. Smith, Mr. Fenner and Mr. Agmondsham, who were appointed to meet this Afternoon at three of the Clock in the Star-Chamber.' [1]

There was a strong Protestant tide running and the Commons were determined to press forward the work of reformation, by abolishing pluralities, non-residence, licences and dispensations; they wanted to make changes in the Thirty-nine Articles and in the Book of Common Prayer. A number of Bills dealing with religion were brought forward from previous Parliaments; the second of them, which Grenville was to consider on his committee, dealt with the order of ministers and doubtless contemplated a departure from strict episcopacy. By what influence he was appointed to the committee, whether by these Protestant members like Strickland and Peter Wentworth, the irrepressible member for Barnstaple, or by the Privy Councillors as likely to support the Queen, we do not know. It is hardly likely to have been the former, especially when we consider that Sir Humphrey Gilbert came forward conspicuously in the debates as an exponent and defender of the Queen's prerogative. But the Queen was in no mind to have the Reformation carried forward a stage further under the ægis of the Commons; and desirable as many of the reforms would have been, she preferred that they should not be made at all, rather than have Parliament interfering in the sphere of her prerogative, the Church. On 29 May, Parliament was dissolved and the members were free to return to their respective counties.

Next year, a new Parliament was summoned, to meet on 8 May; chiefly to strengthen the Government's hands in dealing with Mary Queen of Scots and in bringing Norfolk to execution. For the classes from which the Commons drew their strength, the country gentry and the merchants of the towns, were prepared to go much further than the Government in the attack on Catholicism, the Queen of Scots and the old aristocracy.

[1] ibid. 180.

Grenville was returned, this time for Dunheved; and his young cousin, George Grenville, for Camelford. Peter Edgcumbe and Richard Chamond were Knights of the Shire for Cornwall, as Sir John St. Leger and Arthur Basset, another of Grenville's cousins, for Devon. For Plymouth, the members were again John Hawkins and Edmund Tremayne, who counted as one of the official members, in close touch with the Government. Among the Cornish members were William Killigrew for Helston, another official person, since he was Groom of the Chamber to the Queen, a life-long servant; and Henry Killigrew, for Truro, employed on many diplomatic missions by the Crown, envoy in turn to Scotland, France and the German Princes. But these West Country members were no mere royal nominees as is sometimes thought; it happened that they agreed with the Government, or where they disagreed it was in wishing to go farther and faster; was there not among them, for example, the notorious Peter Wentworth, member for Tregony, or his brother Paul, member for Liskeard? [1]

The Government lost no time in consulting Parliament about the business of the Queen of Scots. On 12 May, Lord Keeper Bacon signified to the Lords and Commons the Queen's pleasure that twenty-one of the Upper House and forty-four of the Lower should meet on the morrow 'in the Morning at eight of the Clock in the Star-Chamber, then and there to consult and deliberate upon matters concerning the Queen of Scots.' The most influential members of the Commons were chosen, both of the official and unofficial elements; among them were the Treasurer, the Comptroller, the Lord Deputy of Ireland and Sir Hugh Paulet, Grenville's old guardian; Henry Killigrew, Peter Wentworth and 'Mr. Greenfield Sen.,' who must be Grenville so described to distinguish him from his younger cousin, George, the only other Grenville in the House.[2]

The House was almost entirely taken up with its proceedings against Mary Queen of Scots – in its way an advantage, for it meant that there was the less time for it to badger the Government with its protestantising proposals. A 'Bill for the Continua-

[1] *Official Return of Members of Parliament*, 1, 408.
[2] D'Ewes, *Journal*, 206.

tion of certain Statutes' was read on 25 June and committed
to a small Committee of whom Grenville was one; next day he
was among a larger number who were appointed to confer with
the Lords on the same matter.[1] In the end, Elizabeth did not
proceed to extremes against Mary; it was enough to inculpate
her and hold her under the perpetual threat of proceedings for
high treason. Parliament was more than willing, and had given
Cecil enthusiastic support in bringing Norfolk to trial, proceedings which, in the case of the highest peer of the realm, were so
repugnant to the Queen that she could hardly bring herself to
sign his death-warrant. However, after many hesitations she
yielded, and the Duke was executed on 2 June. On the last day
of the month, Parliament was dissolved.

It is to the year 1571 that we owe the one portrait-painting of
Grenville which we possess, that which now hangs in the
National Portrait Gallery. Elizabethan portraits are apt to be
not good; and the portrait of Grenville is only a fair specimen
of its class. Fortunately, however, the head is the best part of
it and carries conviction. The lettering upon it says: AN. DNI.
1571. AETATIS. SUAE. 29. This too is convincing: the inscription is undoubtedly contemporary and, what is interesting,
agrees with 1542 as the year of his birth.[2] It is a handsome
young man that is portrayed, of a very recognisable Devonshire
type: oval head, fair hair and blue eyes. The hair is brushed
well back from the forehead, where it is already beginning to
thin at the temples, while it is full and thick round the ears
and at the back. The moustaches and beard are those of a
young man, not very full or thick, and revealing a noticeably
prominent underlip. The real interest of the portrait is in the
eyes, which are full and expressive, beneath beautifully curved
brows, rather low upon the eyes and so exposing a fine and lofty
forehead. But the impression of the character they give is
curious and arresting: the eyes are intense, watchful, giving the
impression of a man very much on the alert, a quick and in-
flammable temperament.

It is an effective portrait, in its way. One does not have to

[1] ibid. 224.   [2] v. ante p. 37.

attach too much credence to the colouring; yet the high colour in the cheeks goes with the fair Devonshire type. The whole personality is that of a man of action on the *qui vive*. Moreover, one can see how it is possible that this handsome man in the late twenties might become the person portrayed in the later engraving in Holland's *Heroologia*.

Drake's first portrait, the little miniature done by Isaac Oliver some time after the voyage to Nombre de Dios, affords a curious contrast; for though Grenville and Drake were much the same age, it portrays Drake as yet so very immature: a round babyish face with no beard and only incipient moustaches, but with the high arched eyebrows which all the portraits of him show. Yet they were both of the Devonshire type, high-coloured and fair-haired; unlike Gilbert and Ralegh, who were dark and black-haired like Cornishmen.

Drake was now employed in getting his own back on the Spaniards for the losses of San Juan de Ulloa. The circumstances of these years of crisis were favourable; and in 1570 he fitted out two ships, the *Dragon* and the *Swan* with which he went out again to the West Indies, the beginning of his daring career of private war on the Spaniards. Next year while Grenville was occupied with his duties as member of Parliament, Drake went out in the *Swan* alone. These were rather reconnoitring expeditions, but the latter was successful in more ways than one. For one thing it paid handsomely; from Carthagena harbour he succeeded in cutting out a ship of 180 tons. There were other prizes too which he made and carried off to his hiding-place, a pleasant natural harbour abounding with fish and game, which he named Port Pheasant, in the recesses of the Gulf of Darien. More than this, it was on this expedition that he conceived the scheme of a raid on Nombre de Dios, got his information about the mule-trains crossing the Isthmus from Panama with the treasure, and took all his soundings for the next expedition.

He set sail again from Plymouth at Whitsun 1572, in the *Pascoe* of 70 tons and the little *Swan*, on the voyage which made his name and fame; his brothers John and Joseph were with him, as also John Oxenham. It was very much the character of a family enterprise; but no voyage ever made from Plymouth achieved such a height of daring and adventure, not even his own later voyage round the world. From his lair in the Gulf, which despite the Spaniards' discovery of it he continued to use as his base, he made his attack on Nombre de Dios; with only seventy men he made himself master of the town and was only forced to retire from the very 'mouth of the Treasure-House of the World' because, severely wounded, he was carried off by his men. But undaunted he went on collecting prizes and plunder, and in the New Year planned his raid into the interior of the country in alliance with the revolted cimaroons, which was intended as an attack upon Panama itself, but turned into a coup against the treasure-train at the very gates of Nombre de Dios. Leaving his men loaded with treasure upon the coast, he got off in a raft to look for his pinnaces, promising them 'if it pleased God he should put his foot in safety aboard his frigate, he would, God willing, by one means or other, get them all aboard in despite of all the Spaniards in the Indies.' Rich and successful beyond their expectations, they sailed home from Cape Florida to the Isles of Scilly in twenty-three days –

'and so arrived at Plymouth on Sunday about sermon-time August 9, 1573; at which time the news of our captain's return did so speedily pass over all the Church, and surpass their minds with desire and delight to see him, that very few or none remained with the preacher, all hastening to see the evidence of God's love and blessing towards our gracious Queen and country, by the fruit of our captain's labour and success.'

Meanwhile, Hawkins at home was engaged in his own more devious way of inflicting revenge upon Spain; a typical Elizabethan piece of double-dealing by which the new Spanish Ambassador, Don Guerau de Spes, a fool and filled with a fanatical hatred of England, was inveigled into supposing that Hawkins would aid Philip and Alva's plans for an invasion by going over at the critical moment with his whole western squadron guarding the entrance to the Channel. Burghley, of course, was privy to the scheme; the price Philip paid for services never intended to be rendered was the return of Hawkins' men who had been taken at San Juan and imprisoned in

Spain, with a considerable sum of money in addition. When the moment was ripe, and Burghley had unravelled the Ridolfi plot, the plan was blown into the air and Don Guerau, shown up for the fool he was, sent packing from the country. For a time, it looked as though there would be war between England and Spain; certainly these things accounted in part for the exacerbation of the Parliament of 1572 against Mary Queen of Scots, upon whom these designs pivoted.

But both England and Spain were too much occupied otherwise, and the fundamental antagonism between them not yet sufficiently apparent, for them to embark on war. The mercantile interest, particularly in London, was in favour of peace; and an effort was made to patch things up. With the beginning of 1573 a new temporising policy, to the confusion of her friends, was observable on Elizabeth's part. A convention was arrived at by which the mutual embargoes on trade with each other were removed; and the Queen sent a few warships down-Channel, taking some twenty sail of the Huguenot privateers and some eight hundred of their men. It was a very profitable proceeding; Elizabeth, having gained at the expense of her enemies, was now profiting at the expense of her friends; so winning on both scores and, as usual, making the best of both worlds.

CHAPTER V

THE GREAT SOUTH-SEA PROJECT: GRENVILLE AND DRAKE

To seek new worlds, for gold, for praise, for glory . . .
SIR WALTER RALEGH: *Book of the*
Ocean to Cinthia

THE restiveness of these years, the signs of a new orientation of English policy, the uncertainty of our future relations with Spain were the symptoms of new forces at work, driving the country irresistibly forward along new untried paths. These men of the western ports, but not they alone, felt that it was on the seas that the destiny of their country lay. 'For discovery of sundry rich and unknown lands, fatally (and as it seemeth by God's providence) reserved for England, and for the honour of your majesty' – such were Grenville's words in petitioning the Queen to allow the great enterprise he planned in 1573-4. For he was at length affected by the new currents flowing, somewhat later than the seamen of the West Country, his contemporaries, the Hawkins' and Drake, or than his cousin Humphrey Gilbert. But his position was rather different from theirs; he was younger than the rest of them, except for Drake; to the Hawkins' it was their business. Gilbert was a younger son, while Grenville was the head of his family, whose tradition in any case was martial rather than maritime.

In the early seventies, as a concomitant of these sea-changes, there was a great growth of interest in geographical matters. It was, as these things are, confined to a small circle; but it was an influential one. There was great interest, for example, among the men at Court who were directing the country's destiny; Burghley was much alive to the new tendencies and

83

lent his support to the Hakluyts, to the elder and younger Digges, the mathematicians, and to the universally learned Dr. Dee. It became the fashion – though in some cases it was more, a real enthusiasm – among the leading spirits at Court, Leicester, Walter Earl of Essex, Sir Christopher Hatton, as later with Ralegh.[1]

The real significance of this interest in geography was the passionate excitement aroused in the question of a North-East or a North-West Passage to Cathay. It was a matter of the greatest importance for the future of English expansion. The riches of the trade with the Far East had been revealed by the Portuguese voyages via the Cape of Good Hope; but southward expansion up to the time of the Hawkins' voyages was blocked by the Portuguese and Spanish monopoly, and it was now being made abundantly evident that any attempts to penetrate their privileged sphere would mean fighting. The Government's attitude towards open war beyond the line was an equivocal one; they did not recognise the monopoly, but those who fought their own way into it, did so at their own risk and were liable to be disclaimed at any time. And so the question of a northern Passage to the Far East was a vital one; if there were one at all, and most geographical opinion agreed that there was, it would fall naturally into the sphere of English control, and being nearer than the Cape of Good Hope, give this country the larger control of the trade in Far Eastern commodities at cheaper rates.

Opinion was divided into two schools; those who favoured the North-Eastern Passage and those who supported the idea of a North-Western. The former had a first innings, with the brilliant navigator Richard Chancellor, and the brothers Stephen and William Borough. Humphrey Gilbert made himself the exponent of the North-Western school, collected a great deal of material on the subject and in the winter of 1565–6 debated the project against Anthony Jenkinson before the Privy Council. He then started to put this material into shape, the 'Discourse to prove a Passage by the North-West to Cathay and the East Indies'; but service in Ireland and in the Netherlands inter-

[1] cf. Taylor, *Tudor Geography, 1485–1583.*

vened, and it was not published till 1576, having been prepared for the press by the poet George Gascoigne. Meanwhile, the 'Discourse' circulated in manuscript and had a considerable influence on opinion; for it was a brilliant piece of work, having all Gilbert's vigour and inventiveness, and seemed convincing.

Ortelius and Mercator were agreed, by about 1569, that America was an island, and that between it and the continent of Asia there was a strait; this contemporaries mostly called the Strait of Anian. This strait, if it existed and was at all passable, would obviously be a quicker route than that by the north-east along the Arctic coast of Asia. Gilbert took his stand upon this and upon the argument, which men were by no means all convinced of yet, that the New World of America was separated from Asia and not merely an extension of it.

'When I gave myself to the study of geography,' he wrote, 'after I had perused and diligently scanned the descriptions of Europe, Asia and Africa, and conferred [i.e. compared] them with the maps and globes both antique and modern: I came in fine to the fourth part of the world, commonly called America, which by all descriptions I found to be an island environed round about with sea, having on the south side of it the fret or straight of Magellan, on the west side Mar del Sur, which sea runneth towards the north, separating it from the east parts of Asia, where the dominions of the Cathaians are: on the east part our West Ocean, and on the north side the sea that severeth it from Greenland, through which northern seas the Passage lieth, which I take now in hand to discover.' [1]

He argued, Elizabethan-like, from a variegated collection of authorities, from Plato's views of Atlantis in the *Timaeus* and the *Critias* and from Marinaeus Siculus to the Spanish gentleman from the West Indies, who in Ireland affirmed before the Lord Deputy and himself that Urdaneta had told him only eight years before that he had come from the Pacific into Germany through this North-West passage. This story was current in Spanish America at the time;[2] and neither the English nor the

[1] Hakluyt, *Principal Navigations*, VII, 160.
[2] Taylor, *Writings and Correspondence of the Hakluyts*, I, 80.

Spaniards had means of knowing whether it might not be true. Amid the rather fantastic medley of authorities, there do emerge some sound critical points. If America were not an island, but a part of the continent adjoining Asia, he argues, the people of the latter would by now have made some inroad into it, or at least have established contact. But the peoples of Tartary and Cathay and those of America 'have not had any traffic with each other.' He cites the information that came to Jaques Cartier of 'a great Sea at Saguinay, whereof the end was not known: which they pre-supposed to be the passage to Cathay' – probably a rumour of the great lakes of the American interior. Through the tract there runs the imperial idea that England might control the northern route to the east, as Spain and Portugal controlled the southern; and that

'through the shortness of the voyage, we should be able to sell all manner of merchandise, brought from thence, far better cheap than either the Portugal or Spaniard doth or may do. And further, we should share with the Portugal in the East, and the Spaniard in the West, by trading to any part of America, through Mar del Sur [i.e. the Pacific], where they can no manner of way offend us.'

It was a brilliant tract and Gilbert had a distinct literary gift. The only thing that was wanting was the strait itself; the new continent interposed an altogether insurmountable obstacle between England and the riches of Cathay. Hardly anyone, until Ralegh and the younger Hakluyt, conceived that the real colonial future of England lay in the far less exciting and less profitable way of settling the American continent. In this Grenville was to bear an important part.

Bound up with the question of the passage to Cathay was a second problem, even more obscure and no less exciting: what was there in the unknown spaces of the great South Sea, the Pacific?[1] This was the question which haunted the minds of Spanish and Portuguese seamen since the marvellous voyage of

[1] In the following paragraphs I am indebted to Dr. J. A. Williamson's Introduction to his edition of Sir Richard Hawkins's *Observations* (Argonaut Press, 1933).

Magellan in 1519, and of the geographers like Mercator and Ortelius. It occupied the thoughts of Dr. Dee in his study at Mortlake in the early seventies, and investigation into it was the primary object of the great voyage Grenville was planning in these years. At the beginning of the century, the South Sea was by no means so great in men's minds; for all that they knew it did not even exist, and the same sea that surrounded the Portuguese Moluccas in the East washed the western shores of Europe and was the Atlantic. So Columbus believed and to his death refused to face the truth that various indications were forcing upon him. In 1513 Balboa first saw the new ocean; but until Magellan's voyage no one knew how wide it was. After that, the problem became, what was it that filled those vast untraversed spaces to the south and east of his diagonal tract from the South Atlantic across the Pacific to the Philippines?

The answer that contemporary thought in the sixties and seventies gave was that there was a great Pacific continent stretching from Java and the Spice Islands in a south-easterly direction through the temperate zone to the Antarctic. Terra Australis began to appear upon the maps. From the time of Marco Polo the fabulous wealth of those imagined lands had stirred men's wondering curiosity; for he was understood to have reported that to the south-east of Asia there lay other rich countries, in particular the Kingdom of Lochac, or Beach, ruled by an independent monarch, with abundance of gold and brazil wood, of elephants and rare fruits, and seldom visited 'for that it standeth out of the way.' Beyond Lochac was the island of Pentain, abounding in aromatic trees, and southward again was the Kingdom of Malaim, remote but rich in spices and drugs. Marco Polo was, of course, speaking of the Malay peninsula; but the Elizabethans identified these lands with the unknown continent in the South Sea.

It does not so much matter that much of what they thought was incorrect; this was

'the geography accepted by the Elizabethans and the basis of their expeditions into the South Sea. With the identification of

Terris Australis with the fabled Lochac and Malaim the system was almost complete. One had but to traverse the Straits of Magellan and follow the Fuegian shore. It would stretch in a long sweep north-westwards to the tropics embracing all latitudes from 52° to 20° or even nearer to the Equator. So placed, it must contain a variety of useful products, and of peoples and kingdoms worth discovering. To its explorers and exploiters there would fall an Empire of the South no whit inferior to the Spanish Empire of the West and the Portuguese Empire of the East. Moreover, having discovered this long coast and established bases upon it, a goal in the region of established knowledge was in sight – the Moluccas, which had shipped priceless cargoes to Lisbon for half a century past. That was the dream of the speculators of the 1570's.' [1]

Just at this moment, amid the excitement of so much theoretical speculation, two contributions of the first importance were made by the Spaniards to the real knowledge of the region. In 1564 Legazpi sailing west from New Spain rediscovered the Philippines, and next year Urdaneta made the passage back from the islands to the Mexican coast. In 1567 Mendaña sailed out of Callao and steered west-south-west for a great distance in search of the hidden continent; but baffled by the vastness of this ocean, he finally turned north-westwards and instead of finding New Zealand or Australia, he reached the Solomon Islands. He thought them to be the fringe of a continental coast, as indeed they are not far from Australia; and the Spanish expectations of what they would yield stand expressed in the name he gave them.

The news of the discovery reached England not long after, perhaps through Spaniards as well as through the English merchants in Seville. But one source of information we know for certain. Henry Hawks, one of the Seville colony, was in Mexico from 1567 to 1571, the very year of these voyages; and when, escaping from the arms of the Inquisition, he reached England in 1572, he brought with him all the latest information. In Mexico he had known the younger Diego Gutierrez, who had

[1] Williamson, p. xxi.

been with Urdaneta on the Philippines voyage. He knew too of
the discovery of the Solomon Islands – the Isles of Gold. And
he mentions in his report a voyage of exploration sent out from
Mexico to seek the western end of the Straits of Anian (i.e. the
North-West Passage) 'which they call the Englishman's strait' –
perhaps because of Cabot's entry into Hudson's bay, its supposed
eastern end. 'They say,' he wrote, 'that strait lieth not far from
the main land of China, which the Spaniards account to be
marvellous rich.' [1]

Here we have brought together the two main themes – the
twin secrets of the Pacific – which Grenville's Project was intended to elucidate and which appear again among the objects
of Drake's voyage round the world in 1577–80. Whether there
was any contact between Henry Hawks and Grenville we do not
know, and are not likely to know now; it is a region of obscure
inference and fascinating surmise that we are working in. But
it is worth noting that Hawks's view regarding the Straits of
Anian is that expressed in the Grenville Project.

This Project, upon which Grenville must have been working
for some time previously, first comes into the light of day with
the Petitions which he presented in his own name and those of
his partners to the Queen and the Lord Admiral on 22 March
1574.[2] This means that preparations must have been going on
at least through the winter of 1573–4. There can be no doubt
what the objective was: it was the unknown Pacific continent,
the fourth part of the world yet to be discovered, reserved (by
God's Providence) for England. Amongst the arguments for
the voyage enumerated amongst the Articles presented to the
Lord Admiral, we find:

'The aptness and as it were a fatal convenience that since the
Portugal hath attained one part of the new found world to the
east, the Spaniard another to the west, the French the third to
the north, now the fourth to the south is by God's providence
left for England, to whom the others in times past have been
first offered.' [3]

[1] Taylor, *Tudor Geography 1485–1583*, 113–17.
[2] S.P. Dom. Eliz. 95, nos. 63–4.   [3] ibid. no. 65.

The point is made doubly sure by the description of the purpose of the voyage:

'The discovery, traffic and enjoying for the Queen's Majesty and her subjects, of all or any lands, islands and countries southward beyond the equinoctial or where the Pole Antarctic hath any elevation above the horizon; and which lands, islands and countries be not already possessed or subdued by or to the use of any Christian Prince in Europe, as by the charts and descriptions shall appear.'

It was a matter of the utmost importance, if the voyage into the South Seas were to be permitted, that the Government should be assured that no attack upon the Spanish dominions was intended. At any time from 1569 to 1572, Elizabeth would probably not have minded – her relations with Spain could hardly be worse. But beginning with 1573, negotiations were entered upon to clear up all outstanding problems between the two countries and to achieve a basis for improved relations. This was arrived at in 1574 with the Convention of Bristol, an ominous event for the forward school of western seamen. It was in effect the reef upon which Grenville's Project foundered, for Elizabeth could hardly afford to risk the new agreement by permitting an expedition, led by a prominent subject, to sail into the closed Southern Sea, regarded by the Spaniards as their monopoly; while an attack upon the Spanish treasure-ships between Peru and Panama, the standing temptation of such an expedition (Drake later succumbed to it, or, more probably, intended it from the first), might have brought the whole might of the Spanish Empire down upon her before she was ready for it.

So, in the Petition to the Queen, to incline her mind favourably towards the enterprise, and tempering their purpose to the new winds of policy, the adventurers underline the point that their scheme would incur no offence or injury to any other Christian prince. Of their enterprise, they say, 'we have good and probable reasons to assure us, easy and feasible means to attain it, and the commodities be large, without injury or just offence to any Prince of Christendom.' Perhaps they assured the Queen a little too eagerly!

With the Lord Admiral, they were more specific as to the business side of their plans and their means of carrying them into effect. They describe themselves as

'certain gentlemen of the West Country desirous to adventure ourselves and our goods in matter of service honourable and profitable to the Queen's Majesty and the Realm, with like hope of benefit to arise unto such as shall be adventurers therein, and having sundry ways good and probable causes to lead us, both by our own understanding and the help of such whose skill and experience we have used, have thought upon and conceived a means by discovery of certain new trades of navigation and traffic to advance the honour of our sovereign Lady and Country, with enlarging the bounds of Christian religion, the beneficial utterance of the commodities of England, the increase and maintenance of seamen, the relief of the people at home, and sundry other commodities such as your wisdom can easily see to ensue thereof.'

They then go on to argue that the voyage is feasible. We have to remember that up to this time English navigation was almost exclusively confined to northern waters. It was mainly the Hawkins circle, the West Country seamen, who had only recently launched into equatorial waters with the voyages to Guinea and into the Caribbean; and to Elizabethan ships with their uncoppered bottoms, the warm waters of these regions offered special problems. In answer to these difficulties, the Articles state that Magellan had crossed the torrid zone six times, and that in the yearly voyage of the Portuguese around the Cape of Good Hope to the Moluccas it is passed four times, and on every voyage by the Spaniards to Brazil twice. Moreover, 'sundry of our own nation and some such as are to go in these voyages have passed it to Guinea, Brazil and other places' – a most interesting hint, where so much is dark, that support for this voyage was forthcoming from the Plymouth circle, that among the men who were to go were some who had been on the Hawkins' voyage to the south. Besides, they argue, 'the countries that we seek, so lie, that our course continueth not near the line but, crossing the same, still hasteth directly to the temperature of our own regions'; that is, Terra Australis. Here in these temperate climes, similar to England, there should be good vent for English commodities, particularly of cloth, 'wherein we most abound and the transportation whereof is most necessary for our people at home.'

As for the means which they have for accomplishing the voyage, they put forward the following considerations: 'Ships of our own well prepared. The West Country being the aptest of all parts of England for navigation southward. Mariners and sailors to whom the passage almost thither is known.' And those who are backing the enterprise propose to equip it at their own charges, setting forth four good ships, upon which they will spend some £5,000; £2,000 in shipping and equipment, £2,000 in victuals and necessaries for the company, and £1,000 in cloth and merchandise for trading. Among the advantages of the enterprise which they enumerate is 'the enlarging of Christian faith which those naked barbarous people are most apt to receive and especially when it shall not carry with it the unnatural and incredible absurdities of papistry.' This was more or less common form in all these early ventures in imperialism; or perhaps not merely common form, for nothing is more surprising than the devoutness of these sea-marauders and pioneers of empire, Hawkins, Drake, Gilbert. The farther they went and the more they ravaged, the more pious they became. Did not Elizabeth on one occasion protest of Hawkins that he had gone away a seaman and returned home a prating divine?

More substantial are the economic objectives, mercantilist in character:

'the abating of the prices of spices and such commodities that we now have at the Portugals and Spaniards hands, whereby they increase their riches upon our loss, when much spices and such like here spent, and bought dear of them, do with the less quantity consume the value of our cloths that they receive. The increase of the quantity of gold and silver that shall be brought out of Spain itself into England when the commodities coming out of Spain becoming this way cheaper,' etc.

There remains the danger of conflict with the Portuguese or the Spaniards. To this they answer:

'Our strength shall be such as we fear it not, besides that we mean to keep the ocean, and not to enter in or near any their ports or places kept by their force . . . In the places already subdued and inhabited by the Spaniard or Portugal we seek no possession nor interest; but only, if occasion be free, to traffic with them and their subjects which is as lawful and as much without injury as for the merchants in Portugal or Spain itself.'

Here was the rub; here they were treading on dangerous ground: the fact was that neither Spain nor Portugal regarded trading with their empires in the same light as trade with themselves: to them it was an incursion into forbidden territory. The more the adventurers argued, the more it raised awkward memories. They appealed to the Hawkins's voyages to Guinea and their trafficking in Mexico as a precedent, since they have 'been defended by her Majesty and Council, as friendly and lawful doing: much more this, which is but passing in the open sea by them to places that they neither hold nor know.' And they go on to claim that not only traffic, 'but also possession, planting of people and habitation hath been already judged lawful for other nations in such places as the Spaniards or Portugals have not already added to their possession.' They cite the grant made by the Queen, back in 1563, to Thomas Stukeley – who was a connection of Grenville's – for the discovery and occupation of Florida.

In conclusion, therefore, they asked that Letters Patent might be conferred upon them, constituting them into a corporation, and establishing 'some form of governance and authority in some persons of the Company of this adventure, so as by some regiment, obedience, quiet, unity and order may be preserved.' They prayed further that rules for the conduct of the voyage might be confirmed by the Queen's authority, as also

'for the agreement and obedience of the parties, for the contribution and charge, for the equality and partition: and severally orders to be appointed by her Majesty for the stablishing of her

Majesty's dominion and amity in such places as she shall assign unto: and for the rate and true answering of her Majesty's portion.'

This last shows that it was contemplated that the Queen herself should have a share in the enterprise, as she had had in Hawkins's voyages and was to have in Drake's. It was this factor of her own contribution to such ventures which gave her all the more power of calling them off, if for political reasons it became necessary.

Until recently it was not known what response, if any, this request for Letters Patent had. Owing to a mistaken endorsement upon the Petition, in a later hand, it was connected with the names of Sir George Peckham and others, with whom Grenville was never in association. While the draft of this very Patent in answer to the Petition, giving the names of Grenville and his associates, being misdated to the year 1590 in the *Calendar of State Papers*, failed ever to be connected, where it properly belongs, to the Grenville voyage.[1] In consequence, no one had realised how near the voyage came to being tried out three years before Drake set out upon its tracks and so was led on to the circumnavigation of the world. Nor was its importance grasped, even as a project. For it gave a new and original direction to English plans for expansion and was the first to put into shape the idea of an English empire in the southern seas. In the fuller and more complete form it took in the following year, it combined this idea with that of an attack upon the problem of the North-West Passage from the Pacific end, sailing up the west coast of America from the Straits of Magellan to the supposed Straits of Anian which were to be discovered somewhere in the latitude of California.

Just as the news of Spanish attempts upon these two problems had been brought home to England by Henry Hawks in 1572, so some attempt was made, if perfunctorily, by Drake on the great voyage of 1577 to 1580 to throw light upon them both. It was fortunate for him that when he got into the South Sea,

---

[1] These two mistakes were first cleared up by R. P. Chope in *Trans. Devon. Assoc.*, 1917.

he did not make either of them a main objective, but made for the gold coast of Peru. How do we know that Grenville would not have done the same if he had been allowed by the Queen to set sail? The very fact that he was not permitted to go, her relations with Spain in these years being amicable, shows what the Government must have suspected. In practically every respect, therefore, as far as intentions go – no doubt the emphasis on different purposes would differ with the man – Drake's voyage followed the Grenville Project. It is impossible not to conclude that Drake was acquainted with this earlier plan. Though there is no evidence that he knew Grenville at this time – there were others among the adventurers whom he did know, for example, William Hawkins. At this time, after his notorious triumphs in the Isthmus, he was lying low in Ireland and when he sailed in 1577, it was as his own master, to reap where Grenville had sown.

The draft Patent gives us the names of the adventurers:

'Richard Grenville, of Stowe in the county of Cornwall, Esquire, Piers Edgcumbe, Arthur Basset, John Fitz, Edmund Tremayne, William Hawkins, Alexander Arundell, Thomas Digges, Martyn Dare, Esquires, Dominic Chester of Bristol, Merchant, and divers other of our good and loving subjects.' [1]

There they all are: it is almost a muster of Grenville's family circle. Many of them have already appeared in these pages and do not need explanation. But it is clear from the special position which is assigned to Grenville throughout the document that he is the prime mover and the leading spirit of the enterprise. Not in the sense that he had more experience than the rest, but that he was the chief adventurer and had put more capital into it. His capital resources were considerable, probably larger than any single co-adventurer's, even Edgcumbe's or Hawkins's; and he could always raise money by selling some outlying property, such as the tenement in Launceston which he sold in April 1572 [2] – there may have been other sales we have now lost track of.

[1] S.P. Dom. Eliz. 235, no. 1.
[2] Peter, *Histories of Launceston and Dunheved*, 204.

Edgcumbe too was a man of considerable landed estates, and we find him interested in the contemporary developments of tin-mining and the search for other metals going on in Cornwall. Hawkins was wealthy and had inherited the position of the leading citizen in Plymouth. Out of a list of ships owned there in 1570, thirteen out of the sixteen named, including all the larger vessels, are listed under his name;[1] in addition he owned more property in the town than any other citizen. To him, the Grenville voyage – though he was closely associated with Grenville later in the ownership of the *Castle of Comfort*, which was to have been the flagship of it – was one in which he had but a subordinate interest, as compared with numerous ventures of his own. Of the others interested, Arthur Basset, son of John Basset and grandson of Lady Lisle, we know; and the ubiquitous and competent Edmund Tremayne. Alexander Arundell was Grenville's half-brother, some eight years junior to him, to whom he was very much attached; we hear of them together later on, associated in various other undertakings. John Fitz of Fitzford was a cousin, the son of Agnes, daughter of Roger Grenville of Stowe. Thomas Digges, the mathematician and geographer, who was evidently designed to accompany the expedition as its scientific expert, much as Thomas Harriot accompanied Grenville's Virginia voyage in 1585, though not himself a Devonshire man, was also connected with the circle by marriage, for his wife was a daughter of Sir Warham St. Leger. Dominic Chester was a well-known Bristol merchant who had lost heavily by the embargoes on trade in Spain and Portugal; perhaps his motive in supporting the enterprise was not unlike Hawkins's. Only Martin Dare remains unidentified; but the Dares were associated with Virginian exploration from 1587; Virginia Dare was the first English child to be born in America.

The Patent was drawn in very wide terms, granting them full licence

'to discover lands, territories, islands, dominions, peoples and places unknown which are not possessed by nor subject to any Christian prince . . . and specially such as have the Pole

[1] S.P. Dom. Eliz. 71, no. 75.

Antarctic elevate and the dominions of the great prince commonly called the great Cham of Cathay . . . and with the peoples so by them discovered to traffic, and the lands and peoples to join to the Christian faith and also to our dominion and amity so far as the same may be done . . .'

What could be fuller or more comprehensive as a grant for exploration or for settlement and possession? It is to be observed that their powers included the joining of lands discovered, if need be, to our dominion or amity – an objective which stands out clearly among the purposes of the expedition in the light of later information.

That the actual preparations for the voyage were now well advanced we know from the report of the Spanish Agent in London to Don Luis de Requesens, Governor of the Netherlands, as well as from the information sent by the French Ambassador to his home government. The interest aroused was significant. Antonio de Guaras, for it was probably he, wrote to Requesens on 17 May 1574:

'An English gentleman named Grenfield, a great pirate, and another called Champernowne, Vice-Admiral of the West, a co-father-in-law with Montgomeri, with others recently armed seven ships, four large and three small, with the advowed intention of going on a voyage of discovery to Labrador, but the real intention was to help Montgomeri in Normandy, which is very near the west coast. Since Montgomeri's defeat, it is said they will be too late to help him, and they consequently assert that they are going to the straits of M[agellan], their fleet being increased by three sail making ten ships in all, amongst which is the *Castle of Comfort*, a celebrated ship of 240 tons, the largest of them. The fleet is very well fitted and found, and will carry 1,500 men, soldiers and sailors, 500 of them being gentlemen. The real design is not yet known, as there are so many plans afoot, but, as they are going in this guise, they probably mean to sack some of the islands and lie in wait for the ships from the Indies and other merchantmen. They say they are taking with them a store hulk of 600 tons, with provisions, but I believe it is more likely to carry their plunder than to take stores. They sail this month. It is to be hoped that measures of precaution will be taken in the Canaries and elsewhere, as so many ships are leaving and it is very necessary that some remedy should be provided. Whilst things remain as they are these people will continue their present proceedings, which are the accursed result of their false religion. I have already written at length as to what the remedy should be, as these raids are increasing so greatly in consequence of the immunity they enjoy, and bye-and-bye it will be too late for redress.' [1]

It is evident from de Guaras' report that a good deal of activity was on foot, and that he had not yet penetrated fully what the South Sea scheme was. But the alarm was certainly given in Spain. A copy of his report was sent to Martin Enriquez, the Viceroy of Mexico – the same whose arrival at San Juan de Ulloa had so discomfited Hawkins. The upshot was an investigation in December of that year by the Audiencia in Guadalajara as to how Grenville could get into the South Sea, and in particular whether he could enter it by some strait to the north. [2] They took the testimony of the famous navigator Juan Fernandez de Ladrillero, who had gone out to New Spain with Mendoza in 1535, had conducted an expedition to explore the Straits of Magellan in 1558–9 and whose experience of the South Sea now extended over some thirty-five years.

From the French Ambassador, La Mothe Fénelon, writing on June 4 to Charles IX, we derive further information, some corroborating the Spanish agent, some entirely new. To the Spaniard, Grenville, though a gentleman, was also 'a great pirate.' Probably all the West-Country gentry were pirates to him; he did not distinguish. In point of fact, there is no evidence that Grenville had been engaged in piracy – this was his first sea-venture; nor even later is there evidence of piracy, his activities in this kind come under the heading of legitimate privateering. The distinction between privateering and piracy was a clear one. To the French Ambassador, who was in a

---

[1] *Cal. S.P. Spanish 1568–1579*, 481.
[2] H. R. Wagner, *Spanish Voyages to the N.W. Coast of America in the Sixteenth Century*, 63.

much better position to know, Grenville was a 'gentilhomme tenu en très bon compte en ceste court.'

He reports that since the beginning of the winter, Grenville has been engaged in setting forth and arming seven ships, with the intention of discovering some passage towards the north; but that having let the season for such a voyage pass, he nevertheless continues to prepare at this very moment, with all haste, to put to sea with these seven ships and three more which have newly joined him. He has already left court to make embarkation in divers places, for the above ships are distributed in different ports of the kingdom, where many gentlemen are to be of the company with some fifteen hundred soldiers and mariners. In short, La Mothe says, 'I hold the said equipage to be very suspect; the more so because I was told that the said Grenville has associated Sir Arthur Champernowne with him.' In consequence, he had at once set on foot inquiries in every direction where he might gather the intent of the enterprise. And this is what has been reported to him:

'That the said Grenville, having for long time solicited permission to make this voyage of discovery, and having been held back, up to the present, by those who support the cause of the King of Spain and the King of Portugal, has at last so well demonstrated the utility which will arise from his voyage to the whole kingdom if he is allowed to achieve it, that with the favour of his friends he has obtained permission to go, on condition that before undertaking it he renders some service which has been prescribed for him, to the Earl of Essex in Ireland. And from there he will afterwards take his journey to where he intends, without its being permissible for him nevertheless to enter upon places which the Spaniards and Portuguese have already discovered, and without his being able to attempt anything against the friends of this kingdom, particularly against your Majesty. So that my advertisements are that I need take no alarm, nor give you any, from the said Grenville's enterprise.' [1]

This corroborates the main outline of the preparations that were taking place for the voyage, such as we know them –

[1] La Mothe Fénelon, *Correspondance Diplomatique*, VI, 127–8.

though here too its secret destination was unknown to La Mothe's informants. But he takes us a stage further; apparently by now, June, Grenville had got permission to go – information which is supported by later evidence from a remote and unsuspected source.[1] But the permission was contingent upon his rendering some service to the Earl of Essex in difficulties in Ireland.

The Irish situation was again disturbed; the Earl of Desmond had escaped, or rather ridden away into Munster from his easy confinement in Dublin and was now ranging the province, attired in native Irish dress, the acknowledged leader of his people stirring up trouble along with his cousin James Fitzmaurice. The latter was again in correspondence with foreign powers. Simultaneously Philip was collecting a large fleet in his Biscayan ports to carry reinforcements to the Netherlands and his troops on the Rhine. There was instant alarm in England at the prospect of a Spanish fleet in the Channel and preparations were made for setting the Queen's ships to sea. There was no question of allowing a small squadron of ships such as Grenville's to depart the country at such a time.

Moreover there was work for him to do at home in the west. The Government decided to send down the Earl of Bedford, on 1 June, to his Lieutenancy of Devon and Cornwall to put the whole force of that country in readiness, to take general musters of men, horses and arms, and to make preparations for their defence.[2] The Justices of the Peace were to aid as his subordinate officers in the work. On 14 June, commissions were sent to the Earl in the West and to the Lord President of Wales, to raise 1,000 men for service in Ireland.[3] On 17 July, a letter was sent to Bedford 'commending his Lordship's diligence and the rest of the gentlemen of those counties under his charge for the accomplishment of such services as were committed unto them by her Majesty's commandment.'[4] The Irish situation looked less threatening, and the soldiers levied for service there were to be stayed for the time, though still kept under arms 'in case there

---

[1] See below, pp. 106–7.   [2] S.P. Dom. Eliz. 97, nos. 1–2.
[3] ibid. no. 12.   [4] *Acts of the Privy Council*, VIII, 270.

shall be any occasion to employ them hereafter.' There was still anxiety on the score of the Spanish fleet, and on 12 July, the Earl was directed 'to consult with Sir Arthur Champernowne, or some others thought meet, to send forth to the seas some bark under some skilful man to learn the coming forth of the Spanish fleet, and to give understanding thereof with all diligence.' [1]

In August, 200 of the men still under arms, 100 from Wales and 100 from Cornwall, were ordered to be sent to Ireland. [2] But the crisis passed; Desmond made his submission, and the Spaniards sent their reinforcements from Italy up the Rhine. In the autumn, when the danger was over, the Council sent its letters of thanks to the Deputy-lieutenants of the western shires, 'for their forwardness, diligence and good conformity to her Majesty's service when the Earl of Bedford was among them as Lieutenant; they are required to continue their good doings, and promised that it shall be holden in remembrance to their comfort upon all good occasions offered.' The Deputy-Lieutenants named for Cornwall were Sir John Arundell, Mr. Edgcumbe, Mr. Grenville, Mr. Arundell of Trerice and Mr. Mohun. [3]

The excitement and activity of that summer meant that it was now too late to start on the voyage: a whole year had been lost. Moreover, following the Treaty of Bristol in August there was a diplomatic *détente*; and the lessening tension meant that the motive not to give offence to Spain moved once more into the foreground of Elizabeth's calculations. The atmosphere was distinctly less favourable for the voyage, or indeed for any southward voyage now; and this gave an opportunity for those who favoured a direct attack upon the North-West Passage through the northern seas to the coast of Labrador, the chance of raising their head. They would be greeted with favour, for it promised a peaceful approach to the great problem. Frobisher, backed by the Earl of Warwick, seized his chance and gained the ear of the Council; in February 1575 he was granted his licence and set on foot his first voyage to the North-West. In the next year, Gilbert's 'Discourse,' the classic statement of the North-Western school, was published.

[1] ibid. 272.   [2] ibid. 282.   [3] ibid. 304.

Grenville does not appear to have given up all hope of carrying out his plans; for it must be to this time that we have to date the 'Discourse' which he presented to Burghley.[1] Burghley endorsed it in his own hand 'Mr. Grenville's voyage'; it is undated, but its heading gives one to suppose that it was written before Frobisher's departure. The tract is distinctly polemical: 'A discourse concerning a Strait to be discovered toward the north-west passing to Cathay, and the oriental Indians, with a confutation of their error that think the discovery thereof to be most conveniently attempted to the north of Baccalaos' (i.e. Labrador). Another impression that the tract gives, is that it was written in reply to Sir Humphrey Gilbert's. That might indeed well be, since there were copies of the latter circulating in manuscript before it was printed; and it would not be difficult for Grenville, Gilbert's cousin, to come by one. But Grenville's 'Discourse' is a remarkable document in itself; its importance has been totally overlooked, most probably for the reason that it was never printed in Hakluyt. The younger Hakluyt, as a skilful and staunch upholder of mainland plantation in North America, was not much interested in southward projects, though one wonders on the other hand whether the elder Hakluyt, the lawyer, whose geographical interests were much more widely scattered and diverse than his young cousin's, may not have had some hand in drafting the 'Discourse' for Grenville's project; the economic ideas put forward, though perhaps common enough at the time, are so very like his expression of them in other connections.

The 'Discourse' had as its purpose to show the superiority of a southward voyage for an attack on the problem of the North-West Passage and from the Pacific side. Very little is said about the lands that might be discovered in the Pacific, though they are not forgotten; any argumentation about Spain's possessions there would now have been tactless. It is the question of the Passage itself which has moved into the centre of interest and the tract is concerned almost entirely with that. It starts with the position that the seas to the north of Labrador are open, so that the Strait cannot be there, and since America is known to

[1] Lansdowne MSS., no. 100, f. 4.

be an island, unless it is joined to Cathay, then the Strait must be there in the north-west of America. So much is agreed with Gilbert's 'Discourse.' The question that he poses then, is

'which were the more convenient way to discover the said strait, either passing under the congealed Arctic circle, for so high the main of America reacheth; or by passing the Strait of Magellan, so ascend from the equinoctial along the western course of that Atlantical Island, as Plato seemeth in his *Timaeus* to term it.'

He admits that the way round into the Pacific by the Straits of Magellan and up the west coast is longer; but considers that the advantage of sailing in mostly temperate zones, along a route to a great extent known, outweighs that disadvantage.

'But considering that in discovery of new unknown seas I must neither bear stiff sail by night, nor yet in the day when fog or mist shall happen (which in these parts are almost continually); whereas contrary wise, in the other, passing altogether by seas known and already discovered even till we come to the Strait sought, I need not refuse night or day to pack on sail for my most speed, being no less clear in those whole and temperate zones than dark and misty in the other. And, therefore, albeit in quantity the grades differ, yet, all circumstances duly weighed, I may well affirm, that in one natural day, and so consequently in one week or month, I will pass more grades of my southern voyage than can be passed of the other.'

He then proceeds to outline the scheme of the voyage. Leaving England in the summer, he reckoned to reach the Straits of Magellan before the autumn equinox and to 'bestow three weeks at the least in platting and discovering the island and other commodities for fortification of the said Straits need were).' By Christmas, coasting northwards along the Pacific coast of America, he expected –

'I may with facility arrive to the Straits of Anian. So have I now one whole quarter of a year to discover (i.e. explore) the said straits, and to make plats of every bay, road, port, or channel therein; and to sound all such places as in that passage may cause peril. In which time the summer will be arrived again to the equinoctial, approaching to the congealed *Arctic circle*. And so have I the whole summer to return from the Northern Seas, and the first three months to employ in traffic with Cathay or any other islands to the said strait adjoining, which may sufficiently occupy the fleet till the seas be resolved.'

The conception of the Strait underlying this, was that it ran south-west to north-east, so that its supposed Pacific end, which would be in the latitude of California, was in a temperate clime, while its eastern end would be in Arctic waters and would need to be navigated, if discovered, in late summer.

The disadvantages of the Southern voyage, namely its greater length and the double crossing of the Equator, he considers not to be compared with the difficulties arising from cold in the north – an argument in its way sound enough.

'In the north, both day and night being freezing cold, not only men's bodies but also the lines and tacklings are so frozen, that with very great difficulty mariners can handle their sails. I omit the rages of the seas and tempestuous weather wherewith we shall be far more oft endangered in the north than in the south.'

Further, he advances the objection that from any northern island that may be discovered, no gold or precious metals could be expected, but merely the same commodities as the Muscovy Company brings from Russia, 'seeing they are both subject to the Arctic circle.' This was the view generally held, until the excitement over the supposed gold ore brought back by Frobisher, which caused Philip Sidney to write to his friend Languet that a new Peru had been discovered. This objection in itself is proof that the 'Discourse' must have been written before Frobisher's return in 1576.

On the other hand, 'from any land that shall in the other voyage be found, we are assured to expect gold, silver, pearls, spice, with grain, and such most precious merchandize, besides countries of most excellent temperature to be inhabited' – a glancing reference to that other object of the voyage, the unknown lands of the South Sea.

He concludes that once the Straits in the north are found, and all the channels and currents charted,

'that both day and night in the clear and fog, a man need not fear to pack on sail with all celerity to exploit his voyage without any doubt or scruple, but that this way he may safely, commodiously and most speedily pass into that rich and bountiful sea abounding with innumerable islands of incomparable riches and unknown treasure. But whosoever shall before such exact discovery made that way attempt the same, I aver he shall proceed to the shame and dishonour of himself, to the destruction and ruin of his company and to the utter discouragement of this nation, further to adventure in this gainful, honest, honourable enterprise. And report me to the judgment of the wise, these reasons before alleged well weighed.'

The tone of personal vexation in these concluding words point to something more than theoretical polemics; they can only be intended against the Frobisher enterprise now going speedily forward.

Such was the defence of the project. It was a conception of the greatest importance for English power. The idea was to gain control both of the Straits of Magellan and of the Straits of Anian in the north, and so to gain a counterweight to Spanish power in Central America. As it was conceived, it should lead to English control of the Pacific at both the northern and southern entrances into it. There was this implicit in it, it is clear, no less than the personal desire of the Elizabethan, so well expressed by Ralegh, Grenville's junior, who must have been influenced by the elder man:

'To seek new worlds, for gold, for praise, for glory.'

For the next three years, public attention was directed to the attempts Frobisher was making to force the Passage in the north. In each of the years 1576, 1577 and 1578 he made a voyage to the Labrador-Greenland region; and after bringing home the sample of ore which they thought to be auriferous, on his first voyage, he had very influential and extensive backing. He himself thought too, in 1576, that he had found the Passage through the broken lands north of Labrador, and that he had only to follow it through to get to Cathay. It promised a peaceful surmounting of the greatest barrier to English expansion.

But there were other minds which had not given up the possibilities of the southward route – notably Drake and his comrade at Nombre de Dios, John Oxenham. There was another way of getting into the South Sea besides the strait but narrow path through the Straits of Magellan – that was, a smash-and-grab run upon the Isthmus of Panama. It offered no chance for a permanent English route, but only the opportunity for a raid upon the treasure-ships coming up the coast from Peru. This was the plan which Oxenham, conceiving it after the pattern of Drake's exploit of 1572, now proposed to carry out as a private venture of his own, after Grenville's failure to get permission to go through with his. Oxenham, there is no doubt, was to have served under Grenville; and it is possible that when Grenville sold some of the ships he had preparing, Oxenham bought one of them and sailed in her to the Isthmus.

The story of Oxenham's venture is well known and there is no need to repeat it; it has all the excitement and the astonishing adventurousness of Drake's exploits in 1572. Oxenham fitted out a ship of 140 tons, with a company of seventy men, and slipped away some time in 1576 to the Spanish Main. Arrived there, he crossed the Isthmus, built himself a pinnace on the Pacific coast that he had so longed to see, and with this tiny craft captured two Spanish treasure-ships. With the treasure he tried to get back to his ship on the other coast, but it had been discovered and destroyed by the Spaniards. Meanwhile a strong force was scouring the Isthmus for him, and in the end tracked down his camp in the wilds and captured him. Most of his men were hanged as pirates at Panama; but Captain John, his ship's master and his pilot, were reserved to grace an *auto-da-fé* at Lima.

While in the prison of the Inquisition there, they were examined as to what they knew about English designs upon the Straits of Magellan and the South Sea. The recent find of their very depositions, taken on 20 February 1579, just at the time when their former comrade Drake, having at last broken through into the Pacific was hovering off the coast of Callao (so little a distance away and yet so incapable of helping them) – is one of the romances of historical research.[1] Its importance to us is that it gives the last information we have on the Grenville voyage, and since Oxenham was in Grenville's confidence about it, it sheds a little further light into its darkness.

We have to remember the motive that would be strong, for his own sake, not to say too much on the subject. For example, Oxenham confessed that Grenville had many times spoken to him about it, and tried to persuade him to accompany him, but that he was unwilling to go. But John Butler, the pilot, deposed outright that Oxenham had agreed to go with Grenville on the expedition. On most other points, the three Englishmen, all of whom knew about the intended voyage, were at one in their evidence. Let us take Oxenham's:

'Questioned whether, while in England or since he had left there, he had heard or understood that Queen Elizabeth or any other person had entertained the project to arm a certain number of vessels for the purpose of establishing settlements, or for other purposes, on the coast of the North Sea [i.e. the Atlantic], or in the region of the Strait of Magellan or on the coast of the South Sea, he answered that four years ago an English gentleman named Richard Grenville, who lives at a distance of a league and a half from Plymouth, [i.e. at Buckland], and is very rich, applied to the Queen for a licence to come to the Strait of Magellan and to pass to the South Sea, in order to search for land or some islands where to found settlements, because in England there are many inhabitants and but little land. The Queen gave him the licence and witness saw it. It was very large. The said Grenville bought two ships, and was about to buy two or three more, when the Queen revoked the licence, because she had learnt that beyond the Strait of Magellan there were settlements made by Spaniards, who might do them harm. The said Grenville sold the ships after the licence had been taken from him . . . Grenville's project was to come and found

[1] Mrs. Zelia Nuttall, *New Light on Drake* (Hakluyt Society, 1914), Introduction and pp. 1–12.

a settlement on the River Plate and then pass the Strait and establish settlements wherever a good country for such could be found.'

The desire to be politic is unmistakable: Oxenham puts Grenville's intentions in the most favourable light, even then dissociating himself from any part in them; while the purity of the Queen's attitude is a charmingly loyal trait in his account. What he goes on to say is equally revealing and important; it shows that before he left England, Drake was meditating plans on the same line as Grenville's. Oxenham was known to both, though on more equal terms with Drake: he could not fail to be a channel of information between the one and the other.

'The witness thinks that if the Queen were to give a licence to Captain Francis Drake he would certainly come and pass through the Strait, because he is a very good mariner and pilot, and there is no better one in England than he who could accomplish this . . . Witness thinks that the Queen will not, as long as she lives, grant the licence, but that after her death, there will certainly be some-one who will come to that strait. The said Captain Francis Drake had often spoken to witness saying that if the Queen would grant him licence he would pass through the Strait of Magellan and found settlements over here in some good country . . . Questioned whether they had discussed how and by what route they were to return to England after having passed through the Strait, he said that it seemed to him that some said that it was to be by the same Strait, but others said that there was a route through another Strait that passed into the North Sea [i.e. the Strait of Anian], but nobody knows this for a certainty or has passed through it.'

To this information, the deposition of John Butler, the pilot, adds a few more touches. He says that Grenville had bought four ships; but that 'the Queen had demanded that they were to give a security of thirty to forty thousand pounds that they would not touch the lands belonging to King Philip, and on this account the expedition was frustrated.' Butler was not acquainted with the full design of Grenville's voyage, as Oxenham was; but he adds something to our knowledge of Drake's position in regard to it.

'Questioned whether he had understood or known whether the said Captain Francis Drake had agreed with Captain John Oxenham to come and explore the Strait of Magellan or any other seas, and to pass into the South Sea, he answered that he did not know about this and that the said Captain Francis Drake was a poor man who did not have the means for doing this, for he owns nothing more than what he had taken in the Indies, and all this he had spent on certain islands over there towards Ireland. Only a man having great power could possibly come here.'

This about describes the position so far as Drake was concerned, regarding such an enterprise; it would have to be backed financially by others, for he could not possibly have raised the money himself. Whereas Grenville was rich enough to finance it mostly himself.

The third Englishman, the ship's-master whose name is given as Thomas Xerores or Xervel [1] adds nothing to our knowledge of Grenville's voyage; but he knew of it and knew also that it was intended to pass through the Straits. Only one thing else he adds, but in it we seem to see the brave spirit of this unknown man revealed as in a lightning-flash before going down into the darkness. When asked if he knew Captain Francis, he replied fearlessly, 'Yes, he knew him and had been with him on the voyage when they robbed the mule-train on the road to Nombre de Dios.' So much for the depositions: the men who made them were led out to be hanged, a few days after the *auto-da-fé* at Lima, a year later.

So Grenville's hopes of his great scheme were frustrated, mainly because he was too early; he suffered the fate that all too frequently attends upon the first originators of projects, of being beforehand with time. As we have seen, it was more than a project that he advanced; he had actually gone far with the preparations for the voyage, and had obtained the Queen's licence,

[1] Mrs. Nuttall was not able to identify this name; but I would suggest Sherwell, a name well known in Plymouth at this time.

only to find it withdrawn at the last moment. Many others, among them Drake, were to suffer a like chagrin in later years; but with none of them was it a matter of such overwhelming importance, or so decisive as in Grenville's case. For the opportunity that should have been his, at the least, of achieving fame as the first Englishman to pass through the Straits of Magellan fell to another.

Drake, during these years when Grenville's voyage was being prepared, was mostly in Ireland, aiding the Earl of Essex with his ships: it was a convenient way of employing himself in obscurity after the excessive light that the exploits of 1572–3 had concentrated on him. Moreover, the Queen's desire to be at peace with Spain, for the time at least, upon which Grenville's scheme had broken, also kept Drake from any important venture. Grenville, so far as we know, sold most of his ships, except for the most powerful of them, the *Castle of Comfort*, which in this year 1575 ran up a series of charges against her for doubtful doings in and about the Channel: exploits which will be dealt with later. By the end of 1575, Elizabeth began to veer again in her relations with Spain – the Netherlands were becoming more disturbed; and Drake, through the intermediary of Essex, was in touch with Walsingham and through him with the forward school of policy.[1] Drake's ideas for his southward voyage began to take shape.

The recent discovery of the missing draft project for the great voyage,[2] has thrown a good deal of light upon its intended designs, which had hitherto remained obscure; it enables us to see that Drake's voyage was in origin a continuation of Grenville's plans. The draft shows that the lands in the south to be explored and occupied were not the South American coast, which was already under Spanish obedience as far as 40° S., nor the unoccupied parts of South America, Patagonia and South Chile, which offered no attractions. The inference is that the lands to

---

[1] Corbett, *Drake and the Tudor Navy*, I, 213.

[2] v. E. G. R. Taylor, 'The Missing Draft Project of Drake's Voyage of 1577–80,' *Geographical Journal*, Jan., 1930; 'John Dee, Drake and the Straits of Anian,' *Mariner's Mirror*, 1929; and 'More Light on Drake, 1577–80,' *Mariner's Mirror*, 1930.

be sought for were those of Terra Australis, which were depicted on Mercator's map of 1569 and Ortelius' of 1570, now in the hands of every English cosmographer, and which were regarded by Dr. Dee as the main objective of British enterprise. The official plan then became that of visiting Terra Australis and so making for the Moluccas along its supposed coast; and failing this, to make for the Straits of Anian by which he might return. That is, the two main elements in the Grenville Plan reappear in Drake's first draft.

But the objectives were flexible as they had been with Grenville; it was necessary to have alternatives since some of the objectives were yet to be discovered and not known certainly to exist. Moreover the emphasis laid on them varied with political circumstances. While in March 1576, everything looked promising for Drake, by the autumn and throughout the winter of 1576–7, it seemed as if he would not be allowed to go after all. Grenville had now retired to the West Country, doubtless in bitter disappointment – the doings of the *Castle of Comfort* may have been an expression of it; he occupied himself in building at Buckland Abbey, and in local affairs as a Justice of the Peace; at the end of the year he became Sheriff of Cornwall.

Then in the spring of the New Year, the political atmosphere changed again. Elizabeth disliked Don John of Austria's progress in the Netherlands and was suspicious of his designs in English affairs in association with Mary Queen of Scots; in consequence, she became ready and willing to see some damage inflicted upon Philip in a totally unexpected and vulnerable quarter. So that the central design of Drake's voyage when he came to set sail – a design which was kept a close secret in connivance with Elizabeth herself, not even Burghley was to be told – was the attack upon the treasure-trade upon the coast of Peru. When Drake got through the Straits of Magellan, he did make an attempt in a westerly direction as if to find the coast of Terra Australis; but the belt of the Brave West Winds, which he here encountered and which blew him back well to the south towards Cape Horn, gave him the excuse to turn northwards and make for Peru. After his exploits upon that coast he ran up to California, evidently in an attempt to search for the entry to the Straits of Anian, though he could not have entertained much hope of returning through it. He beat up in stormy weather to 48° N., beyond the New Albion to which he returned to re-fit, being driven back by the north-westerly winds and discouraged by the icy cold. So he made for the Moluccas and completed his circumnavigation of the world. But these two attempts, even if they were no more than feints, may be regarded as passing tributes to Grenville's scheme, the salutes of the greater, more fortunate captain.

On 15 November 1577, Drake put to sea: and one day at the end of September 1580 he returned, the most famous Englishman of his day. The laurels that might have been Grenville's were his.

CHAPTER VI

WEST COUNTRY OCCUPATIONS: BIDEFORD, THE *CASTLE OF COMFORT*, BUCKLAND

> The sea of Fortune doth not ever flow,
> She draws her favours to the lowest ebb,
> Her tides hath equal times to come and go,
> Her loom doth weave the fine and coarsest web:
> No joy so great but runneth to an end,
> No hap so hard but may in fine amend.
>
> ROBERT SOUTHWELL

So these years, 1573 to 1575, had been mainly taken up by the projected voyage; making ground for it with the Queen, carrying through the preparations for it, stating the case, in the end in vain. Then there were the various occupations of a local character which fell to his lot as a Justice of the Peace and a large landowner in the west; in addition to his private concerns of which we know so little, and his family life, of which we know nothing. But in these same years, though living at Buckland when he was not in London, where he lived at St. Leger house in Southwark, he was also busily engaged upon the affairs of his town of Bideford, getting a charter of incorporation for it and setting the town on the path to a more vigorous corporate and trading life.

Bideford, along with Kilkhampton, was the earliest possession of the Grenvilles in the west, going right back to the second generation after the Conquest. But the town was of no consequence, it had no trade; its only importance was, as its name shows, that it was the lowest ford over the Torridge near the sea and so the main thoroughfare along the coast passed through it. As a ford, it must always have been dangerous: the waters are swift here, as they come round the loop from Wear Giffard to the sea. The importance that the ford had, was continued in and centred upon the bridge, which was built, mainly by the efforts of the Grenvilles fortified by episcopal indulgences, in the fourteenth century. It was often repaired and rebuilt, with great lamentations by the inhabitants; but in its sixteenth-century shape, a long stone bridge of twenty-four arches, it was the pride of the town, and in a sense, the centre of its life.

Nevertheless, its trade did not prosper; right on into the reign of Elizabeth it made no progress: all the more mortifying because of the close proximity of Barnstaple, with its long tradition of civic life – it is one of the most ancient boroughs in the country: one of the Wessex burghs before Domesday, and the hub of a thriving trade. Whether Bideford's backwardness was due to its dependence upon its lord, and a consequent lack of corporate institutions, we can now hardly tell. But Grenville determined to put it to the test and to infuse new life into the town, something of his own energetic spirit.

In 1574 he took up the question with the leading men in the town, prepared to give up something of his own rights over it, for the sake of seeing a more thriving, active existence develop. Having no doubt settled the terms himself, he pressed the Government to grant a charter, incorporating the town, upon the agreed basis. The charter was granted on 10 December in the same year.[1]

By it Bideford was constituted a free corporate town – a 'politic body and one commonalty of itself in deed, fact and name for ever having perpetual succession,' governed by a Mayor, five Aldermen and seven capital burgesses. The five Aldermen were for the first time to be chosen by the inhabitants; the former were then to elect the seven chief burgesses. Together they formed the Common Council and were to elect a Mayor annually from among the Aldermen. Whenever an Alderman died or was removed from office, Common Council was to elect one of the chief burgesses into his place; and whenever there was a vacancy in the place of a chief burgess, Council was similarly to elect another from among the most worthy and discreet inhabitants. It must have been settled beforehand who

[1] Chancery Warrants, File 1268; J. Watkins, *History of Bideford*, 19–28.

most of the five Aldermen and seven burgesses were to be; the leaders of a community's life, then as now, in spite of the difference of forms, indicate themselves. Grenville himself was chosen as first Alderman.

The town was granted the usual privileges, a weekly market and three fairs a year, in February, July and November, with the customary right to hold court of pie-powder and the tolls and other dues arising from them. The Mayor, Aldermen and burgesses obtained the right of holding a court of record in their Guild Hall every three weeks, and to have cognisance of a number of civil pleas, such as debt, trespass, contract and contempt. One Alderman each year was to be a Justice of the Peace for the borough; and the borough was to enjoy the usual profits arising from felon's goods, outlaws, waifs and strays, and the assizes of bread, wine and ale. These privileges followed very much the usual run of such grants, but they were restricted in character. In spite of its new-found corporate status, there was no doubt whose was the guiding hand in Bideford. Upon receipt of the charter, a meeting was held at which Grenville was present, which chose the five aldermen, who elected the seven burgesses, who together elected John Salterne, merchant adventurer, to be their first Mayor.

Next year, in order more clearly to define the respective rights of the new corporation and Grenville's, they entered into an agreement with each other, on 4 September 1575. By this the corporation covenanted that Grenville was to enjoy all the revenues, issues and profits within the manor and town of Bideford which he and his family had enjoyed before the town's incorporation, with the exception of the fee-farm rent of 10s. 6d. per annum, together with the office of portreeve – signs of the town's previous subjection to the lord of the manor – which Grenville now released to the mayor, aldermen and burgesses and their successors for ever. In return, of any increase in the town's revenues from fairs and markets and other sources, over and above the necessary charges for maintenance and wages, Grenville and his heirs and assigns were to have half.

The borough agreed not to erect any house or building upon the premises of the fairs or markets, nor to pay any wages without the advice and consent of the Grenvilles. Finally, Grenville grants the borough, for stallage and standings for the markets and fairs, and for the use of their guildhall, prison or any other corporation purpose, the use of the chapel standing near the west end of the bridge, and of ground 'whereon certain limekilns sometime stood, and where a quay, or wharf, is now lately builded; and also of all the streets, lanes, ways, and waste soil within the said manor, borough and town of Bideford.'

In the following year, on 19 June 1576, a writ of *quo warranto* was brought into the court of Queen's bench, a formal process by which the borough's new privileges were legally confirmed.

It was a very important stage in the history of Bideford; in fact it may be regarded as the beginning of its civic life. Not that the liberties granted by this first Charter were at all excessive; on the contrary, they were considerably restricted: so much so that, in the next generation, application was made for a new charter, which was granted by the Crown in 1610. Nevertheless, this first impulse given to the town's active corporate life, was Grenville's work. Still more important was the way in which he followed it up, particularly in the eighties, by pushing forward its shipping and trading connections abroad. From that anchorage in front of his town house upon the quay, there departed his expeditions to Virginia and upon the high seas; here he brought home his prizes, his Indian native, from here he set forth against the Armada.

In the next century were to be seen the fruits of his enterprise, for Bideford prospered greatly from being first-comer in the trade with Newfoundland and Virginia. A number of local fortunes were made in the tobacco trade with Virginia and Maryland; till the middle of the eighteenth century, more tobacco was imported into Bideford than into any other English port except London. Then, with the revolt of the colonies, all was at an end, and Bideford became a shadow of its former self. But a charming eighteenth-century shadow it is, with the mark of an even earlier age and hand upon it. For though the old chapel which stood at the west-end of the bridge is gone, the guildhall, though it has been re-built, still stands in the same place that Grenville granted, looking across the bridge to East-the-Water.

In his time, particularly after he sold Buckland and shifted his main centre of interest to his North Devon affairs, there was much coming and going from that house on the town quay, which has now vanished – 'my house of Bideford' he calls it in his letters. As early as 1573, we find him interested in shipping; for in that year, he agreed with Philip Corsini and Acerbo Velutelli, two of the chief Florentine merchants in London, to transport certain goods to Newhaven in France (Havre). He had entered into a bond in £2,500 on 7 May, that before 1 June he would 'lade or cause to be laden in one ship, crayer or vessel for the port of Newhaven (Havre) in the realm of France, all such goods, wares or merchandizes as lately were discharged in Cornwall out of the ship called the *Marie* whereof was master John Mouton D'Anyon,' except such goods as were remaining in London and 'one bag of ginger being lacking'; and 'with so much speed as conveniently may be, after shipping and lading thereof as wind and weather will serve . . . transport and convey the same to Newhaven,' where the goods were to be delivered into the hands of the Florentine merchants. After this arrangement was made and the bond entered into, it was decided between the parties that the goods should be transported to Calais and not to Havre. Grenville apparently sent the ship to Calais, and the Florentines threatened to sue him for breaking the original agreement. He therefore initiated a Chancery action against them to protect himself. We do not know what happened; presumably all was well.[1]

This is only one piece of evidence as to his shipping concerns at this time. The ship or crayer in which he was to transport the merchandise may well have been one of the smaller craft which he had gathered for the South Seas Voyage. But there is rather more evidence about the activities of the largest and most powerful of them, the *Castle of Comfort* – a pretty name for a ship with such a privateering record as she had! She was a ship of some 240 tons, and in the sixties when she was built, of a new type, being a private warship with a powerful armament. Her type was called into existence by the exigencies of the Guinea Coast trade, after which the Portuguese took to arming

[1] Chanc. Proc. Eliz. G 14/9.

themselves heavily against intruders. The secret of her success was her overmastering gunfire, and she had a long record of exploits to her name; for, frequent as is her appearance in the maritime papers of the time, she is 'never once found engaged in peaceful trade.' [1]

She was based mainly upon Plymouth; she was there in the spring of 1570, when she was to be sold by her owners, a London syndicate. A few years later, Grenville bought her for the expedition to the South Seas; the very fact that it was the *Castle of Comfort* which was to lead it cannot have given the government much confidence in his pacific intentions. Once within that closed sea, with the *Castle of Comfort* he could have inflicted even greater damage upon Spanish shipping than Drake's *Golden Hind*, which was only of a burden of 180 tons and less heavily armed. It is curious to think it might have been the *Castle of Comfort*, instead of the *Golden Hind*, which might have garnered all that fame.

On the collapse of the South Sea scheme, and having been jointly owned for a time by Grenville and William Hawkins in partnership, she was at sea again in the spring of 1575. For in May, serving under licence from Huguenot Rochelle, she captured a ship of Catholic St. Malo, belonging to one Guillaume Le Fer and worth some £5,000. Sir Arthur Champernowne, Vice-Admiral of Devon, wrote to Burghley in September that she was then riding in Cawsand Bay (the red cliffs of Cawsand), having taken a ship of Queenborough which she refused to deliver. [2] He asks for a special Commission from Burghley and the Lord Admiral against her – in itself some indication that by now, Grenville and Hawkins, a relative and a friend, had ceased to be responsible for her. Such was in fact their plea when the case brought by the St. Malo merchant was brought before the Court of Admiralty. Le Fer had gone on with his efforts to obtain redress; it appears that the ship, *Le Sauveur* of St. Malo, was taken off the coast of Ireland, when coming from the Levant; that her crew were set on land at Baltimore and the ship brought into Chepstow. [3] They valued her goods at

---

[1] Williamson, *Hawkins*, 159. [2] *Hatfield Papers*, 11, 113.
[3] *Cal. S.P. Foreign 1575-7*, 215.

60,000 crowns. But nothing was done until next year; meanwhile the *Castle of Comfort,* under her captain Anthony Carew, went merrily on collecting fresh charges against her.

On 29 April 1576, the Privy Council summoned Grenville and Hawkins 'to make their appearance here with as convenient speed as they might, for the answering of certain goods and merchandizes taken by a ship called the *Castle of Comfort* from a ship of St. Malo's, the particularities whereof they shall more fully understand at their coming.' [1] We do not know whether they made their appearance then or sent written answers; probably one of them attended and it appears to have been Grenville upon whom rested the burden of the defence. On 27 May, the Council wrote to the Judge of the Admiralty

'committing to him the consideration of the cause betwixt the Frenchman of St. Malo and Mr. Grenville, for which purpose there is sent unto him certain examinations taken in the behalf of the Frenchmen and Mr. Grenville's answer to the same; he is required to consider thereof by conference with the parties if he shall so think good, and to return his opinion thereof by Friday next in the Star Chamber.' [2]

When Friday came, the report of the Judge on the issues in dispute was by no means clear; and, on 1 June,

'for so much as it appeared that sundry points stood upon proof so as the very truth could not be discerned, it was ordered by their Lordships that the said Judge should with all expedition proceed to the further examination thereof according to the due course of the law, that thereupon the matter might be determined according to justice.' [3]

In consequence, we have the deposition of 19 July 1576, entered into one of the large parchment-bound books of the Court of Admiralty [4] – one of the few personal appearances that Grenville makes before us, in which we can hear him, as if in the flesh, answering in his own words. Almost one imagines the large paper volume with its clasp being handled by Mr. Doctor

[1] *A.P.C.* IX, 111.   [2] ibid. 130.   [3] ibid. 132.
[4] H.C.A. Examinations, vol. 22, 19 July 1576.

Lewis or Mr. Doctor Caesar, Judges of the Admiralty, the broad pages smacking, not unlike ship's canvas, the scratching pen of the scribe on that summer's day. We derive a very definite and convincing impression of Grenville on this occasion of his appearance; his behaviour and his replies are uncompromising. He denies the content of the first four articles – 'non credit eosdem articulos esse veros in aliquo.' On the fifth, he is more informative and replies that

'the captain and owner of the *Castle of Comfort*, being a Frenchman, and the mariners and soldiers of that ship having licence from the Prince of Condé, and being first assaulted and shot at, by the articulate ship called *The Saviour*, and after a number of the *Castle of Comfort* were hurt and one slain, did prevail against the said ship, and boarded and apprehended the same, and brought her to the ports mentioned in this article. Et aliter non credit articulum esse verum in aliquo, saving that he believeth, that the said captain and company did by the way of sale and otherwise dispose of the said goods, as they thought good.'

To the sixth article he replies that he

'was not owner of the said ship called the *Castle of Comfort*, at the time of the apprehension and taking of *The Saviour*, for that he had made full sale thereof to the said French captain called Jolliffe, when she was furnished and before she did go to the seas.'

The next three articles he denies according to the formula. To the tenth, he makes a characteristic reply; he says that 'he believeth that he is not bound to answer to these particular values for that he cannot being no merchant esteem the values of the commodities mentioned in the schedule.' To the eleventh, he will not reply at all; but he has next to admit that 'the victuals and furnitures mentioned . . . came, before the said sale made to Joliffe, from the houses of this respondent and Mr. Hawkins, by their consents and with their knowledge.' The next articles also he refuses, and then again admits 'that this respondent, having then an intent to make a lawful voyage to the Newfoundland, did before the said sale appoint such officers, masters and persons in the said ships as are mentioned . . . who after, were wholly at the direction of the said Joliffe.' The sixteenth and seventeenth he denies, 'saving that this respondent had two of his servants in the said ship, appointed by this respondent to receive money for the said ship and furniture according to the covenant made between this respondent and Joliffe.'

Such was his story. It is impossible not to conclude that the sale of the ship to Jolis was a put-up job. Here was the ship victualled and furnished by Hawkins and Grenville, manned entirely by Englishmen engaged by him, though under a French captain, and with two servants of Grenville aboard as receivers. It is permissible to suppose that if Jolis really had purchased the ship, the purchase-money was to be raised as they went along from the prizes they took – only another way of Grenville's receiving the profits from her privateering. Of course, the sale was a fiction, and more than likely was thought of after the lucrative capture of *The Saviour*. Grenville and Hawkins were determined not to lose their hold upon the prize; and the fiction provided them with an ingenious defence. But such a *coup* could not be repeated; and it is probable that having made their gain, they did then sell the ship, for we do not hear of her again in their ownership. The St. Malo merchants received no redress; for two years later we find the French King writing to Elizabeth, drawing her attention to their grievance, 'neither our letters in their behalf nor their own suit having so far profited them.' [1] So the *Castle of Comfort*, in spite of remonstrances, arrests, executions of writs, went sailing on out of our ken, beyond all remembrance.

The week before his appearance in the Court of Admiralty, Grenville had obtained licence to alienate his London house. [2] Evidently he had determined to return to the West Country, upon the failure of his great project, and to make that the main centre of his activities henceforward. The house where he had been living of late years when in London, was the great St.

---

[1] *Cal. S.P. Foreign 1577–8*, 479.
[2] 12 July 1576. Pat. Rolls Eliz. 1145, mem. 36.

Leger house in the parish of St. Olave's, Southwark. It looked out upon the water between the quay next St. Olave's Church on the west and the bridge-house on the east; on the south was the lane leading up to it. The house then was in the shadow of London Bridge. It was a great house of stone and timber, 'an ancient piece of work and seemeth to be one of the first built houses on that side the river over against the city.'[1] It had formerly been the town house of the abbot of St. Augustine's, Canterbury, had passed to Sir Anthony St. Leger, the Lord Deputy, then to Warham St. Leger and from him to Grenville.

There are other indications which point to Grenville's interests turning permanently to the West Country. A series of entries upon the Close Roll at this time dealing with his financial and business transactions, reveals that he was buying land there.[2] It would seem that the capital he had hoped to employ more spectacularly in the South Sea Voyage, was now free for domestic investment. At the end of May he entered into a number of indentures, mainly with his cousins the Bassets, by which they released to him for certain sums of money, the manor of Lancras in Devon. George Basset of Tehidy in Cornwall, the head of the Cornish branch of the Bassets, sold his interest in the manor for £1,300, with the proviso that if within two years from then (28 May 1576) he should repay Grenville that sum 'at or in the mansion house of the said Richard Grenville wherein he now dwelleth in Stowe,' the bargain should be void. Sir Arthur Basset of Umberleigh sold Grenville his interest in the manor, and, for £200, the little hamlet called Upcott Snelard by Bideford.[3] From Edward Hungerford, the heir of the Hungerfords, who had held considerable estates in Cornwall, he bought the manors of Wolston and Widemouth, properties conveniently near Stowe. This purchase was spread over a year.[4] On 10 July 1576, Hungerford acknowledged that he had received 200 marks from Grenville according to his bond 'between the hours of one and four of the clock in the afternoon of

[1] Stow, *Survey of London*, 155.   [2] Close Rolls Eliz. 987, 18 May 1576.
[3] ibid. Roll 990, 12 May 1576.
[4] ibid. Roll 990, 28 May; Roll 1007, 2 February 1577; Roll 1013, 10 July 1577.

the same day, in the Temple Church in London, at the font stone there'; and on 2 February 1577, between two and four in the afternoon at the same place he received the remaining sum of £300. Probably in order to raise these sums conveniently and speedily, he entered into two recognisances with George Fletcher, hosier, of Southwark – evidently a near neighbour to St. Leger house – the first for 1,000 marks, the second for £500, to be paid on the Feast of St. Bartholomew next, 24 August 1576.[1]

In these same years he was spending largely upon the building operations at Buckland. He was engaged, as were so many others of his class, in transforming the Abbey into a comfortable and up-to-date Elizabethan mansion. But where others were taking the obvious line – like his northern neighbour William Abbot at Hartland, or the Eliots at St. Germans – making their house out of the existing domestic buildings and leaving the monastic church to go to ruin or become a parish church, Grenville was making his house out of the church and leaving the cloister and domestic buildings. It was certainly very queer, but in the result, extraordinarily successful.

Amicia, Countess of Devon, had lighted upon an attractive spot for her foundation in 1278 of a Cistercian house at Buckland. The Abbey stands protected from the blasts that blow upon the high downs above: a green sheltered nook fed by the streams running down to the Tavy, doubly secured among its walls, the same that the monks built confirming the narrow closes, some of which are gardens, another Sir Richard's bowling green, shadowed by the yews the monks planted and which yet stand sentinel there. From the south side of the house, the silver streak of the Tamar is visible in the distance; on the slopes around are the woods of the Abbey – the park is now beautifully treed with beeches – and in the middle distance, hiding the Tavy are the woods still belonging to the Edgcumbes. All about are the little winding lanes running down to Bere Alston, and around to Milton Combe and such places. From the slopes higher up, above the hollow in which the house lies, all the country is within sight of the Cornish hills on the further side of

[1] ibid. Roll 1000, 18 July 1576.

the Tamar valley. From Buckland Monachorum, the attendant village about a mile away, the whole distance to the south-west is dominated by the lovely rounded form of Kit Hill, above Callington, where in those days the tinners held their assemblies. So that this little cut-off patch of Devonshire, between the great Roborough Down and the junction of Tavy and Tamar, gives the impression of being singularly in touch with Cornwall, as indeed it looks westward towards it. But in addition, it is very well placed in relation to Plymouth, near to it though itself remaining withheld from it, not too accessible. It was an ideal position for the Grenvilles, if they wanted to remain close at hand to a town growing so rapidly in trade and in maritime importance. No doubt, if they had remained there, they would have come in time to exercise a great influence over it.

From the time of Grenville's grandfather, Sir Richard the Marshal, little or nothing had been done at Buckland. If his son Roger had lived to succeed him, almost certainly the alterations, the transformation of the Abbey into a habitable mansion, would have come earlier. For it appears that Roger lived here a little, since the year before he was drowned, his eldest child Charles was buried at Buckland Monachorum, on 28 August 1544.[1] Then, for the remainder of old Sir Richard's life and during the long minority of the grandson, it is not likely that there was much family life there. But in these years after the South Seas project, particularly the later seventies, Grenville chiefly resided here. On 1 November 1578, his daughter Bridget was baptised at Buckland Monachorum; and on 19 September 1579, Cecil Grenville, son of John, Grenville's uncle.[1]

The transformation of the Abbey church into a mansion was complete by 1576 – at least that is the date given on the frieze of the great fire-place in the hall. On the whole it is remarkable how conservative Grenville was in the changes he made: perhaps that was the point of the plan he adopted, it enabled the change to be carried through at a minimum of cost. He left the external arrangements of the monastic buildings virtually un-

[1] Buckland Monachorum Parish Register.

touched; the great tithe-barn of superb proportions – it is the finest in the West Country, remained with the farm-buildings as they were; so also with the gate-house and its little tower, and the girdle of walls with the screen of yews, around the inner precinct of the monastery. The external structure of the church, with its central tower, he kept almost intact, contenting himself with pulling down the two transepts so as to straighten the line of the building and to enable his great hall within to be lighted from without.

Within, the changes were more drastic; three floor-levels were inserted throughout the building, keeping the ceilings low in accordance with Elizabethan taste. The nave of the church was divided up into three reception rooms, with bedrooms and a withdrawing room above. A floor was inserted over the whole space and carried through the choir, which then became the hall. This, as may be expected with an Elizabethan house, is the finest and most elaborately decorated room of all. Its proportions are beautifully simple; it is a regular rectangle, broad in relation to its length, so that with the low-pitched ceiling, it subtly conveys the impression of being more a square than it is. Its chief decoration is the plaster ceiling, with exquisite rib-work and pendants, and with great brackets in the form of caryatids. At the west end is a decorative frieze portraying a scene which, being allegorical, such as the Elizabethans loved, may throw some light on the mood, at the time, of him who had it made. Under a vine, there is a knight resting, his arm against the tree, upon which he has hung up his shield. All his harness and armour lie in a heap away from him alongside his war-horse at rest; beside the knight are an hour-glass and a skull. It is a mood of retirement and reflection.

It is curious to think how little the house has changed since then – how what it is now we owe to him, not to his great successor who needed not to change anything; still more, this being so, how little memory of that association remains. For Grenville's name at Buckland has entirely gone out of mind; there are only those few entries in the early Register at Buckland Monachorum, so carefully written in by the Elizabethan vicar. To most people who are attracted by the historic memories of the place, it is not Grenville they think of: his name counts for nothing in the story of the house. And yet he made it what it is; it is the one indubitable thing he did that still remains to us. The house is his memorial; his mark is on everything there: the lay-out of it is his, his is the great hall and its frieze, the Grenville clarion is his signature upon the stone fire-places of the house. Here then, where everything at Stowe and at Bideford has perished, we move among the things amid which years of his life passed; occupied about his business, making his plans for the future, begetting his children, carrying out his duties to his family and to the state.

The latter, in the nature of things, became more weighty as time went on; particularly after he became Sheriff of Cornwall, to which office he was appointed at the end of this year. It is to this time too that we owe another of the very few occasions upon which we can, through the documents that remain, come into any personal touch with him; even so, it is tantalisingly impersonal in character. We know from the delightful Richard Carew of Antony how sociable was the life of the Cornish gentry at this time. Because they lived in an out-of-the-way corner of the land and were driven back upon their own society, they were even more hospitable and given to visiting each other's homes than elsewhere:

'They converse familiarly together, and often visit one another. A gentleman and his wife will ride to make merry with his next neighbour; and after a day or twain, those two couples go to a third; in which progress they increase like snowballs till through their burdensome weight they break again.' [1]

Grenville, with his many interests, his houses in South Devon near the Cornish border, and at Stowe and Bideford, and with relations everywhere, had extended opportunities.

So it is that we have notes of some of the visits that he made, chiefly to his friends and relations at Roscarrock, or to his cousin George Grenville at Penheale, in whom he had great trust and liking, from a curious and interesting diary kept in this year by a fellow Cornish gentleman who knew him well.[2]

[1] Carew, 179–180.   [2] S.P. Supplementary, vol. 16.

Elizabethan diaries are few and far between, so that the man who kept this one must have been interesting and in his way remarkable. He was William Carnsew, of Bokelly in St. Kew. His family came from Carnsew in the parish of Mabe, where they still had property.[1] He was a man of substance, having a good deal of property in several parishes; and with Peter Edgcumbe he was among the small group of Cornish landowners who were interested in mining speculation.

The Diary gives us what is so rare to find, a picture of the man himself, his interests, what he did with his time, what he thought about and speculated and read. It is somewhat surprising to find, a country gentleman of no importance living in a remote corner of the land, how interested he was in contemporary affairs, and what an impression they made on him. It is clear how concerned he and his friends were in what was happening abroad, in the struggle between Catholics and Protestants, Spaniards and Netherlanders on the continent. On 4 November 1576, the Spanish soldiery sacked Antwerp, the richest city of the north; some seven thousand lives were lost in the 'Spanish Fury.' On 29 November, Carnsew heard of it at home in Cornwall: 'this month the Antwerp was sacked and burnt by the Spaniards, the 4 day as I have been informed.' A few days later, after noting the great storm which blew some of his house away and the large number of shipwrecks brought in upon the coast, he has the tell-tale entry: 'at home all day, talked of the burning of Antwerp.' At the very end of December, the last day of the old year, he notes: 'rain, mists, read the destruction of Antwerp.' It made an impression upon his mind much like that made by the events in Spain upon ours.

In addition to these high matters, and such reading as Calvin's *Institute* and his *Epistles*, there were the ordinary country pursuits, planting trees, shearing sheep, harvesting, walking about his grounds, administering a potion to the vicar who was sick (he soon after died), paying and receiving visits. It is upon these that we get occasional glimpses, all too few, of Grenville at ease among his friends. On 13 March, we read: 'Went to Roscarrock, whereat I met Mr. Richard Grenville and Mr.

[1] C. Henderson, *History of the Parish of Mabe*.

Arundell Trerice; lay there.' Next day: 'at Roscarrock all day playing and trifling the time away; lay at Roscarrock; a gray horse fell down and would not stand.' On the 15th, they were evidently up early and away: 'breakfast at Cannys house: rode to Tintagel with Mr. Grenville.' In August, which was very wet and stormy this year, Grenville was again at Roscarrock, this time with Sir Arthur Basset and others, where Carnsew joined them. Again in October, on the 17th, another rainy day, Carnsew rode over to meet 'Mr. Basset, Mr. Grenville, Mr. Monk and Mr. Alexander Arundell, which all rode away gan we rode to Fowey.' The Roscarrocks would seem to have been very hospitable, or else Grenville very much liked their company. Thomas Roscarrock, who was living there then, was a man of forty-five; he had a numerous family and a large number of brothers, two of whom were Catholics, Nicholas who was afterwards racked, a man of antiquarian pursuits, who retired to the shelter of Lord William Howard's house at Naworth, where he compiled his large volume on the lives of the Saints; and Trevennor, whom we hear of in prison later for the Faith.[1] But these divisions had not yet attained their later acute form, dividing and embittering the relations of families. However, the time was not far distant: the sack of Antwerp which so excited Carnsew was a portent.

In the second week of November, he has a note in the margin to say 'Mr. Richard Grenville buyeth the manor of Stratton of Mr. Danvers,' which seems to be our only reference to the transaction. But it shows Grenville going on with the process of adding to his properties in that area around Stowe. December brought dry weather and on the 12th, Carnsew 'rode to Penheale: met Mr. Edgcumbe there with whom I charged Mr. Richard Grenville for the Sheriffwick of Cornwall. George Grenville was sworn commissioner of the peace.' In January of the new year, Carnsew himself was entertaining at Bokelly: '6: Many hawked with me. George Grenville, Richard Carew, Richard Champernowne, their brethren.' On the 18th, he had a visit from Grenville:

[1] Sir John Maclean, *History of Trigg Minor*, 1, 556–63; *The Household Books of Lord William Howard* (Surtees Society 1877); *Catholic Record Society*, vol. 1.

'Walked about my ground, Mr. Sheriff with me, who rode to William Vyell's to make a marriage for George Grenville with Jill Vyell. 19: rode to Camelford with the Sheriff: met George Grenville there. The Queen's or Council's letters were considered there. 21: At Trevorder: met Mr. Arundell Trerice, Mr. Carew, George Grenville who promised to marry Jill Vyell.'

It looks as if the Sheriff were the prime mover in the marriage of his cousin George, who had remained unduly long unmatched; the latter very dutifully obeyed, for before long we find him duly married to Julyan, daughter and a co-heiress of William Vyell.

Grenville now as Sheriff for the year 1577 – he had been appointed in November 1576, had a good deal of public business to attend to. Much of the correspondence between the Government and the county relating to local or to public affairs passed through the hands of the Sheriff; he stood at the head of the Justiciary, the gentlemen of the county. In later medieval times the office had lost something of its earlier importance, but it was still an onerous responsibility – so much so that men did not seek it and many hoped to avoid it. Nevertheless it was a position of honour which the leading gentry knew must come round to them once in their lives. Moreover, its actual importance varied with the stress of the times; a year of threatened invasion, of internal crisis – and it was an important matter who the Sheriff was, whether he were capable of giving a firm lead: the emergency brought out the character of the man.

It is well to bear this in mind, for Grenville's year of office was made memorable by a course of action which left its mark in the history of the country.

CHAPTER VII

GRENVILLE AS SHERIFF: THE ATTACK
ON THE CATHOLICS

THE outstanding-problem within the country was that of the Catholics. In Europe the issue between Catholicism and Protestantism was being fought out in sanguinary civil wars; only the integration and strong cohesion of the English state prevented the same thing happening here. That good fortune we owed to the nature of the Elizabethan settlement – a political arrangement if ever there was one—and to Elizabeth's sensible pursuit of purely political objectives. She was, providentially, no religious believer. All the same, her government was in a quandary – the Established Church aroused no one's ardour or belief. It was a political compromise and most minds were incapable of the subtlety necessary to appreciate the inner reason of compromise. Spiritual fervour and devotion were to be found either on the side of the Catholics or of the Puritans. It is fair to say that the finest minds, those most refined and philosophical, though at the same time most unyielding and selfless, men like Edmund Campion or Robert Southwell, the poet, were Catholics. Hardly anyone cared for the Anglican church – it was filled with time-servers; the Queen herself did not care for it and had a well-merited contempt for most of its ministers. However, it was politically necessary: that was her attitude; and, given time, it would develop an ethos of its own and a case for itself. That happens; since men are so easily moulded, any regime, given long enough, will mould them to its pattern – they have so little capacity by which to resist. After Elizabeth was dead, men began to discover, as they would, beauty in the English church, satisfaction in its formularies.

In the seventies the problem of Catholicism became acute:

twelve years of Elizabeth's sceptical compromising and men began to lapse back into the old Faith, which was at any rate a faith. The Papal Bull of Excommunication had marked the dividing line; the issue could not be left in doubt any longer; one side or the other must win. Catholicism was making great progress, particularly at the universities, where minds were most sensitive to the winds of doctrine and had least judgment of political realities. A considerable number of young Fellows of colleges went over to Catholicism. How could they help it? – it had so much greater appeal to the sincere than the new State-made Church. Besides, there was a nucleus of able exiles abroad, of whom the centre was Dr. William Allen, later Cardinal, who founded the Catholic seminary at Douai, which drew them as a magnet. Oxford was especially susceptible to its impulse – the seminary had been created by Oxford men. When the time came to make martyrs of them – if they were to be held in check – of the first thirteen seminarists to be martyred, ten were Oxford men.

I

In Cornwall, the situation was not dangerous, for after the lesson of 1549, when Cornishmen had been killed in their numbers on the heath outside Exeter, the county accepted tranquilly the religious forms the Government, in its greater wisdom, thought fit to impose. But it was awkward that the richest and most powerful family, the Arundells of Lanherne, had not accepted the new Establishment and continued in their old ways, devout Catholics. For this meant a certain radius of Catholic influence, where they held their property and where they had relatives. Their influence in the county had become less in late years by the very fact of their Catholicism; but also because in recent generations they had been making very exalted marriages, which carried them beyond the ranks of the other Cornish gentry. The eleventh Sir John Arundell, of Henry VIII's reign, who refused the offer of a peerage at the time of the Field of the Cloth of Gold, married the sister and co-heiress of Thomas Grey, first Marquis of Dorset and half-brother to Elizabeth of York, Henry VII's Queen. His son, Sir Thomas Arundell, married Lady Margaret Howard, sister of Queen Catherine Howard. In the third generation, the grandson, the thirteenth knight, married a daughter of the Earl of Derby and widow of Lord Stourton. These marriages perhaps aroused the jealousy of the other Cornish gentry; in spite of an occasional alliance, the Arundells did not move on a footing with the others: there was not the same friendly equality as among the Grenvilles, the Edgcumbes, the Arundells of Trerice, the Godolphins. And their Catholic and Spanish sympathies provided an opening for their enemies. At the time of the taking of the Spanish treasure at Saltash, Sir Arthur Champernowne wrote to Cecil that there were only three people in the town who favoured the cause of the Spaniards and of these one was 'Clowborowe, servant to Sir John Arundell.' [1]

But in the affairs of the county at large, the Arundells, though unsympathetic to their direction, were discreet; they were indubitably loyal and they lay low. They were extremely popular with the people in Cornwall, in their own neighbourhood greatly beloved, and they remained so until they left Cornwall at the beginning of the eighteenth century for Wardour. But there was a prominent connection of theirs who was altogether less discreet, and perhaps not even loyal.

This was Francis Tregian of Golden, a charming Tudor house not greatly changed, though now it has descended to being a farm-house, lost among the winding lanes off the main road to Truro, in the rich farming lands between Probus and the sea-coast. Francis was the son of that John Tregian, whom Grenville's grandfather, old Sir Richard, might have had as the husband of his daughter Margaret, with a good jointure to boot. [2] Sir John Arundell, the twelfth, took advantage of the lost opportunity and married his daughter Katherine to Tregian. The Tregians, though a new family, were among the richest in Cornwall. They had made a fifteenth-century fortune in commerce, then married an heiress of the Wolvedon family

---

[1] S.P. Dom. Eliz. 48, no. 60.   [2] v. ante p. 33–4.

who brought Golden with her, and now were possessed of a large number of goodly manors in the Roseland country and in other parts of the county. Francis Tregian was the child of this Arundell marriage; and, completing his assimilation to the old aristocracy, he married the daughter of Lord Stourton, whose widow, we have seen, became the wife of the thirteenth Sir John Arundell, Tregian's uncle. This made them a closed circle, Catholic, devout, self-consciously aristocratic.

All that we know of Francis Tregian reveals him as an obstinate though ineffectual *dévot*, but a man of culture and taste – something of the type of the Venerable Philip, Earl of Arundel, who followed the Court gaily in his young days and then either through disappointment or marriage fell out of temper with it and took to religion. We find that in 1570, shortly after his marriage and at the height of the struggle with the Catholic aristocracy, Tregian was 'upon causes of great importance enforced by the space of almost ten months suppliantly to follow the Lords of the Council.' [1] Some years later, after Norfolk had been brought to the block and the Catholic opposition reduced, Tregian's name appears with several other well-known Catholics on a list headed 'Fugitives from England,' begging for the Queen's favour and pardon to return to England, 'and desiring to spend their lives in her Majesty's service . . . and they will discover themselves upon her Majesty's good acceptance of their dutiful affection and zeal.' [2] From an altogether less reputable source, a silly seventeenth-century life of Tregian by his grandson Francis Plunkett, a very low example of Catholic hagiography, [3] we learn that several attempts were made upon his virtue while at Court by no less a person than the Queen, who developed a passion for him and sent to him in the night. But he was a miracle of chastity: no less than sixty-five crosses (we do not learn the significance of the number) appeared upon the sheets of his bed, as the providential traces of his virtue; and to avoid such embarrassing attentions, even though stimulating in

[1] Quoted from the Oscott MSS. in Morris, *Troubles of our Catholic Forefathers*, vol. 1.
[2] Hatfield Papers.
[3] Boyan, Plunkett's 'Life of Francis Tregian,' *Catholic Record Society*, vol. 32.

grace, he fled from the Court, and Elizabeth out of vexation ordered the laws against Catholics to proceed!

So much for hagiography. But there is nothing inherently improbable in the story that Elizabeth took favour on him and offered to make him Vice-Comes – for the grandson, being an Irish exile living abroad, did not know that all that meant was to be Sheriff of the county; nor in the information that at Court he encouraged Catholics not to yield and was a proselytiser. Whatever the reason, thwarted and fanatically believing, he retired to his Cornish estates where he could enjoy the private consolations of religion, thereby endangering the safety and well-being of all those who joined in them and the very life of the poor misguided priest who administered them.

The priest, Cuthbert Mayne, was a Devonshire man, coming not far from Grenville's part of the country, for he was born in the parish of Sherwell, near Barnstaple, in 1544, so that he was three years younger than Grenville.[1] Mayne's uncle, who had conformed and was the holder of a fat parsonage, had sent him to Oxford, where he entered St. John's College. Oxford, we have seen, was at this time under the influence of the Catholic revival; some of her most distinguished sons were already abroad working, and many of her best men remaining felt the impulse. Certain colleges were particularly affected by it, notably Exeter, where the Rector himself was a Catholic and went into exile with several of his Fellows, and St. John's, where the brilliant Edmund Campion became a convert and went to Douai in 1571. At Trinity the Devonshireman Thomas Ford, also afterwards martyr, was converted in 1570 and went abroad.

These events, for Ford was his friend and he must have known Campion well, had their influence upon Mayne; two years before he left Oxford, his sympathies were already Catholic. Some letters from his friends overseas came into the hands of the Bishop of London, who sent a pursuivant to Oxford to arrest him and others of his circle. Mayne happened to be in the West Country, and warned by his friend Ford, did not again return to Oxford. Early in the year 1573, he 'took shipping on the coast of Cornwall, and so went to Douai when the seminary

[1] McElroy, *Blessed Cuthbert Mayne*, 29.

there was but newly erected.'[1] Here he remained for three years, studying theology; he was ordained priest in the Jubilee year 1575, in February 1576 took his degree as Bachelor of Divinity and in April left with another priest, John Payne, for England.[2]

Arriving in England, the two priests separated and Mayne made for his own West Country. On the night before he died, in his final examination, he said that

'coming from beyond seas to London, about a two years hence, he had a desire to place himself in the west country. Moving certain of his friends thereof they procured him unto Mr. Tregian, but what his friends' names were he will not utter lest they should be troubled therefore.'[3]

In the next article, he admits to having brought in letters for Tregian, so that it may be that the arrangement was already made by which Tregian was to receive him into his household, and that Mayne was concealing it for his benefit. It was not long before the authorities were aware that the two priests had slipped into the country; for apparently their papers had been seized on landing. And there is a curious entry in June in the Diary at Douai of news of their death arriving at the college; either it is wrongly dated, or more probably it was due to a rumour that the authorities had captured them.

Anyhow, Mayne reached Cornwall safely and lived in the household at Golden for a year before anything happened. Ostensibly he went about the country as Tregian's steward; and since the latter's estates reached as far as Tremolla near Launceston, this gave Mayne an opportunity of travelling about, visiting Catholic families, reconciling the lapsed and administering the sacraments. He admitted in his last examination to having said mass, but would not say where or who were present. All this was, of course, contrary to the laws, and there were heavy penalties attached to the breach of them, though sub-

[1] Allen, *A Briefe Historie of the Glorious Martyrdom of XII Reverend Priests* (ed. Pollen, 1908), 106.
[2] Knox, *First and Second Douai Diaries*, 100.
[3] S.P. Dom. Eliz. vol. 118, no. 46.

sequently they became still heavier. For the Government was really alarmed at the progress Catholicism was making; and the threatened subversion of the established religion by the filtering in of Allen's seminary priests, impossible as it seemed to stop them, threw the authorities into a panic. Cuthbert Mayne and John Payne were only the first; from now on a regular supply flowed into the country, and from Rome, Louvain, Valladolid, as well as from Douai. Orders were issued to keep stricter watch on recusants, and pressure was put on the secular and ecclesiastical officials to certify them.

The authorities in Cornwall could not be unaware of the fact that there was a priest at work in the Tregian household, for his ministrations went beyond to a wider circle. Catholic recusants had not yet learned the technique of secrecy, of hiding-places, and of keeping strict watch such as later enabled the Arundells in London and at Chideock in Dorset to retain Fr. John Cornelius as their chaplain for thirteen years. Mayne later admitted that 'he hath often been at Sir John Arundell's at Lanherne with his master, where he hath sometimes remained sevennight or fortnight together, and that he went not otherwise thither unless he were sent in some message of his master's.' [1]

It was not to be expected that what was going on in the county could continue unnoticed or that the authorities should not intervene. The difficulty was on what authority could a Justice of the Peace intervene without a writ, and how was he to obtain a writ without evidence. It needed someone of determination to deal with the situation; several of the Cornish Justices were not without the will, and some of them exhibited a most unpleasant vindictiveness throughout the proceedings against Mayne and his fellow Catholics. The Sheriff for the year 1576, however, made no move: he was George Kekewich, a courteous and easy-going old person. What was characteristic of Grenville when he came to face the situation left by his predecessor was his determination to force the position.

From the exactness of his movements when he determined to strike, it is clear that he had been carefully informed about the interior arrangements of the Tregian household; he knew

[1] S.P. Dom, Eliz. no. 47.

exactly where to find Mayne: someone must have turned in-
former. In June, the Bishop of Exeter was holding his visitation
at Truro, some half a dozen miles away from Golden; Grenville
with some other Justices sought him out there and requested
him to aid and assist him in searching Golden for the seminary
priest who was lying there. After some deliberation it was
agreed that not the Bishop, but the Bishop's Chancellor, a legal
official, should accompany the Sheriff and his company: a nice
distinction such as the Inquisition was accustomed to make
between the condemnation of a heretic and handing him over to
the lay arm for execution.

When they reached Golden, there was an altercation between
Grenville and Tregian as to the right of entry and search.
Tregian being weak allowed himself to be overborne: he might
at least, if he had been at all effective, instead of being a passive
dévot, have barricaded the house and enabled the priest to get
away. To quote Cardinal Allen's informant, who may have
been an eye-witness of the scene:

'As soon as they came to Mr. Tregian's house the Sheriff first
spake unto him saying, that he and his company were come to
search for one Bourne, which had committed a fault in London,
and so fled to Cornwall, and was in his house as he was informed. [Anthony Bourne was a fugitive from justice, who had
fled into Cornwall and later across the seas.] Mr. Tregian
answering that he was not there, and swearing by his faith that
he did not know where he was, further telling him that to have
his house searched he thought it great discourtesy, for that he
was a gentleman as he was, for that he did account his house as
his castle: also stoutly denying them, for that they had no
commission from the Prince.

'The Sheriff being very bold, because he had a great company
with him, sware by all the oaths he could devise, that he would
search his house or else he would kill or be killed, holding his
hand upon his dagger as though he would have stabbed it into
the gentleman. This violence being used he had leave to search
the house.' [1]

All this, one cannot but think, was very tame on Tregian's part, first to have allowed himself to be caught napping, to have had no one on guard of all his servants; and secondly, to have put up no resistance to give Mayne the alarm. For the account goes on to say that, just before, Mayne had been in the garden 'where he might have gone from them.' He had now returned to his room and shut it fast. Grenville made straight for it and beat upon the door, which the priest then opened.

'As soon as the Sheriff came into the chamber,' the account relates, 'he took Mr. Mayne by the bosom and said unto him "What art thou?" and he answered "I am a man." Whereat the Sheriff being very hot, asked whether he had a coat of mail under his doublet, and so unbuttoned it, and found an *Agnus Dei* case about his neck, which he took from him and called him a traitor and rebel with many other opprobrious names.'

Grenville now had his evidence; it was characteristic of him that by carrying himself with a high hand he should have obtained justification for his proceeding after the event. For to possess an *Agnus Dei* (it was a little wax imprint of a figure of a lamb made from the Paschal candles), or beads blessed by the Pope, was a penal offence under the Act of 1571, punishable by imprisonment and confiscation of goods. Anyhow, Mayne was a fool to be wearing it – perhaps he thought it might be efficacious as a protection; that was not the sort of mistake made by the subtle, eel-like Jesuit, Parsons, when he came into the country three years later disguised as a soldier: he got away again. Mayne's books and papers were seized and himself haled off to Truro, where he was examined by the Bishop. Then in the custody of the Sheriff he was taken 'from one gentleman's house to another' across the eastern part of the county to Launceston, where he was lodged in close confinement in the gaol within the Castle. Tregian, meanwhile, as a gentleman of standing, was given bail.

These proceedings were at once reported to the Council, for on 19 June they wrote to Grenville and his fellow Justices thanking them 'as well for their pains taken in the diligent search for Bourne as for the apprehension of Mr. Tregian and others for

matters of religion.' [1] The various papers and things found at
Golden were sent up to the Council; for on 1 July, at a session
at which the Earl of Bedford, the Lord Lieutenant of Devon and
Cornwall, was present, a letter was sent to the Judges of Assize
for Cornwall, enclosing the Bull of Indulgence taken at Golden
'and divers other relics used in popery, with some declaration
of lewd matter prejudicial to the present state, with a special
treatise against the Book of Common Prayer,' and directing
them to proceed in their examination of the matter and 'administering of justice according to the desert of their facts.' [2]

The hunt was up. Grenville's independent and forceful
action had set in motion the machinery of government; from
now on the Council was to take the main burden of responsibility and to order the steps taken. They were grateful for so
active and energetic a drive as Grenville was making against
Papists throughout the county. The trouble in some parts of
the country was that the local Justices could not be got to move,
as in Lancashire: hence the survival of Catholicism there. Some
trace of what was happening in Cornwall this summer remains
in the Borough Accounts of Launceston, where we read: 'To
Mr. Sheriff when he searched St. Katherine's for papist books,
a potell of sack, and a potell of claret wine, 22d.' [3] No doubt it
was hot work! St. Katherine's was one of the chapels attached
to the old buildings of the ruinous priory: one wonders if it was
among the remnants of its library that Grenville was doing
destruction.

The Council was very encouraging: on 4 August, they wrote
again to the Judges requiring them to examine Mayne and
others at the next assizes, 'and also to understand what others
there are of that condition lurking in this realm, and in what
place.' [4] Already as the result of the investigations proceeding,
a number of Catholic gentlemen had been sought out; for the
Bishop of Exeter was ordered to take bonds of Robert Becket, a
gentleman of a very good Cornish family and of considerable
property, living at Cartuther near Liskeard, and of Richard
Tremayne and Francis Ermyn, for their appearance before the

[1] *A.P.C.*, IX, 364.   [2] ibid. 375.
[3] Peter: *Histories of Launceston and Dunheved*, 212.   [4] *A.P.C.*, X, 6–7.

Council. A number of others too were being indicted along with Mayne and Tregian. In fact, there was proceeding a general round-up of the Catholic elements in Cornwall, all except the Arundells themselves, who were too important to touch and against whom there was not as yet any evidence.

Mayne waited for his trial in close imprisonment until the Michaelmas Sessions, when the Judges of the Western Circuit, Manwood and Jefferys, came to Launceston. It was Grenville's duty as Sheriff to impanel the grand and petty juries. It is not necessary to suppose that they were packed,[1] except in a sense in which all sixteenth-century juries were packed; that is to say, that the authorities did not choose to nominate those whom they thought would show favour to the accused. The grand jury was representative of the Cornish gentry, who supported the established order: there were on it, among others, Richard Carew of Antony, Peter Courtenay, John Arundell of Tolverne, Hannibal Vyvyan, Diggory Tremayne, Peter Killigrew, John Kempthorne, George Carnsew. They returned a true bill against the accused. The petty jury were impanelled from among the bourgeois of the towns, shopkeepers and traders: Sampson Piper who was Mayor of Launceston for this year, Thomas Hicks who had been Mayor the previous year, John Wills, a well-known resident of Saltash. They came from a class even more hostile to Catholicism than the gentry.

Cardinal Allen's account tells us that the Earl of Bedford was 'present at Mr. Mayne's arraignment and did deal most in the matter.' There is no other evidence for this, but Bedford was in the west this summer and at his house at Tavistock would be conveniently placed for the proceedings at Launceston. Mayne was tried upon several indictments, for saying mass, for bringing in and delivering an *Agnus Dei*, for upholding the Pope's authority within the realm; upon each of these he was condemned and sentenced to various penalties amounting to perpetual loss of lands, goods and liberty. But it was upon the charges of obtaining a Bull of absolution from the see of Rome, and of publishing it, that he was condemned of treason and sentenced to be hanged, drawn and quartered. Tregian,

[1] McElroy, 65–8.

as his accessory, was condemned to loss of lands and goods, and imprisonment for life. On the charges of aiding Mayne upon each of these counts, a varying number of persons of Tregian's Catholic circle, from ten to fifteen on each indictment, were condemned: theirs are the names given above.[1] Upon a seventh indictment, that for simple recusancy and not coming to the church, several new names appear in addition to Tregian and those we know: they were Sir John Arundell, Nicholas Roscarrock (a cousin of Grenville's), Joanna, the wife of Richard Tremayne, Mary Hame, Margaret, Winifred and David Kemp, Philip and Jane Tremayne, Robert and Jane Smith, Thomas Becket and Thomas Pickford. These were all persons of substance and sentenced to fines for the luxury of not attending Church.

There was some disagreement between the Judges over the point made in Mayne's defence that the Bull of Absolution made out for the Jubilee Year 1575 had expired: was it therefore executable? Manwood, the Chief Justice, over-rode his dissentient colleague and gave the death sentence. But it was respited until the pleasure of the Council should be known. Allen says, 'after the twelve had given the verdict Guilty, the Judges gave sentence on him that he should be executed within xv days, but it was deferred until St. Andrew's day, upon what occasion I know not.' Meanwhile Grenville rode to London to inform the Council of the issue; for on 28 October, the Bishop of Exeter, who had been ordered to make a return of all the recusants in his diocese, wrote to the Council,

'for the Cornish travail, where are the greatest number of papists, and where I proposed first to begin, knowing that Mr. Richard Grenville was then ridden to London, I sent to Mr. Edmund Tremayne, praying him to supply his place, which he gladly did accomplish, and brought with him Mr. George Grenville, a very earnest and learned Justice of Cornwall, and in the mean season, sent also for Sir John Killigrew who readily came.' [2]

They were all ready for the work, and as the result of their

[1] v. ante p. 139.   [2] S.P. Dom. Eliz. 117, no. 25.

joint labours, a schedule was sent up containing the names of all the chief recusants, including several new ones.

On 12 November, the Council sent down their orders that the execution of Mayne was to go forward:

'the place of his execution to be at Launceston upon a market day; where after he shall be dead and quartered, his head to be set upon a post and placed in some eminent place within the said town of Launceston, and his four quarters to be likewise set upon four posts and placed the one at Bodmin, the second at Tregony, the third at Barnstaple and the fourth at Wadebridge.' [1]

And so it happened that when the last ghastly rites were performed in the market-place at Launceston, upon a market-day for the better edification of the people, Grenville was not there, and his place was taken by his deputy, the Under-Sheriff.

Mayne will always continue to be somewhat impersonal to us, we know so little about this first of the Douai martyrs. Far less, for example, than we know of Fr. John Cornelius, a Bodmin lad who came in his time too to be martyred: he was the clear type of the mystic, with whom the inner life was so strong that the life of this world seemed uncertain in comparison. [2] But on the night before Mayne suffered there was a final examination of him taken, which enables us to see something of what sort of man this was who resisted all their force and their persuasions alike. [3] Nothing could move him: he had the whole intellectual position worked out, from which he answered all their questions: his was the mind of the complete Counter-Reformation type.

He told them, now that he was past all hope, that 'any that is a Catholic may not in any wise receive the Sacrament, come to the Church or hear the schismatical service, which is established in the same here in England.' It must have been gall and wormwood to those who heard, for their first memories

---

[1] *A.P.C.*, X, 85.

[2] Martyred at Dorchester, 4 July 1594, having been taken at Chideock Castle, the Dorsetshire house of the Arundells. *Records of the Society of Jesus*, vol. 3.

[3] S.P. Dom. Eliz. 118, no. 46.

were those of the Catholic Faith. Further, he gave them his belief

'that the people of England may be won unto the Catholic religion of the see of Rome, by such secret instructors as either are or may be within the realm. But what these secret instructors are he will not utter, but hopeth when time serveth they shall do therein as pleaseth God; and that those with others use secret conference to withdraw the minds of the subjects of this realm from the religion established in the same.'

He explained to them that the text of the Lateran Council found in a book of his, 'signifying that though Catholics did now serve, swear and obey, yet if occasion were offered they should be ready to help the execution etc.,' had been ratified by the Council of Trent, and that it meant 'that if any Catholic prince took in hand to invade any Realm to reform the same to the authority of the see of Rome, that then the Catholics in that Realm invaded by foreigners should be ready to assist and help them and this was the meaning of the execution.'

It was a declaration of war: it was this theory of Papal absolutism overriding national sovereignty which justified the Elizabethan government in its harsh repression of Catholics; and if only Mayne knew it, or rather his superiors, Allen and Parsons, it was this setting of themselves against the trend of national feeling which made the position of the Catholic Church hopeless in England. No wonder the Justices who heard it were provoked to fury by it.

Next day, St. Andrew's day, 30 November, Mayne was dragged on a hurdle through the streets of Launceston from the castle to the market-place. At the gibbet, he would have spoken to the assembled crowd, but was prevented; and one of them made a last attempt to incriminate Sir John Arundell, probably for the benefit of the mob. He called out, 'Now, villain and traitor, you are at the moment of death; tell us then truly whether Mr. Tregian and Sir John Arundell knew of the things you are to die for.' Mayne was not to be caught by this, and took all the charges home to himself, as being 'known only to me and no others.' A moment later he was cast off the ladder, saying *In manus tuas, Domine*, the words which so many others were to say after him in years to come, and as much in vain.

It is a mistake to treat this chapter of events, as previously it has been treated, in all hagiographical literature, as a personal matter between Grenville and Mayne, or even between Grenville and the Arundells. It was much more important than that. We have seen that, from a personal point of view, it was at least the whole ruling gentry of Cornwall that accepted the Elizabethan system against those who did not. The poor Douai priest, the proto-martyr of the seminarists, was but the occasion for the destruction of the Catholic remnant in Cornwall. It was a very considerable remnant, much greater and more influential than what remained in Devonshire; and if left to itself it would have grown, for there must have been some underground sympathy for Catholicism among the simplest people. It was Grenville's great service to the Elizabethan government, during his year of office as Sheriff, to have seized his opportunity to strike at this influential minority, and as might be expected, he struck hard and passionately. The result of it was the virtual end of Catholicism in the west.

For his services in this hectic year of office, Grenville was awarded his knighthood: in itself no great matter, for his family was a knightly one and the head of it in each generation was accustomed to receive the honour. It would have come to him some time in any case; the occasion upon which he received it, the services for which it was conferred, were much more important.[1]

II

In addition to the main business of his term, there was a miscellany of other matters belonging to the routine of the office, of which the most burdensome, though perhaps to Grenville, since he was a martial man, the most congenial, was the taking of Musters. These were as yet early days to what the Musters, and the duties attendant upon them, subsequently

[1] He was knighted at Windsor in October. Shaw, *Knights of England*, 11, 78.

became. Though there had been a war-scare in 1569–70, there was not yet the insistent pressure for defence which led Carew to claim with justice that Cornwall was burdened out of all proportion to Devon and the neighbouring counties. Training the able-bodied men of the shire had rather fallen behind with the early peaceful years of Elizabeth's reign; and as yet, the authorities were content to draw out and train, if it could be called training, a number of men each year, mustering what weapons the country and themselves could provide, mainly pikes and bills, with a few arquebuses and muskets. Perhaps it partook more of a holiday, when the men were drawn together from their fields and woods and pastures to some central place, to undergo a few summer days' training, in those years when the danger of war was but a cloud upon their pastoral horizon.

On 20 April, the Commissioners for Musters, Grenville among them, wrote that they had received the Council's orders for levying, furnishing and training 200 soldiers, and that they had ordered the exercises to begin on St. George's Even and to end on St. Mark's Day.[1] But by 26 September, the Council's orders had still not been put into execution.[2] A new and terrible factor had intervened: now 'considering the general infection of the plague, which presently is very great in divers places in this shire and that the assembly of the people might be a great occasion of the farther spreading thereof' they have with the advice of the Judges of Assize postponed general musters till its mitigation. Meanwhile they had given commandment to the constables to view and take order of the parishioners in every parish to see that they were furnished with weapons.

There is something affecting in these simple measures which it was the habit of our forefathers to take for defence of hearth and home. If the training in arms that they received was perhaps perfunctory, no doubt an amiable sociability was encouraged, particularly in the towns, by the occasions it afforded. We read, for instance, in the accounts of the town of Plymouth, where Sir Richard was this year upon the same business: 'Item

[1] S.P. Dom. Eliz. 112, no. 22.   [2] ibid. 115, no. 26.

paid to Mr. Westlake for sugar when Sir Richard Grenville did muster upon the Hoe vɪᴅ.'[1] In 1580, when John Blitheman was Mayor, there was paid 'for a dinner and a supper bestowed upon Sir Richard Grenville Knight, Mr. Paget and others, xʟs,' and 'for their horse meat vɪɪs vɪᴅ.' Mr. Paget was the parson whom Grenville this year presented to the living of Kilkhampton, upon the death (at last!) of his old great-uncle, John Grenville. Probably the two were on their way to Kilkhampton, where Paget was to be inducted. The appointment was not a success: Paget was a Puritan hot-gospeller, whose eventual eviction from the living led to another turbulent, though in this instance rather comic, episode in Grenville's life. Such was the simple but deferential hospitality bestowed by the town of Plymouth, at Walter Peperell's or Martin White's or Chris. Harris's, upon the neighbouring notables who happened to be passing through.

Still more of his time was taken up, at the orders of the Council, by investigations into piracy with which the Channel was again rife and with which many persons living on the sea-board of Cornwall were connected. There were in particular two notorious pirates, Captain Hicks of Saltash, and Captain Hammond, whose deeds filled the Channel ports with lamentations. It needed persons like Grenville and William Hawkins, who were already sufficiently familiar with the more exalted art of privateering, to deal with these smaller fry. In August 1577, in the midst of the Mayne business, he was appointed to a commission, to inquire into the taking of a ship called *Our Lady* of Aransusia, which, laden with iron, was captured off the coast of Galicia by Captain Hicks, and, it was thought, brought into the Helford River.[2] They were to search there and find out into whose hands her lading had come. By October, Hammond had been caught and a serjeant of the Lord Admiral sent down to bring him up; Grenville was ordered to see Hammond safely guarded through Cornwall under the serjeant's conduction, 'forasmuch as it is doubted lest there may be some practise used for the rescuing of the said Hammond

[1] Plymouth Muniments: Widey Court Book.
[2] *A.P.C. 1577–8*, 14.

146

within that shire.' [1] At the end of the year, as the result of the activities of a Commission of Piracy which had been appointed, a number of dealers in pirates' goods were brought to light. They were for the most part persons of substance, such as Thomas St. Aubyn of Clowance, John Reskymmer, John Penrose and Peter Killigrew. Grenville was to take bonds of them for their appearance before the Council. [2]

Among other matters that fell to him was the job of inquiring into the quarrels of his choleric relation, Sir John Killigrew, whose differences first with Ambrose Digby and then with Henry Farnaby led to much disturbance of the peace in Cornwall. We learn from the invaluable Carnsew that Killigrew and Digby fought a duel at Truro this summer. It appears that the quarrel was over the matter of Anthony Bourne who had escaped from Pendennis Castle overseas. Since Digby was Vice-Admiral, he may have charged Sir John with being privy to it. This indeed seems to have been likely since Killigrew was in debt to Bourne. [3] Grenville and Edgcumbe were appointed to a Special Commission of inquiry, which found that Bourne had left the country without license at Falmouth on 2 June in the previous year. [4] Sir John, having meanwhile repaired to the Council to answer the charges and lay others of his own against Digby, the whole matter was committed to Grenville and Edgcumbe and others to inquire into. They did their best to smooth things over; certainly nothing incriminating transpired as regards Killigrew's relations with Bourne. Later on both Killigrew and Digby were sworn to abide by the arbitration of Bedford; in the end Bedford awarded a sum of money to be paid as compensation to Digby, so that it is clear Sir John was, as usual, in the wrong. [5]

The dispute between Killigrew and Farnaby was even more tiresome and took longer; it is only of any interest now since it provides one of the few notices remaining of the Truro family of Farnabys, which produced in the next generation the charming Caroline musician, Giles Farnaby. Over some matter of

---

[1] *A.P C. 1577–8*, 67.   [2] ibid. 82.
[3] Exchequer K.R. Special Com., 3017.   [4] ibid. 542.
[5] *A.P.C. 1577–8*, 142, 175, 177, 210, 215; *A.P.C. 1578–80*, 339.

debt, Sir John took the law into his own hands and seized some of Farnaby's property – with all the more gusto because he knew Farnaby was too poor to go to law about it. The matter had been committed by the Council, at the end of 1578, to Richard Trevanion and Robert Trencreek to inquire into. They did nothing about it, it is easy to see why: they clearly did not want to embroil themselves with a powerful old ruffian like Sir John, nor would they want to find a neighbour and connection in the wrong. Someone more powerful was needed. So on 31 May, the Council wrote to Grenville placing him at the head of Trevanion and Trencreek in the Commission and, since nothing was returned from them, requiring him

'to signify unto them that they have forgotten their duty, and to require them to send up such examinations under both their hands as they have taken; or if the matter be not examined, then the said Sir Richard to join with them, and so to end the matter between them by both their consents if they can, or else to make certificate of their doings unto their Lordships.'

It is clear that the Council had confidence in Grenville as a competent servant of the Government; a confidence which, in spite of certain turbulent passages in the past and others which were yet to come, was not misplaced. Forceful, too forceful, as he was, he was a man to get things done; and as time went on, he came more and more to emancipate himself from the pull of his own private interests, and became more of a public servant, accepting his own disappointments without complaint and sacrificing his own course at the call of duty. In a month's time, the Council received the report they had desired, and they were able to commit the case to the Justices of Assize where it went on its lumbering way, in the manner of Elizabethan justice.[1]

This was not the last time that Grenville, at a word from the higher command, had to descend upon his kinsman, Sir John. The family at Arwennack, in spite of their high connections at Court, were going a rake's progress to the fate that overtook Sir John's son, disgrace and imprisonment in the Gatehouse at

[1] *A.P.C. 1577–8*, 246, 255; *A.P.C. 1578–80*, 148, 201, 331.

Westminster. Grenville seems to have dealt justly by them, without fear or favour.

His own private affairs, in marked contrast to the Killigrews and the St. Legers, were fortunately prospering, though as they prospered, they became increasingly complex. The St. Legers of Annery, his wife's family, were pursuing a headlong downward course; it is not difficult to see, even through the impersonality of these documents, that they were an easy-going, good-for-nothing, hard-drinking lot. In October 1574, John St. Leger, the son, was one of a band of three who committed a highway robbery on Hounslow Heath: they set upon a certain Thomas Phillpott, robbed him of a gold chain worth 100 marks, beat him and left him wounded there.[1] Next year, Sir John St. Leger was borrowing a large sum, £500, from a London merchant-taylor, at an exorbitant rate of interest: he was to repay the capital with a sum of £100 as interest, within a year! This was contrary to the Statute of Usury, which only permitted up to 10 per cent.[2]

But Sir John was by this time far gone and could not stop: he could only sell off his lands bit by bit, until he had made away with all his inheritance. Grenville came to his aid once and again, but being a man of business, upon good landed security. By 1577 he had advanced £800 to him. Against that and for a further sum of £200, a debt of Sir John to Hugh Jones, a London mercer, for which Grenville made himself responsible, St. Leger granted away to him the fee-simple of the island of Lundy. It is a very complicated and involved document by which the transaction takes place;[3] and it makes pathetic reading, for behind its legal complexities may be discerned the very human hope of the St. Legers some day to regain this strip of their patrimony. It is provided that if they perform their agreements to pay the sums of money owing, then they might re-enter into possession of the Island and Manor. But they never did; and this is how Lundy came into the hands of the Grenvilles. It is curious to reflect as one looks out to sea from the high ground between Kilkhampton and Bideford, to that fine

[1] Middlesex Sessions Rolls, 1. 89. [2] ibid. 93.
[3] Close Roll a⁰ 20 Eliz. part 1 (C 54/1024).

formal shape upon the horizon, sometimes clear, more often withheld in mist, that this was the manner of its passing.

A little more information about Grenville's father-in-law may be gathered from a Star Chamber case a few years later.[1] One Thomas Hilling of Bodmin brought a bill of complaint against Grenville, Christopher Walker and others on the ground that Grenville had brought a suit against him for slander, in the name of Sir John St. Leger, in the Stannary Court of Blackmore. He pleaded that this had been done intentionally and corruptly, without the knowledge or consent of St. Leger, when neither himself nor Sir John were tinners or liable to the jurisdiction of this Court, and that he was condemned 'by a partial jury corruptly returned at the nomination' of Grenville and his creature Walker, who was clerk of the Court. Having been found guilty, he 'was like to have been spoiled and undone if the said Sir John St. Leger being a gentleman of good conscience' had not remitted the heavy damages – further testimony to Sir John's good nature.

No less revealing was what Hilling had said. Sir Richard testified that his wife had complained to him of the 'various abuses' offered to her father; and that Sir John 'being his father-in-law in whose house and lineage the defendant's posterity is to continue,' he wrote to inquire into the matter. Sir John replied that Hilling 'in words and otherwise had to his face used him very proudly and disdainfully,' and that he said in public to one of St. Leger's servants 'thy master is an old drunken bankrupt knave, a rogue, and a raskally villain – and so go tell him.' It was Hilling's misfortune that some part of what he said was true; but having the temerity to say it is another matter: perhaps he was an unsatisfied creditor. At any rate Grenville had him arrested within one of the Stannary Courts near his dwelling, and here he was imprisoned. These smaller prerogative jurisdictions were the source of great discontent to the middle-class townsmen, as they afforded such opportunities to the gentry to enforce their will. The attack upon them in the next century was part of the general attack upon the prerogatives of the Crown which led to the Civil War.

[1] Star Chamber Proc. Eliz., Hilary 1582 (H 6/16).

As the St. Legers went down, so the fortunes of the Grenvilles under the husbanding hand of their present head went up. As one after the other the St. Leger estates were dispersed, the manor of Canonleigh, the Isle of Lundy, the manor of Cullompton and Upton Weaver, then the site of the priory at Canonleigh,[1] so Grenville added to his domains. Two years after acquiring Lundy, he bought the fifth part of the manors of Trenant, Manely Colshill, St. Ewe, and of the advowson of St. Ewe, from Thomas Bodenham for, apparently, £1,500; but this was probably for the purpose of some family settlement, perhaps providing dowers for his daughters.[2] In 1577 he brought an action in Chancery, and in 1578 one in Star Chamber against three tenants of his manor of Lancras who claimed to hold for three lives by copy of court-roll; he was bent upon reducing them to the status of tenants at will.[3]

His experience of business meant that he was entrusted with other people's affairs, as, for example, the sale of the manor of Colquite, a Cornish property of Lord Thomas Howard, Viscount Bindon. The latter was troubled by an ill-disciplined and irrepressible son, Henry Howard, who ran himself and his father into a mountain of debts, so that his father was driven to sell land to meet them. To Grenville and Sir Arthur Basset was committed the sale of Colquite, a goodly manor of the clear yearly value of £50 10s. 8d. But they could not get an offer of more than £1,500 for it, for the manor was assured to Mr. Thomas Howard and his wife for their lives. Grenville wrote on 10 January 1580 that

'I and others in whom the trust for the said sale to have been made was reposed, have done our best endeavours and practised as well with the tenants who manure the same, as with others for purchase thereof. But with all our travails could not make the price (the land being as it is so assured unto Mr. Thomas Howard and his wife as they are to receive all the lands, rents, fines, etc., so long as they live) . . . But if it might be freed of

[1] Pat. Rolls Eliz., 1181, 1194, 1252.
[2] ibid. no. 1194; and Close Rolls Eliz. no. 1073.
[3] Star Chamber Proc. Eliz., 9 February 1578.

that estate of Mr. Thomas Howard, your Lordship's son and his wife, then was there a far greater offer made, of which I thought good to advertise your Honour, praying you to accept our good minds who were the dealers herein and ready to be employed in this or any other like service.' [1]

It seems that Grenville was on terms of personal acquaintance with Lord Bindon, which was natural enough since he was the person of chief authority in Dorset, as Grenville was by now in Cornwall. What adds interest to the connection is that Bindon, a cousin of the Queen, was great-uncle of Lord Thomas Howard, under whose command Grenville was killed.

III

So much for his private affairs in these years: it is all that remains to us. To return to his public occupations: the Council continued to use his services in all manner of business. They came in this period chiefly to depend upon him in Cornwall, and continued to do so as long as he remained in the west.

In December 1579, the Judges of the western circuit returned their certificate of the Cornish Justices of the Peace who had sworn the Oath of Supremacy.[2] Grenville's name appears at the head along with Sir John Killigrew, in place of Sir John Arundell now in London, answering to the Council for the images and pictures of Christ and the Virgin Mary found in his house at Lanherne.[3] In March in the New Year, a commission for General Musters had been sent down, to him and others, under the command of Bedford.[4] They made an expeditious return of the forces of the county in May.[5] The fact was that the military organisation of the county was becoming better organised. The hundreds of the shire were grouped into four larger districts, under the command respectively of Grenville, Edgcumbe, William Mohun and John Arundell of Tolverne. Altogether there were some 6,968 able-bodied men to be drawn upon, of whom they selected 4,000, in addition to the garrisons

[1] S.P. Dom. Eliz. 136, no. 3.
[2] ibid. 133, no. 12.
[3] *A.P.C. 1578–80*, 265, 345.
[4] S.P. Dom. Eliz. 136, no. 52.
[5] ibid. 138, nos. 5, 6.

of Pendennis, St. Mawes and the Mount; 2,000 were appointed for supply into Devonshire in case of necessity, as in Devon 4,000 men were to re-inforce the Cornish forces in similar case. It all reads like a rehearsal for 1588.

For affairs were becoming critical again, especially in Ireland, the weak spot in the English defences. For two years and more, Thomas Stukeley and James Fitzmaurice had been abroad in the courts of Rome and Madrid, and in the sea-ports of Brittany and the northern coast of Spain, preparing their wildcap schemes for a foreign descent upon Ireland. Stukeley in the end deflected himself to serve the King of Portugal in his African campaign, where he perished with the flower of the Portuguese nobility in the fatal battle of Alcazar. Fitzmaurice came home to Ireland to raise the standard of that rebellion which brought untold suffering upon Munster and ruined the house of Desmond. In the summer of 1578, 1,000 men had been levied in the four western counties and transported to southern Ireland from Bristol and Barnstaple; 200 of them were Cornish and some of the shipping provided may have been Grenville's.[1]

It was necessary to think of the defence of the sea-coasts. In Spain, it was rumoured, there was an armada preparing and no one knew what its destination might be. At the beginning of the year 1580, the Council sent out general orders to all the maritime counties of the south from Norfolk to Cornwall to put 'in a readiness such numbers of men as have heretofore been allotted to repair unto the sea coasts for the defence of the places of descent.' On the Channel coast each county was to survey its forts and castles to see that they were in a state of defence: in Cornwall, the duty was committed to Grenville, William Mohun, John Treffry, John Godolophin and John Arundell of Trerice.[2] In the autumn, the careful Burghley, making his preparations for what he hoped would not eventuate, drew up a list of the martial men in each county, men who had had experience of war; for Cornwall he notes, relying on who knows what memory of their past association, 'Sir Richard Grenville, Mr. Specott.'[3]

[1] *A.P.C. 1577–8*, 240–1.   [2] *A.P.C. 1578–80*, 381–2.
[3] S.P. Dom. Eliz. 143, no. 46.

IV

For three years now, Drake had been absent upon his Pacific voyage; for more than a year he had been overdue. During that time (he was engaged upon the long journey across the Pacific from North America, exploring the Spice Islands, returning home across the Indian Ocean and round the Cape of Good Hope) there had been no news of him whatever. A year before, when he was already in mid-Pacific, a report had come home that he had been captured and hanged: it may have arisen from Oxenham's execution at Lima. Soon after came the dispatches from the Viceroys of Peru and New Spain, telling the full tale of Drake's depredations on their coasts. In August, an express from Seville reported that Drake had captured 200,000 ducats of the King's property and 400,000 of private owners in his break-through into the South Sea. The forward party at Court, particularly those who had invested in the enterprise, were according to the Spanish Ambassador, Mendoza, 'beside themselves with joy.' In the city there was great anxiety at what might happen to the trade with Seville and the English merchants there. Then there was quietness; the Government deliberately reassured the commercial interests, and there was a tacit agreement to say nothing until the great depredator returned.

Suddenly, without a word of warning, at the end of September, he was there. He did not dare as yet set foot on shore; his wife put out to see him, and the Mayor, John Blitheman, who must have told him of the curious posture of affairs: the war-party prepared to welcome him with open arms, the peace-party ready to sacrifice him for the sake of peace with Spain. He took warning, warped out of harbour and anchored behind St. Nicholas Island. Word, meanwhile, was sent to the Queen, who, as we now know, unknown to Burghley, was an adventurer in the voyage. Soon her assurance arrived that he had nothing to fear and that he was to come to court; after some hesitation, as over the Spanish treasure of 1569, and after the strongest representations from the insistent Mendoza, the Queen threw in her lot with the forward party. Her warrant

SIR FRANCIS DRAKE.

was sent down to the faithful Edmund Tremayne, to assist Drake in sending up certain bullion that he had brought into the realm (the little ship was literally ballasted with silver), but 'to leave £10,000 worth in his hands, which sum is to be kept most secret to himself.' It was a pledge of her approval. The bullion was stored for the time under guard in Trematon Castle, across the water. Drake, having seen that all was set fair for him at Court, came down again to escort the treasure by a train of pack-horses (memento of the road to Nombre de Dios!), which the country people flocked to see on its way to Sion House and thence into the Tower.

In London, Drake was the hero of the hour.

'The Queen,' complained Mendoza bitterly, 'shows extraordinary favour to Drake and never fails to speak to him when she goes out in public, conversing with him a long time. She says that she will knight him on the day she goes to see his ship.'

'The people generally,' wrote Stowe, 'applauded his wonderful long adventure and rich prizes. His name and fame became admirable in all places, the people swarming daily in the streets to behold him, vowing hatred to all that misliked him.'

He had become at a blow not only the most famous man in the country, but the darling of the nation.

What Grenville thought of it all, we do not know; there is utter and absolute silence: no word that we know ever escaped him on the subject. But his actions are revealing. Not much more than two months after Drake came into harbour, Grenville sold Buckland, which he had made what it was and which gave him such a favourable position in relation to Plymouth, to two intermediaries, John Hele and Christopher Harris, who paid him £3,400 for it.[1] That money, so large a sum at once, could only have come from Drake, to whom, within six months, they passed the property over. So Drake reigned at Buckland in his stead. There needed nothing to be done to the house, it was now in such finished perfect state: so it comes that there was

[1] Pat. Roll Eliz. 1209; Lady Elliott-Drake, *The Family and Heirs of Sir F. Drake.*

nothing added at Drake's hand, save only a fine plaster mantel-piece in the Tower room, on which are his arms, the two pole stars granted him by the Queen, and the lovely crest of a ship in full sail upon the globe.

For Grenville, it was in a way, a confession of defeat: some-body else had made his South Sea Voyage, and made history by it. Grenville withdrew from Plymouth, making way for Drake who henceforward took first place there. The entries in the town's accounts relating to Grenville come to an end; the messages go to and fro between Buckland and the town as much as ever, but not to Grenville. It is Sir Francis and his lady whom the town entertains to supper or to a banquet.[1] As the years go on, and we approach nearer to the crisis of 1588, the relations between Plymouth and the house at Buckland becomes ever closer and more intimate. From that time the Drakes have been there ever since.

[1] Worth, *Calendar of Plymouth Municipal Records*, for many entries, pp. 124-37.

CHAPTER VIII

CORNISH PIRACY AND LAW-BREAKING

As England swung into the eighties, the country moved forward gradually, yet not imperceptibly, into the leading place in the alignment of European forces against Spain. It was indeed high time. While Drake was marauding on the other side of the world, the independence of the Kingdom of Portugal was at its last gasp with the life of the old King Cardinal Henry, last of his line; and immense preparations were being pushed forward in Spain for Philip to enter upon his inheritance, the farflung Portuguese Empire. It was not only within the Iberian Peninsula and upon the outer oceans that Spanish power moved forward, but at the heart of Northern Europe, in the Netherlands.

Here Don John of Austria had been succeeded by Alexander, Prince of Parma, as diplomatic a politician as he was brilliant in the field. Within a short time of his arrival he had succeeded in dividing the Netherlands and setting the southern provinces against the north. The States in despair were reduced to offering their sovereignty to Anjou, the French candidate for their overlordship. But the situation in France as between the Catholic Guises, supporters now of Philip, and the Huguenot party of Navarre, with the miserable Henry III in a precarious equilibrium between them, kept France immobilised so that no support could be given to Anjou. This meant that the Netherlands were forced back upon the surreptitious aid that Elizabeth alone could give. It was an exposed and hazardous situation for this country; but fortunately it was one to which the abilities of Elizabeth conspicuously rose, and for which her wits were peculiarly adapted.

On 31 January 1580 the King-Cardinal died; Alva was

placed in command of the large Spanish army which moved upon the Portuguese frontier, as the great Admiral, Santa Cruz, was of the fleet which blocked the Tagus. Within a few months Philip was in possession of his new Kingdom, and Don Antonio, the claimant of the throne, an illegitimate son of a previous king and the candidate of the Portuguese people – for what that was worth – a refugee in France. The whole of the Portuguese dominions, with the singular and important exception of the Azores, were ready to accept Philip as King. Of these islands, which occupied the most important strategic position in the Atlantic in those days of sailing ships, for they were the rendezvous of ships coming and going from the West Indies and South America as well as from the East Indies, only the largest, San Miguel, had accepted Philip and a Spanish garrison. All the rest, Terceira, Graciosa, San Jorje, Pico, Fayal, and at the extreme north-west, Flores (a name eloquent of the future) held out for Don Antonio.

The Pretender had got away with some of the Crown jewels, and in 1581 he was in England trying to induce Elizabeth to support an expedition under his flag to seize the Azores as a basis for future operations. Drake, at a loose-end after his triumphant home-coming, was strongly in favour of it; and Walsingham, who was now sole Secretary and wishing to drive the Queen into a forward policy, drew up a scheme under which Drake, with six ships, eight pinnaces and a thousand men, was to establish himself at Terceira under Don Antonio's flag, thence to operate against Spain's sea-communications with the Indies and to intercept the Plate Fleet.[1] It was an audacious scheme; but it would have meant war, and Elizabeth had no mind for embarking on a war single-handed against Spain, and without a French alliance. Upon this the project foundered; France, hopelessly divided against itself, was in no position to contemplate a war with Spain. The project of an English conquest of the Azores was abandoned and Don Antonio went back to France.

In the next year, however, he succeeded in getting together, with French aid, a large armament under the command of

[1] Corbett, *Drake and the Tudor Navy*, I, 347.

Philip Strozzi. It was badly organised and worse led; Strozzi, under the influence of the old Mediterranean ideas of naval tactics, had committed his fleet to grappling with a superior force—the Spaniards being ably commanded by Santa Cruz. The expedition was annihilated and Don Antonio's shadow-realm in the Azores collapsed. A curious consequence of the battle was that the Spaniards conceived a very low opinion of the fighting qualities of English ships; for they were convinced that an English contingent had taken part—there could not have been more than two or three merchant-ships of the smallest size, if that—and that they had fled at the onset of the action. A reverberating reversal of this opinion was one day to be delivered in the Azores! Santa Cruz advised an attack upon England as not only feasible, but not to be feared; while in 1580, Mendoza had written from London that the English fleet could not withstand a quarter of the Spanish maritime forces. The Prince of Parma was of the same opinion; it was known, he said, that the Queen of England could not arm more than forty ships; and as for the boasts of the English captains, he made little of them, since at the battle of the Azores their ships were the first to run away.[1] So that this earlier action in the Azores was not without its influence in bringing about that invasion of England on the grand scale, whose defeat was a smashing blow to the power and prestige of the Spanish Empire.

I

It was in this year 1580–1 that the first Jesuit mission reached and was at work in this country. Campion and Parsons had landed in June 1580, the most powerful combination of personalities of all that the Catholic Church sent into the country throughout the reign; for Campion was an exquisite and saintly character, of brilliant and persuasive gifts, while Parsons was the very idea of a Jesuit, a subtle politician, intriguing and pertinacious, a born controversialist, wary, impossible to lay hand upon. These two remained at work in the country for a

[1] Merriman, *The Rise of the Spanish Empire*, IV, 516.

year, reconciling people to the Church, secretly printing and distributing literature. The very secrecy, and the success of it, was what was frightening; nobody knew how many they were or what effect they were having; there was a widespread consternation. So it went on till Campion was captured in July 1581, and Parsons escaped to the continent.

To arm itself with further measures of severity against Catholics, the Government summoned Parliament in January 1581. It was the third and last session of the Parliament which had been returned in 1572. The second session had been held in 1575. There is nothing to show that Grenville took part in its business, at any rate by serving on committees as he had done in 1572; though his friends Edgcumbe and Sir Arthur Basset were active enough in this way. Probably he was too much occupied with the preparations for the South Seas Voyage and with the *Castle of Comfort*'s proceedings, to give much attention to Parliamentary business in that year. Nor is there any record either of his serving on committee in the 1580 session. Parliament passed an act greatly increasing the penalties for recusancy; fines for non-attendance at church were raised to £20 a month—a sum which the Arundells of Lanherne regularly paid from this time onwards, lesser people who could not raise the money frequently languished in prison; a year's imprisonment with a large fine was the penalty for saying mass; while anyone who sought to withdraw men from the established church and so from their allegiance was to be adjudged liable to the penalties of treason. Having passed this, along with some lesser legislation, Parliament was dissolved.

In Ireland, the Desmond Rebellion had become a war of attrition; the Irish were holding out in the hope of foreign aid. At length, in August 1580, when the rebellion had already lasted a year, it came: a miserable contingent of 600 men, mostly Italians with a company from North Spain, under the Papal banner. They took up a position at Smerwick and entrenched themselves. As the weeks passed and no more reinforcements reached them from abroad, while the English forces blockaded them in their hopeless position, it was obvious that they could not hold out. They surrendered and to a man were

put to the sword, one of the two Captains in charge of the
butchery being Walter Ralegh.[1] It was his first appearance
upon the public scene.

Just immediately before, the order had been sent down to
Cornwall to raise another 100 men for service in Ireland; they
were to be embarked at Padstow or Ilfracombe, upon warning
being given from Ireland. At the same time, on 5 July, the
Council appointed Grenville and Godolphin to make provision
within Cornwall and Devon for certain quantities of grain,
butter and cheese for the English garrisons in Ireland.[2] Grenville and his fellow Justices performed their duty; but they felt it
necessary to register a protest: only two years before, 200 men
had been levied from Cornwall for Ireland; the brunt not only
of the Irish war but of the increasing necessity for defence of the
sea-coasts fell upon the south-western counties, and particularly hard upon Cornwall.[3]

The deterioration in the European situation was reflected
once more in the increase of piracy on the high seas. Sir Julian
Corbett says:

'Ever since the Treaty of Bristol had cleared the air, the
English rovers had been growing more and more active. So entirely were they in command of the Narrow Seas, so powerless
was Philip to protect his commerce even on his own coasts, that
the dangers of the northern navigation had come to be regarded in the counting-houses of Seville and Cadiz as an ordinary trade-risk, and the practice had grown up amongst merchants and under-writers of concealing their losses from their
ambassador in London in order to make terms behind his back
with the pirate's agents. This impunity only increased their
daring and their profits.'[4]

Where the larger fish could so play about, there was plenty of
scope for the smaller fry. It meant a great deal of work for local
justices, particularly for those like Grenville who were qualified
for such matters. On 12 May 1580, we find the Council directing the Masters of the Court of Requests to make out a Com-

---

[1] Bagwell, *Ireland under the Tudors*, III, 75.   [2] *A.P.C. 1580–1*, 78–9.
[3] S.P. Dom. Eliz. 140, no. 21.   [4] Corbett 1, 327–8.

mission to Grenville and Richard Edgcumbe to take the oath of Peter Edgcumbe and his answers to certain charges made against him by William Hawkins.[1] It appears that a ship of Sir Henry Ratcliffe's had been stayed at Plymouth by Hawkins, but upon information given to Edgcumbe that she was suspected of piracy he had had her removed from Plymouth to Stonehouse, where she had perished upon the rocks. Grenville was to examine into the matter and report to the Council.

Two further piracy cases which it fell to Grenville to examine into, in autumn 1581 and spring 1582, and of which the detailed examinations remain, enable us to see with extraordinary and sudden clarity the pathetic human figures engaged in this business against that dark background of barbarity. After Captain Hicks of Saltash, of great fame as a pirate, Captain Piers of Padstow, who was no less renowned. He had had a long run, the success of which was attributed to his mother being a witch. It was just before his capture that he had his greatest triumph; with his small bark of 35 tons and his consort of 18 tons, he blockaded the harbour of Rye so that, according to the lamenting Mayor and jurats of the town, 'none can go forth or come in.'[2] A month later, he was taken 'by chance' in Studland Bay, a favourite haunt; and the Council wrote to inform Bedford of the apprehension of this 'very notorious pirate born in Cornwall, who hath an old mother dwelling at Padstow, noted to be a witch, to whom by report the said Piers hath conveyed all such goods and spoils as he hath wickedly gotten at the seas.'[3] Bedford was to make choice of someone to examine Piers's mother and 'to discover whether she be a witch indeed, and what spoils and goods she hath received from her son.'

Bedford made choice of Grenville and his cousins George Grenville and Thomas Roscarrock to probe into the matter. One can imagine them all stopping at Roscarrock, as Carnsew depicted them in his Diary, 'playing and trifling the time away' – alas that what we have left of his Diary should stop short so soon! But the examinations which they produced are a no less human document, not without its element of silent tragedy.[4]

[1] *A.P.C.* XII, 12.   [2] *Victoria County History of Cornwall*, 490.
[3] *A.P.C.* XIII, 227–9.   [4] S.P. Dom. Eliz. 150, no. 49.

Piers William, Captain John's old father, when examined, confessed to having been aboard his son's bark at Padstow with the vicar of St. Merryn and one William Amy, but only for the sake of procuring payment of a debt of £7 which his son owed the latter; and he 'saith that he never was more aboard his said son, nor that he ever after did speak with his son . . . for it is well known that he had renounced his said son for his lewdness.' The mother, however, was made of sterner stuff, and admitted that 'she was often on shipboard with her said son.' In spite of denials, she was driven to admit that she had received a great coverlet or rug from him which she had fetched from the water-side at twelve o'clock one night and left in a barn at Padstow. One John Bath deposed that 'he being upon the shore, fast by where Piers rode, saw Piers come a land with ten of his company with their swords, every man having a caliver; but he saith he had no talk with him other than that Piers asked him for some of the town' – a friendly endearing touch.

'The same night about xii of the clock he went to the water side again and there met with Piers's mother sitting by a mow of corn; and there he saw two men bringing a great rug fardled up upon a staff between them . . . And this examinate did help the said Piers's mother to bring the same to the town and at the town's end he left the same in a barn with her and went his way.'

What a picture it is! – the water-side at Padstow, midnight, and the old woman sitting in the shadow of a mow of corn waiting to receive her son the pirate's stolen goods. John Pentire, searcher of Padstow, deposed that, aboard, Piers had shown him

'a purse where he thinks there was fifty pounds or thereabout in gold, and that the said Piers had also a bag about him of silver containing by estimation £20: Also he saw in a chest that Piers opened before him by chance, a bag containing by estimation £60. And he saith he saw no plate there saving one silver bowl wherein they drank.'

Henry Horn's wife gave evidence that her husband coming from Bristol was aboard Piers at Lundy, and 'had of him a parrot, a little firkin of soap and two calivers. The parrot, the Vice-Admiral had; the calivers she hath in her house.' Finally the vicar of Padstow testified that 'the young Piers's mother was at Bodmin at the time of the last Sessions, and there had with her xv ounces of plate and sold the same there to a goldsmith being one of Plymouth'; – but before she received the money a seizure of the plate was made in the Queen's name, though the cover of a double gilt cup was restored to her, it being her property apparently. The vicar also deposed to Piers's delivering calico to certain persons while in the roads, 'among others to the vicar of St. Merryn, which vicar was aboard the said Piers's ship' – a scandalous betrayal of one parson by another.

It is pleasant to record that when Grenville and his fellow Justices inquired of 'some of the better sort and of most credit of the town of Padstow and of the said parish . . . whether they know or ever heard that Anne Piers of Padstow did practise witchcraft or had the name to be a witch,' they answered in the negative; for one knows what might have happened to the poor woman if it had been otherwise. Meanwhile the son had been taken to Dorchester gaol to await trial; whence he escaped 'by the corruption of the keeper,' but before he could embark was taken 'by the great pains and industry' of that scapegrace Henry Howard, Lord Howard of Bindon's son – a very suitable occupation for him.[1] Piers was put on trial and afterwards, it appears, executed.

The investigations at Padstow must have made their own small sensation at the time, but nothing compared to that of the next piracy-case Grenville was called into, for it concerned no less a person than the chief Commissioner for Piracy himself. Sir John Killigrew of Arwennack, Captain of Pendennis Castle, had been appointed at the head of the Commission for Piracy in Cornwall in September 1577. At Court he was very well placed for influence, since his brother William was Groom of the Chamber to the Queen and Henry, another brother, was a leading diplomat constantly sent on missions to France, Scotland, the Netherlands and the Empire. At Arwennack, by the

[1] *A.P.C. 1581–2*, 272, 355.

water-side within the crook of the headland of Pendennis, Sir John was very conveniently, too conveniently, placed in relation to the sea. It was, alas, his temptation and the cause of his downfall. For Sir John at home in Cornwall, whatever he may have been in the presence of his grand (if Puritan) relatives at Court, was a genial old ruffian, fast degenerating into an unmitigated nuisance. He kept up a large establishment and spent freely; he alternately terrorised and cajoled the countryside and bullied his lesser neighbours; he had got badly into debt and took more and more to dubious courses. He had long had a hand in trafficking with the pirates around the coast, himself the responsible authority for putting them down. Now, Sir John, driven to desperate straits, took to a little piracy on his own.

On New Year's Day 1582, a Spanish ship the *Marie* of San Sebastian, 140 tons burden, was driven on her way down Channel by stress of weather into Falmouth Haven.[1] When she arrived her masts were cut down, and what with repairs and then lack of wind, she was forced to remain some six days. On the seventh, at midnight, she was entered by a number of Killigrew's servants and other Penryn men, her goods rifled and the ship carried out to sea. The pinnace which had carried the men out to her, so it was said, was Sir John's own. Upon hearing the protest of de Chavis, the merchant-owner, and de Orio, the ship's master, the Council at once wrote to Sir John to come up. He went up to London, remained there in cover for a while, and when he thought it safe, returned home to Cornwall.

Sir John must have thought that in London the coast was clear; certainly he had taken what steps he could as regards the regrettable occurrence, before leaving home. There had been a very speedy investigation of the affair by the Commissioners for Piracy, with himself at the head.[2] It was perhaps not surprising that the story they elicited was hard to make out; but still it looked suspicious. As regards the whereabouts of Sir John's servants that Sunday night, they were oddly innocent. Henry Kendall and John Hawkins, two of them, agreed that they had spent from nine o'clock at night to midnight at Penryn, in the

[1] *A.P.C.*, XIII, 315, 356. [2] S.P. Dom. Eliz. 152, no. 5.

house of one Bess Moore; they were there so long, because the lady was 'a drying one of their shirts': the lady agreed with this, though she did not remember whose. Then they went straight home to Arwennack 'without any man calling of them.' Before leaving Arwennack that evening, they had tied the pinnace to the stake outside the house, it being then half-ebb. But Ambrose Cox when examined, said that one Timothy Duncalse's boy knew who carried the boat to and fro the Spanish ship in the harbour the night she was taken away, and that he had named two of Sir John's servants, Bewse and Kendall.

It was evidently necessary to probe further into the affair. Sir John who had ridden from Falmouth immediately before the capture and stayed away while the ship was carried off to Baltimore in Ireland and there disposed of, now returned to the West but remained in hiding. The Council wrote in March to Bedford as Lord Lieutenant in the West, either to go into the affair himself or to appoint his deputies to inquire thoroughly into it, 'to do their best endeavour to come by Sir John himself' and to take bonds of him in a thousand pounds to make appearance before the Council. Bedford transferred his authority to Grenville and Edmund Tremayne, both of them experienced in such matters. They held their inquiry at Penryn on 27 and 28 April; it was a very full story, with many picturesque details that they elicited in the end.[1]

Ambrose Cox, the keeper of the tavern in Penryn to which the Spaniards resorted the night before the capture, deposed that two servants of Sir John's had come to him at nine o'clock that night, requiring him 'as so commanded by their master, that the Spaniards should go presently aboard, alleging the cause to be, for that there was sickness in the ship.' Henry Piper of Penryn, to whose inn they that carried the ship away often resorted, had come to him that night and required the return of the boat which he had lent to the Spaniards for a groat a day; 'for if the Spaniards happen to be robbed and carried away,' he said, 'it will be said that my boat doth put them aboard that shall do it. And so shall I forfeit my boat to the Vice-Admiral.' Henry Piper could not be called himself, for,

[1] S.P. Dom. Eliz. 153, no. 37.

as a note in the margin has it – 'Nota that this Piper is now gone to the sea with Don Antonio' – a tiny tell-tale bit of evidence which shows that there were at any rate some Englishmen with Don Antonio in his expedition this year to the Azores. One wonders whether this Cornishman ever came back again; or whether he was one of the hundreds of sailors hanged by Santa Cruz after his victory.

Next there came evidence that considerable parcels of holland cloth had been handed about the district. One John Bailie of Mawnan had had twenty yards sent to him by Mistress Wolverston, Sir John's daughter, in part payment of a debt. Then it was found that various persons, including one of the constables, had become sureties for Sir John's servants, Henry Kendall and John Hawkins, who were chiefly implicated; and that it was Lady Killigrew who had entreated them to it, by her son Mr. Knyvett who gave them his word to discharge them. Armed with these promises, Kendall and Hawkins had previously denied all knowledge of the affair. But being brought face to face with Mrs. Wolverston, who had deposed to receiving a bolt of holland cloth from Kendall and two leather chairs, Kendall confessed all.

He admitted

'that he and John Hawkins did carry aboard about a dozen persons that went away with the Spanish ship, who met altogether at the lime kiln. And after the setting of them aboard, this examinate and the said Hawkins came back with the boat and moored her unto the stake by the smith's bridge near Sir John Killigrew's house.'

Then came the tale of cloth which had been rifled from the ship; four bolts each for Lady Killigrew, himself and Hawkins, one bolt each for the maids of the house, 'old Renodon and long William, servants of that house,' young Mistress Killigrew, Mrs. Wolverston, Mr. Knyvett and eighteen yards for Piper's wife. He had also brought ashore six leather chairs, one each for Lady Killigrew, and Mrs. Killigrew, two each for Mrs. Wolverston and Mr. Knyvett. The false evidence of the poor folk was breaking down: Bess Moore now denied her former story protecting Kendall and Hawkins, while Mrs. Piper admitted to receiving a parcel of holland cloth, which Hawkins 'fetched out of a ditch . . . by the way as they went' and which she was to keep safe for her Ladyship.

John Hawkins thereupon made a full confession, from which it appeared that

'he was not made privy to this enterprise of taking the ship till the same Sunday at night, after that he came from the Road. Then my Lady Killigrew brake it unto him . . . And when they came aboard the ship they bound the Spaniards. But two of the Flemings that were aboard the ship were agreed before to go with this company and help to bind the Spaniards and had put away all their weapons before'.

– an interesting indication of how national feeling could be worked upon in such cases. There were some thirteen or fourteen Spaniards aboard, whom they carried out to sea beyond the bar, before they began to cut open the packs of holland. It appeared that Lady Killigrew was the leading spirit in the undertaking, led on by the report which the Flemings put about of the ship's great wealth; when the stuff came in 'she found herself very ill contented that it was of no more value.' Hawkins confessed that she

'did often deal with him to keep this matter secret, and took an oath of him to that purpose, saying for her own part she would never confess it. And she, misliking that any of the chairs should be brought into her house, gave order to this examinate to put them in a cask and bury them in the garden.'

What a picture of the times it affords! – it is not very often that the documents which remain permit such a view into the heart of an affair like that and the motives and feelings of those who took part in it.

II

This period in Grenville's life – he was now, in 1581, in his fortieth year – was one of a peaceable and uneventful enough activity. He was kept busy, and increasingly so, by all sorts of private and public affairs. He was an active and hard-working man, the leading figure in his county, a public servant who came more and more to be relied upon by the Government in the west. Soon we shall find him called in to give his advice in a wider sphere. All the same, to a man of Grenville's ambition and temper, we cannot but think it must have been a source of disappointment to him that so far no opportunity of rendering a first-class service, of making a great name, had yet presented itself. It may not be fanciful to suppose that something of the passionate outbursts that were characteristic of him may be due to the effects of disappointment working upon a naturally impatient temper. The one great opportunity he had forged for himself, the projected South Seas Voyage, had been denied him and its fruits had fallen to another; there is evidence later that he bore no good will to Drake, who was more fortunate. Very curiously, Grenville's great chance came when Drake was in disgrace and retirement; it was almost too late, so that no wonder Grenville snatched at it so avidly, and in the event achieved death and fame together.

These middle years were full of the ordinary business of a country gentleman of the time, private responsibilities, public duties, law-suits, disputes, attendance at sessions and in Parliament, things which in themselves give us a picture of the life of the time. On 15 September 1580, his friend John Arundell of Trerice died: that delightful mansion of Cornish elvan, of which something still remains, time- and weather-beaten, near Newlyn East in the church of which Arundell was buried. He left a large family of children by his two wives; and by his will he appointed Grenville, with Sir John Arundell of Lanherne, Sir John Chichester and others as overseers.[1] Since Sir John Arundell could hardly act now, as he was a recusant and much away from the county, while Chichester lived in Devon, the responsibility fell mainly upon Grenville. The young Arundells, John, Dorothy and Mary, became his wards.[2]

Various law-cases at this period, though it is hard to come at the truth of them, portray Grenville in a less favourable, though no less characteristic attitude. At Michaelmas 1580, one

[1] P.C.C. 40 Arundell.   [2] Pat. Rolls Eliz. 1198, 1200.

William Spencer sued Grenville in the Exchequer. Spencer was the lessee of some of the extensive woods attached to Launceston Castle; he had assigned his lease to Anthony Carew, who some five or six years before, had conveyed it to Grenville. That would be about 1574-5, when we found Grenville much engaged with property transactions, no doubt to raise money for his voyage. At any rate he had cut down and sold the trees, on those slopes on the steep hill going out of Launceston by the Castle gate, and so taken, as the plaintiff said, the whole benefit of the lease without paying any rent. Grenville's answer was that he had bought the lease from Carew discharged of the rent, and that it was by 'the folly of the said complainant' that he got no assurance beforehand from Carew.[1] It seems to have been sufficient.

We have already seen how, in the case of Thomas Hilling of Bodmin *v.* Grenville and Christopher Walker in the Star Chamber, Grenville was not averse to using the Stannary jurisdiction to serve his turn.[2] Whether technically right or no, Grenville seems to have been justified in bringing Hilling to book. He was a noisy braggart; in addition to his insulting remarks about Sir John St. Leger, he stirred up trouble at the tavern in Bodmin kept by George Mapowder, a tenant of Walker's. This gave Walker his opportunity, who took him to various justices in the neighbourhood to make out a warrant against him. When this failed, according to Hilling, 'the said Walker then called to mind that the said Sir Richard Grenville was capital enemy of your said subject and was the likeliest man in that country to favour and farther any action against your said subject,' took horse and rode off to Stowe to procure a warrant. Sir Richard, being at home, made out the order and appointed a number of persons to execute it in as public a manner as possible and to bring Hilling 'strongly guarded as if he were a felon before the said Sir Richard at his house.'

Next day, when they all arrived at Stowe, Sir Richard 'minding to prevent the testimony of Malachias Mallett who came as a witness on Hilling's behalf, 'sent forth one of his servants to

[1] Exchequer Bills and Answers Eliz. Cornwall, no. 24.
[2] v. ante p. 150; and Star Chamber Proceedings, Eliz. H 6/16.

command the said Malachias Mallett to stay without the doors
and not to come into the said house until he was sent for.' When
Hilling was brought in, he was 'so threatened, taunted, and re-
viled, the said Sir Richard calling him "rascal" "rogue" and
other opprobrious names and threatening him to make him flee
his country, that your said subject a good space might not be
suffered to speak or answer one word.' One can imagine the
scene: it sounds veracious enough, when one considers Grenville's temper and Hilling's previous provocation. On Hilling's
refusal to find sureties for good behaviour, he was committed to
Launceston gaol where he cooled his heels for three weeks. At
the end of March the Council wrote to Bedford committing the
whole affair to his judgment.[1] The judgment went entirely
against Hilling; and on receiving Bedford's report, the Council
called the pertinacious man before them and committed him to
the Marshalsea until he had put in his bonds for good behaviour.[2] Moreover, since it was considered he had demeaned
himself ill towards the Justices of the Peace in Cornwall, at
which they had written their protest to the Council, he was
ordered upon release to make open submission before the Bench
there at the next Assizes. So was law and order vindicated, and
authority in the person of Grenville backed up by the Lord
Lieutenant whose good opinion of him we know, and by the
Council no less.

Two years later, in June 1584, we find another Star Chamber
case in which Grenville and some of his supporters were defend-
ants; this time a conflict about property, which had led as usual
to some disorder.[3] In sixteenth-century society, which was even
more primitive than our own and where human beings acted
and reacted more spontaneously, more vigorously and with
a still more infantile unself-consciousness, no dispute seems to
have been capable of being settled without disorder. This was
a dispute between one Richard Taverner of St. Teath, a gentleman, and John Stidson, a retainer of Grenville's, over some
property in the parishes of St. Teath, Advent and Blisland.
Grenville had naturally, but according to Taverner by undue

[1] *A.P.C. 1581–2*, 367.   [2] ibid. 416.
[3] Star Chamber Proceedings, Eliz. 5T 13/21, and 19/39.

means, supported his retainer. Taverner had leased the premises to one Saunders, and to try his title had served a process upon Stidson, which was to be tried at the next Assizes, 1583. According to Taverner, Stidson had held up the due course of law and was backed by Grenville in so doing;

'the said Stidson, being a retained servant with one Sir Richard Grenville, Knight, a man of great countenance and power in these parts, and having received the badge and livery of the said Sir Richard Grenville and usually ever since weareth the same, being neither his domestical servant, nor any way tolerated nor allowed by your Majesty's laws or statutes to take any such badge or livery.'

He complained that Sir Richard had influenced the sheriff and under-sheriff to return among the jury persons favourable to Stidson's cause and even 'hath conferred and instructed the said jurors or some or one of them . . . to think well of the cause.'

Knowing what we do of Elizabethan justice, and of Grenville's behaviour in the Mayne case, it does not sound at all unlikely. Taverner pleaded that the judgment had gone in his favour, but that Grenville had dealt with Richard Carew, the sheriff, not to execute the writ. Then Stidson had been advised to take away the doors of the house in dispute and to expel the plaintiff, so that if he resisted he would be indicted under the Statute of 8 Henry VI; Grenville was to be present as a Justice of the Peace, consenting unto the same. This was accordingly done in April last; Sir Richard was present 'with a great multitude all armed,' and requiring the plaintiff to yield possession, had read the Riot Act. Sir Richard had 'brought an hourglass with him and did hang the same up in the view of your said subject upon a pole'; while Stidson on the feast of St. Philip and St. James, 'in the time of divine service came to the parish churches of St. Teath and Michaelstowe and willed the persons there assembled to leave off service and prepare themselves in armour to expel your subject giving out that the said Sir Richard should bear them out therein.' And so he, the plaintiff, was ejected.

Grenville's answer was that Stidson

'was one of the first men that served this defendant in his youth, which was about six and twenty years past . . . And so continued in his service until he married; since which time because this defendant found the said Stidson a trusty and faithful servant, he appointed Stidson bailiff of some of his lands and tenements.'

He declared that as a Justice of the Peace, he had been present at sessions at Bodmin when an indictment was found against the plaintiff upon the Statute of 8 Henry VI, for forcing an entry and disseizing Stidson of the land. The Justices awarded Stidson a writ of restitution, but the under-sheriff wrote to Grenville that when he went to execute it, 'certain of the persons who kept the said tenements with force did shoot guns at him and made great resistance'; he had therefore called upon Grenville as a Justice to assist him. 'Coming thither they found the said messuage farded and defended with a multitude of people in warlike manner in such sort as the like hath seldom been seen in these parts.' Grenville had accordingly

'caused the statute of rebellion to be read . . . and the more to terrify the said lawless and rude people, the said defendant having a dial about him and the sun there shining, took forth his dial and showed to them by the same what the hour of the day then was, advising them not to continue in their riotous and rebellious manner more hours than the statute required.'

He thought this wise, for if he and the under-sheriff 'upon their first coming had used violence or force in putting forth the said unruly persons, this defendant feareth lest some inconvenience would have happened.' This apparently was enough; after a little they quickly laid down their arms and allowed the writ to be executed. One cannot but admire the gesture and its effectiveness; Grenville evidently understood how to handle people.

But it is the gesture that remains to us long after, the centuries passing: certain persons of great force have the gift of expressing themselves in so immediate and memorable a way, leaving the imprint of their personality upon time and circumstance in their action. It is not different in kind, though less memorable, than

Grenville's refusing to leave the *Revenge*; it is only a little more circumscribed: an unruly mob in a Cornish parish, armed and prepared to resist, while Grenville takes out his dial, shows them what
hour of the day it then was, 'the sun there shining,' until quietened
they go home. What children, what fools, human beings are!

The Council Registers are missing from this time, 1582 to
1586, years which cover a very important period in Grenville's
life, the first voyage to Virginia. A good deal that might throw
light on both his public and private activities is therefore missing. He seems to have been involved, in his private capacity,
in more trouble in this last year before the Virginia voyage, this
time over the case of the parson of Kilkhampton and the ejection
of his wife from the parsonage. It led to some disorder and
riotous assembly, with Grenville at the centre of it. Again we find
him resorting conveniently to the Stannary jurisdiction in dealing with his opponents, and again having to exculpate himself,
which as usual he does very plausibly, with the higher authorities.

The person whom Grenville had presented to the rectory of
Kilkhampton on the death of his great-uncle in 1580, was Eusebius Paget, already well-known as a Puritan. We heard of him
first in the company of Grenville, supping very pleasantly at
the expense of the town of Plymouth.[1] Paget had begun in the
world as a chorister at Christ Church, Oxford, where according
to Fuller, 'he broke his right arm with carrying the pax'; so
that in later years he was in the habit of signing himself 'lame
Eusebius Paget' – clearly a suitable subject for Puritanism. At
the time of his presentation, he had informed Grenville, as
patron, and Wootton, the Bishop of Exeter, that 'he could not
with quietness of conscience use some rites, ceremonies and
orders appointed in the service-book'; on this understanding
he accepted the charge and was inducted.[2] No doubt he was
godly, and his ministrations were apparently popular; he was a
preacher, travelling indefatigably up and down the neighbouring country. But there was, as always with such devout persons,
a vein of self-righteousness in him which roused others of his
clerical brethren to fury.

[1] v. ante p. 146.   [2] Neal, *History of the Puritans*, 1, 297.

The Cornish clergy were certainly in an interesting condition at this time: many of them were pluralists and most were ignorant. The Rector of Philleigh, so the Puritans said, was 'a good dicer and carder both night and day'; the vicar of Lanteglos-by-Fowey was 'a common gamester and the best wrastler in Cornwall'; the vicar of St. Issey was 'a common dicer and burnt in the hand for felony and full of all iniquity'; the vicar of Gulval was 'a drunkard and hath lately married a common harlot.' Of the Rector of Week St. Mary it was said, 'he keepeth his house for debt; he payed so much for it (i.e. the living) to Sir Richard Grenville.' Such were the Cornish clergy according to the brethren in Christ, the Puritans.[1]

A person such as Paget who set himself up for righteousness, rendered himself a conspicuous target, and he opened himself to his enemies by not conforming to the Prayer Book, omitting to use certain portions of the prescribed services, and objecting to the surplice and the sign of the cross in baptism. Just at this time, the Queen who had no love for the Puritans appointed Whitgift as Archbishop, a strong disciplinarian, to reduce them to order. Paget was informed against and brought before the High Commission; on refusing to follow the prescribed forms in every particular and appealing to his bishop's promise to refrain from urging him, he was suspended. Paget proceeded to show the stuff these fanatics were made of, by producing a list of articles against Wootton, the Bishop of Exeter, charging him with never visiting the whole diocese in person, nor attending at preachings, 'yea he will be in his bed, or be in his stable among his horses, or in his kitchen among his servants, when there are sermons in the Church hard by his house, and he not come at them' (unpardonable offence!); and winding up by charging him with nepotism, and that 'he had two harlots begotten with child in his own house, which accused two of his men, and none of them brought to penance, yea the men do yet wait upon him.'[2] It was perhaps a pity that he could not accuse the Bishop of begetting them himself; but there was something in his charge. The Bishop was under the unfortunate necessity

[1] *The Seconde Parte of a Register* (ed. Peel), 11, 98–110.
[2] Lansdowne MSS. 45, no. 42.

of making a lengthy explanation. But to Paget it was of no avail; he was put out of his living.

Grenville must have been sympathetic to Paget in the first instance to have presented him to it. But there is no evidence that he was actively Puritan in his sympathies, as Drake and Hawkins were. He was a Protestant, and by now probably a convinced one; but he was a supporter of the Crown and of the Church as by law established. He was probably the less reluctant to see Paget put out of his rectory, since he had now another candidate of his own, a cousin, a certain William Tucker. But though Eusebius had gone, Mrs. Paget was by no means so easily disposed of. She had but recently recovered from childbirth – the minister's quiver was full of arrows – and filling the parsonage-house with her friends and connections, including two Scots, David Black and his wife, and one Fullerton, she determined to remain on. She had a whole party of sympathisers in the country-side, headed by John Kempthorne (of the delightful manor of Tonacombe) –

'one John Kempthorne,' Grenville wrote scornfully, 'whom Mr. Paget called his Justice of peace, otherwise a mean person, came thither, who not only advised them to stay there, but further offered himself to assist them with his authority, which he hath only almost used as an engine of small account to oppugn me in these causes with Mr. Paget.' [1]

One day in the winter of 1584–5 Grenville arrived at Stowe from his house at Bideford; the day before being Sunday, there had been a sermon in the parish church, and Fullerton and the inhabitants of the parsonage not coming, the churchwardens sent to ask them why not. Mrs. Paget's supporters barricaded themselves in, put the house into a state of defence and appealed to Kempthorne as a Justice to help them. Grenville upon this warned them to depart, and procured a precept from the Stannary Court to arrest them as trespassers. Under this he arrested Kempthorne and Black's wife, and himself went – so he put it – with a company of gentlemen to reason with Mrs. Paget, who was in no mood for reasoning and challenged him to throw her

[1] S.P. Dom. Eliz. 176, no. 58.

out of the house. Grenville stated afterwards that he had offered her to remain there for a month or two or three, provided she gave up some room to the incoming incumbent, Mr. Tucker, and would accept the same at his hand.

The account of these proceedings we derive from Grenville himself; for the rumour of them reached the Court – somebody had been busy reporting them – and he thought it necessary for his credit with Walsingham and other Puritan sympathisers who were his friends, to make a full explanation. He was just about to depart on his voyage to Virginia, and would certainly need Walsingham's support and good opinion in the future, as he had had it in the past. Untrue reports had been put about to lower his credit with sundry honourable personages, he wrote to Walsingham:

'whereas I being now prepared to commit myself to the pleasure of God on the seas, having a desire not to leave so great an infamy as this laid on my poor name unanswered before my departure, have thought it convenient even in plain sort to set down to your honour and other my honourable friends the whole and true course of all my dealings in this behalf.'

He wrote out a full account of his proceedings, claiming that he was entirely within his rights, since Paget had been lawfully deprived, and in the vacancy the living lapsed to him as lord of the manor and patron of the parish; and protesting that he had acted with courtesy and politeness to Mrs. Paget. His account was subscribed by various persons, Richard Prideaux, Richard Bellew, Arthur and Diggory Tremayne, John Harris – almost all of them his relatives. Having cleared his conscience, or, what was more important, re-established his credit with his friends at Court, he was free to depart for Virginia.

Perhaps Grenville protested too much, for in all the affairs of these years there is an element of violence which one cannot fail to observe. It was not entirely due to the rawness and crudity of the time; Francis Godolphin for instance managed his affairs in the westernmost part of the county with smoothness and ease. It was Grenville's way of doing things; we cannot but regard it as in part the character of the man.

CHAPTER IX

THE JUSTICE OF THE PEACE

In spite of the absence of Council Registers for these years, and with them information about many of Grenville's activities, there is evidence to show a constant increase in the pressure of public business upon him. Nor is it so miscellaneous in character. As the years move on to the great crisis of the war with Spain, we find him more and more caught up into the work of organising the defence of the country, overlooking the annual musters in Cornwall, surveying forts and likely places of descent upon the sea-coast, superintending the building and repair of fortifications, in which last sphere he had come to be regarded as an expert. Evidence of his private avocations becomes, if anything, rarer even than before: no word of his family, not a single letter to his wife has survived, hardly a mention of his business transactions which must have been considerable.

In 1583 we find him serving on two special Commissions of the Exchequer; the first, in June, to inquire concerning debtors of the Crown within the county – a more or less routine inquiry set on foot by the Exchequer from time to time.[1] The second was more interesting; it concerned the lands which had been given in time past for the endowment of a chantry in the parish church of St. Michael Penkivel.[2] It brings back vividly to mind the not far-distant time when mass was celebrated in these Cornish churches with all the old rites, the annual obits and commemorations of the faithful departed. The manor of Fentongollan had been left by one Trenowth for an obit in the Church of St. Michael Penkivel on St. Gregory's day. John Harry deposed before Grenville at Launceston, that mass used to be celebrated on that day with great solemnity. John Michell

[1] Exchequer K. R. Special Commission 139.   [2] ibid. 541.

of Truro 'saith that about fifty years past he, this examinate, repaired with his mother to the parish of St. Michael Penkivel and saw to the number of—people and upwards and mass [was said].' Every priest coming to the mass received a groat for his attendance; and there was usually great concourse in the church on that day. The scene appeals movingly to the historical imagination: the faithful people, the priests hurrying along the tangled woodland lanes of that Roseland parish to church.

In December he was appointed along with Bernard Drake to examine into a case of suspected popery at Great Torrington [1] – one finds him rarely employed in the capacity of a Justice now in Devon, his work in Cornwall occupied so much of his time. One Alexander Barry examined before him, deposed that William Edmunds, servant to Mr. Chappell, had brought with him to church at Great Torrington, a popish catechism by Laurence Vaux, a well-known Catholic frequently imprisoned, a relative of Lord Vaux's. Edmunds protested that he brought the book from Mr. Coplestone's, who was further inculpated by Barry for his views on the sacraments; for he held the suspicious view that though only two were essential, the other five 'were sacraments and had their mysteries and significations as matrimony did express the unity betwixt Christ and his church.' A distinctly high-church view; but nothing further emerged to incriminate Coplestone, which would have been a serious matter, for he was the head of a family important in the county.

Among the State Papers there has survived too a certificate of this year, from Michaelmas 1582 to July 1583, of the amounts of corn which had been exported abroad under Grenville's license as Commissioner.[2] The quantities were considerable: it must have been a year of plenty or permission would not have been given, for the Tudors were guided by the conception of the well-being of the whole in their economic policy. What is remarkable is that though some went to Ireland, most of it was exported to Spain; and it is amusing to find that the biggest individual shipment (280 quarters of wheat and a little barley) was made from Padstow by John Sparke, the Plymouth mer-

[1] S.P. Dom. Eliz. 164, nos. 59–61.   [2] ibid. 161, no. 42.

chant who went with Hawkins on his second voyage to Guinea and the West Indies in 1564, and wrote the delightful account of it in Hakluyt's *Principal Navigations*.

By this time, he was much more occupied with the preparations for national defence, in the widest, not merely a negative sense: he was naturally drawn along with the ablest and most energetic leaders of the nation into the work of keying up the spirit of the people for the struggle to come. In the summer of 1583, the Council ordered the Cornish Justices to take the Musters again; it was very short notice, and as the county extends a great way in length, they reported, there were many deficiencies 'too intricate to trouble your Honours withal.' [1] And so they gave the gentlemen of the county a new day, till 6 November to remedy defaults in the musters, by which time they would be sufficiently provided. At the same time the Council ordered the leading Justices to make a return of all the parks and commons in the county, evidently with a view to discovering what number of horses it could support in case of war. They returned a full report, and wrote with Grenville at the head,

'we have signified to your Honours of the barrenness of our said commons, being wet moors in some part. And for the most part very dry heath-grounds, altogether unable and unmeet to nourish and breed such mares and horses as should be serviceable for the wars.'

Cornwall was at this time very poorly off for horses and cattle: the local breeds were undersized and in number very few. Only the gentry, and a few of the most substantial yeomen were in a position to supply a horse in case of need.

On 6 October, orders were issued by the Government for the survey and repair of forts along the coasts, in Essex, the Isle of Sheppey, Dorset, the Isle of Wight, and in Devon and Cornwall.[2] For the last a Commission was made out to Bedford, Grenville, Godolphin and others.[3] They were to survey the forts, castles, platforms on the sea-coast, and to place fit persons

---

[1] S.P. Dom. Eliz., 162, no. 38.   [2] ibid. 163, no. 5.
[3] Westley Manning MSS.: Elizabethan Exhibition Catalogue, no. 371.

to look after them; at the same time they were to have 'some care and foresight not to increase her Majesty's charges at this time, but with that shall be very needful, in respect her Majesty's charges (even for this kind of service) is like to be very great through the realm.' It has been well said that finance was the essence of Elizabeth's success; without the constant and increasing pressure of the Government for strict watchfulness as to every item of expenditure, English resources would have been fatally dissipated as Spain's were. It was 'the disparity between Elizabeth's resources and achievements' which was 'the miracle of her age.' [1]

It was clear that the main responsibility in the work would fall upon Grenville; Bedford's name was placed at the head of the Commission, but he hardly ever crossed the Cornish border, though he was frequently enough in Devonshire. On 9 December, the Council wrote to Grenville specially to view the state of the castle at Tintagel – that fantastic headland stronghold going back into remote antiquity. At the end of the month, he reported: [2]

'I presently rode thither and sending for him that hath the charge thereof went up into it. At the entry of the island there is a door and certain walls standing with certain ruinate rooms which were lodgings and may yet with some small charges be repaired and made fit to be dwelt in. From the utter great gate on the main there hath been within the memory of some that dwell thereby a drawbridge which is now gone, by reason that the seas have undermined and fretted out some part of the rocks whereon the bridge stood.'

He goes on to give a complete and practised survey of the island, the state of its fortifications and landing-places and makes a number of suggestions for repairs. This was evidently a strong point with him: we find him being used shortly by the Government to give advice about the important works going forward at Dover at the entrance to the harbour.

Then he goes on to consider the keeping of the castle, for

[1] Neale, *Queen Elizabeth*, 284.   [2] S.P. Dom. Eliz. 164, no. 62.

'the Isle itself as it is now left, is a dangerous receptacle for an evil affected person that shall attempt to take it, either by land or sea, for he who now hath the charge of the castle and the island, is one John Hendey a very tall young man and one that is thought to be evil affected in religion; his father now dead who had the charge before him, was accounted a papist and accused and long imprisoned in the gaol for seditious words against her Majesty; this young man's mother known to be a papist and not caring for her bonds wherein she stood bound to her Majesty's use to appear before us at the Sessions as a recusant for not coming to the Church, forfeiting the same, hath forsaken this house and her county and is gone to a house of Sir John Arundell's in Dorsetshire called Chideock, where she and many such are received and harboured, and where this John Hendey hath of late been with her, coming and going this Michaelmas term last to and from London where he hath had access to Sir John Arundell, no cause known.'

It was true that Sir John Arundell's Dorsetshire house, Chideock Castle, had become a refuge for a number of his Catholic dependants and sympathisers who resorted there. And the withdrawal of Sir John from Cornwall to residence partly at Chideock and partly in London, which later became confinement, left all this part of the coast void of its natural guardian. Grenville had been asked to certify whom he thought meet for the charge, and he replied,

'that part of the country is so barren of such gentlemen [i.e. those well-affected in religion] of any account . . . as I know none more fit dwelling near to the place than Mr. Geo. Grenville, now sheriff of the county, whom I assure your honours to be a gentleman well inclined to religion and to her Majesty's service.'

The Government was not content with the way in which the organisation of the Musters was being handled in most counties – in Devonshire the Justices were not even making any efforts, which they certainly were in Cornwall, and the Council addressed a pretty stiff remonstrance to the former.[1] It was

[1] S.P. Dom. Eliz., 170, no. 32.

arranged to send into each county a person experienced in martial matters to serve as Muster Master and organise the levies professionally. Thomas Horde was sent down to Cornwall.[1] While his cousin George Grenville, the Sheriff, and other Justices were tackling the Musters with Horde's expert advice, Grenville was away from the county giving his advice on the question of the harbour-works at Dover.

It was a very considerable problem; for some time the harbour had been silting up, there were extensive repairs to be undertaken, and it was a question on which side of the Crane to open the mouth of the haven. Work had been going on, but there was much dispute and doubt about it. In Spring 1584 Grenville and George Cary of Cockington were appointed at the head of a Commission to go down to Dover and take evidence on the matter.[2] The work was of great complexity and difficulty, and gave rise to innumerable disputes among the experts. It occupied Grenville all the early summer.

By 6 August, he was back again in the west, at Penheale with the Sheriff; for together they wrote from there to the Council explaining why they had not yet moved the county to contribute to the relief of Nantwich, which had been burned and for which an appeal was being made throughout the country.[3]

'Because our poor country hath been somewhat busied ever sithence and before the receipt of the said letters with musters, and since with the trainings and the constables continually followed the same . . . and now those charges being intermitted and the people ready busily to employ their harvest,'

they ask that they may forbear for the time to move the county for a collection. Captain Horde, they report, has won golden opinions in the county, having shown himself 'among all degrees to be a man of a very modest expert and discrete government in all his actions and thereby hath won the good commendation of all men.' The bands have very much profited by his instructions, and by his discreet and courteous usage of them he has

[1] ibid. 171, no. 8. [2] ibid. 170, no. 99; 171, nos. 17, 18, 30, 31.
[3] ibid. 172, no. 57.

'won them generally to such a willingness to be employed and trained that they that erst were abashed, yea and as would have given good sums of money to have been exempted from the service, rejoice in that they have profited by this training. And generally they wish that there were allowance of powder for them that they might the more often be exercised.'

Such was the spirit of the country in the golden days before the war.

Nor did Grenville lose much time in getting into touch with the work in building a new pier at Boscastle, which had been begun under his direction in April and was now two parts done; he forwarded the account of the charges as delivered to him by the townsmen.[1] The pier and quay at Boscastle, that narrow little entry between the cliffs, but so necessary since it was the only harbour in forty miles between Padstow and Ilfracombe, had been twice built within recent memory and had cost the poor inhabitants and their well-wishers £200. 'But the same quay,' so the townsmen say, being 'now begun and set in a new place by the good aid and directions of the right worshipful Sir Richard Grenville Knight, is thought of the skilful workmen and others by God's grace most like for ever to continue.' One is not sure whether it is the aid and directions of Sir Richard Grenville, or God's grace, which is expected to be the more effectual.

On 17 October Grenville wrote to Walsingham to report the result of his and the Sheriff's endeavours to raise a subscription for the relief of Nantwich, at the same time taking the opportunity to introduce his cousin to the Secretary's favourable notice and assuring him of their family's good wishes and support:

'We having motioned the county thereunto do find them generally to complain of the great burdens that have of late been laid on them, and yet nevertheless there is collected to the value of £20, which is to be delivered at your honour's direction, by the sheriff of this county my kinsman the bearer hereof; who also most humbly presenteth himself to your honour as one that

[1] S.P. Dom. Eliz., 172, no. 57 (i).

184

will be always most ready at your commandment, as myself and the residue of my poor house are by your honourable favour most bounden, therein so do we most humbly desire the continuance of your favour towards us, and we shall rest ready with hand and heart at your honours commandment during our lives as knoweth our good god, to whom we continually pray for your good preservation, and so most humbly I take my leave, from my poor house of Stowe this xvii of October 1584.' [1]

It is not merely politeness, the form of the time, that accounts for the excessive courtesy of the letter; it signifies that Grenville looked to Walsingham for his lead, and for the protection of his interests at Court. Nor was it an empty expectation: what significance Grenville attached to it may be seen from the alacrity with which he wrote to defend himself in the affair of Mrs. Paget: it was important to him to maintain his credit at Court through the Secretary.

He was, then, at Stowe in the middle of October: one thinks of the leaves falling in the woods below the house, the evenings drawing in, and around the great house on the hill the autumn gales beginning to blow. The days were full as ever of business, but no doubt – since those were more leisurely days all told – there was time for hawking and hunting, coursing the hare and for bowls in the bowling alley.

The days moved on: towards the end of the month a messenger brought him a letter from the Secretary concerning the works at Dover for his opinion. 'Whereupon I rode presently to a place called Dodding-castle,' he wrote, meaning Boscastle, 'where I caused a pier to be made this summer which as yet is not fully finished, to the end I would confer with the master workman, who hath great experience as a manual workman in that kind of work.' [2] He has there tried out the use of stone mixed with chalk in building the pier, and is opposed to it, as the stone sinks into the chalk and soon comes loose. His letter is full of protestations of service and devotion, because 'the work is commanded by her Royal Majesty.' He is grateful for being sent a full account of what was done at Dover this sum-

[1] ibid. 173, no. 76.   [2] ibid. no. 95.

mer, and to see the good effect of his directions, 'wherein it plainly appeareth that to observe the course of nature with the unruly seas is the best school-master.'

With the questions and answers of the master-workmen, and his own comments on them, he enclosed a sketch of his device for a pier at Dover, the core of which was of chalk, but entirely encased in hard stone. It is interesting to observe that though he was reluctant again to embark upon computations, perhaps because he was unable, he very competently performed the drawing of the sketch-plan to indicate his design. This is the last we hear of him in connection with the works at Dover; George Cary continued to act as Commissioner for a time. Grenville became caught up in the Virginia projects of his cousin, Walter Ralegh, now rapidly rising to power and wealth. By April, a new Commissioner for Dover was appointed;[1] Grenville was at Plymouth awaiting a favourable wind, and on the ninth sailed.

Before this, however, one or two more services in the county and at Westminster remained. In January he was drawn into the investigations proceeding as regards the Winslade inheritance. It was a complex and tangled affair, going back to the Rising of 1549; but it was an extremely moving story that was revealed, involving as it did the ruin of a whole family, the formal depositions of witnesses unfolding layer upon layer of human suffering.

John Winslade, with whom the trouble began, was a leader along with Humphrey Arundell in the Rebellion; and like him was executed and his lands, which were extensive, forfeited to the Crown. Some time before, perhaps fearing some such trouble in those unquiet days, he had made over to his wife Agnes a number of his manors, Bochym, Tregarrick, Talcarne, Penfugh and Killiow, as her jointure. He seems to have been a generous, good-hearted nature, just such a man as the Rising would have swept in with it. After his death, his widow married John Trevanion of Carhayes, bringing her jointure saved from the wreck of Winslade's fortunes with her. When she was dead, the lands were to go to Winslade's son William, or his heirs.

[1] S.P. Dom. Eliz. 178, no. 2.

But Trevanion kept the evidences, nor would he give them up when his wife lay on her death-bed beseeching him to deliver them to the Winslades. Instead, Trevanion handed them over with the lands which he granted partly to Francis Buller, partly to Sir William Mohun and John Trelawny, for certain sums of money paid down and so much income for life. Poor Agnes, the wife, was kept from knowing the details of the transaction; she was willing enough for him to be made secure for life, but anxious that the children of John Winslade should come into their rights after. Buller and Mohun made themselves as sure as they could legally. Then, on 17 November 1582, she died.

The position of the Winslades was weakened by the fact that William Winslade had fled the country some time before. But there was evidence enough to warrant a full inquiry, and on 28 December 1584, Grenville was put at the head of a Commission to investigate.[1] They sat at Launceston on 21 January. Evidence was brought that Daniel Winslade, William's son, had come to his grandmother at Tregarrick, and asked her 'by the way of conscience' to deliver the evidences which he thought to be in her keeping. It was clear that she meant them to come to the Winslades after her death, she 'had already taken such order with Master Trevanion.' But upon her death-bed she was cheated of her wish by Trevanion and her daughter and son-in-law. The scene in her house at Tregarrick was pathetically described by an old serving-woman there, Alice King of Talland: how again and again Agnes besought her husband to give her the deeds that belonged to the Winslades, and was continually put off; how on the day of her death, her daughter and son-in-law called for a fire and a wad of straw to burn evidences of a debt due by the latter to Winslade, and how John Connock, a lawyer from Liskeard, handed over certain deeds to Trevanion, with the words: 'Keep you that safe and I will keep this; which if we do, the Winslades shall never be able to recover their lands except they seek it out above, which through poverty they shall never be able to do.'

And so it came about: the Winslades never came by their

[1] Exchequer K.R. Special Commission 531.

lands again. The stumbling-block seems to have been, not so much that, John Winslade having been attainted, they were corrupt in blood, but that William Winslade was a fugitive from the country. Evidence was given by a number of mariners from round about Helford Passage, who said 'that about four years past, William Winslade in a small bark called the *Peter* of Helford, in the company of these deponents, passed from Helford into the parts of Brittany being the dominion of the French King, to a place there called Lantrégan.' That would have been about 1581. And so all was lost, and the Bullers came to live in the hall at Tregarrick, where they were comfortably seated by the time Carew came to write his *Survey of Cornwall* and had adopted a satisfactory legend how they came by it.

'The warmth of this hundred, siding the south,' says Carew, 'hath enticed many gentlemen here to make choice of their dwellings, as Mr. Buller, now sheriff, at Tregarrick, the Wideslades' inheritance, until the father's rebellion forfeited it to the Prince; and the Prince's largess rewarded therewith his subjects. Wideslade's son led a walking life with his harp, to gentlemen's houses, wherethrough, and by his other active qualities, he was entitled Sir Tristram: neither wanted he (as some say) a "belle Isoult," the more aptly to resemble his pattern.'[1]

And sure enough, we find that in his wanderings, by 1583 he had reached the kindly shelter and hospitality of Douai; for we find an entry in the Diary of the College saying that on 28 August there arrived 'Tristram Winslade.' [2] It shows where his sympathies were: his family had lost everything by their loyalty to Catholicism: at Douai at this time he would find the solace of several other Cornish Catholics.

But the Mohuns and the Trevanions went on; the former till they came to an end with the fifth Baron, an infernal brawler and duellist who was no better than a murderer and was himself killed in a duel with the Duke of Hamilton in Hyde Park on 15 November 1712 – an affair of which Swift sent such a vivid account to Stella; while the latter, the Trevanions, went on at

[1] Carew, 308-9.   [2] Knox, *Douai Diaries*.

Carhayes until early in the nineteenth century they came to an end in a riot of drink and wild escapades.

So much for the characteristic and many-sided activities of a leading Justice of the Peace at this time in his county – a position to which Grenville had attained in these years by his assiduous attention to business, by the force and vigour of his character and the historic place of his family in the county's affairs. It was a position which he was to continue to occupy until, after the Armada, he found a wider sphere of service, at first in Ireland and then at sea. Nevertheless it is easy to underestimate the importance of these local and very varied services rendered within the bounds of his own county. In fact, it was upon this structure of efficient and voluntary local administration that the success of Tudor government rested.

As difficulties thickened round the Queen's government, so the gentry as the natural leaders of her people drew in around her person. At the end of 1583, Throckmorton's conspiracy against the Queen's life, and for combined invasion and insurrection, was unveiled. Mendoza, the Spanish Ambassador, had been acquainted with it at every stage and even instigating it. He was told ignominiously to leave the country. It was too much for his intolerable pride; he said to Elizabeth in his farewell audience: 'Don Bernardino de Mendoza was born, not to disturb countries, but to conquer them.' 1588 was the answer to all that. On the day that Throckmorton was executed, 10 July 1584, the great William of Orange died at the hand of an assassin. In September, Elizabeth heard of the plots of Guise and Allen for replacing her by Mary. The Earls of Northumberland and Arundel were arrested and sent to the Tower. All this aroused a fever of resentment and indignation. Throughout the country Instruments of Association for the preservation and defence of the Queen were signed by all the leading persons, binding themselves with all their power to serve and defend her against 'all Estates, Dignities, and earthly Powers whatsoever,' and to pursue to utter extermination all that should attempt anything against her Royal Person, or claim succession to the Crown. The Instrument of Association for the county of Cornwall was very widely signed – it contains twice the number of names on that for Devonshire; at the head of it stood the names of the Sheriff and Grenville.[1]

A new Parliament was elected in the autumn of 1584; by the time it met, at the end of November, feeling had somewhat subsided. Grenville and Sir William Mohun were returned as Knights of the shire.[2] Sir Francis Drake sat for the borough of Bossiney; Sir John Killigrew's brother, William, Groom of the Chamber to the Queen, and the son, John, sat for Penryn. Old Sir John St. Leger, now very decrepit, was returned for Tregony. Grenville and Drake, on the other hand, were very active and served on several Committees of the House, on some of them together.

Parliament was opened by the Queen on 23 November, 'in her accustomed Pompous and Royal manner.'[3] Its first bill legalised the Association for her defence. The second banished all Jesuits and seminary priests who would not take the oath and prohibited their return on pain of treason. Parliament was prepared to go much further than the Government, which had no desire for merciless measures; and the Queen amended the bill legalising the Association so as to restrain the possibility of private vengeance. After this, their passion somewhat abated. Parliament settled down to less important measures.

The one which occupied a good deal of time and gave rise to much dispute and discussion, was a Bill for the better and more reverent observing of the Sabbath day. On Friday, 27 November, it was given a second reading, and committed to a large committee, upon which both Grenville and Drake served.[4] On 3 December, an unimportant Bill concerning Hue and Cry was read a second time and committed to Grenville, Sir Henry Cock, Mr. Richard Lewkenor and others.[5] On the same day the Bill for the true answering of tithes was given a second reading and committed to Grenville, Sir John Petre, Sir William Herbert and Mr. Dale, one of the Masters of Requests.

Much more important for the next phase in Grenville's life was the Bill for the confirmation of Walter Ralegh's Letters Patent for the discovery of foreign countries. Humphrey Gil-

---

[1] S.P. Dom. Eliz. 174, no. 5. [2] *Official Return*, 1, 413.
[3] D'Ewes, *Journal*, 311. [4] ibid. 333. [5] ibid. 335.

bert, Ralegh's half-brother, had been granted a Royal Charter in June 1578 to discover and occupy 'such remote and barbarous lands . . . not actually possessed of any Christian prince or people.' [1] It was in fulfilment of this charter that Gilbert made his last voyage to Newfoundland in 1583; and upon his death, Ralegh, who had been associated with his enterprises, immediately sued for the renewal of Gilbert's Charter for himself. In March 1584, his Letters Patent were made out, and he at once dispatched a small scouting expedition under Captains Amadas and Barlow to North America. They came back with a favourable report of the bounty and good prospects of the land they had hit upon – the later Virginia. Ralegh at once set in hand preparations for an expedition on a large scale, which was to occupy and colonise the newly discovered territory. He intended to go himself at the head of it and take possession.

The Bill before Parliament was to confirm the very wide powers which Royal prerogative, and the Queen's personal favour, had conferred upon him. It received its first and second reading on the same day, Monday 14 December; and upon that was committed to a Committee consisting of the Vice-Chamberlain, Secretary Walsingham, Sir Philip Sidney, Sir William Courtenay, Sir William Mohun and others, with Grenville and Sir Francis Drake.[2] It was a powerful Committee, with a strong West-Country representation, wholly sympathetic to Ralegh's colonising project. No wonder therefore, as D'Ewes tells us, three days later the Bill 'was brought in by the Committees not altered in any word; and upon motion for ingrossing, was after some arguments upon the Question, ordered to be ingrossed.' Next day, it had its third reading, and 'after many Arguments and a Proviso added unto it, passed upon the Question.'

There followed the Christmas adjournment:

'Her Majesty graciously considering the great pains and careful travail of this House in the service and affairs of the Realm, hath determined upon Monday next to adjourn the Court of Parliament until some other convenient time after Christmas, that such Gentlemen and other Members of this House may the

---

[1] Edwards: *Sir Walter Ralegh*, 1, 84.   [2] D'Ewes, 339.

more conveniently repair home to their houses in the mean time for their better ease and recreation.' [1]

It is to be noticed that Grenville who had taken a very active part in the business of the House before the adjournment, took none of which there is any mention after. At some time during the proceedings over the Bill in Parliament, Ralegh not being permitted by the Queen to go on the voyage himself, persuaded Grenville to take the command in his place; and Grenville out of the 'love he bore unto Sir Walter Ralegh, together with a disposition he had to attempt honourable actions worthy of honour, was willing to hazard himself in this voyage.' [2]

[1] D'Ewes, 342.   [2] Holinshed, *Chronicle*, 1402.

PUBLIC LIBRARIES ERITH

SIR WALTER RALEGH.

CHAPTER X

RALEGH AND VIRGINIA

'I marvel not a little that since the first discovery of
America (which is now full fourscore and ten years) after so
great conquest and plantings of the Spaniards and Portingales
there, that we of England could never have the grace to set
fast footing in such fertile and temperate places, as are left as
yet unpossessed by them.'

RICHARD HAKLUYT, *Divers Voyages*, 1582

It was at this time, and in this way, that Walter Ralegh makes
his first known entry into Grenville's life. Hitherto, there is no
evidence of their having come into contact; which, although
they were cousins, is not surprising, considering the largeness of
the cousinage and the disparity of age between them. Ralegh
was some ten years younger than Grenville, so that, though
their early careers followed the same pattern, service in the wars
abroad and in Ireland, they never coincided. Their relation-
ship was in the first instance on their mother's side, through the
Champernownes. Ralegh's mother was Katherine Champernowne, sister of Sir Arthur and widow of Otto Gilbert – hence
the Gilberts were Ralegh's half-brothers; while Grenville's
uncle, William Cole of Slade, his mother's brother, married
another Champernowne sister. But further back than this, their
families had intermingled. Sir Thomas Grenville, whose tomb
is in Bideford church, had married a Gilbert; while a daughter
of Sir Thomas's, Joan Grenville, married Wymond Ralegh, Sir
Walter's grandfather.

Such were the connections of the families; they both belonged
to the gentry of long-standing in the western counties, though
the Grenvilles were the more prominent, and the Raleghs had

become somewhat impoverished in recent generations. Both too, as befitted their social class, were in favour of the changes consequent upon the Dissolution and the reforming movement, from which they drew advantage.

The career of Walter Ralegh is too well known to need describing here; it is sufficient to note the close parallel its early stages afford to those of Humphrey Gilbert and Grenville, and those are less well known. At the age of fourteen or fifteen he was at Oxford, at Oriel College. Then in 1569, when Gilbert and Grenville were in Ireland at the time of the Fitzmaurice Rebellion, Ralegh was a young volunteer with his cousin Henry Champernowne going to the aid of the Huguenots at the battle of Moncontour in October; this was three years after Grenville's similar venture in Hungary. Ralegh's sojourn abroad lasted much longer; he was in France for some six years, in the midst of the civil wars, and he must have become an experienced soldier. By 1576 he was back in England, a resident at Islington, a hanger-on of the Court. Gilbert was at this time living at Limehouse, plunged in his schemes for a voyage of discovery and colonisation; his early Irish exploits and his expedition to the Netherlands were behind him. In 1578 he was fitting out his first voyage, a large affair into which he threw all his resources. In June he obtained his Charter from the Crown to hold and occupy the lands he discovered; Ralegh in September was at Dartmouth helping him. When it set sail it was largely a family enterprise, Gilbert being in command of the admiral, Carew Ralegh of the vice-admiral and Walter of the *Falcon*, a bark of 100 tons. But the enterprise came to no good. What happened to it is something of a mystery; it seems that it became engaged in an encounter with Spaniards, of which no details are known, except that Gilbert lost a tall ship and came back with the rest 'sore battered and disabled.'

Next year Gilbert and Ralegh intended to make another attempt and perhaps exact retribution for their losses; but before they could leave Dartmouth, word came down from the Council that they were 'to surcease from proceeding any further' and Gilbert was to put in sureties for his good behaviour. He went straight to Ireland, a field of action always open to the disgruntled Elizabethan, and took part in the fighting against Fitzmaurice and Desmond. Ralegh followed next year, being given command of 100 soldiers. Here he remained for a year, making a reputation for valour and severity. He rescued a fellow west-countryman from an ambush with great daring and at much personal risk to himself. In November he commanded on the first three days and the final day of the assault on the Spaniards and Italians at Smerwick, and on their surrender had them all put to the sword. But he was not contented with Ireland; we find him writing in August 1581 to Leicester who had become in some sort his patron: 'I have spent some time here under the Deputy, in such poor place and charge, as, were it not for that I knew him to be one of yours, I would disdain it as much as to keep sheep.' [1] It is the true Ralegh spirit, pride and discontentment with his present lot.

It was soon to be remedied; in December he was in England with dispatches, and somehow or other – it is still a mystery how or when – he gained the favourable attention of the Queen. Posterity has enshrined its romantic suddenness in the story of the cloak laid for the royal feet to pass over a muddy place. There is nothing inherently improbable in it – tradition is often a useful guide; and there is a worldly parable to be read into the action. The next generation was not even certain how it was that Ralegh gained the Queen's ear. Sir Robert Naunton suggests that it may have been over some variance with his superior Lord Grey in Ireland, which drew them both to the Council-table, where Ralegh had a marked advantage; 'but true it is, he had gotten the Queen's ear at a trice, and she began to be taken with his elocution, and loved to hear his reasons to her demands: and the truth is, she took him for a kind of Oracle, which nettled them all.' [2] Perhaps a more lasting recommendation to a lady so susceptible to masculine charms as Elizabeth was his handsome personal appearance; moreover he was unmarried. Naunton witnesses: 'He had in the outward man, a good presence, in a handsome and well-compacted person, a strong natural wit, and a better judgment, with a bold and

[1] Harleian MSS. 6993, f. 3.
[2] Naunton, *Fragmenta Regalia* (ed. Arber), 48–9.

plausible tongue, whereby he could set out his parts to the best advantage.' It should be added, what posterity knows, that he was a man of scintillating and original genius; and that Elizabeth, whose judgment of men was faultless, was justified in her choice.

Armed with these advantages, he rose rapidly into the splendour of royal favour. The pay of his Irish establishment he continued to receive – it was a way of providing for him till better could be found. It was not long in coming; in 1584 and later he was given very profitable grants of licences to export woollen cloths, and in the same year a very lucrative grant of the farm of wines, power to grant licences for their sale and to regulate prices. This latter brought in a large regular income; the impecunious second son of impoverished though gentle family ('the Queen in her choice never took into her favour a meer new man, or a Mechanick') was financially safe and able to support the position of conspicuous splendour to which he had so suddenly risen. Thereafter lands also were granted to him, and he obtained possession of the desired Sherborne from the see of Salisbury, with the aid of a tart letter from the Queen to the reluctant Bishop.

In July 1585, while Grenville was captaining his expedition on the other side of the Atlantic, Ralegh had succeeded Bedford as Lord Warden of the Stannaries; and in September as Lieutenant of the county of Cornwall, and Vice-Admiral of both Devon and Cornwall. In 1587 he became Captain of the Guard in succession to Sir Christopher Hatton, a position of constant personal attendance upon the Queen, with all the great advantages that it offered. The position was complete: Ralegh from being one of the obscurer and unprosperous members of the great West Country cousinage, was through the favour of the Queen raised to a pivotal position within it. He was from now on the most important man in the government of the western counties; the Devon and Cornish gentry looked to him for their support – Carew, when he came to write his *Survey of Cornwall*, dedicated it to him; he was in a position to advance the interests of his friends and relatives. From now on we find Grenville and Ralegh working in close and friendly association, not only as regards the Virginia schemes but in the government and defence of the West Country.

It is to Ralegh's eternal honour that he used his good fortune and new-found wealth to advance the great schemes for discovery and colonisation which he had set his heart upon. In 1583 Gilbert set out upon his last voyage. The Queen had tried to hold him back, as Gilbert wrote pathetically to Walsingham:[1] 'Her Majesty of her especial care had of my well-doing and prosperous success hath wished my stay at home from the personal execution of my intended discovery as a man noted of not good hap by sea,' – one more indication of the rightness of her judgment. But Gilbert had gone too far: he had sold his lands and even spent his wife's jointure upon his dream of discovery. When the time came for him to sail, the Queen gave him a meaning little token, 'an anchor guided by a lady,' but prudently forbore to subscribe to the adventure. Ralegh contributed £2,000 in equipping the *Ark Ralegh*, but the ship returned early to harbour with fever aboard her.

A sort of fatality overhung the expedition from the first. Gilbert sailed with his remaining ships for Newfoundland, which he took possession of and then turned south to explore the American coast. But he lost two of his ships and turned home defeated and discouraged. The rest we know from the famous words of Edward Hay's report in Hakluyt:[2] how Gilbert shifted into the tiny ten-ton frigate the *Squirrel*, where

'the General sitting abaft with a book in his hand, cried out unto us in the *Hind* (so oft as we did approach within hearing): "We are as near to heaven by sea as by land"; reiterating the same speech, well beseeming a soldier, resolute in Jesus Christ, as I can testify he was.'

The same night the lights of the little ship went suddenly out; 'whereof as it were in a moment we lost the sight, and withal our watch cried, the General was cast away, which was too true. For in that moment, the frigate was devoured and swallowed up of the sea.' The single surviving ship,

[1] S.P. Dom. Eliz. 157, no. 59. [2] Hakluyt, VIII, 74.

the *Golden Hind*, arrived in Falmouth, not without peril, on Sunday 22 September.

Ralegh was the heir to Gilbert's originating spirit; and at once he set about to resume the enterprise. His half-brother's charter had now expired and in March he obtained a new one, with somewhat larger powers. The objective that Gilbert had had in mind was not merely Newfoundland but the mainland of North America. The English claim to possession was based upon the voyages of John and Sebastian Cabot nearly a century before. The early promise of these voyages for this country was somehow not fulfilled; the difficulties and problems of the Reformation years for a time confined English energies and directed our attention inwards. In consequence, not only the Spanish but the French had stolen a march upon us in North America. Jacques Cartier and others had explored the St. Lawrence and into Canada; while at the southern end, in Florida, to the short-lived Huguenot colony under Ribault, there had succeeded the permanent Spanish settlements at St. Augustine and St. Helen's. But there remained all the American coast north of Florida; and this was what these and succeeding voyages were designed to bring into English possession: as Edward Hay wrote, 'God hath reserved the same to be reduced unto Christian civility by the English nation.'

Ralegh's determination to carry forward his half-brother's projects for colonisation in North America, in spite of his ill-success, attracted the ardent support of the younger Hakluyt, already well known for his geographical knowledge and a passionate believer in England's fortune upon the sea and in the New World.[1] Ralegh had requested Hakluyt to set down in writing his views on the question of colonisation; and in July 1584, he came over from Paris and working through the summer in London, in close proximity to Ralegh, wrote his famous *Discourse of Western Planting*. Its real purpose was to persuade the Queen to take up the project and give it the backing of the state; Hakluyt seems to have realised that only the resources of the state could ultimately see the thing through to success. But Elizabeth was in no mood for such commitments; she was per-

[1] Taylor, *Writings and Correspondence of the Hakluyts*, I, 32-44.

fectly willing to see the favourite whom she had raised to afflu-ence spend his wealth, if not himself, upon the venture. Not all Hakluyt's eloquence could persuade her. While he was writing away through the hot summer in London, Ralegh's first scout-ing expedition, two small barks under Captains Amadas and Barlow, were already in the new country.

Immediately upon the issue of his charter, Ralegh had sent out the two barks to spy out the new country and prepare the way for a larger enterprise later. Philip Amadas, of that Ply-mouth and Launceston family which was connected with the Hawkinses, and Arthur Barlow, who had served under Ralegh in Ireland, were in command. The latter in addition wrote the delightful report of the voyage which is printed in Hakluyt;[1] fresh, taut and vigorous as is always the writing of Elizabethan sea-captains, this one, an otherwise unknown man, surpasses most in the natural ease and beauty with which he wrote. There is a singular nostalgia about his writing: one can only put it down to this time being the morning of the language.

They departed from the west of England on 27 April. They took the southward course via the Canaries and the West Indies; the prevailing winds and currents on this route and thence up the coast of Florida being better known and more favourable than the northern route. After remaining for a little in the West Indies to refresh themselves with sweet water and fresh victual, they struck up the coast of Florida. And on

'the second of July, we found shoal water, when we smelt so sweet, and so strong a smell, as if we had been in the midst of some delicate garden abounding with all kinds of odoriferous flowers, by which we were assured that the land could not be far distant. And keeping good watch, and bearing but slack sail, the fourth of the same month we arrived upon the coast, which we supposed to be a continent and firm land; and we sailed along the same a hundred and twenty English miles before we could find any entrance, or river issuing into the sea.'

At the first entry that appeared, they entered and took possession in the name of the Queen; 'the land about us, being, whereat we

<hr />

[1] Hakluyt, VIII, 297–310.

first landed, very sandy and low towards the water's side, but so full of grapes, as the very beating and surge of the sea overflowed them.'

When they passed from the sea-side to the higher ground, they found that there was sea on both sides and that they were on an island. The fact was that they had hit upon the long chain of narrow islands running for some two hundred miles or more, roughly north and south, off the coast of what is now North Carolina. They had struck this low sandy coast somewhere to the north of the modern Cape Lookout, the most southerly point of the sequence; thence their northerly run of a hundred miles had brought them to the New Inlet, as it is now called, and the island they were at was the isle of Wokokon. Inside the barrier stretched the great inland seas, now known as Pamlico Sound and Albemarle Sound, which they began straightway to explore. They were at once struck with the richness of the woods and the variety of game.

'Under the bank or hill whereon we stood, we beheld the valley replenished with goodly cedar trees, and having discharged our harquebus-shot, such a flock of cranes (the most part white) arose under us, with such a cry redoubled by many echoes, as if an army of men had shouted all together.'

The islands were not much peopled, and it was not until the third day that a few native Indians appeared in a boat; one of them allowed himself to be rowed over to the ships, 'never making any show of fear or doubt.' There they gave him a shirt and a hat, and 'made him taste of our wine, and our meat, which he liked very well.' Next day there came several boats, bringing some forty or fifty men, 'very handsome and goodly people, and in their behaviour as mannerly and civil as any of Europe.' Among them came the King's brother with great ceremony. 'After he had made a long speech unto us, we presented him with divers things, which he received very joyfully, and thankfully. None of the company durst speak one word all the time: only the four which were at the other end, spoke one in the other's ear very softly.' A few days after, they fell to trading with the Indians, exchanging a few shiny metal things

for chamois, buff and deer skins. 'We exchanged our tin dish
for twenty skins, worth twenty crowns, or twenty nobles: and a
copper kettle for fifty skins worth fifty crowns.'

Gaining greater confidence, the King's brother brought his
wife and children to see the ships. The English noted that 'she
was very well favoured, of mean stature, and very bashful,'
and with even greater interest that 'in her ears she had brace-
lets of pearls hanging down to her middle (whereof we delivered
your worship a little bracelet), and those were of the bigness of
good peas.' Each day the King's brother, who was very friendly
and just of his promise, sent them

'a brace or two of fat bucks, coneys, hares, fish the best of the
world; with divers kinds of fruits, melons, walnuts, cucumbers,
gourds, peas and divers roots, and fruits very excellent good,
and of their country corn, which is very white, fair and well-
tasted.'

Indeed, Barlow wrote, 'the soil is the most plentiful, sweet,
fruitful and wholesome of all the world.'

Several days later, a party went some miles farther up into the
Sound and came to the large island of Roanoke, where their
friend the King's brother lived. Here they were entertained to
a solemn banquet in the large family-house in the native village.
All was as friendly as could be: 'We found the people most
gentle, loving, and faithful, void of all guile and treason, and
such as live after the manner of the golden age.' Roanoke was
near the mainland, and while there they gathered as much information as they could about its geography, inhabitants, the
state of the tribes and their relations with each other – like most
groupings of human beings external to each other, their relations were those of incessant warfare. Beyond Roanoke was
another great inland water [Albemarle Sound] and many
islands 'very plentiful of fruits and other natural increases, together with many towns, and villages, along the side of the
continent, some bounding upon the islands, and some stretching
up farther into the land.'

So Barlow rendered his report of this goodly, pleasant land
to Ralegh. He brought home with him two Indians, 'being

ERITH PUBLIC LIBRARIES
& MUSEUM

lusty men, whose names were Wanchese and Manteo.' What is interesting is that when at the end of his report he gives the names of the chief persons who were of the company on the voyage, a William Grenville stands at the head. We do not know for certain who he was, though it is to be presumed that he was a relative of Sir Richard's. George Grenville of Penheale had a brother called William, and it may have been he. Next year in the great expedition with which Drake went running 'through the Indies like a conqueror,' storming San Domingo and Carthagena, there was a Captain Grenville among those who were killed. It is not fanciful to identify these two, since we know that George Grenville's brother William died unmarried and he was not among those who accompanied Sir Richard to Virginia. However, he may well have given the latter some verbal report of it.

Encouraged by this report of the new country, Ralegh redoubled his efforts to plant a new England beyond the seas. The literary powers of the Hakluyts were further drawn upon to create an atmosphere favourable to the enterprise.[1] The younger Hakluyt completed his *Discourse*. The elder Hakluyt, who had not been yet superseded as a colonial adviser by his more brilliant and more enthusiastic cousin, was called in to write a pamphlet to encourage the venture: *Inducements to the liking of the voyage intended towards Virginia*. This tract was intended for the information and instruction of the prospective colonists. As such it dealt chiefly with the commodities and trading prospects of the colony. The region marked out for the enterprise, lat. 40° to 42°, lay in the latitude which Hakluyt had always regarded as best for settlement, with a climate like that of Spain and Italy, and similar produce, olives, vines, mulberries, sugar and other Mediterranean products. All this was part of the psychological preparation for the enterprise; and it is notable that when it set sail, it included a number of friends from the circle of the Hakluyts, Cavendish, Harriot and Ralph Lane among them.

In the winter of this year, in order to give Ralegh's project the greater security, a Bill was introduced in Parliament to con-

[1] Taylor, 36–40.

firm his Charter. He certainly intended to lead the expedition which was to plant the first English colony in America himself; and when this was made impossible by the Queen's desire to retain him by her side, it was arranged that Grenville, who had taken part in the committee-work on the Bill in the House and so was acquainted with Ralegh's plans, should take his place. After the Christmas recess, Grenville devoted himself to the preparations for the voyage, at first in London, but mainly in the West Country. We hear no more of him in Parliament, nor indeed was he ever returned to Parliament again: for the last crowded years of his life, action and constant service abroad and at home claimed him.

It was at this time (February 1585) that we found him writing *à propos* of Mrs. Paget, 'being now prepared to commit myself to the pleasure of God on the seas.' We realise with a start that this was actually Grenville's first voyage; so far as we know, his experience of the sea up to this had been mainly concerned with the ownership of ships. At the same time there was a project on foot, and preparations were being secretly made at Plymouth and elsewhere for a very different voyage by a more practised hand. Elizabeth had at last been brought round, owing to the critical posture of affairs in Europe, the assassination of William of Orange, and the growth of Spanish sea-power, which was now reaching its apogee under the far-reaching plans of the great Admiral Santa Cruz, to sanction an unmistakable and responsible act of aggression against Spain, a powerful armament under Drake to attack the very strongholds of Spanish power in the West Indies. The Queen, as usual having committed herself to so decisive a step, which could not but mean open war, hung back. Drake was in London up to March and perhaps later, making what headway he could; in the summer he was at Plymouth gathering and victualling the fleet, and having got his commission signed, he slipped away to sea on 14 September.

Grenville was by that time on his way homeward, making no great hurry, hanging about off the Azores to pick up what he could. He had departed from Plymouth on 9 April. The Black Book of Plymouth, in which the town recorded events of historical importance under its successive mayoralties, has the following entry under that of Christopher Brooking for 1584–5: 'Sir Richard Grenville Knight, departed from Plymouth with VI ships and barks for Wingane Dehoy, where he carried VI hundred men or thereabouts.'

CHAPTER XI

THE FIRST VIRGINIA VOYAGE

The little fleet which Grenville commanded consisted of seven sails: the *Tiger* of 140 tons, a flieboat called the *Roebuck* of the same burden, the *Lion* of 100 tons, the *Elizabeth* of 50 tons, and the *Dorothy*, a small bark, with two pinnaces for speedy service. There were aboard a number of gentlemen, mostly young men, who had volunteered to make trial of the new country. There was Ralph Lane, one of the Queen's equerries, whom Grenville appointed to take charge of the colony on his return. Thomas Cavendish, the brilliant young navigator who repeated Drake's exploit of circumnavigating the globe, was another; he was now twenty-five, and it seems to have been his first introduction to the sea. Equally interesting was the presence of Thomas Harriot, who became the foremost scientist and mathematician in England; he was now about the same age as Cavendish, but unlike him he remained a whole year in the new country under Lane's government, and later wrote the *True Report of Virginia*, a document full of close observation and scientific curiosity. Grenville took with him a considerable west-country contingent: there was Philip Amadas, who remained on under Lane as 'Admiral of the country'; John Arundell, Grenville's half-brother; his brother-in-law, John Stukeley, a Kendall, one of the Prideaux of Padstow, a Courtenay, Anthony Rowse, the friend and later an executor of Drake's, along with others.

Five days out from Plymouth, after a storm in which Cavendish was separated from Grenville in his flagship the *Tiger*, the rest of the fleet fell in with the Canaries and continued their course across the Atlantic to the West Indies. They reached Dominica on 7 May, and three days later came to anchor at Cotesa, a little island off Porto Rico, 'where we landed, and refreshed ourselves all that day.' [1] Grenville was determined to land in Porto Rico, in spite of the Spaniards, to build a new pinnace in place of that which had been lost in the storm. So on 12 May they anchored in the Bay of Moskito,

'within a falcon shot of the shore: where our General Sir Richard Grenville, and the most part of our company landed, and began to fortify very near to the sea-side: the river ran by the one side of our fort, and the other two sides were environed with woods.'

Next day they began to build their pinnace within the fort, with the timber which they felled in the country, some part of which had to be fetched from three miles inland, the Spaniards not daring to offer any resistance.

A few days later, a small company of eight Spanish horsemen appeared out of the woods, and stayed some distance from the fort viewing the English forces: Grenville dispatched 'ten of our shot' against them, and they retired into the woods. On the 19th, Cavendish came up with the rest of the fleet, arriving at Cotesa, within sight of the *Tiger*:

'we thinking him a far off to have been either a Spaniard or French man-of-war, thought it good to weigh anchor, and to go room with him, which the *Tiger* did, and discerned him at last to be one of our consorts, for joy of whose coming our ships discharged their ordnance, and saluted him according to the manner of the seas.'

A very natural, if somewhat schoolboyish exhibition of good spirits; for there they were in the great spaces of the Caribbean with their diminutive forces: any reinforcement must have been highly welcome in the unfriendly temper of the Spaniards on the island.

Three days later, a troop of twenty Spanish horsemen showed themselves on the other side of the river. Grenville sent twenty footmen against them, with two horsemen mounted upon

[1] All quotations in the following account of the voyage, unless otherwise stated, are from Hakluyt, VIII, 310–18.

Spanish horses which they had taken. The Spaniards produced
a flag of truce, and made signs for a parley; whereupon two men
from each side went half-way to meet each other upon the sands.
'The two Spaniards offered very great salutations to our men,
but began according to their Spanish proud humours, to ex-
postulate with them about their arrival and fortifying in their
country.' The Englishmen explained discreetly enough that
their only intention was to furnish themselves with water and
victuals, and other things which they needed, and that they
wished to obtain them by fair and friendly means, otherwise
they would be reduced to relieving themselves by the sword.
Upon this the Spaniards 'yielded to our requests with large
promises of all courtesy and great favour, and so our men and
theirs departed.'

Two days later, when the pinnace was finished and launched,
Grenville marched with his captains and gentlemen some four
miles up into the country, where

'in a plain marsh they stayed expecting the coming of the
Spaniards according to their promise, to furnish us with
victuals: who keeping their old custom for perjury and breach
of promise, came not, whereupon our General fired the woods
thereabout, and so retired to our fort, which the same day was
fired also, and each man came aboard to be ready to set sail the
next morning.'

It was like Grenville to fire the woods: Drake would have done
the same; the Spaniards recognised very well what it meant.

Before leaving the island, Grenville sent Ralph Lane in a
frigate which they had taken round to the south-west side to
fetch salt, being conducted by a Spanish pilot. Here too they
met with the same unfriendly reception and refusal to traffic
with the English. Lane landed twenty men who entrenched
themselves upon the sands, encompassing one of the salthills,
and so brought away as much salt as they wanted, unmolested
by the Spaniards who did not dare attack. They returned on
the 29th to St. Germans' Bay, and from here the fleet sailed the
same day, 'being many of us stung before upon shore with the
mosquitoes.' That night they took a Spanish frigate which its

crew had deserted upon sight of them, and next morning another one 'with good and rich freight, and divers Spaniards of good account in her, which afterwards we ransomed for good round sums and landed them in St. John's' [i.e. Porto Rico].

On 1 June they anchored at Isabella on the north side of the island of Hispaniola. Here their reception was very different, for the rumour had reached the Governor of the town and the Captain of the port that there were a number of English gentlemen aboard, and that they had very civilly entertained the Spaniards on their ships. More probably, the Governor thought discretion the better part of valour and was unwilling to bring down an attack upon his head and depredations upon the island. There thereupon followed an elaborate exchange of courtesies and a singular entertainment, which very curiously reflects the fluctuating state of international relations in the Caribbean, with England and Spain on the verge of war in Europe.

The Spanish Governor, accompanied by 'a lusty friar' with some twenty other Spaniards attended by their servants and negroes, came down to the sea-side where the ships rode at anchor. Grenville immediately

'manned the most part of his boats with the chief men of our fleet, every man appointed, and furnished in the best sort: at the landing of our General, the Spanish Governor received him very courteously; and the Spanish gentlemen saluted our English gentlemen, and their inferior sort did also salute our soldiers and seamen, liking our men, and likewise their qualities; although at the first they seemed to stand in fear of us, whereof they desired that all might not land their men, yet in the end, the courtesies that passed on both sides were so great, that all fear and mistrust on the Spaniards' part was abandoned.'

Underneath it is clear that suspicion and mutual watchfulness remained in spite of the formal courtesies that ensued.

While Grenville and the Spanish Governor conversed, mainly

of matters concerning the island, its population and commodities,

'our men provided two banqueting houses covered with green boughs, the one for the gentlemen, the other for the servants, and a sumptuous banquet was brought in served by us all in plate, with the sound of trumpets, and consort of music, wherewith the Spaniards were more than delighted.'

What a picture it is: the amenities of this marauding, seafaring life at the other end of the new routes across the Atlantic. It was like them, too, to make such a show; we are reminded of Drake, who on his world-voyage did not 'omit to make provision also for ornament or delight, carrying to this purpose with him expert musicians, rich furniture (all the vessels for his table, yea, many belonging even to the cook-room being of pure silver).' [1] Moreover, the Spaniards well might be grateful, while keeping a sharp look-out: colonial life in the island of Hispaniola must have been tedious in the extreme and such a visit a conspicuous excitement. Nor to Grenville, dining with the Spaniards under a canopy of boughs to ward off the hot summer sun, can it have been without a spice of mingled bravado and irony: the more so if he could have had any intuition of what would some day befall him at their hands!

The banquet, which was the English contribution to these gaieties, over, the Spaniards provided the sport. They had drawn together from the mountains a great herd of white bulls and kine, and they provided a horse ready saddled for every gentleman and captain that would ride. Then they singled out three of the best bulls 'to be hunted by horsemen after their manner, so that the pastime grew very pleasant for the space of three hours, wherein all three of the beasts were killed, whereof one took the sea, and there was slain with a musket.' After the sport, presents and gifts were exchanged; and next day 'we played the merchants in bargaining with them by way of truck and exchange of divers of their commodities, as horses, mares, kine, bulls, goats, swine, sheep, bull-hides, sugar, ginger, pearls, tobacco, and such like commodities of the Island.' To obtain

[1] Fletcher, *The World Encompassed*.

these things was the real object on the English side of those courtesies; for Grenville it was vitally necessary to obtain cattle to stock the new colony with. His dealings with the Spaniards in Hispaniola were, therefore, a triumphant success, and without any further delay they departed 'with great good will from the Spaniards.'

So much for the English account, as given in Hakluyt, of their doings in the West Indies. It so happens that one or two Spanish documents remain, which have hitherto been over-looked by English writers, that enable us to see these events from the Spanish side.[1] They entirely corroborate the English account, and add some illuminating and picturesque details which complete the picture for us. At the end of this month, on 22 June, the Spanish Governor of Havana, Diego Hernandez de Quiñones, wrote home to Philip a report containing the information which had come in to him.

He was alarmed for the trading fleet from Mexico, which, with the ships of the Honduras, Jamaica and Campeche, had just arrived in harbour at Havana, under their commander Pedro Menendez Marques. At the same time warning came from the Governor of Porto Rico that two big English ships had arrived there, at a port called Guardianilla, ten leagues from Porto Rico; that here they had landed some 400 men and were building an entrenched fort and cutting timber to build pinnaces. The Governor had sent a Lieutenant, living at San German, with 40 men to view the position, and dispatched 35 arquebusiers to harass the enemy whenever they left the fort to cut wood or get water. When the enemy were embarking, having finished their pinnaces, the Lieutenant sent two men to parley with them and ask who they were. The pirates raised a flag of truce and sent two men in return, who told him that they were Englishmen, bearing hostages for a good sum whom they were going to set to ransom in New Spain. As they were sailing towards La Mona they captured a bark on its way from San

---

[1] Colección Navarrete, XXV, nos. 48, 49. These documents, which derive originally from the Archives of the Indies and the Secretariat of New Spain respectively, are merely referred to by Duro in his *Armada Española*, II, 392.

Domingo, and next day a large frigate with a great cargo of cloth for Porto Rico, causing much loss to the dwellers round thereby.

At the time of writing, the Governor had reported that there were still three big ships and two pinnaces at San German, that they were asking for horses, pigs, calves and mares; and that they had on board two Indians, richly dressed. They said that they were going to settle, but did not say where. Upon this, the Spanish Commanders in the Islands took alarm for the safety of the *flotas* and the Governor of Havana wrote to Philip to send out some warships to protect them, since the trading ships of the *flotas* were incapable of defending themselves. Little did they know that a far more powerful force, under the redoubtable Drake, was shortly to follow Grenville to the Islands, to wreak destruction upon their commerce and security.

A little later news came to the Governor of Grenville's five ships anchored in the port of Isabella, one of them a big galleon, and that they were demanding horses, dogs, cattle and sheep. The information was that they had been given some horses for ransoms and that they were staying on that coast. There were two more big ships on the south coast at the Cabo de Cruz, which tallied with the news sent out from Seville; but who they were, the Spaniards did not know, nor do we. The Governor thought they were the ships which had a little while before been at Cape St. Anthony, preying upon commerce. The purpose of Grenville's expedition, and 'whither their thoughts are set' the Spaniards could not make out. Pedro Menendez was, however, reporting his opinion to his Majesty; and since the Governor and he agreed that he should return to Florida, it seems that his suspicions lay in the right direction.

A second Spanish document gives us a much nearer close-up of Grenville and his proceedings, since it is an account of what happened by a Spanish gentleman, Don Fernando de Altamirano, who was captured in the frigate taken by Grenville and held to ransom. The frigate had been taken in the Straits about four leagues from the Island of Porto Rico. There were four English ships present, the largest about 200 tons, another of about 100 according to his estimation; there was the small vessel they had taken the day before and the pinnace they had built on the Island, on the southern side at a place called Mosquetal, where they had made a fort and set up a forge to make nails for the pinnace. Altamirano says that they had been twelve days repairing their ships because they had been damaged by a storm, in which thirteen or fourteen ships as they said, had been separated from them and they were looking for them there. We do not know that Grenville's squadron set out in company with any other ships from Plymouth. The information seems designed to spread the rumour of much larger forces than they had at their disposal. Altamirano was also told that they had the intention of peopling Trinidad and Dominica, and other lands which the King did not wish to settle, since he had so much on his hands already. Here again the English were disguising the real destination of the expedition. They told Altamirano a tall story of their wanting the Indies to be the joint possessions of England and Spain, and that they had been commanded not to kill anybody by a great lord of England (i.e. Ralegh) who had so instructed the General of this fleet, Fulano de Verde Campo, a certain Grenville, many times.

There were in the fleet some twenty people who seemed persons of distinction, and among the rest were officers in all posts; they were served upon much silver plate, chased and gilt. They brought with them two Indians who were tall of stature and well cared for, and who already spoke English. They also brought much music, clarions and other instruments, and some organs, because they said the Indians were lovers of music. And they brought the Bible translated into Spanish in their fashion and begged him to take a copy to Porto Rico so that people should understand how their preachers were deceiving them. At San German, Altamirano relates, they asked to be given horses and mares and other animals, in exchange for his person and the others who were with him. When the people on shore refused, they threatened to hang him and the other captives. The day before they set sail they set him and his companions ashore, so that they should not see what course they were taking; and next day, since they had been becalmed, they saw them go towards the Cape to deceive the island of San

Domingo. When Don Fernando and his companions had been taken, the papers which they found in their possession were read to them by a Portuguese whom they had as their pilot and who was a Lutheran; there was another odd Portuguese who went with them too. All this time they were asking if there was any news of their ships in the Indies. They carried a great many plants, plantains and other fruits that they found on the sea-shores, and they drew pictures of both fruits and trees. They brought with them a Treasurer and Comptroller from their home; and they asked questions about the forces holding Porto Rico and San Domingo and whether the Inquisition were there.

From this it is clear that Grenville was expecting Drake's expedition to follow close upon his heels; but it was delayed all through the summer by the hesitations of the Queen. It was not until September that Drake was at length free to set sail; and by then, the Spanish authorities had received a warning from Grenville's presence. Drake's task was made all the more difficult, and the board swept correspondingly clean before his appearance. As we have seen from the Governor of Havana's dispatch, Pedro Menendez went on immediately with the *flotas* of New Spain, and so they at least eluded Drake's grasp. But it is an interesting deduction from this, that it was the function of Grenville's squadron in part, to act as a scout for Drake's larger force coming behind. Had their movements synchronised as was intended, the damage done to Philip's dominions in the West Indies and on the mainland would undoubtedly have been far heavier than it was. But Grenville could not wait on indefinitely in the Indies; his prime object was to plant his colony and he was already delayed in arriving upon the coast of Virginia – as Lane was later to complain, very unfairly, for it was not Grenville's fault. More amusing, though less important, are the glimpses that Altamirano gives us of Grenville and his ship: the distinguished company, the honoured position of the two Anglophile Indians, John White drawing the strange fruits and plants, the plate upon which the gentlemen were served, and the many instruments of music. Doubtless the clarions had an heraldic significance, as much as musical; for the three clarions were the crest of the Grenvilles. Whether the

Indians were lovers of music or no, we know that Elizabethan Englishmen were.

To resume the English account of the expedition: leaving Hispaniola on 7 June, they took a north-westerly course towards the Caicos Islands, a sort of connecting ridge with Florida, to the north of Cuba. Next day they anchored at a small island to take seals, which they had heard were in great quantity there. But instead, Grenville was almost cast away by some accident that happened to the pinnace, in which he and others were sailing, presumably, to or from the shore; 'but by the help of God they escaped the hazard, and returned aboard the Admiral in safety.' Next day they landed upon Caicos, to search for salt-ponds, 'upon the advertisement and information of a Portugal: who in deed abused our General and us, deserving a halter for his hire, if it had so pleased us.' In the next four days they passed along the other islands of this northerly group, landing at Guanima and at Cyguateo. On the 20th, they came to the mainland of Florida, three days later were 'in great danger of a wreck on a beach called the Cape of Fear,' and next day came to anchor in a harbour 'where we caught in one tide so much fish as would have yielded us twenty pounds in London.'

This was their first landing in Florida, and on the 26th they came to anchor at Wokokon. They weighed anchor again three days later to bring the *Tiger* through the inlet between the islands into the Sound; but the passage was very difficult among those shoals, and 'through the unskilfulness of the Master whose name was Fernando, the Admiral struck on ground, and sunk.' The ship was not lost, only grounded; but we learn from Hooker's account that a good deal of damage was done to the stores she carried for the provision of the colony, the 'ship was so bruised, that the salt water came so abundantly into her, that the most part of his corn, salt, meal, rice, biscuit, and other provisions that he should have left with them that remained behind him in the country was spoiled.' [1]

On 3 July, word of their arrival was sent from Wokokon to the King Wingina at Roanoke: Amadas and Barlow in the pre-

[1] Holinshed's *Chronicle*, Continuation to 1586, p. 1402.

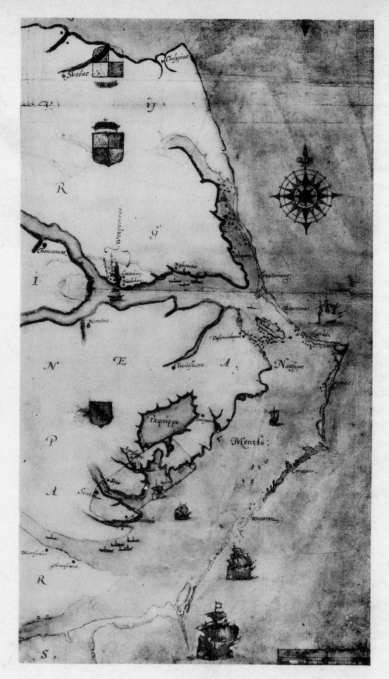

CHART OF VIRGINIA.

vious year had not seen him, for he had been wounded in battle with a neighbouring people and during the time that they were in the country was lying at his chief town, some six days' journey off. Granganimeo, his brother, was their particular friend. The geography of this region has changed a good deal since then, for it is all low-lying swampy ground liable to be silted up; some of the inlets have become closed in course of time and certain of the long islands of the barrier been joined together. Wokokon, however, which was their first anchorage, seems to be the modern Ocrocoke between Portsmouth island and Hatteras which has kept its old name.

On the sixth, Captains Aubrey and Bonython were sent up the next island, Croatoan, where they 'found two of our men left there with 30 other by Captain Reymond, some 20 days before.' Evidently he had arrived there considerably ahead of the other ships. It took two days to bring these men back to the base at Wokokon. On the same day, John Arundell was sent across to the mainland, that would be to Secoton and the district round, now known as Hyde county: it was then much more cut up by inlets of the sea and by a great inland sea called Paquipee, later Lake Mattamuskee. He was accompanied by Manteo as guide, one of the two Indians whom Amadas had taken back with him to England. Manteo remained a staunch friend to the English all the time they were there under Lane's governance; indeed it was due to him that Lane heard in time of the chief Wingina's conspiracy against him, and so was saved. The other Indian, Wanchese, later turned against the English. The two are commemorated in the two townships upon Roanoke island which are called by their names.

Grenville led an expedition a few days later to the mainland. He went in his tilt-boat, with his relatives Arundell and Stukeley; Lane, Cavendish, Harriot and others went in the new pinnace; and two ship's-boats followed with a score of others. They were victualled for eight days, and they spent a week exploring the country about the mouth of the Pamlico River. They discovered several native settlements, Pomejok, Aquascogoc and Secoton, where they were well entertained by the natives, 'and also the great lake called by the savages Paquipee.'

But at Aquascogoc one of the Indians stole a silver cup from them; and Grenville, sending a boat to demand it and not receiving it according to promise, set fire to the settlement and burnt and spoiled their corn, 'all the people being fled.' It was a characteristically harsh, and probably unfortunate, way of enforcing a lesson upon them.

The expedition returned on the 18th, and three days later the fleet sailed for Hatteras, a good deal farther up the coast towards Roanoke. They arrived there on the 27th, and there the King's brother Granganimeo came aboard Grenville's ship with Manteo. During August, Grenville explored up the other great sound (Albemarle Sound), mainly it appears on the north side to Weapomeiok, about where the modern Hertford is, and to where the Chowan river, which has retained its old name, comes into the Sound. At this time Lane was very busy writing letters home to England, to Walsingham and Sir Philip Sidney, explaining the situation there between himself and Grenville as he saw it. On the 5th, John Arundell left for England, and on the 25th, Grenville, leaving the command in the hands of Lane and a plentiful supply of provisions for the colony, sailed for home too. Some 107 men elected to remain behind under Lane's command, among them Harriot, Acton, Edward Stafford, and among the west-countrymen, Philip Amadas, Kendall, Prideaux and Anthony Rowse. Grenville had performed his task.

On the voyage home, when not many days out from Virginia – the name conferred upon the new country with the Queen's good liking – Grenville, according to the account in Holinshed,

'descried a tall ship of four hundred tons or thereabouts, making the same course that he did, unto whom he gave chase, and in few hours by goodness of sail overtook, and by violence won, richly laden with sugar, hides, spices and some quantity of gold, silver and pearl: she was the vice-admiral of the fleet of Sancto Domingo that year for Spain.' [1]

The account in Hakluyt says that the Spanish ship was of 300 tons, 'richly loaden'; but its brief entry as to the manner of her

[1] Holinshed, 1402.

capture is more excitingly specific, if it is to be believed. It says that Grenville boarded her 'with a boat made with boards of chests, which fell asunder, and sunk at the ship's side as soon as ever he and his men were out of it.' He then shipped in the prize and completed his journey in her in a short time, 'having a merry gale.'

On 10 September, he lost sight of the *Tiger* in foul weather, which came in at Falmouth on 6 October. Grenville arrived at Plymouth on the 18th, 'and was courteously received by divers of his worshipful friends.' Drake had left harbour just a month before on that destructive West Indies expedition which marked the opening of the war. But the Chronicle says that Ralegh met with Grenville at Plymouth, where he 'did presently resolve upon another voyage, to supply Ralph Lane, and his company that were left with him in Virginia, the next spring following.' [1]

It so happens that for the taking of the Spanish prize and other accidents of Grenville's homeward journey, we have much new detailed information in another Spanish document, an account given by Enrique Lopez, a Lisbon merchant, who was a passenger with other merchants on board the ship taken by Grenville.[2] We learn that her name was the *Santa Maria* of St. Vincent. She set out from San Domingo as flagship of seventeen other merchant ships, the San Domingo *flota*, carrying a cargo chiefly of hides and sugar. At Havana in July, after Grenville had left the Islands, the San Domingo contingent joined the *flota* of New Spain and the Mainland, under the command of Don Antonio Osorio. When they all set sail for Spain, they were some thirty-three sail.

Two days out they were caught in a storm, and the *Santa Maria* was forced to drop anchor and lay to all night. Next morning there were only six or seven sail of the *flota* in sight, and these the ship, being a poor sailor, could not catch up. However they went on their course lagging behind in the rear, until

---

[1] Plymouth Muniments: Widey Court Book, 1584-5. Ralegh was at Plymouth about this time, for in the Town Accounts we find Mr. Hawkins paid £4 and Martin White £8 11s. 4d. for his entertainment.

[2] Colección Navarrete, XXV, 53.

they were in line with the Bermudas. Here, on 4 September, about 10 o'clock in the morning, they suddenly saw a sail following in their track, which they took to be one of their company which had waited for them; so they took in sail to await her, so that they might go on together in company. As the ship came up with them, to windward, they fired a round from a gun to greet her as a sign of friendship. Immediately the ship opened fire on them, disabling their rigging and partly cutting down their shrouds. Since they had no arms nor artillery, they tried to fly; but they were outsailed, the pirate-ship firing shot after shot at them, killing one of the crew and wounding several, and then gave them two rounds of cannon at the waterline so that they feared they were going to the bottom. So they took in their sails and lay to: there was nothing else to be done.

Immediately a boat from the pirate-ship came to board them with thirty armed soldiers, and among them an officer whom they called the General, whose name is Richard Grenville (Richarte de Campo Verde). He said that they had set out from England for the Indies armed with fourteen ships. Coming on board, the General ordered the master and the other passengers to deliver up all the gold and silver and other things they had, promising to spare their persons. The passengers gave him the keys of the boxes; he opened some, broke open others and took out of them many packets of gold, silver and pearls that they were carrying. He took also the inventory of the ship and went through it asking for the gold, silver and pearls catalogued in it. They were handed over to him without exception, to the value of more than 40,000 ducats. In addition there were some 200 boxes of sugar of about 40 arrobas [1] each, 7,000 calf-hides and 1,000 quintals of ginger, and other things, worth altogether 120,000 ducats. Grenville ordered twenty sailors to be taken out of the prize into his own ship, leaving only some 20 Spaniards all told, merchants and sailors, in the prize. With his 35 men he stayed in her, continuing the voyage together with his own ship, until they were some 400 leagues from the Bermudas, when they were separated in a storm and did not see

[1] An arroba = 25 lbs.

the English ship again. So the *Santa Maria* continued on her voyage alone, suffering great hardship from lack of supplies, for they had hardly any left; Grenville had taken off most of what they were carrying into his ship which was in want. They were driven in the end to eating no more than a little rye cooked in salt water. So they went on until 12 October (Spanish Calendar) when they got sight of the Island of Flores.

As soon as they sighted land they drew near so that some boat might come out and show them a harbourage; and Grenville arranged that no English should be found or appear, but only the passengers and sailors of the ship. So they had speech with some of the islanders and asked them to send a boat to board them because they were in want; and the islanders recognising them for their countrymen sent out a boat with five men. When they came alongside the General forced them to come into the ship and seized them, saying that he would not let them go until they gave him the supplies of which there was need, for payment. The islanders, knowing him for a pirate, refused. One of the most important passengers went ashore and begged the islanders to give them the supplies they asked, for payment; for if they did not, he said that they would throw him and the rest of them, passengers and sailors, into the sea; the General seemed to be so resolved. When the islanders saw that he was so, they gave them the supplies they needed in return for money. As soon as the General had got his supplies on board, he set the Spaniards, some 22 in all, on shore; before they left the ship he stripped them to see if they had anything hidden on them.

The Portuguese merchant reports that Grenville's ship was a galleon in type, which made good sail and was well-armed and rigged. She had two tiers of artillery on each side, besides many other firearms; as pilot she had one Simon Fernandez, a Portuguese of the island of Tercera. He says that he had talked with some distinguished persons whom Grenville had with him; they told him that they had been in the Indies, on the north side of Porto Rico, where they had taken two frigates carrying merchandise, and that thence they had gone towards Florida, where they were to lose themselves among certain islands; the General had set ashore some 300 men there with orders to begin building a fort for settlement. He had dispatched a frigate to England – this must have been that which left under the command of John Arundell on 5 August – to get tools and munitions and men ready on his arrival to return at once to where he had left his men.

'This Richard Grenville appeared to be a man of quality, for he was served with much show, and vessels of plate and gold, and servants, and many musical instruments which they played while he ate; and in his appearance he seemed a distinguished person, (en su aspeto del parecia hombre principal).'

CHAPTER XII

THE FIRST ENGLISH COLONY IN AMERICA: VIRGINIA 1585-6

Grenville arrived home to find himself under the necessity of defending his conduct, not so much over the taking of the Spanish prize, but as regards certain particulars in his conduct of the voyage. He waited for some days, doubtless rendering a full report to Ralegh, and then on 29 October, wrote to Walsingham.[1] He does not make much of the unfavourable rumours; he merely says, 'by the ignorance of such as have come before me a large report hath been made of great quantities of pearl and metal of gold and silver' taken in the prize. On the contrary, he says:

'I do assure your honour that I have found but little; neither doth any such quantity pass from St. Domingo from whence they came unto Spain. That which was here belonged only to private persons who were passengers into Spain from St. Domingo. And the same when the ship yielded, was embezzled by the company.'

We need not attach much importance to this last statement, any more than to his account of the manner in which the prize was taken:

'In my way homewards I was encountered by a Spanish ship, whom assaulting me and offering me violence, god be thanked, with defence and safety of my self and all my company, after some fight I overcame and brought into England with me; her lading is ginger and sugar.'

Such statements were more or less *pro forma* in such circumstances

---

[1] S.P. Colonial, 1, no. 7.

with Elizabethans: everybody would know how much importance to attach to them. What was of more importance to Walsingham, for he was a co-adventurer in the voyage, was the value of the prize. Grenville says that the whole estimate of the ship by the confession of the Spaniards and view of their books 'amounteth only to 40,000 or 50,000 ducats.' One must allow a good margin to this, the figure is so very round. But whatever the precise value was, the voyage was 'made': he was enabled to pay back what each adventurer had subscribed with a profit, whatever there was left over for Ralegh and himself. 'The same being sufficient to answer the charge of each adventurer, wherein I am glad that my hope is to yield your honour the return of your adventure with some gain.'

That was a strong argument with which to meet any difficulties that might be brought up as regards his conduct of the voyage. Nor does Grenville anticipate objections; he was conscious of his own rectitude in having accomplished his mission.

'I have, god be thanked,' he writes, 'performed the action whereunto I was directed as fully as the time wherein I have been absent from hence and all possibilities would permit me. I have possessed and peopled the same to Her Majesty's use; and planted it with such cattle and beasts as are fit and necessary for manuring the country and in time to give relief with victual, as also with such fruits and plants as by my travail by the way thitherwards I might procure.'

For any further report of the commodities of the new country he refers him to his cousin Ralegh, and promises to let him have a report later of such as he has brought with him, 'the account whereof with other relations of the whole course of the voyage at my repair to the Court, which god willing shall be shortly, I will my self impart unto you.' One notices the increased godliness of the language with Grenville as with the seamen generally, as time went on and the impending struggle with Spain drew nearer: it was no impediment however to their somewhat pragmatic attitude towards telling the truth.

It does not appear that Grenville was acquainted with Lane's charges against him; but for some time Lane had been boiling over. There had evidently been open quarrelling between the two men on the voyage, and Lane may have been the head of a second party within the expedition, opposed to Grenville, as was frequently the case with Elizabethan enterprises. Drake had only obtained the unity necessary for his great scheme of circumnavigating the globe, by trying and executing his rival, Thomas Doughty, who led the opposition to his command. Lane laid the charge against Grenville that the latter had purposed to do the same by him:

'he not only purposed but even propounded the same, to have brought me by indirect means and untrue surmises to the question for my life, and that only for an advice in a public consultation by me given, which if it had been executed, had been for the great good of us all, but most chiefly of himself.' [1]

Lane arrived at this charge in a long indignant letter to Walsingham, written on 8 September from Roanoke.

But he had already begun his campaign as early as 12 August, writing 'from the Port Ferdinando, in Virginia' – the first letter to be written from Virginia that survives.[2] Either it is wrongly dated by a fortnight, or Lane took Grenville's departure to explore the Sound beyond Roanoke as his departure for England. He begins circumspectly enough, writing to Walsingham: 'The General's return in his own person into England doth presently cut me off from using circumstances in report of the particularities of this country.' He goes on to hint that they have arrived in the country late in the year, 'and that wholly through the fault of him that intendeth to accuse others.' It should be said that there is no evidence whatever to show that Grenville did accuse Lane; he seems to have been content with establishing his authority. And the fact that he left Lane in command on his return, and next year hastened to bring him supplies, suggests that, the perils and disputes of the voyage over, Grenville bore him no grudge.

Lane wrote at the same time to Walsingham and Sir William Russell, commending the bearer of these letters, a Mr. Atkinson,

---

[1] S.P. Colonial, 1, no. 6.   [2] ibid. no. 3.

who had borne himself honestly and industriously throughout the voyage, 'notwithstanding the General's displeasure towards him and his complaints.' [1] It is not difficult to see that Atkinson was one of Lane's supporters. But there were others according to Lane. In the letter in which, after Grenville's departure when he was now left in control, Lane's indignation reached its height, he names particularly Cavendish, the high marshal on the expedition, Edward Gorges, Francis Brooke, the treasurer, and Captain Clark, Captain of the fly-boat. Lane thought that Grenville had returned home to accuse them, for he wrote to inform Walsingham

'that it is not possible for men to behave themselves more faithfully and more industriously in our action . . . Contrary wise how Sir Richard Grenville, General, hath demeaned himself from the first day of his entry into government at Plymouth, until the day of his departure from hence over the bar in the Port Ferdinando, far otherwise than my hope of him, though very agreeable to the expectations and predictions of sundry wise and godly persons of his own country, that knew him better than my self.'

The circumstances of Elizabethan seafaring, with high-tempered and explosive men cooped up in small ships for long spaces together, and when they commanded separate ships so apt to disagree about the course to be followed, were conducive to disagreement and quarrelling. But Lane felt venomously about Grenville, who had evidently given him a fright when Lane ventured to disagree, if indeed he had intended in his passion to make him pay the death-penalty. Lane refers Walsingham for a full account of all the General's dealings, especially towards himself, to 'an ample discourse of the whole voyage' dedicated and sent to Sir Walter Ralegh. It is a pity that this book has not survived; it perished along with most of Ralegh's private papers in the wreck which overtook his fortunes. Lane concludes:

'So as for mine own part, I have had so much experience of

---

[1] S.P. Colonial, 1, no. 4.

his government, as I am humbly to desire your honour and the rest of my honourable friends, to give me their favours to be freed from that place, where Sir Richard Grenville is to carry any authority in chief. Assuring you, Sir, with all that the Lord hath miraculously blessed this action, that in the time of his being amongst us, even through his intolerable pride, and insatiable ambition, it hath not at three several times taken a final overthrow.'

However, it had not, and that was the strong point in Grenville's case; his great argument, if it came to that, was the success of the enterprise.

We know no more than this of the quarrel between the parties within the command: through the perishing of the documents it has remained obscure. But it left Lane in a queer temper, at the beginning of a difficult and nerve-racking task. He sought relief in letter-writing; in a stream of letters at this time, to Walsingham, Sir Philip Sidney, Richard Hakluyt, he sings the praises of the new country. To the last, he writes that before Grenville's departure and after, they have

'discovered the main to be the goodliest soil under the cope of heaven . . . and the climate so wholesome, that we had not one sick since we touched the land here. If Virginia had but horses and kine in some reasonable proportion, I dare assure my self being inhabited with English, no realm in Christendom were comparable to it.' [1]

Left to his own resources, with his company of 107 men, Lane built a fort at the north end of Roanoke Island, and with this as his base started upon the exploration of the country. We are greatly aided in following him about his travels, and in gathering the character of the country and the people, their villages and manner of life, by the charming water-colour maps and drawings made by John White, the artist and cartographer of the expedition, as Harriot was its scientist—a fine series now reposing in the British Museum, the first artistic product of the new country. The farthest Lane travelled to the South was, like

[1] Hakluyt VIII, 319–20.

Grenville, to Secoton, the district that lies now between the Pamlico and Neuse Rivers. To the north, their farthest discovery was the country of the Chesapians, 130 miles distant, on the way towards Chesapeake Bay. This country earned Lane's enthusiastic commendations, and he had some intention of moving up the coast to it. His inclination was right, for it was upon one of the inlets of Chesapeake Bay that the final and permanent planting of Virginia took place.

But Lane did not get so far up the coast as this; indeed exploring by water was made dangerous by the shallows of these wide Sounds; as he says, once come to grief upon one of them, there was no hope of obtaining help, the shore was so far away. To the North-West they explored as far as Chawanook, beyond Weapomeioc which Grenville had reached: it was the country lying on both sides of the modern Chowan River, 'where it groweth to be as narrow as the Thames between Westminster and Lambeth.' [1] The chief of this country was called Menatonon, 'a man impotent in his limbs, a very grave and wise man, and of a very singular good discourse in matters concerning the state, not only of his own country, but also of his neighbours round about him as well far as near.' He certainly entertained Lane with some strange tales of a country four days' journey to the North-East (again on the shores of the Chesapeake Bay), where there were pearls to be had in great quantity. Of the second great river which flowed into the Sound, the Moratoc (now the Roanoke), he told an even stranger tale. Its head, they gathered, was some thirty or forty days' journey away, where it sprang out of a rock, 'which standeth so near unto a sea, that many times in storms the waves thereof are beaten into the said fresh stream, so that the fresh water groweth salt and brackish.' This aroused their excitement: did the river rise somewhere close by the Bay of Mexico? Or could it be that they were so near the Pacific, or at least an arm running into it: the long-sought North-West Passage at last?

Lane and his men determined to put it to the trial. The difficulty was that the river was almost impossible to navigate with oars, there was such a violent current from the west: 'for the

[1] Hakluyt VIII, 320–45.

Their rype corne

Their greene corne.

Corne newly sprong.

Their sitting at meat.

the place of solemne prayer

The house wherin the Tombe of their Herounds standeth

SECOTON.

A Ceremony in their prayers w the strange testius and soug dansing abowt posts carued on the topps lyke mens faces.

7

THE INDIAN VILLAGE OF SECOTON.

space of thirty miles rowing, it is as broad as the Thames betwixt Greenwich and the Isle of Dogs, in some places more, and in some less: the current runneth as strong, being entered so high into the river, as at London bridge upon a vale water.' To this, there was added the greater difficulty of a complete change of attitude among the Indians. After the death of Granganimeo, the friend of the English, his brother the King Wingina had changed his name to Pemisapan, and with that his attitude of former friendliness to secret hostility. He played upon the powerful Indian tribes along the course Lane was to take, with tales that the English meant to kill them; 'on the other side he told me (Lane), that they had the like meaning towards us.' The consequence was that the Indians by concerted action withdrew as Lane went up into the country, taking their corn and victual with them, which 'made me and my company as narrowly to escape starving in that discovery before our return, as ever men did, that missed the same.' Still the English struggled forward, led on by the hope of a mine of 'marvellous and most strange mineral' at the end of their journey; until all their corn being exhausted they were reduced to making the two mastiffs they had brought with them into a pottage with sassafras leaves, and subsisting on that, they dropped exhausted down the river again to Roanoke.

Pemisapan never expected to see them again, having taken good order as he thought to get rid of them. On their return he was suitably impressed and ready to submit to their demands again for a while. Some of the Indians thought that the English could not be killed, for 'we be dead men returned into the world again, and that we do not remain dead but for a certain time, and that then we return again.' Pemisapan sowed his ground at the end of April, besides giving the English a plot to sow themselves; by July when the harvest came, they would be safe. But during the intervening months, Pemisapan suffered a relapse and took to his old courses of starving them out, putting off their demands for corn with excuses, while he brought together a confederacy of the Indians against the colony. Lane was forced to disperse his forces about the islands to live off crabs and oysters, while he sent Prideaux to Cape Hatteras and Stafford to Croatoan to feed themselves and look out for shipping.

The Indians were gathering in force, planning to fire the settlement and kill Lane and Harriot in the confusion. Lane preferred to precipitate matters rather than to wait, and in an attempt to surprise all their canoes upon Roanoke, which miscarried, Pemisapan and his chiefs were set upon, Lane giving the watchword, 'Christ our victory,'

'and immediately those his chief men and himself had by the mercy of God for our deliverance, that which they had purposed for us. The King himself being shot through by the Colonel with a pistol, lying on the ground for dead, I looking as watchfully for the saving of Manteo's friends, as others were busy that none of the rest should escape, suddenly he started up, and ran away as though he had not been touched, insomuch as he overran all the company, being by the way shot thwart the buttocks by mine Irish boy with my petronel.'

The Irishman, one Nugent, pursued him into the woods alone, and later came back with Pemisapan's head in his hand.

A week after this unhappy event, there came news of a large fleet of twenty-three sail upon the coast; not knowing whether they were friends or foes, the whole colony stood on guard. But it was Drake returning from his triumphant rake's progress through the Indies, in which he had stormed and taken Santiago, San Domingo, Carthagena and St. Augustine, inflicting a vast amount of damage and carrying away their defences, besides much booty. Drake anchored in the roads outside, being unable to venture in because of the shallows. Lane went out to him, and Drake offered them forthwith a bark, the *Francis*, two pinnaces and four small boats, with victual for 100 men for four months, and all kinds of necessaries, hand weapons, boots, match, besides artificers and masters to take them back to England if need arose.

Lane, who was very discouraged by the accidents that had happened and 'seeing our hope for supply with Sir Richard Grenville, so undoubtedly promised us before Easter, not yet come, neither then likely to come this year, considering the doings in England for Flanders, and also for America,' derived a new lease of hope and courage from Drake's generous offer and elected to remain on in the new country. But immediately after, a great storm arose which lasted for days and Drake's fleet had to put out to sea before it, if it was not to be wrecked upon those shoals, and with it the bark *Francis* with all Lane's provisions and hopes was driven clear to sea. It was too much to endure. The storm subsiding in a few days, Drake made a new offer, putting the bark *Bonner* at their disposal to take them and all their provisions home. This time it was the wish of all the colony to accept: they had had enough. Setting sail with the fleet on 19 June, they arrived in Portsmouth 27 July.

It was the end of Ralegh and Grenville's first and chief attempt at founding the colony,

'being of all others' wrote the judicious Harriot in his admirable *True Report of Virginia*, 'the most principal, and as yet of most effect, the time of their abode in the country being a whole year, when as in the other voyage before they stayed but six weeks, and the others after were only for supply and transportation, nothing more being discovered than had been before.' [1]

Harriot was inclined upon reflection to lay some blame for the unfortunate turn of events upon this, that 'some of our company towards the end of the year, showed themselves too fierce in slaying some of the people in some towns, upon causes that on our part might easily enough have been borne withal.' Perhaps it was that the strangeness of the conditions, and the strain of their labours and of constant watchfulness, had an effect upon their nerves, for when they left it was by a sudden panic. When they saw Drake's fleet being driven from their anchors to sea, we learn that 'the rest on land perceiving this, hasted to those three sails which were appointed to be left there; and for fear they should be left behind they left all things confusedly, as if they had been chased from thence by a mighty army.' It seemed little enough that remained from so much

---

[1] Hakluyt VIII, 348–86.

effort – a few letters and writings, John White's drawings and some confusion.

And yet in reality the colony achieved something of the highest importance: it founded the tradition; from that everything else sprang. Voyage after voyage, often after an interval of years, was despatched – and so strong was the tradition that they made for Roanoke, when the country was not really favourable for colonisation and that to the north along the shores of Chesapeake Bay offered a far better foothold; until in the end, in the latter area, a permanent colony was planted. But all went back to these earlier efforts, in particular to Grenville's colony of 1585. A more curious, though not less far-reaching, by-product of this year's residence in the new world, was the introduction of tobacco into the old. One can never be sure who has the first claim to the honour, or according to Camden, the dishonour; but we may be certain that tobacco was among the commodities that Grenville brought back in the *Tiger*. Harriot wrote immediately after: 'We ourselves, during the time we were there, used to smoke it after their manner, as also since our return, and have found many rare and wonderful experiments of the virtues thereof.'

CHAPTER XIII

LATER VIRGINIA VOYAGES

'I shall yet live to see it an English nation.'
SIR WALTER RALEGH, 1609

RALEGH and Grenville were not unmindful of the colony and spared no pains in the winter of this year to gather reinforcements and supplies. Ralegh was extremely pressed with business at this time; he had only just been appointed to his new and important offices in the west, and at the same time he was engaged upon schemes for the colonisation of Munster, laid waste and depopulated in the Desmond Rebellion, and where he had been granted some twelve thousand acres. The main responsibility as regards Virginia fell therefore upon Grenville; and during this winter and spring he was gathering supplies and fitting out ships, this time at his home-port of Bideford.

In February the Council wrote him and the deputy-lieutenants of Cornwall concerning the plantation of Munster; they were to treat with the gentlemen of the county, making offer of certain grants of land there to be taken up and settled.[1] On 27 April, the deputy-lieutenants wrote back: 'We have generally made known through this country her Majesty's offers, and do find none of sufficient ability offer to undertake the same.' They suggested that it would 'further the people's willingness if some principal gentleman of each county, of whose discretion and fidelity the people are persuaded, be sent with them as their captain or governor'; the people then would follow.[2] This was indeed the crux of the question of planting Munster as of other colonies: to be successful it needed the transplantation of the

[1] *A.P.C.* XIV, 8–9.   [2] S.P. Dom. Eliz. 148, no. 42.

social structure men were accustomed to, with its dependence upon the gentry. It was not until Grenville turned his attention to Munster that Cornwall took a part in the plantation, a band of a hundred men following Grenville's lead into this new field of enterprise, so much nearer home than Virginia, but in the end no less heart-breaking.

Then too there was Grenville's place in the defence of the country to be filled in his absence: he commanded a body of 300 trained men, the forces of Stratton hundred. The deputy-lieutenants advertised the Council that

'Sir Richard Grenville now being ready to depart to the sea, hath signified unto us that he hath left the charge of the 300 men whereof he was by your Lordships appointed captain unto Digory Grenville, John Facey and John Bligh gent. his petty captains, and to his kinsman George Grenville as their captain, whom we do for the present necessity confirm and allow so to be, until it shall please your lordships otherwise to direct.'

Before leaving for whatever perils the new voyage might hold, Grenville put his affairs into order, executing a trust deed on 16 March to regulate the uses of his real estate and the succession thereto.[1] The trustees whom he appointed were Ralegh, Sir Arthur Basset, Sir Francis Godolphin; Henry Killigrew, Richard Bellew, his brother-in-law, John Hele and Christopher Harris; Thomas Docton and John Facey, gentlemen. His estates are set out in full: the mansion house and demesne lands of Stowe, the manor of Kilkhampton with all lands, tenements, hereditaments, etc., in the parishes of Kilkhampton, Stratton and Morwinstow; the manors of Wolston and Widemouth; the manor of Swanacott and lands in Week St. Mary; the manors of Bideford, Littleham and Lancras, with all lands in Devonshire; and the manor and island of Lundy.

All these were to be held by the trustees to the use of his wife after his death, so long as she remained unmarried, in recompense of the jointure she might claim. After her death, or second marriage, the trustees are to pay the debts, marriage of the daughters and performance of Grenville's will, and then the

[1] Granville, 124–7.

estate is to go to the use of Bernard, his son and heir, and in turn to the next heirs in carefully elaborated succession. On Dame Mary Grenville's marriage after his death, her interest in the premises determined, and she was to be paid an annuity of £200 per annum – a goodly sum, indicative perhaps of the jointure he obtained with her. Finally, it is provided that if Grenville at any time in his natural life, in person or by writing, demand of the trustees at the parish church of Kilkhampton the sum of £50,000 and is not paid, the above grant is then void and all the estates and rights in it shall stand to the only use and behalf of Grenville and his heirs. This sufficiently safeguarded himself; for £50,000 was out of all proportion to the value of his estate.

Having made his preparations, Grenville was ready to depart by the middle of April. It was already late. Ralegh had despatched a 'bark of aviso,' a small express-boat 'freighted with all manner of things in most plentiful manner for the supply and relief of his colony then remaining in Virginia: but before they set sail from England it was after Easter, so that our colony half despaired of the coming of any supply.' [1] By the time the bark reached Cape Hatteras, the colony had already been taken off by Drake; and after spending some time in seeking for them up in the country, the ship returned with all its provisions into England. A slight accident on leaving harbour at Bideford delayed Grenville a little further. We hear from the useful Philip Wyot, Town Clerk of Barnstaple, who kept a diary:

'16 April Sir Richard Grenville sailed over the bar with his fly-boat and frigate; but for want of sufficient water on the bar, being near upon the neap, he left his ship. This Sir Richard Grenville pretended [i.e. intended] his going to Wyngandecora, where he was last year.' [2]

The fly-boat and frigate were the *Roebuck* and the *Tiger*, each of 140 tons; it would seem that Grenville was sailing in the Span-

[1] v. the account of the Third Voyage, Hakluyt VIII, 346–8; cf. W. Strachey, *Historie of Travaile into Virginia* (Hakluyt Society), 149, and W. Stith, *History of Virginia* (New York 1865), 22.

[2] Chanter, *Literary History of Barnstaple*, 91.

ish prize, in which he had returned last year, and that being of much greater burden got stuck on the bar.

However, he arrived in Virginia fourteen or fifteen days after Ralegh's bark had departed;

'who not finding the aforesaid ship according to his expectation, nor hearing any names of our English colony there seated, and left by him anno 1585, himself travelling up into divers places of the country, as well to see if he could hear any news of the colony left there by him the year before, under the charge of Master Lane his deputy: but after some time spent therein, not hearing any news of them, and finding the places which they inhabited desolate, yet unwilling to loose the possession of the country which Englishmen had so long held: after good deliberation, he determined to leave some men behind to retain possession of the country: whereupon he landed fifteen men in the Isle of Roanoke, furnished plentifully with all manner of provisions for two years, and so departed for England.' [1]

It must have been a great disappointment to him and even more, matter for bewilderment. He cannot have known at this time that it was Drake who had taken off the colony and was even now bringing them home; nor, we may be sure, would it have contented Grenville any the more if he had known. The score against Drake was running up; later on we shall find an unmistakable indication that their personal relations were not good. On his way home, not long after this, we read, Grenville

'fell with the Isle of Açores, on some of which Islands he landed, and spoiled the towns of all such things as were worth carriage, where also he took divers Spaniards. With these and many other exploits done by him in this voyage, as well outward as homeward, he returned into England.'

This seems to have been his first landing in the Azores; no wonder his name afterwards aroused such terror among the islanders. It was out of this and similar experiences that the islanders conceived the great fear they had of him; and fear gave rise to the sort of stories reported by the Dutchman, van

[1] Hakluyt, VIII, 347–8.

Linschoten, who was in the Islands at the time of the last fight of the *Revenge*. There is, for example, the tale that everybody knows that 'while at dinner or supper, he would carouse three or four glasses of wine, and in a bravery take the glasses between his teeth and crash them in pieces and swallow them down, so that often times the blood ran out of his mouth without any harm at all unto him.' [1] All sixteenth-century people relished incredible tales of this sort: nor to them were they incredible; a later, more critical generation regards them, not so much as true, but as having their value in revealing the age no less than the man.

There is no need to extenuate or excuse Grenville's descent upon the Azores; it was now open war with Spain. The long period of doubt and hesitation, when it was neither war nor peace, was considered by the English seamen to have passed into war with Philip's arrest of the English cornships in Spanish ports in May 1585. Even Elizabeth regarded Drake's West Indies expedition as an act of retaliation; and in descending upon the Azores Grenville was following in his footsteps. We do not know what spoil he brought home with him, nor even when he arrived again in England.

On 2 June of this year, his daughter Mary was married to her cousin Arthur Tremayne of Collacombe.[2] It is unlikely that her father was present; after all, privateering was a more profitable occupation than even marrying one's daughters. Again, we do not know if the interesting entry that Wyot records in his Diary for December, means that Grenville kept the seas all the latter part of this year, or put out a second time; there may be a mistake simply in the month, when he says: 'In December this year Sir Richard Grenville came home bringing a prize with him, laden with sugar, ginger and hides.' [3]

These incursions into what he considered his own privileged sphere of the New World were watched with close attention by one great person in Europe, the King of Spain. To the English,

[1] *The Last Fight of the Revenge* (Arber's Reprints 1871): J. H. van Linschoten: 'The Fight and Cyclone at the Azores,' 91.
[2] Kilkhampton Parish Register.   [3] Chanter, 92.

Ralegh and Grenville's new country was Virginia, named so by
the Queen; to the Spaniards it was the northward extension of
their Florida. Sitting into the early hours at his writing-table in
the Escurial, endlessly annotating the reports from his agents
concerning his interests all over the known world, Philip was
astonishingly well-informed, if a little late. He knew very well
what was going on in England and had no desire to be involved
in war. From the days when he had reigned as King in England
– gone were the happy days when he could rely on the English
alliance to protect his sea-communications in the Channel –
from those days he had remembered a good deal of the political
life of the country and had taken trouble since to keep in touch
with innumerable Englishmen. But the new generation growing up he did not know. He would hardly have known a Drake,
who had only recently thrust himself into the forefront from
obscure beginnings; but neither did he know Grenville.

It so happened that when Grenville was at Plymouth in 1585
preparing for his first Virginia voyage, he pressed a German
captain into going with him. At some time this German con-
trived to remain behind in the West Indies, whence his account
of Drake's expedition was dispatched to the King. In July 1586
Philip wrote to Mendoza, now in Paris, urging him to send constant reports of what was happening in England, and take
occasion to note as regards the German who had recently arrived in Spain: 'I do not understand that he was a prisoner of
Drake's, but of him whom he mentions in his relation.' [1] This
was Grenville: evidently Philip had not yet heard of him.

On 7 August, Mendoza wrote a letter of information, which
must have crossed Philip's; he says:

'The ships of Richard Grenville, on board of which he (the
German captain) says he was pressed at Plymouth, are those
which I mentioned to your Majesty as soon as I came to France
were being fitted out by Ralegh, the Queen's favourite, to sail
for the coast of Florida; which voyage was under discussion for
two years before the ships left England as I informed your Majesty. The ship that this captain says was captured from Santo

---

[1] *Cal. S.P. Spanish 1580–6*, 591.

Domingo with so large a treasure in gold, silver, pearls, cochineal, ivory and hides, was one I advised your Majesty of months ago as having arrived in England, and that Ralegh himself had gone down to the port to take possession of her cargo and not to allow it to be distributed among the sailors.' [1]

Mendoza goes on to describe the way in which the English pirates undertook these long voyages to the West Indies, plundering ships on the way to provide them with victuals, or at least with goods to barter with the King's subjects there when short of stores. The voyages were evidently self-subsisting. In the Indies traffickers on shore even made fires at night in the creeks as a signal for them to come and take victuals in exchange for merchandise, which they give at a fair price. At this, Philip wrote in the margin, in his rapid, crabbed hand: 'Notice! I believe this is true. It will be advisable to have it remedied. Remind me.' Mendoza states that so long as this continued, there was no hope of extirpating the pirates; and that the King's officers had not acted with energy in this respect, as the German captain's Relation shows that in Porto Rico and Santo Domingo, Richard Grenville was offered victuals for money. He corrects the statement that 'General Grenville' had sailed with twenty-eight, and Hawkins with fifteen, of the Queen's ships: the Queen had not so many in all, and they were all in England on 20 July.

On 13 August, Mendoza sent the King a report of the sailing of Cavendish's expedition, with the design of getting to the East Indies through the Straits of Magellan, a design which, as we know, was brilliantly accomplished. He adds that

'news had arrived in England that Richard Grenville with seven ships had been captured by five of your Majesty; that the story went round that the Spaniards seeing the English superior in number pretended to take to flight; that the English gave chase and encountered separately were captured.' [2]

Mendoza had no certainty of the news, except that it was sent from England. The air was thick with such rumours; the inter-

---

[1] ibid. 599–600.   [2] ibid. 611.

est of this one is that it relates to Grenville's homeward voyage from Virginia via the Azores: the rumour curiously pre-figures what was to happen to him at no distant date in those very waters. But Philip had heard nothing of it, nor perhaps as yet of Grenville's descent upon the islands. He wrote upon the margin: 'I do not know what ships these could be. I do not believe it.' The point remains that Grenville's name was becoming known to the King: the account against him was mounting up in Spain.

From now on, with an open state of war at sea and in the Netherlands, and an invasion impending, the situation had very much worsened for Ralegh's hope of carrying through his plans for a colony to success. Moreover, both Ralegh and Grenville were exceedingly occupied in the work of concerting measures for the defence of the country against the approaching emergency, overseeing the defences, drilling the trained bands. They were both members of the small body of 'experienced captains' which was called into consultation by the government to consider and report on the defences of the Realm. Since the most exposed position, the western coast-line, was in their charge, they were both kept hard at work, particularly Grenville who was resident there. Nevertheless they continued to carry on with their Virginia enterprise, in spite of increasing difficulties and great losses in these years.

In 1587, 'intending to persevere in the planting of his country of Virginia,' Ralegh sent out a new expedition of three ships with 150 men under John White, as Governor.[1] They followed the old route to the West Indies and up the coast, but they were directed by Ralegh after making search at Roanoke for the fifteen men left there the previous year by Grenville, to make farther up the coast and plant their settlement in Chesapeake Bay. This last the master and sailors flatly refused to do, on the ground that the summer was too far spent;

'wherefore it booted not the Governor to contend with them, but passed to Roanoke, and the same night at sunset went

---

[1] Hakluyt VIII, 386–404.

The manner of their attire and
painting them selues when
they goe to their generall
huntings or at theire
Solemne feasts.

A NATIVE INDIAN OF VIRGINIA.

aland on the Island, in the place where our fifteen men were left; but we found none of them, nor any sign that they had been there, saving only we found the bones of one of those fifteen, which the savages had slain long before.'

Next day, John White and some of the company walked to the north end of the island, where Lane had built his fort and some dwelling-houses.

'When we came thither, we found the fort rased down, but all the houses standing unhurt, saving that the nether rooms of them and also of the fort, were overgrown with melons of divers sorts, and deer within them, feeding on those melons: so we returned to our company, without hope of ever seeing any of the fifteen men living.'

Nor did they ever see them.

At the isle of Croatoan, which being inhabited by Manteo's mother and kindred was ever friendly, they heard how the year before, the fifteen men Grenville had left on Roanoke had been set upon by a company of Indians from the mainland, men of Secoton and Aquascogoc with whom the hostile Wanchese and the remnant of Wingina's men kept company. The Indians had come suddenly out of the wood upon the houses where the Englishmen were living carelessly off their guard, killed one of them in a parley and drove the rest into a house which they set fire to. The English fought their way out to the water-side where their boat was, and retired to 'a little island on the right hand of an entrance into the harbour of Hatorask, where they remained a while, but afterwards departed, whither as yet we know not.' On 13 August, Manteo for his faithful service, was by Ralegh's commandment christened in Roanoke, and named Lord of the island. Five days later, a child was born to Eleanor, the Governor's daughter, and wife of Ananias Dare – the first English child to be born in America, and so they named her Virginia.

Soon after there arose disputes among the colonists as to who should be sent back to England for supplies; in the end they all settled upon Governor White. White allowed himself to be persuaded and set sail with two ships, leaving a hundred or so persons to form a plantation in his absence. There was some idea that they were to go fifty miles up-country to settle; it was all very vague, and in the event, the fate of the settlers equally so. Of all the attempts so far made, this should have been the most promising for a permanent settlement, since there was a proportion of women to accompany the men; instead, it was the most ignominious and its fate the most mysterious.

In spite of discouragements, on hearing White's plea for supplies, Ralegh appointed a pinnace forthwith with such necessaries as the colony was crying out for, and promising them

'a good supply of shipping and men with sufficiency of all things needful, which he intended, God willing, should be with them the summer following. Which pinnace and fleet were accordingly prepared in the west country at Bideford under the charge of Sir Richard Grenville.' [1]

This was now 1588: the country had entered the danger-zone of imminent invasion. It was hardly to be expected that Grenville, a leading captain, would be permitted to leave the country at such a moment; though after the insubordination displayed by the colonists under the leniency of White, it must have been evident to Ralegh that what was needed was the hard hand of Grenville.

The ships were got together at Bideford, by the usual time in April; they were probably the same three in which Grenville sailed in 1585 and 1586, with two pinnaces; or they may have been five in number: it is not certainly known. Just as they were about to sail, 'this fleet being now in a readiness only staying but for a fair wind to put to sea,' the news that the Armada was ready to sail came to England; practically all ships capable of fighting were stayed for service at home, 'and Sir Richard Grenville was personally commanded not to depart out of Cornwall.'

This was a serious situation for the stranded colonists in Virginia, if they, poor things, had known of it: 'the voyage for Vir-

---

[1] v. account in first edition of Hakluyt 1589, reprinted by R. P. Chope in *Trans. Devon. Assoc.*, 1917, 274–8.

ginia by these means for this year thus disappointed.' Governor White pleaded so earnestly with Ralegh and Grenville that he obtained two small pinnaces, one of 30 tons called the *Brave*, the other of 25 called the *Roe*, and departed with fifteen planters and their provision, with some relief for those that were wintering in the colony. But the relief never reached them. In the disturbed state of the seas in that year, it was too much to expect two heavily-armed if diminutive boats not to think of gain by the way rather than of distant relief. Their course from Bideford to Madeira was one of continual giving chase and being chased; one of them, after a disastrous fight with two much bigger French ships, in which she suffered very badly and was ransacked and spoiled of everything worth carrying away, staggered home at the end of May, anchoring 'between Lundy and Harting [Hartland] point near unto Chavell [Clovelly] Quay, where we rode until the next tide, and thence we put over the bar, and the same day landed at Bideford.' Some weeks later, the other pinnace from whom they had parted company, after similar experiences, also returned 'without performing our intended voyage for the relief of the planters in Virginia, which thereby were not a little distressed.' They were more than distressed, they were irretrievably lost.

Ralegh was by now so discouraged, and so taken up by other and more necessary work at home, that he was prepared to give over for the time; and with him Grenville. The former had spent, so he claimed, £40,000 on these enterprises. He made an agreement granting liberty to carry on the planting of Virginia to Thomas Smith, Governor White and a number of London merchants and adventurers. A curious relic of Grenville's arduous efforts at establishing the colony is to be found in the Parish Register of Bideford. An Indian whom he brought back with him on one of his two voyages was baptised in Bideford church on Sunday, 26 March 1588. He was given the name of Ralegh. It was just before Grenville hoped to go on his third voyage; and perhaps he intended to take the Indian back with him, like the faithful Manteo who had behaved with the utmost constancy to the English. But Grenville was to be disappointed; and next year the Indian died, and was buried in

Bideford churchyard on 7 April 1589. He is described in the Register as a native of Wynganditoia.

The London adventurers seemed in no great hurry to take up their appointed task – though we must remember the excitements and stress of these years 1588, 1589, 1590; so that it was not until the last of these years that John White departed once more from Plymouth with three ships for Virginia.[1] They made first for the West Indies and plunder, gaining considerable booty. Passing by Wokokon and Croatoan, they came to Hatteras, whence they descried smoke rising at the place in Roanoke where the colony had been left three years before. On landing, White found traces of their having been there; engraved upon a tree in 'fair Roman letters' he recognised the sign CRO which had been agreed when he left them should instruct him where to look for them on his return; if they were in distress a cross was to be carved over the letters.

Arrived at the settlement he found all the houses had been taken down and the place enclosed with a high palisade of great trees. On a post at the entrance there was again engraved the word CROATOAN, without any sign of distress. Within, various heavy pieces of iron and lead and sacre-shot had been thrown down and were now overgrown. Some of the sailors found traces of chests having been buried and again dug up. White went to the place,

'which was in the end of an old trench, made two years past by Captain Amadas: where we found five chests, that had been carefully hidden of the planters, and of the same chests three were my own; and about the place many of my things spoiled and broken, and my books torn from the covers, the frames of some of my pictures and maps rotten and spoiled with rain.'

White concluded that this had been done by the hostile Indians of the mainland, who had watched until the colony had departed for Croatoan and dug up wherever they suspected things to be buried; but he was 'greatly joyed' to find some certain token of the colony being safe at Croatoan.

Almost inexplicably, they never went there to seek them.

[1] Hakluyt VIII, 406–22.

Travelling about in the shallow waters of these sounds was always dangerous, and several accidents had already overtaken them. At last, when they came to depart for Croatoan, foul weather arose and their ship lost two of its anchors; frightened of the narrow escapes they had along these shoals, they put to sea intending to make again for the West Indies to winter there and return in the spring. It was only an excuse they made to themselves for their unforgivable behaviour; at sea they were forced to run before a westerly gale to the Azores and so made straight for England. No doubt it was the profits they had in hold and which they wanted to see safely home, which made them put to sea and shirk their duty to the colony.

No one knows, or will ever know, what happened to those hundred or so English men and women, who left for their last token that they were going to Croatoan. They must have been too many for the inhabitants of that island to support indefinitely; they may have left for the mainland and been set upon there. Or again, some of them giving up all hopes of rescue, may have been received into the Indian tribes. There is a tradition that remains that in the veins of some of these Indian tribes there flows the blood of white people; and that is all.

After this humiliating end to so many attempts, nothing more was done for twelve years. Grenville was killed; Ralegh turned his attention to the fabulous wealth of Guiana. In 1602 a voyage was made by Bartholomew Gosnold, who made a landfall much higher up the coast, at Cape Cod: it was 'the first that came in a direct course to America.' [1] Four years later there set sail the expedition which arrived in Chesapeake Bay, where Ralegh had directed White to plant his colony in 1587. Now, twenty years later, when Ralegh was a prisoner under attainder in the Tower, it was under other auspices that the first permanent settlement at Jamestown was made. But there can be no doubt who was the real founder of English rule in North America; a year before his fall, Ralegh had written, 'I shall yet live to see it an English nation.' In this work, Grenville had been his right hand.

[1] W. Stith, *History of Virginia*, 31.

CHAPTER XIV

THE ARMADA AND THE DEFENCE OF
THE WEST

WHEN at last the war came which so many had done their best to make inevitable, but which Elizabeth had always hoped to avoid, the country was by no means unprepared for it. The popular conception of an innocent defenceless isle, fighting with the aid of the Almighty against the overwhelming might and wickedness of Spain, is like most popular conceptions untrue – untrue in both its terms. The English chances in a war with Spain were very good; all the better for thirty years' careful husbanding of resources under Elizabeth. They were under-rated, certainly by the Spaniards, and by a good deal of contemporary opinion abroad; but not by those who were in the best position to know – the sea-captains. When the war actually came, English sea-power was at the highest level of efficiency it had yet attained; the great efforts made by Henry VIII reached their fruition and their reward under his daughter.

For years now, since the early seventies, Hawkins at the head of the Navy Board had worked unceasingly to equip the state with first-class fighting ships; when the test came, the seamen were as proud of them as Hawkins himself. 'The ships sit aground so strongly and are so staunch as if they were made of a whole tree,' wrote William Hawkins from Plymouth in February 1588 to his brother John, who had had the labour and anxiety of making them.[1] When the latter himself came down to Plymouth in July, to see the Queen's ships riding there, he wrote back to Burghley, 'the four great ships, the *Triumph*, the *Elizabeth Jonas*, the *Bear*, and the *Victory* are in most royal and perfect estate'; you could not tell that they have been at sea, he

---

[1] S.P. Dom. Eliz. 208, no. 72.

THE ARK ROYAL.

said, 'more than if they had ridden at Chatham.' [1] Yet they had been out sweeping the Channel and off the coast of Spain in all the gales and storms of that summer.

Spanish sea-power was at its height too in these years, when the maritime resources of Portugal had been joined to those of Spain. But the nature of that sea-power was different in its basis from the English; with Spain it depended upon the strictly regulated traffic with the Indies, it was shaped and controlled from the top downwards by the royal government – in the end by Philip's own command. In England, it had a healthier basis – the manifold and natural activities of the sea going on all round the busy English coasts. And when the crisis came, the English had the advantage of a numerous body of seamen all with their own individual experience of the sea, and, thanks to the disturbed conditions that had long prevailed, practised and skilful fighters. In this struggle, it was the English who were the professionals.

The sea, then, was England's front-line of defence – or offence – it came to the same thing. From 1585, when the embargo had been placed upon the English ships in Spain, there was a tightening up of the government's activity. As the full extent of the preparations in Spanish harbours became known, the English government came more into the open. In December 1586, Drake's cherished plan for a raid on these preparations, after the pattern of his West Indies raid the winter before, was sanctioned. He set sail from Plymouth in April 1587, and in two months, by his attack on the shipping in Cadiz harbour and his seizure of Cape St. Vincent, did a great deal of actual damage to Philip's preparations and disorganised the concentration of his fleets upon Lisbon. In consequence, the sailing of the Armada had to be postponed till next year, with all that meant in increasing the burden of upkeep and supplies. Nor were Drake and the seamen in favour of using the interval gained to stand on the defensive; they all without exception were in favour of making a great attack in force upon the Spanish coast before the Armada could get going. Elizabeth, however, was engrossed up till the last moment in negotiations

[1] ibid. 212, no. 61.

which she thought might yield a durable peace; not so engrossed, though, but that she kept the fleet ready in skeleton-formation, and continued to put the country in a state of defence on land.

We have already seen that on land, the state of military preparedness had been advancing for some years past. Each year now, musters of all the able men of the county were held throughout the southern and midland counties; a proportion of them were trained, and as far as the resources of the county allowed, they were armed, some with calivers and muskets, most with pikes, bills and bows. There was no professional army, though bands of English troops were becoming seasoned fighters in the Netherlands, in France and in Ireland. The training of the bands at home depended upon captains and gentlemen who had had some experience of war. In addition, in the last few years the Government had sent into each of the southern counties a professional soldier as muster-master, to be actually responsible for training. It was the counties along the south coast which were most exposed to the danger of invasion, and here to other duties was added that of inspecting all likely places of descent for the enemy, and as far as possible arranging for their defence. All this was especially Grenville's field; he was by origin a 'martial' man, not a sea-captain, and so accounted until the fame of his last commission at sea put out of mind his earlier life.

Devon and Cornwall were in the most exposed and dangerous position of all; and of these two, as Ralegh wrote a few years later, 'Devon may better spare men than Cornwall . . . which hath fewer men and is nearer the enemy.' [1] After all, the plan drawn up by the great Menendez in 1574 for an attack upon England, rested on a descent upon Falmouth. Grenville was given the especial charge of the oversight of Cornwall's defences.

We have to remember that, according to Wyot, he had just returned (December 1586) from sea with a prize. Among Burghley's memoranda of business relating to the defence of the

[1] Edwards, *Ralegh*, 11, 96.

country, we find in his notes on the situation in Devon and Cornwall:

'Sir Walter Ralegh to show all the force of the stannary and of the duchy to the Lieutenant's deputies. And that he also see the Musters and make report. Cornwall: the Lord Admiral to do the like. Sir Ric. Grenville, having charge of 300, gone to the seas.' [1]

By January, he was attending upon his duties as Justice of the Peace again ; for we find his name among those of the Justices who had assembled according to the Council's directions and taken order for supplying the markets with grain.[2] Nothing would be more disturbing to the morale of the country-side in time of war than the dearth of corn which was prevailing in the west. We find Grenville named, along with Richard Chamond and John Kempthorne, as responsible for collecting such grain as could be spared for distribution from the hundred of Stratton. Later the Sheriff wrote up to the Council: 'There is found a great scarcity within the country, but the people are very willing to do their best for the relief of their poor neighbours.'[3]

In February, the Council drafted its orders for putting in readiness the forces of the maritime counties.[4] The Deputy-Lieutenants were to call the bands together, and view them, supplying deficiencies in equipment; they were to repair to the sea-side, to view likely landing-places, to cover them with stakes and throw up ramparts. Ammunition would be supplied by the Queen, but they were not to use it for pleasure or it would be charged to them. Watch was to be kept on the beacons, according to the orders sent out in 1585. There were additional instructions 'because of the increasing danger of the times.' Grenville was already taking his part in these exercises, for we read in Wyot's Diary of a general muster at Barnstaple on 24 February,

'before my Lord of Bath, Sir Richard Grenville, Mr. Hugh Acland, and Mr. George Wyot, Justices, of all the able men

---

[1] S.P. Dom. Eliz. 185, no. 36.   [2] ibid. 197, no. 42.
[3] ibid. 199, no. 37.   [4] ibid. 198, no. 63.

with a show of their arms and furniture of the hundreds of Braunton, Sherwell, and Fremington. And on Wednesday following the inhabitants of this town and parish mustered before the said Justices in the Church with a show of their arms and artillery.' [1]

Grenville was residing now at Bideford, for three days later he wrote a letter from there to Dr. Julius Caesar, the Judge of the Admiralty Court, concerning a prize which had come into his possession, a hulk of Amsterdam: we do not know whether it was the same he had brought in in December, or another brought in by one of his ships.[2] A factor of one Lemon had come into the West Country armed with a commission from the Court of Admiralty, to demand certain goods which he claimed to have proved before the Court. Grenville wrote with politic address to the Judge:

'Good Mr. Doctor, I do understand by my servant and others how troublesome some causes which partly concern me have been unto you, and withal your good will professed towards me, for the which albeit hitherto I have not been so grateful unto you as I should, yet in the end I trust to be found neither unmindful nor unthankful to so good a friend.'

With this polite introduction, signifying what previous encounters in the Court of Admiralty we do not know, Grenville goes on to claim that this Lemon is just a common dealer in such causes:

'upon some intelligence that he hath gotten that such a ship is come into my hands, and thereon at hap-hazard hath made some unjust proof of something as by his factor's instructions appeareth; for neither knoweth he the just quantity of the goods, nor the prices, by which means he is inforced to send to his master to understand the same, (as I doubt not but his master hath since sent into Holland to have the promotion of this cause).'

[1] Chanter, *Literary History of Barnstaple*, 93.
[2] Lansdowne MSS. 158, 48.

He then maintains that the goods belonged to Spanish Flemings and had been consigned to liegers in Spain, 'which cause I think the States relinquishing the government and their subjection to the King of Spain, would never allow of.' Besides, the goods were contraband: there was 'some good proportion of victual for the Spanish Fleet, as butter, bacon, cheese, whereby it may appear unto all men that these goods do rather belong to such as are wholly Spanish than any way assured to this estate.' Nevertheless, because of the favourable letters they had obtained from the Lord Admiral, he says that he is willing to deal with Lemon in the matter, but that

'the ship being taken by some of my company, that account hath never come to my sight which Lemon demandeth. And that which hath come hath been so spoiled with wet and other sea accidents, as it amounteth not by far to that quality and quantity, that is imagined; and you know how hardly such a company as men in like actions must use at sea will be kept from spoil of such things as come to their fingers.'

So concluding, he asks the Judge to give him 'that favour that a true English subject to Her Majesty and his country shall deserve.'

It is, as usual, a plausible case that Grenville makes out; but reading between the lines, one suspects that his case in law was not a good one and that the Admiralty Court had declared against him. To give a decision, however, and to get it executed were two different things. The Court was at its wits' ends in these years to hold the balance fairly between English subjects and neutral traders. We do not know in this case whether Grenville succeeded in getting away with it; what is more important is to observe that the ships with which he would have made another voyage to Virginia are engaged this winter in privateering.

Another voyage was out of the question this year, he was so fully occupied in carrying out the government's orders for preparing the defences in the west. In March he was given the special charge of surveying and reporting on the places of descent in both Devon and Cornwall, and giving his opinion on the measures to be taken to prevent the enemy's landing. To this the Council later added the instructions that

'before his coming up he should also take a view of the trained bands of the said two counties, and of their armour and furniture; and to see them mustered and exercised in his presence, to the end he may be able to bring a true and sound report as of the choice of the persons and the sufficiency of their armour, as also of the profit they have made by the exercise of training in the use of the several weapons they are appointed unto, and of such defects as he shall find in their persons, furniture or skill, that order may be taken for repairing of the same.'

Orders were at the same time sent to the Earl of Bath, Lord Lieutenant of Devon and to the Deputy Lieutenants of Cornwall, to assist Grenville 'in the execution of his charge that is laid upon him, wherein her Highness wisheth as great expedition to be used as may be, for that she very earnestly desireth to be truly informed of the state of that country.' [1]

The work must have taken some months, and its impulse went right on through the year. It is to this that we owe the certificates of musters, the abstracts, the returns from the western counties that are so frequent among the State Papers this year. They make dry reading; yet it is not difficult to capture the atmosphere from these scraps of paper – the living urgency, the immediacy of the hour speaks in them no less than in the winged words of a Drake. It was the habit of Tudor government to expect the localities to provide for and look after themselves; but in this emergency the Government sent down a certain provision of powder and shot and ordnance: for Devon 7,200 lb. each of powder and lead, and half as much for Cornwall. [2] Of ordnance, each county received two sacres, two minions, and two falcons, which were to be mounted; together with a proportion of match, and all necessaries for the cannon. Certificates of the musters were delivered to Grenville to be handed on by him to the Council; possible landing-places were viewed by

[1] *A.P.C. 1586–7*, 370–1; v. also *Hist. MSS. Com., Foljambe Papers*, 22; S.P. Dom. Eliz. 199, no. 19.
[2] S.P. Dom. Eliz. 198, no. 43; 203, no. 17.

him, and the Council's instructions to the Deputy-Lieutenants to confer with him for the trenching of these places carried out.[1] In June the certificate of the Cornish musters was complete – it is worth noting that the returns were more fully and perfectly made from Cornwall than from Devon or Somerset – doubtless there was a greater feeling of urgency where the fear of invasion was greatest. The Cornish certificate returns some 1,600 men as trained; they were divided into six divisions, each under its captain: Grenville himself stands at the head of one of the larger divisions of 300 men.[2]

There are few traces of other activities than this, doubtless so much of his time was taken by his charge. But in April we find the Council writing to him 'for the release of the two French men,' probably two ships which had either been stayed by him in port or else brought in by his own company;[3] and in May we find a Devonshire gentleman, James Woodley of Ilsington, who had been bound over by him, making appearance before the Council – probably for some failure to do his duty as regards defence.[4] About this time too, at the christening of the Earl of Bath's son, Grenville stood as godfather for the Lord Chancellor, Sir William Mohun for the Earl of Essex and Lady Denys for the old Countess of Bedford.[5] With the summer there comes a lull; the preliminary work of surveying and organising having been tackled, exercises and training follow and then the harvest. It was now the turn of the seamen.

Drake had been at Plymouth through the winter, organising his expedition for the attack on the preparations in Spanish ports. He was on tenterhooks lest the Queen's permission given in December should be withdrawn before he had sailed. But the revelation of the Babington Plot and the decision to bring Mary Queen of Scots to execution kept the Government firm upon its course; while the news of Mary's death steeled Philip's resolution and determined him upon the invasion of England. Drake had collected a force of some twenty-three ships, to

---

[1] ibid. 199, no. 76. [2] ibid. 202, no. 37.
[3] ibid. 205, no. 28. [4] *A.P.C. 1587–8*, 64.
[5] Wyot's Diary, p. 15 (in Chanter, *Lit. Histy. Barnstaple*).

which the Queen, the Lord Admiral, himself and the West Country ports contributed. On the day of his leaving harbour, 2 April, he wrote from the *Elizabeth Bonaventure* to Walsingham:

'there was never more likely in any fleet of a more loving agreement than we hope the one of the other, I thank God . . . If your honour did now see the fleet under sail and knew with what resolution men's minds do enter into this action, so you would judge a small force would not divide them. Each wind commands me away, our ship is under sail, God grant we may so live in his fear as the enemy may have cause to say that God doth fight for her Majesty as well abroad as at home, and give her long and happy life and ever victory against God's enemies and her Majesty's.' [1]

This was the spirit in which the famous exploit, 'the singeing of the King of Spain's beard,' was carried through. Drake made straight for Cadiz, where he arrived in the Road on 19 April, ran his ships into the harbour beneath the fortifications on either side, and wreaked destruction upon all the shipping gathered in the outer harbour in preparation for the invasion of England. A great Biscayan of 1,200 tons, a galleon of the Marquis of Santa Cruz of 1,500 tons and 30 lesser ships were all burnt. The extent of Philip's preparations was a revelation: 'the like preparation,' Drake wrote home, 'was never heard of nor known as the King of Spain hath and daily maketh to invade England.' [2] Thanks to Drake the invasion had to be postponed till next year. Lisbon proved too strong to be assaulted with his present forces, but he took possession of Sagres and St. Vincent, and from this vantage-point disorganised the Spanish attempts to concentrate their forces. Making for the Azores, he there captured a great East Indiaman, the *San Felipe* – the richest prize that had yet been brought to England, with which he more than covered the costs of the expedition. On 26 June he arrived back again in Plymouth Sound.

When Drake's report of the immense character of the preparations in Spain reached England, it appears that the Government considered sending out reinforcements to him to en-

[1] S.P. Dom. Eliz. 200, no. 2.   [2] ibid. no. 42.

able him to continue the good work of holding them up. The Spanish intelligence from England early in June was that four of the Queen's ships guarding the west end of the Channel, and her armed merchantmen of the West Country ports, were to be sent out to him. But 'it was uncertain whether they would be commanded by Grenville, a gentleman who has been sailing as a pirate, or Frobisher, who they thought would agree with Drake better than the other.' [1] This is extremely interesting news, and this is the only source in which it appears: it may be that this is what accounts for our lack of information regarding Grenville's whereabouts this summer. It is still more interesting, if the Government contemplated appointing Grenville to lead a squadron to reinforce Drake, to know that it was common information that their personal relations were difficult, so that it was doubtful whether Grenville would serve under Drake.

Mendoza's information to Philip towards the end of the month, while Drake was still at sea, was even more positive on this point.

'It was proposed in the Council,' he writes, 'that Grenville, a gentleman who has always sailed with pirates, should command the squadron, but it was objected that he would not serve under Drake, and it was necessary to send some person who would not raise questions but would obey Drake unreservedly, and it was therefore thought that Frobisher would be put into command.' [2]

This is specific enough, whatever the Government's plans might be as regards the reinforcement. Grenville indeed had no reason to love Drake, who had stolen his laurels with the voyage into the Pacific in 1577, and had adversely interfered with his Virginia projects in bringing home the colonists in 1586. It is true that there is no evidence of an open quarrel; there is, instead, the very suspicious absence of any reference on either side to the other. We may presume at least a coldness in their relations; and with the family pride of the Grenvilles which must have made Grenville regard Drake as a parvenu, we may be sure that the Spanish information that he would not serve under him, was correct.

[1] *Cal. S.P. Spanish, 1587–1603*, 93.   [2] ibid. 110.

By the end of the year the government felt that the invasion was inevitable, and full plans for defence were set in motion all over the country. To co-ordinate them and advise the government, a committee of 'noble and experienced captains' was appointed to report on 'such means as are considered to be fittest to put the forces of the Realm of England in order to withstand an invasion pretended [i.e. intended] by the King of Spain.' [1] Members of the Committee were Lord Grey, the Lord Deputy of Ireland under whom Ralegh had served, Ralegh himself, Sir Francis Knollys, Sir Thomas Leighton, Sir John Norris, Sir Richard Bingham, Sir Roger Williams, Ralph Lane and Grenville. At the end of November it presented a report, which was a fully drawn scheme for the land defences of the realm. In December, the Spanish intelligence service reported that feverish preparations were being made; that the Earls of Cumberland and Huntingdon were being sent to the North, Sir John Norris to Milford Haven, Grenville to Plymouth and Ralegh into Cornwall.[2]

Ralegh was at Exeter on 21 December, when he reported to Burghley that he had

'attended the Earl of Bath and conferred with the deputies of Devon and Cornwall for the drawing together of 2,000 foot and 200 horse, and I find great differences of opinion among them. Some are of opinion that this burden will be grievous unto the country standing at this time void of all traffic, the subsidy not being yet gathered and the past musters having been very chargeable. Sir John Gilbert, Sir Richard Grenville and the Earl himself being more zealous both in religion and her Majesty's service, who have always found a ready disposition in their divisions and willingness to bear whatsoever shall be thought meet for her Majesty's service by their people, are of opinion that the matter and service will be very feasible.' [3]

It appears that some of the Commissioners for Devonshire were 'vehemently malcontent,' while the citizens of Exeter refused to

---

[1] q. from Harleian MSS. 168, by R. P. Chope, *Trans. Devon. Assoc.*, *1917*, 255–6.

[2] *Cal. S.P. Spanish 1587–1603*, 174. [3] S.P. Dom. Eliz. 206, no. 40.

bear the part thought meet by the Deputy-Lieutenants of Devon. Ralegh wrote that he was now ready to repair into Cornwall with all diligence to perform the commands laid upon him.

It seems that the plan that was under consideration was for the drawing together of a western army, to concentrate upon whichever of the ports the Spaniards attacked. The view was held that Plymouth was the likeliest of all, for the Spaniards would not care to engage 'too far within the Sleeve [i.e. the Channel] before he have mastered some one good harbour, of which Plymouth is the nearest to Spain.' [1] It was arranged therefore that if Plymouth should be attacked, 6,000 trained men of the western counties should converge upon it for its defence; and some similar proportion for Falmouth in like case. It was also recommended that some one person should be appointed to the head of the western forces in both Devon and Cornwall, where there were ten Deputy-Lieutenants in all, 'so that there may be no straining of courtesy, lest there be confusion and delay to the advantage of the enemy.' By April, the certificates of musters, as the result of the work put in, were able to show much fuller returns: Devonshire had a total of 10,000 able men, of whom 6,200 were furnished with some sort of weapon; of these 3,650 were trained, and 2,550 untrained. [2] Cornwall could show some 5,776 able men all told, of whom 3,600 were furnished, 1,500 were trained and 2,100 untrained. The larger totals of 10,000 and 5,776 respectively represented all the men of fighting age, between sixteen and sixty, in the two counties.

Meanwhile, since returning from Spain, Drake had remained at Plymouth with the nucleus of a fleet; his task was to keep watch on movements in the Spanish ports, and as the time of invasion drew near to collect the contingents of ships from all the ports of the West Country under his command. Grenville, having performed his especial charge, was at Bideford fitting out his ships for the voyage with which he intended to relieve and supply the colony which had been planted the previous

[1] ibid. 209, nos. 49 and 51.
[2] ibid. 210, no. 42; and Harleian MSS. 286, 92.

year under the command of John White. A rumour that Grenville's ships were to be used upon some service of the Queen reached Mendoza in Paris at the end of February; for he wrote on the 28th to Philip that

'the Queen had ordered Grenville (an Englishman who, as I have informed your Majesty, has several times gone on plundering voyages, and was lately on the coast of Spain) to remain with twenty merchantmen and pirate ships on the English coast opposite Ireland.' [1]

The news had not lost anything in the telling, nor was it exact; however, there was something in it.

We hear further too, if belatedly, of the Spaniards whom Grenville took in the prize near the Bermudas on his way home from Virginia in 1585. For two Spanish prisoners in England at this time, writing to Mendoza, suggest that one James Lomas, an English merchant in Seville,

'be held for the liberty of the poor pilots who were captured by Richard Grenville of Cornwall, and are now held prisoners by him. He is a pirate; and brought to England twenty-two Spaniards whom he treated as slaves, making them carry stones on their backs all day for some building operations of his, and chaining them up all night. Twenty of them have died or escaped, but he still keeps the two pilots.' [2]

To a Spaniard, all the English seamen were pirates; they made no distinction between piracy and privateering, especially when the latter was directed against Spain. We know no more of this episode, nor even whether the information of these two Spaniards was accurate. It would be interesting to know what building operations of Grenville's these were – probably at Bideford if anywhere. It is always the misdeeds of the other side that arouse men's moral indignation; it is not likely that the Spanish gentlemen would have been roused to protest by the spectacle of the English prisoners serving in the galleys.

On the last day of March, an embargo was placed on all

[1] *Cal. S.P. Spanish, 1587–1603*, 223.　　　　[2] ibid. 220.

shipping throughout the kingdom; and the Council wrote a special letter to Grenville, saying that

'whereas he hath seven or eight ships and pinnaces ready for a voyage he intendeth to make to some part of the West Indies; forasmuch as her Majesty doth receive daily advertisement of the preparations of the King of Spain to increase, whereupon it is also thought necessary her navies on the seas should be reinforced and strengthened, and to that end order is given both for the stay of all ships in all the port towns of the Realm, and to the said towns to furnish a certain number of vessels etc.; he is also straightway charged and commanded in her Majesty's name and upon his allegiance to forbear to go his intended voyage, and to give the ships so by him prepared to be in readiness to join with her Majesty's Navy as he shall be directed hereafter.' [1]

Grenville's ships, as we saw, were already at this time in readiness for his voyage, 'only staying but for a fair wind to put to sea.' Without a word he complied and wrote to inform the Council of his intention to 'repair unto the Cape of Cornwall or the Scillies for commodity of wind, to be better able upon any occasion to repair where most use might be of his service.' There was no use in being caught on the north coast of Devon, with the Armada in full sail up the Channel.[2]

It may be supposed that beneath this ready compliance, Grenville may have hoped to keep his ships together under his own command and to perform his service at sea. But it was not to be: his services were more urgently required on land. The Council approved of his plan, but directed him

'to send presently unto Sir Francis Drake such ships as were of greatest burden and fittest for service according unto such direction as he should receive from him, the others of less burden, and such as Sir Francis should not think fit to be retained, he might dispose of and employ in his intended voyage as he should think good.'

Since Grenville's ships were already victualled for many months, Mr. Darrell, who was in charge of the victualling of the Navy

[1] *A.P.C. 1588*, 7–8.　　　　　　　　　　　　　[2] ibid. 27.

in the west, was to come to an arrangement with him for payment.

'Moreover, Her Majesty considering the danger of this present time and his knowledge and experience in martial affairs, did think it convenient he himself should remain in those parts where he now was, to give his assistance and advice to the Lieutenants of Cornwall and Devon.'

A letter was sent to Drake informing him of this recruitment to his forces.

Grenville's conduct, regarding only the service of the state and sacrificing his own projects and interests, was in marked contrast to Sir John Gilbert's. In spite of the embargo, and Drake's command, Gilbert had allowed a large ship of his, of great burden and fit for service, to depart out of the Realm, and 'in a letter of his did seem little to regard the authority of the said Sir Francis.' [1] Such were the difficulties of co-ordinating defence in the conditions of Elizabethan individualism. Gilbert was severely reprimanded by the Council. Grenville's ships, according to the Council, were seven or eight in number; at the end of April, as we saw, two small pinnaces, the *Brave* and the *Roe*, were detached for John White to take a supply to Virginia. Wyot's Diary tells us that 'five ships went over the bar to join Sir Francis Drake at Plymouth.' [2] Grenville was still at Bideford on 17 April, for on that day John Hender, a messenger, was paid a shilling 'to run to Bideford with post letters to Sir Richard Grenville that came from Sessions,' probably at Stratton. [3]

Soon after this he set sail, joining forces with the Bristol squadron on the way, for they had arrived together at Plymouth by 12 May. Captains Fenner and Crosse wrote to report to Drake then in London: 'Here are arrived all the ships from Bristol and all the west parts, with Sir Richard Grenville and Mr. St. Leger, for which two we pray your consideration in moneys they demand for victual.' [4] Grenville certainly remained with his

[1] *A.P.C. 1588*, 17.   [2] Chanter, 94.
[3] Goulding, *Records of Blanchminster's Charity*, p. 72.
[4] S.P. Dom. Eliz. 210, no. 17.

little squadron at Plymouth till the end of May, by which time Drake had returned and the Lord Admiral himself had arrived with the main body of the Queen's ships; for Howard writes to Burghley on 28 May, complaining that the fleet has only eighteen days' victual left and they must not tarry,

'for even this morning Mr. Cary, the sheriff of Devonshire, and Sir Ric. Grenville have brought me word of a bark that is newly come from the South Cape [i.e. St. Vincent] and was there within these seven days and did take two or three fishermen of that place who told them that the Spanish fleet was to come out with the first fair wind.' [1]

Of the ships which Grenville brought round to Plymouth to serve under Drake, three were his own: the galleon *Dudley* of 250 tons, the *Virgin God Save Her* of 200 tons and the *Tiger*.[2] The first, which was the largest, may be identified with the Spanish prize that Grenville took on his way home from Virginia in 1585. Against the Armada she was now commanded by James Erisey, Grenville's cousin, who had previously commanded the *White Lion* in Drake's West Indies expedition of two years before. The *God Save Her* had for her captain John Grenville, Grenville's second son, who died on Ralegh's Guiana Voyage in 1595. In addition to these three, there were the bark *St. Leger*, commanded by Sir John St. Leger's son; and the *Golden Hind*, which was the first to bring the news of the Armada's approach.

Grenville returned to Stowe, while the fleet at Plymouth passed these months in an agony of expectation. The seamen were all in favour of a descent upon Spain, seeking out the Spanish fleet and destroying it before it could set sail. Drake had written to the Queen in April:

'The advantage of time and place in all martial actions is half a victory, which being lost is irrecoverable, wherefore if your Majesty will command me away, with those ships that are here

[1] ibid. no. 35.
[2] ibid. 216, no. 54; 237, f. 15; and cf. Chope, *Trans. Devon. Assoc.*, 265–9.

already and the rest to follow with all possible expedition, I hold it in my poor opinion the surest and best course.' [1]

It was not adopted: Elizabeth took the peace negotiations with Parma in the Netherlands seriously and did not want to prejudice their chances. As it happened too, the defensive waiting policy was usually the best in sixteenth-century conditions: they had so much less command then over external forces and conditions that whichever side put forth an aggressive effort on a large scale exposed himself to far greater risk of losses.

The long delay, due mainly to the storms of this summer, ate into the English provisions and put a great strain upon the government's resources to victual such a large body of ships and men. The Lord Admiral wrote at the end of May: 'God send the wind to serve to put us out, for I believe surely if the wind hold here but six days they will knock at our door.' [2] The spirit in the fleet was excellent. Howard scribbled in his own fist a postscript to his secretary's letter to Burghley, saying, 'My good Lord, there is here the gallantest company of captains, soldiers and mariners that I think ever was seen in England. It were pity they should lack meat, when they are so desirous to spend their lives in her Majesty's service.' [3] He concludes with a little joke against the landsmen, knowing full well how much Burghley was in favour of negotiating peace: 'God send us the happiness to meet with them before our men on the land discover them; for I fear me a little sight of the enemy will fear the land men much.'

Then in the middle of June, a storm swept down upon the Channel. Howard wrote to Walsingham:

'Sir, we have endured these three days, Wednesday, Thursday and Friday, an extreme continual storm. Myself and four or five of the greatest ships have ridden it out in the Sound, because we had no room in Cattewater for the lesser ships that were there; nor betwixt the shore and the Island, because Sir Francis Drake with some four or five other ships did ride there. Myself and my company in these ships do continually tarry and

---

[1] S.P. Dom. Eliz. 209, no. 89.   [2] ibid. 210, no. 35.
[3] ibid. no. 36.

lie aboard in all the storm, where we may compare that we have danced as lustily as the gallantest dancers in the Court.'

Still the victuals have not come, and the ships are running short; 'and if it do not come, yet assure yourself we will not lose any opportunity nor we will not lack; there is good fishing in the seas.' [1]

At the end of June, word came that the Spanish Fleet was on the way: Sir Francis Godolphin wrote to say that a little bark of Mousehole had encountered nine sail of great ships at the entrance of the Channel.[2] At the same time, a new supply of provisions came for the fleet, and, writes Howard, 'we will not eat nor sleep till it be aboard us. We must not lose an hour of time.' [3] Ralegh, meanwhile, had taken steps with the land forces for a body of 2,000 foot, and 200 pioneers for incamping, to march from Cornwall to the royal camp upon invasion; 'and if I shall not be commanded down myself, I have thought good to direct Sir Ric. Grenville to have the conduction of this regiment to bring them to the camp.' [4]

But they were not needed: the Spanish ships, an advance division of the Armada, were driven back to Spain by the storms which raged this unnatural June. The English fleet disposed itself in three divisions across the entrance of the Channel, between Scilly and Ushant, to keep watch. For a moment at the beginning of July, the wind was favourable for a descent upon Spain; then it changed to south-west again. There was no hope now of a preventive attack on the Armada; there was nothing for it but to await its arrival. On land, the Deputy-Lieutenants of Cornwall, with Grenville at their head, speeded up their precautions and screwed an increase out of the exiguous resources of the county in horse and weapons. They reported to Ralegh that they had 'dealt with the gentlemen of the best sort, whom we find very willing to increase their proportion to the uttermost of their powers'; but they cannot equip themselves 'with such speed as is requisite, because there is not armour to be bought here for money.' [5] But they had raised the number of

[1] ibid. 211, no. 18.   [2] ibid. no. 47.   [3] ibid. no. 51.
    [4] ibid. no. 90.   [5] ibid. 212, no. 22.

horsemen, and taken order for the little army of 2,000 men to be ready to march when the word was given.

Then at the end of July the Armada was suddenly there. Some fifty sail were first descried off the Scilly Islands, where they waited for the rest to come up; on Friday 19 July, the whole fleet was off the Lizard, 120 sail in all, moving up-Channel in a half-moon formation, the great ships flying their flags with the red cross – the crusade for the conversion of England. All day and night before, the English fleet had been getting their last supply of provisions on board; so great was the haste that not all the ships were fully victualled; when at night, the wind being against them, they warped out under the lee of Mount Edgcumbe and Rame Head, and on Saturday afternoon at three o'clock came in full view of the Armada. That evening and through the night they continued tacking along the Cornish coast, and on Sunday morning, having gained advantage of the wind, they began the running fight which continued off and on all that week up the Channel.

'Sir, for the love of God and our country let us have with some speed some great shot sent us of all bigness, for this service will continue long, and some powder with it': so wrote Howard to Walsingham on 21 July, when the fleet had come up thwart of Plymouth again.[1] The good citizens of Plymouth could see the splendid but dangerous spectacle out beyond the Sound:

'Our last intelligence we gave to your Lordships,' wrote the Mayor, William Hawkins, to the Council, 'was that the Spanish fleet was in view of this town yesternight and that my Lord Admiral was passed to the sea before our said view and was out of our sight. Since which time we have certain knowledge both by certain pinnaces come from his Lordship as also by plain view this present morning, that my Lord being to the windwards of the enemy are in fight, which we beheld.'[2]

The Mayor kept sending out such reinforcements of men as came in from town and country as the fight went on off the coast. The alarm was given throughout the country from the west.

[1] S.P. Dom. Eliz. no. 80.   [2] ibid. no. 81.

Though nothing survives from Grenville to tell us where he was and what he was doing at this moment of crisis, there are traces, footmarks as it were, to reveal the agitation. In the records of Blanchminster's charity at Stratton, there appear these tell-tale entries:

to Harry Juell the 21 July to run to Stowe with a letter in post haste for her majesty's service	iijd.
to Richard Juell of Launceston (with five others) for their horses to go in post to Launceston for Sir Richard Grenville to ride to Plymouth when the Spaniards were come to Plymouth, viijd. for every horse	iiijs.
to John Short for his horse to carry the victuals the same time	viijd.
to Thomas Juell Cordener for his horse to carry the armour to Launceston for the same time viijd; provender for the said horses at Launceston xd; for setting 3 new shoes unto them ixd; for John Juell's labour to go to Launceston to fetch back the same post horses & for going to Stowe with a post letter	xiijd.
paid to Jasper Bedlime the same night to warn the parish that they should be ready at an hour's warning	iijd.[1]

These are but diminutive and unimportant relics of the agitation of that night when the news of the Armada came to one remote Cornish parish: how many thousands in all the parishes of the West Country must have passed that night with their harness, their bills and pikes ready at hand in case the call came!

But in the event it was not needed. The turning-point came with Howard's successfully warping out of Plymouth Sound and gaining the wind of the Armada: had he not done so, the fleet might have been caught bottled up in harbour and no one can tell the consequences. As it was, the Armada passed on up-Channel – the danger to Plymouth was removed by the time Grenville got there; the great fleet sailed on its course to the rendezvous off Calais, the fire-ships, the storms of the North

---

[1] q. by Chope from Goulding, *Records of Blanchminster's Charity*, 73.

Sea and to the wreck of Philip's hopes upon the cruel shores of Ireland.

Throughout August, the levies were kept up throughout the southern counties; but at the end of the month, the danger having passed, Howard and Drake discharged the volunteer ships from the western ports. They asked for payment to be made for Grenville's ships which had been 'taken into service by Sir Francis Drake then over and above his warrant, yet by order from the Council, as Sir Richard Grenville and he hath to show.' [1]

The Council could not be sure that all danger had passed from the quarter of Ireland: it was known that a number of Spanish ships were upon that coast and that numbers of Spaniards were landing. It was decided to send a small force into Ireland, to stay shipping upon the north coast of Devon and Cornwall to transport it, and to form a small squadron to keep a look out in the Irish Channel. Grenville was chosen for the service. The Queen wrote him on 14 September:

'We require you that upon the north coast of Devon and Cornwall towards Severn, you make stay of all shipping meet to transport soldiers to Waterford, and to give charge that the same ships be made ready with masters, mariners and all other maritime provisions needful; so as upon the next warning given from us or from our Council they may be ready to receive our said soldiers, which shall be 300 out of Cornwall and Devon, and 400 out of Gloucester and Somersetshire. We have also some other further intention to use your service in Ireland with these ships aforesaid, whereof Sir Walter Ralegh, Knight, whom we have acquainted therewith, shall inform you; who also hath a disposition for our service to pass into Ireland, either with these forces or before that they shall depart.' [2]

---

[1] The month before, Howard and Hawkins had sent up an estimate of charges for eight ships of this little squadron, mostly Grenville's: 700 men in all for four months, which would amount to £1,960, and for the tonnage of the ships, 800 tons in all, £320. Laughton, *The Defeat of the Spanish Armada*, 11, 163.

[2] S.P. Dom. Eliz. 216, no. 24.

This document is a draft in Burghley's hand, but it has the Queen's signature at the top and the commission went forth.

Next day the Council wrote to Ralegh recommending him to see that the hundred soldiers appointed out of Cornwall for Ireland were well chosen and their officers able and well disposed, and to help Grenville to stay shipping in Devon and Cornwall and in transporting 700 soldiers to Ireland upon intelligence that they were needed there. 'The ships shall be under the leading of Sir Richard Grenville to use them as he informed to destroy the Spaniards' ships, wherein he is required to assist him.'[1] Grenville's device, it seems, was the same that Drake had used so successfully off Calais, to send in a number of fire-ships among the Spaniards; for the Mayor of Bristol was ordered to make provision of fifty barrels of tar, with brimstone, pitch and pitch-boards and 'to deliver the things above mentioned to such as Sir Richard Grenville shall appoint to receive the same.'[2] A general Warrant was issued to all officers to aid and assist Ralegh and Grenville in taking up such ships as they thought needful for the Irish service.[3] Three Queen's ships, the *Foresight*, the *Aid*, and the *Tiger* were allotted to this task, being ready victualled for 370 men for 14 days.

Ralegh and Grenville then kept the western seas with this little force, until all doubt about the capacity of the Spaniards to make a return blow was dispelled. A number of the finest ships of the Armada, some twenty in all, went on the rocks of the Irish coast in the storms of this stormy autumn, and with them there perished some thousands of men and many of the gallantest names among the chivalry of Spain. The remnants of the Armada – forty ships in all with the unfortunate Duke of Medina Sidonia intact – were in no condition but to struggle helplessly back to Spain, their crews dying in hundreds. In November, the last fears from Ireland removed, the Council gave orders for the stay of the western bands that were to have been dispatched there.[4]

So passed that year of crisis, the greatest in Elizabeth's reign, a determining point in the history of the English people. As we

[1] *A.P.C. 1588*, 277.   [2] ibid. 276.   [3] ibid. 278.
[4] ibid. 330–1.

have seen, Grenville played a not inconsiderable part at a danger-point in the English defences. It may have been a matter of disappointment to him that his rôle was not a more spectacular one – like Drake's on board the *Revenge* (for it was Drake's hour), or the Howards, or Ralegh who had rushed down to the coast to join the fleet – that after the Armada had passed by Plymouth, his chance had once more slipped by. If it were so, as it may well have been, no murmur of his disappointment escaped his lips.

CHAPTER XV

GRENVILLE IN IRELAND 1588-90:
THE PLANTATION OF MUNSTER

THE Irish service with which Grenville was charged in the autumn of 1588 brought him once more into direct contact with that field of plantation and colonisation in Munster, in which he had been an early, a too early pioneer, twenty years before. Then, the great Desmond power in the south of Ireland had been still unbroken; it was under a temporary eclipse, while the Earl, upon whom centred the devotion and the national aspirations of the native Irish, wore away his years in confinement in London. In the interval, after many years of partial resistance, semi-rebellion, reconciliations and lapses, that power had been broken; but not without four years of warfare on an extensive scale and of great savagery on both sides.

In November 1583, the last Earl of Desmond – the 'Earl Garrett of the Risings' of Irish Legend – driven to his last desperate lair in the woods of Ahurlow, in the extreme mountainous west, was killed by an Irish clansman. The wide and fertile spaces of Munster, after so much fighting and laying waste on both sides, were a scene of desolation. The orderly mind of the Devonshireman, John Hooker, was revolted by it:

'The curse of God was so great,' he wrote, 'and the land so barren, both of man and beast, that whosoever did travel from one end to the other of all Munster, even from Waterford to Smerwick, about six score miles, he should not meet man, woman or child, saving in cities or towns, nor yet see any beast, save foxes, wolves or other ravening beasts.' [1]

The English Government agreed that it was desirable to re-

---

[1] Hooker's Supplement to Holinshed's *Chronicle*, q. Edwards, *Ralegh* 1, 95.

people the province, as far as might be, with 'well-affected' English settlers; it turned to the gentry of the western counties to provide them. The appeal was not without its effect on Grenville, who had made a premature attempt in this direction in 1569 and must have kept in some contact with southern Ireland through his shipping interests and the port of Bideford; but for the time he was taken up by the Virginia project. Ralegh took an immediate interest in the scheme, in addition to Virginia, hoping to make a princely patrimony for himself in Ireland.

The scheme was to get a number of undertakers, gentlemen of substance, who would take up the lands escheated to the Crown by the treason of Desmond and his supporters. These lands were of enormous extent, but there were many difficulties in the way. A rough survey of Munster was made, and a seignory of 12,000 acres was fixed as the basis of a plantation. The younger sons of gentlemen and substantial yeomen were encouraged to take up leases under the undertakers, who were to provide English artisans and labourers. The scheme hung fire, partly because of the increasing tension in England due to the war, and partly because of the general uncertainty in Ireland regarding the titles to the land. The Irish took advantage of the delay to regain or take possession of the land, creeping back into the fertile lands from their mountains and bogs, welcoming the enforced peace after the horrors of the Desmond rebellion. All kinds of difficulties arose – the troubles that one famous undertaker, the poet Spenser, had with the Lord Roche are well known and typical.

In August 1588 the Government sent over Chief Justice Anderson with a commission to try out and settle all questions of title, and from then on the plantation began in earnest. Ralegh took up a large seignory in Waterford and Cork; with his usual energy he proceeded to settle English families upon it and set to work on the estate, introducing the potato from Virginia, developing the timber trade, building houses for himself at Lismore and Youghal. In the earlier lists of undertakers, Grenville's name does not appear; but Sir Warham St. Leger, who had gone back to Ireland in 1579 as provost-marshal of

Munster, was there to partner Grenville's interests. From a letter of St. Leger's to Walsingham in February 1588, it appears that already by then Grenville had got together a number of settlers for Munster. Though he was as determined as ever to establish the Virginia colony – we saw that on the eve of the Armada he had an expedition ready to sail – he doubtless felt that he could send over his settlers to St. Leger who would look after his interests in Ireland until such time as he was free to see to them himself.

St. Leger was claiming certain lands that had been mortgaged to him by 'the late wicked Earl of Desmond' – it was *de rigeur* among the English to refer to poor Desmond, the sport of fate and ineluctable circumstance if ever a man was, as 'the wicked Earl.' St. Leger's grant, like so many others, was being held up for legal reasons; a most grievous matter, he writes, since he has been put to the charge of £500 in furnishing himself and his company to go there, 'besides the preparation that Sir Richard Grenville and his friends hath bestowed in furnishing themselves to set down here with me.' [1] St. Leger had made over a half of his grant of Kerrycurrihy, the fertile country to the west and south of Cork, the scene of their previous unsuccessful experiment in settling. Grenville was a desirable, or even a necessary partner, having the greater ability to draw followers to settle in Ireland through his influence in the West Country.

By May 1589, Grenville had brought over 99 settlers and St. Leger 46; but as yet the lands which they were to hold as tenants had not been apportioned, because of the delay in making out their patent. The settlers meanwhile had been maintained to their great charges; 'and as many more we have in readiness in England to come over, upon understanding what lands we shall be able to assure them.' But they did not as yet know how many Irish were occupying the land, nor had it been decided how many of their claims to freehold were recognised, if any. Grenville returns that he had had the use of five ploughlands since midsummer 1588; and so far his stock there amounted to

[1] S.P. Ireland 133, no. 85.

'xx Irish kine, two English bulls, vII English rams, xII English oxen, four Irish oxen, one Irish bull, vII Irish caples [i.e. small horses], four English horses able to serve for light horsemen. I have no crops of corn nor able to till any as yet.'

Among the settlers who had accompanied Grenville, the chief were members of his own family circle. There was his second son John, who had fought in the *Virgin God Save Her* against the Armada; and there was his half-brother, John Arundell, who had accompanied him on the Virginia voyage in 1585. Then there were Christopher Harris of Radford, who later married Grenville's daughter Bridget; Thomas Stukeley, who may have been brother of the John who went on the 1585 voyage, and was Grenville's brother-in-law; John Bellew, another brother-in-law; John Facey who signed Grenville's family settlement as a witness in 1586. There were besides a number of farmers and labourers like the family of Cornish Teagues who formed part of St. Leger's following.

Grenville evidently spent the winter months of 1588–9, following straight upon the heels of his temporary service at sea, in Ireland. For St. Leger, who was very dissatisfied with the state of affairs in Munster and the delay in the final arrangements for the land-settlement, wrote to Walsingham on 20 January 1589: 'Sir Richard Grenville now departing hence to the Court of England . . . is so thoroughly able to inform you touching the estate of this Province, as I hold it superfluous to write thereof.' [1] A week later, St. Leger wrote to Burghley, requesting him to have some conference with Grenville regarding the former's proposals for preventing foreign invasion. St. Leger, who was not at all popular at Court because of his hostility to Ormonde, was now in the absence of the Vice-President in charge of Munster. At the same time, St. Leger took the opportunity of sending a letter to the Queen by Grenville as bearer, giving her an account of the situation in Munster, and inveighing against 'those who be undertakers in word and not in action.' [2]

Whether Grenville had an interview with Burghley we do not know; but at any rate his ideas on the situation reached him,

[1] S.P. Ireland, 140, no. 25. [2] ibid. no. 14.

for a draft of his 'Remembrances' exists, which was endorsed by Burghley.[1] Probably Grenville saw him, for it was Burghley's way to fix a conversation which he considered of importance by having it drafted in memorandum. Though it is incomplete, it is a statesmanlike document, combining the political realism of the Elizabethan with a genuine consideration of the course to improve conditions for the Irish no less than the English.

He recommended that the various fees which were chargeable by tribal custom upon the Irish and were a great burden, should be swept away; and in their place a revenue raised by an annual tax upon ploughlands and the sale of cattle. The lords of the countries should be made to let their lands to the Irish for fixed terms and rents 'by which means they shall be freed of the bondage and fear that now they be in under their lords, and so become more obedient to her majesty, they being by her majesty's laws made to enjoy the benefit of their labours.' Officers should be appointed to account for the Queen's profits, fines and other issues at assizes and sessions, and the hundred courts be kept as in England. All the ecclesiastical livings which never yet paid any dues to the Crown should be rated, and those livings, by far the majority, in which there were no ministers should be converted to the Queen's use until such time as they have inhabitants and ministers: these revenues would defray the cost of the President and garrison in Munster. Good care should be taken that each undertaker should have the full number of Englishmen resident on his seignory as he was bound. Finally, he recommended that the question of tenure between the freeholders' titles and the Queen's should be decided; until which time the undertakers could hardly be held responsible for not peopling their seignories.

It is clear that the remedies Grenville saw for the unsatisfactory state of affairs in Munster were first settlement and then assimilation to English conditions. Nor can it be denied that such assimilation would have been to the advantage of the poor Irish on the land, no less than to the incoming English. For the latter, Grenville's proposals were precisely such as to make their position strong, that they might live long in the land. He him-

[1] ibid. no. 16.

self took his part in the scheme with the utmost responsibility
– unlike such nominal undertakers as Sir Christopher Hatton,
who never came near the place, or Sir William Courtenay of
Powderham, who backed out at the commencement. Grenville
contemplated spending a number of years in the country getting
his seignory in order, building himself houses, equipping the
rich but ravaged land; and he saw how important it was that all
the undertakers equally should fulfil their responsibilities. It
was the fact that they did not that ruined the prospects of this
first plantation. It was as much an experiment in colonisation
as Virginia; but in the end, it was for Grenville and his family
no less of a disappointment.

Grenville's attitude on the problem is expressed even more
clearly in the letter which he wrote to Walsingham on 17 March
1589, recommending Nicholas Skiddy, one of that Cork family
which was ever loyal to the Crown and, it will be remembered,
had remained so in the Fitzmaurice Rising of 1569.[1] The letter
is dated from 'my poor house of Gilly abbey by Cork,' a ruined
Cistercian house just outside the walls of the city on the west;
Grenville had built a house within its precincts, repaired the
walls and made it his Irish residence. It is interesting to think
what would have happened if the Grenvilles had held on to
their very large Irish estates – Sir Richard was about to double
their extent. It would have been the Grenvilles who would have
become Earls of Cork, instead of the Boyles, possessors of an
enormous Anglo-Irish patrimony which would have entitled
them to a dukedom in the palmy days of the peerage in the
eighteenth century.

Grenville's letter recommends Skiddy for his honest disposition to the English Government, in relation to which he was in a
position to be notably useful; for he had married the sister of
Cormoke mac Dermod, the chieftain of the Muskerry country,
who was very loyal and willing to co-operate. Further, the chief
practises with his tenants and clansmen

'to draw them from their wandering and uncertain dwelling
[so shocking, and rightly, to an English gentleman used to the

---

[1] S.P. Ireland, 142, no. 53.

settled conditions of the English country-side] and seeks to set his land unto them by lease for xx years, or three lives. If the like course were held by the other lords and captains of countries here, there were nothing that would breed a more assurance to her Majesty for the obedience of the common sort of this country people.'

There speaks the English settler who wanted order and the cultivation of the soil, instead of the roving, restless, lazy tribal life of the Irish hitherto. A very small point here is worth noticing in the manuscript: Grenville has difficulty in mastering the Irish use of 'mac' and 'O'; he first wrote 'O Dermod' and then crossed it out. He was obviously not familiar with the Celtic forms; one imagines Skiddy standing by him in the room prompting him with the correct style.

On 22 April, the Queen wrote to the Lord Deputy directing that a lease of the abbeys of Gilly and Fermoy should be made out to Grenville for forty years.[1] The processes of the Irish law were slow; and there was many a slip between even royal wishes as expressed in England and their execution in Ireland. It was not until June 1591, when Grenville was in the Azores on the eve of his last fight, that the Irish Chancery made out its grant in his name.[2] The site and precincts of Fermoy Abbey, some sixteen miles north-east of Cork in the midst of what was then the Lord Roche's country, contained three acres within; the stone walls of the monastic church remained, a vault, two chambers, a close, a garden, a messuage, six cottages, with various parcels of lands containing 340 acres arable, 160 acres pasture, and mountain, and 40 acres of wood in all: a fine site for a baronial mansion and park at a somewhat later date. At Gilly, late the monastery of St. Finbar, the precincts were four acres, in which were a church, a belfry, several stone walls uncovered and a cemetery; three gardens, a close, a mill, two salmon weirs, 40 acres arable, 20 acres pasture; with all the townland of Kilmoney in Kerrycurrihy containing 120 acres arable, 140 acres pasture and several other lands and islands. So much for the character of the properties which Grenville

---

[1] *Cal. Pat. and Close Rolls Ireland*, 11, 195. [2] ibid. 201.

made his residences upon the wide-spread lands of his seignory. But there was, as the way is with Irish lands, to be more trouble before he came into secure possession of them; and, more surprising, the trouble was to come from a St. Leger.

Some periods of the year 1589, after March and again in the autumn, Grenville spent in England. For on 20 March, the Council wrote to the Mayor, Recorder and Justices of Exeter, putting Grenville's name into the Commission, along with Richard Champernowne and others, to try an important murder case, in which two or three servants of Sir William Courtenay were charged with murdering two of the servants of William Fortescue.[1] In May, we find him at Bideford, contemplating a journey to London to discuss various matters of business with Dr. Julius Caesar, Judge of the Court of Admiralty. He writes to the Judge for his favour to a kinsman, who had made a seizure on a ship laden with wines at Padstow.[2] Others are making claim to it, he says, 'yet I think and hope that the first seizure by a commission of reprisal is good'; from which we understand that Grenville's kinsman, either George Grenville or a Roscarrock, had a ship out with letters of marque to prey on trade with Spain, or else the seized ship had been arrested in Padstow by virtue of a commission of reprisal for some ship which he had previously lost.

Grenville was already in negotiation for the sale of the wines, and had gone so far as to bring down a couple of merchants at their great charge which should be recompensed if the seizure is not valid. But he hopes that it is and begs the Judge's favour for his kinsman to enjoy the seizure. It is interesting to note that the merchant who came down to Cornwall to deal for the wines was a Mr. Guinness, whom Grenville recommends the Judge to see, as he has taken great pains in following the case. One wonders if this is not among the earliest notices of that well-known name in such a connection. Finally, Grenville has taken order with Mr. Guinness to pay a certain Dutchman £120 'for the oils and figs' upon Caesar's making out a discharge for them. For the other causes 'according to my speech with you

[1] *A.P.C. 1588–9*, 111.   [2] Lansdowne MSS. 143, f. 264.

the next week (god willing), I shall be able to advertise you to the performance thereof.'

Whether Grenville got up to London and back in time for his daughter Catherine's marriage on 1 July, we do not know. She was married on that date in Hartland Church, to Justinian Abbot, second son of William Abbot of Hartland Abbey.[1] The Abbots of Hartland were Grenville's obvious neighbours between Stowe and Bideford; but apart from this marriage there seems to have been very little or no relations between them. The Abbots belonged to the new class of Reformation gentry, having obtained the abbey for a song – William Abbot as a Groom of the Chamber had been in a good position for picking up unconsidered trifles – at the Dissolution. We do not find the Abbots interested in any of Grenville's ventures, or among his circle of west-country kith and kin. This marriage was their first introduction into it; but it seems curious, if a match between the families had been arranged by the parents, why Grenville did not marry his daughter to the elder son. Perhaps he was not disposed to be generous enough in the matter of a dowry; or it may have been a love-match; we cannot tell. All we know is that Justinian died early, being buried at Bideford where he lived, 6 February 1602. The Abbots of Hartland died out, as their reverend predecessors before them; and that lovely estate, one long deep valley, twisting between its wooded slopes to its mouth upon the sea, passed from them to the Luttrells, from the Luttrells to the Orchards, and from the Orchards to the Stucleys with whom the Grenville blood enters into long-deferred possession. On 9 June, a family event of a different kind took place: Grenville's fourth daughter, Rebecca, was buried at Bideford.

This summer he was back in Ireland, in time to meet the Commissioners who had been sent over to investigate a number of troublesome questions connected with the plantation of Munster. These were three in number: the confused (and confusing) question of the titles to the chargeable lands; an attempt to change the cess, which was a customary charge upon the land

[1] Granville, 124.

for the maintenance of soldiers, into a regular revenue payable to the Queen; and thirdly, to make a survey of the number of Englishmen each undertaker had brought over.

From the returns, we learn that Grenville had considerably added to his interests and responsibilities: he had taken over from one Hugh Worth, one-half of the country of Kinallmeky, a double seignory of 24,000 acres, which Worth had taken up along with Phane Beecher. The latter asked that an equal division might be made between him and Grenville so that they might know how to place their people.[1] From Grenville's answers we learn that the rent of his portion of 12,000 acres was 100 marks, and that it contained no chargeable land.[2] No settlement had as yet been proceeded with, for one Daniel Granoe 'pretended to be lord of that country, became a rebel, spoiling and wasting that country till March last, whereby no tenants durst to undertake to dwell there.' So far, only one or two undertakers of English birth had been placed in the whole seignory, but he promises that 'the gentlemen that are to enjoy this seignory will before midsummer next, bring over to inhabit upon the same seignory the full number required by the articles so as the rebels that are out upon the same country may be suppressed.' Lastly, Grenville informs the Commissioners that he had bought the seignory on behalf of two of his relatives, one-half for Richard Bellew, his brother-in-law, the other for his half-brother, Alexander Arundell, 'who hath sent over at this present the one his son, the other his brother to view and take the conveyance of the country, and so return in to England to bring over people to plant the seignory according to her Majesty's plat.'

Altogether, the Grenville interests were at this time the largest of any of the Undertakers in Munster. Even Ralegh had as yet no more than one seignory of 12,000 acres; but that was the best cultivable land of all, and Ralegh had already settled more Englishmen than any of the others, 120 men, many of them with families. Sir Christopher Hatton, Sir George Bourchier and Sir Edward Fitton were among the next largest Undertakers; Edmund Spenser had a grant of only some 4,000 acres, which,

[1] S.P. Ireland 146, no. 45 (8).   [2] ibid. 148, no. 36.

he complained, was reduced to less than 3,000 acres by the claims and depredations of Lord Roche.

With regard to the chargeable lands, the Commissioners frankly confessed to the Council the almost insuperable difficulties they had met with. These lands were those upon which the Earls of Desmond had charges by Celtic custom, considerably diminishing their value. There was the right of the Lord with all his followers to take meat and drink from the inhabitants one day in a fortnight. Similarly his huntsmen and hounds had to be fed for a day and a night. The Lord might charge upon them the cost of his journeys to Dublin, or of entertaining strangers. Nor were these by any means all; there were other charges equally burdensome.[1]

It is obvious that these fantastic expressions of the primitive Celtic system of land-tenure would be regarded by the English Undertakers as the unmitigated nuisance, thoroughly uneconomic in character, which they were; and that they would desire some definite arrangement with the occupiers, by which the latter received in freehold a portion of the land they occupied, while the rest went to the Queen to whom all Desmond's rights had escheated. The Commissioners offered a fourth part of the land to the customary tenants, and to those of them who had written evidences, a third part; retaining the remainder in the Queen's hands to grant to her Undertakers. But the occupiers would come to no agreement, and some of them put forward ancient charters to show that their titles to the lands existed before ever the Desmonds had any footing in those parts. The poor baffled Commissioners reported from Dublin:

'The question of the chargeable lands hath often been debated, but it could never be decided whether the chargeable lands were the traitor's inheritance that had the rents and spending thereof, or whether they were the lawful inheritance of such the tenants whose ancestors had enjoyed the possession thereof many descents. It is probable that in the beginning some of the tenants were freeholders, and others but tenants-at-

[1] ibid. 144, no. 84.

will to Desmond, but how to distinguish them, wanting the
traitor's evidences and rentals, we know not.'[1]

It was a matter of the first importance for the success of the
Plantation; lacking this certainty, how could those of the
Undertakers who were affected by it, settle their followers?
Grenville and St. Leger were most of all concerned, for their
cantred of Kerrycurrihy, being of Desmond inheritance, was
largely chargeable land. Upon his coming over to England in
October, Grenville wrote from Stowe a long letter to Walsingham, stating his considered opinion upon each of the three
questions before the Commissioners. It is a very full and statesmanlike document, which enables us to appreciate what must
have been the representative view of the Undertakers, as expressed by one of the most important of them.[2]

'Being newly arrived out of Ireland,' he writes on 14 October,
'I have thought meet to make known to your honour how the
estate of the undertakers standeth in the county of Cork, where
my self is one that have an earnest care for the performance of
that which her Majesty hath directed to be done for the
peopling thereof.'

He continues, after reciting the questions submitted to the
Commissioners:

'The first part concerning the chargeable lands both more
concern Sir Warham St. Leger and me than any other of the
undertakers, because there is not so much chargeable land
found in any other place, which caused me the more earnestly
to follow her Majesty therein, at my being at the Court. At
which time her Majesty having Justice Anderson and Mr.
Attorney before her, they delivered their opinions, that in respect of the charge which was found by office that the traitor
Earl had on the land, her Majesty might justly take three parts
of four parts of the land into her own hands for the undertakers
. . . Yet her Majesty's pleasure was that some sorts of the freeholders should have a third part.'

[1] S.P. Ireland, 147, no. 51.   [2] ibid. no. 20.

From this it is clear that when earlier in the year he had attended the Court, he had had an audience of the Queen, who took a personal interest in the affairs of the plantation.

Now, he continued, the freeholders had been called before the Commission, but would yield to no composition; it was well-known that

'of themselves they will never yield to better conformity. Wherefore except her Majesty please to direct a certain course by the advice of her learned counsel (who have heard all their titles) according to that which by law she may do, her Majesty shall greatly prejudice herself and hinder her purpose of planting that country with Englishmen. As for my own part I mustered before them 100 Englishmen that I brought over with me to plant there, yet have I not five ploughlands to place them in. I was very earnest with the Commissioners to procure them to set down order, according as I had heard the Judge and Mr. Attorney yield their opinions, but nothing was done, which hath been to my great harm.'

Yet he is sure, he says, in spite of the refusal of the freeholders to come to an agreement, that they do not really expect to have more than a fourth; for one of them before the Commissioners came, had sold Grenville the fourth part of his ploughland and claimed no more. The frowardest of the freeholders claim that the earl's charges were by extortion. But this, Grenville says, was not so: there were divers sorts of freeholders, some yielding only a small rent and suit of court, and the Earl never took more than that from those freeholders. He claims that a third part of all the land that he and his uncle St. Leger hold, was held thus only by rent and suit [i.e. were not chargeable]. Of the rest which was chargeable, the Earl often made leases to strangers, when the freeholders would not inhabit the same, by which the Earl was to have three parts and the freeholder the remaining fourth.

'And when my uncle St. Leger and I first planted there, being more than twenty years past, we being then tenants to the Earl, all those that now seek to keep the whole of the chargeable land, yielded then to give us as much rent for every of those

ploughlands, as any lord or captain of the Irishry do make of
their own private land at this day . . . And if this chargeable
land be held as the freeholders now seek the same, I do protest
unto your honour I would not exchange the poor portion I have
in England for the greatest lord's living in Munster.'

As regards the cess which was charged upon the Irish lords
and chiefs for the maintenance of soldiers, and which the
government desired to change into a regular revenue out of
their lands, Grenville reported that they were unwilling to yield
to such a composition;

'for that might somewhat touch themselves, where now though
the cess be very grievous, yet it never hurteth them, for that the
whole burden thereof lighteth on the freeholders and inhabitants, who nevertheless yield unto their lords their whole
demands. But a great number of the freeholders were very willing to agree unto it.'

Short of the decisive intervention of the Government, it was
clear that nothing could be done; each class stuck to its own
interest, with no thought of what was the best interest of the
whole country: the chiefs were only prepared to give way on
what was the interest of the freeholders, the freeholders to accept
what was their own interest against the lords. It was all very
human. We are forced to conclude that the only power which
was looking to the interest of Ireland as a whole was the English
government. The tragedy of the situation was that in the sixteenth century, as in later centuries, it was never strong enough
continuously to impose this solution upon the shifting and
treacherous currents of Irish discontents.

Grenville goes on to attack the uncertain and brief tenures
upon which the Irish chiefs set their lands to their tenants,

'who hold the same not above four years, and so wander from
one place to another; which course being redressed, and they
commanded to set their lands as the undertakers must do, would
do much good to breed civility generally in the country; for
whereas now the poor man is never certain to enjoy the fruits
of his own labour and knoweth not in certainty what his lord

will have of him. For fear, he must depend on him and follow all his actions, be they good or bad; whereas otherwise, if the poor tenant held his land by lease for his life or for twenty-one years at a certain rent, then were he sure of his charge and that the overplus were his own; so would he depend on her Majesty and her laws to be defended against the oppressions which now too commonly every lord useth.'

It was a penetrating diagnosis of Irish troubles; and there can be no doubt that if, as Grenville saw, the Irish system of land-tenure could be assimilated to the English, it would lead to an improved economy, a better social order and much greater prosperity for the ordinary tillers and cultivators of the soil. Unhappily the resources of Elizabethan government were insufficient for so vast a task.

As was usual in that age, though particularly so whenever Grenville was writing to a friend at Court, he concludes with a request for a personal favour:

'whereas I having settled my mind to follow the planting of the Seignory that I have undertaken, am for some years to make my abode in that country, so for my poor credit's sake amongst my neighbours and friends here, I shall become an humble suitor unto your honour that my eldest son, being now of some ripe years, and I hope able to serve her Majesty and his country in civil as in martial actions, may by your honour's means have such charge of private bands of men as are now under me, and to supply a place with the rest in Justice, wherein my care shall be such over him, while I am, as he shall be able to do her highness and his country the better service when I am gone.'

Alas, Grenville did not know how soon that was to be! His idea was to leave his eldest son Bernard to take his place in the West Country – it would be good training for the position he was to occupy when his father was gone, and meanwhile he would deputise for him among the Cornish Justices and in command of the trained bands. We do not know if the scheme commended itself to the Government; Bernard was still very young to be a Justice of the Peace – he was only twenty-two. It would seem that he was not put into the Commission of the Peace

until after his father's death and he had become the head of the
family. His father's plan was now to remain in Ireland building
up a patrimony there for his second son John. It was, as always,
the interests of the family that he had in mind.

This year 1589 witnessed the Drake-Norris expedition to Lisbon, which was England's reply to the Armada. Its failure
meant a loss of some of the prestige gained in 1588; yet the
humiliation to Spain of an English army invading its soil, shook
the country out of the dazed condition the disaster to the
Armada had left it in. New preparations were made in the
northern parts of Spain for concentrating a fleet; and many
of the new ships laid down in Spanish yards incorporated the
lessons learnt in English waters and followed English designs.[1]
The fleets of Spain, and the system of guarding the annual
treasure fleet by convoys of fast cruisers, were being ably and
gallantly reorganised. Spain was becoming stronger again.

In England there was no serious fear of another invasion,
but it was feared that the Spanish preparations meant a descent
upon Ireland. Through the winter of 1589 and the spring of
1590, speedy efforts were set on foot to organise the defence of
Munster, so disorganised by the Desmond Rebellion, where the
blow was likely to fall. In December the Council sent over
Edmund Yorke, an experienced officer, to survey the likely
places of descent and take measures for their strengthening and
defence. He was instructed in Munster to take the advice of
Grenville and St. Leger, 'in what sort the towns of Waterford,
Cork and Limerick may be strengthened and fortified in short-
est time by rampering the said towns within the walls or by
raising up of forts or sconces with earth.'[2] In January, Ralegh
undertook for himself and Grenville to raise 200 of the 600 men
appointed to be levied in Ireland for service.[3] Later Ralegh
changed his offer to that of raising 50 horse in place of 100 foot;
we do not know how far Grenville proceeded with the job
allotted him over his head, but the emergency seems to have
passed with the summer months.

Levies were raised, however, in the early months in the

[1] Corbett, II, 364.   [2] *A.P.C. 1589-90*, 299, 331.   [3] ibid. 333, 372.

counties of Pembroke, Somerset, Shropshire, Warwick and
Chester, and the work of fortifying the towns in Ireland proceeded.[1] Grenville and St. Leger were to meet Yorke and Sir
Thomas Norris at Waterford in February; but for some reason
they failed to appear. Nevertheless, the works went merrily
forward, and by the end of May Yorke could report: 'Dun-
cannon is one of the prettiest fortresses in Christendom, and so
is the Rock over the water' [i.e. at Waterford]. He was so much
in love with his handiwork that he desired to have the keeper-
ship of the former.[2] By October, there was a considerable body
of troops in Ireland under the command of the great Sir John
Norris, Black John Norris, the most famous of English soldiers
of the time. All was ready for the attack which, as usual, did
not come.

Throughout 1590, at least right up to the end of October,
Grenville remained in Ireland, working upon his land; for at
the end of that time we hear of his having built a house for
himself at Gilly Abbey,

'purchased other lands adjoining to it, erected a mill and made
divers other commodious and necessary things, greatly to the
ease and good of the inhabitants of that part of the country and
to the furtherance of our service there, with his great costs and
charges.'[3]

Having got this much into order, he found himself up against
a difficulty which all too frequently dogged the steps of the
sanguine undertaker: a legal claim advanced to the property
by his cousin, Warham St. Leger the younger, nephew of Sir
Warham, who doubtless thought it would be a nice little thing
to succeed to, now that some work had been put into it.

Some seven years before, at the time of the Desmond Rebellion, when all was wasted, he had been offered a grant of the
property, but refused it at the rent demanded by the Crown.
Now that Grenville had improved it and made the place habitable again, he procured letters from the Lord Deputy, with
whom he was in closer contact than Grenville, who confined

---

[1] *Cal. S.P. Ireland 1588–92*, 315.   [2] ibid, 348.
[3] S.P. Ireland, 155, no. 14.

himself to the south, to have Grenville's grant stayed, and accepted the abbey himself at the rent he had previously refused.

'Whereby,' wrote the Queen to the Lord Deputy in her magnificent style, her large late signature scrawled across the top of the brief, 'this being as it is informed us, we may have good cause to conceive no direct nor sound dealing in St. Leger, both in respect of the hindrance grown to us through want of the said best rent for so long time, and otherwise also. And do find it likewise strange that you should in such sort grant the same to him, who had so long time refused it.'

Apparently the distracted Deputy had also promised the grant to Grenville upon the strength of the royal letters of 22 April 1589, upon which assurance Grenville had begun to build and lay out his charges. The Queen commanded the Deputy forthwith to resume into his hands the letters-patent granted to the younger St. Leger, and to report on the whole proceedings to her or the Council. Meanwhile he was to take order that Grenville should not be disturbed in the quiet occupancy and enjoyment of the property and that no disorder or quarrel should be suffered by occasion of it: 'Being our meaning nevertheless, in lieu of this, to extend our gracious favour to St. Leger in some other thing there to the like value.' This seems to have been sufficient: there was no quarrel or disorder, such as were endemic over Irish land; and shortly after, St. Leger was appointed to the Irish Privy Council.

Four months elapsed, and Grenville, now in England with a more exalted sphere of service before him – his great opportunity come at last – took the occasion to petition the Queen for a more favourable grant of the fee-farm of Fermoy and Gilly abbeys.[1] The Queen's missive of April 1589 had been for a lease to be made out to him for a term of forty years. It was like Grenville to use the fact of his service being required, to extract a further concession; but in that he was very typical of his class and time. It was the way these men made their own greatness and the greatness of their country.

[1] S.P. Ireland, 157, no. 19.

True, it was no great suit; and since Grenville intended to make Gilly and Fermoy his Irish residences, the nuclei of his estates, it was only natural that he should wish to obtain a freehold of the houses and demesnes, at least. The Queen was very willing and wrote forthwith her letters to the Lord Deputy to expedite the grants to 'our wellbeloved servant, Sir Richard Grenville.' [1] It was the first time that he was addressed according to the formula which indicated the new service of the crown to which he had been called. It was a foretaste of its rewards: the first-fruits of which the full harvest was his own heroic death.

'In consideration of the good service of the said Sir Richard,' the Queen now commands the Lord Deputy to make out patents for Grenville and his heirs male to enjoy the sites and demesnes of the two abbeys in fee-farm at the regular rents of £40 7s. 6d. and £33 9s. 4d. respectively; the remainder of the properties, outlying lands, parsonages, tithings, were granted on lease, with fines payable on renewal. So that the Crown was not being unduly generous with its own; it was fortunate rather to have a tenant who meant to put all he could into the property. After Grenville's death, we learn from a petition of his son John, that he had expended in his efforts to plant an estate in Ireland and by his losses in the Fitzmaurice Rebellion in 1569, some £8,000.[2] In his lifetime there was no return whatever on this large outlay of capital: time was not granted him to see any fruit for all his efforts. Whatever return they might yield in the end could only depend upon the continuance of his work by his posterity.

In the matter of the chargeable lands, the Queen directed the Deputy to make out a Commission to the Vice-President of Munster and others to hear Grenville and St. Leger's case for their enjoying the lands; and to call all parties advancing titles to the lands before them and hear their claims, 'and thereupon to decide their titles to the benefit of the said Sir Warham St. Leger and the said Sir Richard Grenville, as far forth as by law

[1] S.P. Ireland, 155, no. 17. The correct date is 7 March 1591 not 24 October 1590 as given in the *Calendar*; cf. *Hatfield Papers* (*Hist. MSS. Com.*), IV, no. 98 and *Cal. Pat. and Close Rolls Ireland*, II, p. 207.

[2] ibid. 169, no. 7.

and justice, the same ought to be.' Thus prodded by the Queen, the long delays of the Irish Chancery came to an end. On 26 June, the patents were made out: [1] Grenville was already in the Azores.

For, sandwiched into the State Papers between the Queen's letters relating to Gilly and Fermoy, on the back of the draft of the first, is the following docquet: 'A letter to Sir Richard Grenville to make his repair to her Majesty, for some causes of service as he shall understand, and to make the Deputy acquainted with this her pleasure.' [2] This was at the end of October, and Grenville must have repaired to Court immediately. It is all that we have of the Commission which was to lead to such fateful consequences in the Azores.

[1] *Cal. Pat. and Close Rolls Ireland*, II, 201.
[2] S.P. Ireland, 155, no. 16.

CHAPTER XVI

IN THE AZORES

Drake's great expedition to Lisbon, which was our reply to the Armada, had failed. It was a very spectacular affair, and its failure produced a corresponding sense of disappointment. From the first its success had been jeopardised by divided counsels, a divided command, and the usual delays inseparable from the conditions of sixteenth-century warfare, and particularly from the subtle hesitations of the Queen's mind.

It was intended to be both a land- and sea-enterprise. As such the troops and landsmen were placed under Sir John Norris, Black Norris, most famous of our commanders in the Netherlands, and the command was divided between him and Drake. The magic of their names – for it was a semi-private enterprise, to which the Queen contributed six of her ships, including the *Revenge* in which Drake sailed – brought together a motley crowd of men and ships. When they set sail, ill-fed, over-crowded, delayed by bad weather so that provisions were running short, they were some 130 ships in all and 23,000 men. The objectives of the expedition were confused from the start. Drake and Norris were to attempt to establish Don Antonio upon the throne of Portugal, and if possible to capture some of the Islands, the Azores, as a base from which to sever the sea-communications of the Spanish Empire. But they were instructed first to scatter the remnants of the Armada which had collected in the Biscayan ports, and this led to the attack upon Corunna which delayed the expedition, gave warning to the Spaniards of its presence and an opportunity, owing to the wines which the men took in the sack of the town, for disease to spread through the fleet.

After this all went wrong. Norris landed his troops at Peniche some fifty miles from Lisbon, but marched them through the country in vain, for he could not get at the capital. Drake arrived at the mouth of the Tagus, but could not take the city without the troops whose movements had failed to synchronise. Now starving and with a gale blowing upon the coast, all they could do was to re-embark the troops and return home, giving up the projected descent upon the Azores. Off the coast at the height of the storm, the *Revenge* sprang a leak, and it was only with the greatest difficulty that Drake managed to bring her into Plymouth.

The consequences of this ill-success were important. Our naval strategy was overhauled and a new plan of action adopted. Drake was left to languish in retirement at Buckland; though he was still the chief influence at Plymouth and was employed about its fortification. But he was not given another command at sea, until that of the expedition to the West Indies in 1595 which proved to be his last. For six years he was virtually unused, at the height of the war, when the new phase of the sea-fighting most suited his genius. In the curious way in which his fortune was connected with Grenville's, indirectly, almost as if by mutual exclusion, Drake's reversal opened the way to Grenville's opportunity.

The connection, as is the way these intricate strands of circumstance are woven, was not obvious; it may even seem inconsequent: but time brought them together. While Grenville was oblivious of them, hard at work in Ireland, the new plan of campaign was worked out and set in being. It was mainly the work of Hawkins, who expressed its guiding principle of policy to be, 'that first we have as little to do in foreign countries as may be (but of mere necessity), for that breedeth great charge and no profit at all': [1] a principle which became the classic tradition of English policy. The plan was to hold the seas between Spain and the Azores by successive small squadrons of six of the Queen's ships, with their supports, so as to exert continuous pressure upon the vital route by which the *flotas*, the treasure-fleets from the Indies, replenished Spain with the resources of her Empire.

[1] Williamson, *Sir John Hawkins*, 451.

It was a good plan, but it depended upon two assumptions: first, that the squadrons should succeed each other without intermission upon the Azores station and the coast of Spain, so that the *flotas* should not slip home unobserved in the interval: a matter very difficult to accomplish in the conditions of those days, dependent as they were upon wind and weather, with very inadequate provisions for supply and a faltering and discontinuous command of material resources. Secondly, these tactics assumed that Spanish sea-power was so crippled by the disaster of 1588 that Philip would be unable to raise forces sufficient to sweep even these small squadrons from the sea. But it was a matter of life and death for Spain that he should do so.

Slowly, laboriously, but surely, as his manner was, Philip planned to repair the damage, and to construct the nucleus of a fighting force which he might send to sea to keep his communications open. In 1589 he contracted for twelve galleons, the twelve 'Apostles,' to be built on the English model in the Biscayan ports; nine more were laid down on the Portuguese model at Lisbon. Next year he contracted for twelve Ragusan galleons to enter his service.[1] With the assassination of Henry III, the religious wars in France entered upon their final phase and Philip was drawn into intervention on the side of the Catholic League, as Elizabeth was on behalf of Henry of Navarre. Philip sent an expedition to Brittany; its presence there, right on the flank of the Channel opposite Plymouth and the Cornish coast, occasioned far more alarm in England than its actual strength warranted.

Most important of all was the question of safeguarding the homecoming treasure from the Indies. For this purpose, Alonso de Bazan proposed a small number of fast vessels of a new type – gallizabras – small but heavily armed, in which the treasure was to be carried, capable of outsailing whatever they could not fight. The reconstitution of Spain's naval forces was proceeding under the influence of Bazan, a commander of long experience in the Mediterranean and on the Atlantic coasts; he was the brother of the great Admiral Santa Cruz and the in-

[1] C. F. Duro, *Historia de la Armada Española*, III, 79; Corbett II, 364.

heritor of his tradition. It was Bazan who had led the attack of the galleys upon Drake in Lisbon harbour; now he was placed in charge of the collection of an ocean fleet in the northern harbours.

But that would take time; meanwhile the hour was to the English. For a variety of reasons, chiefly through difficulties of supply and in the way of co-ordinating movements, they did not do so well as expected. Cumberland was out in the Azores with a few ships of his own all the summer of 1589 and right up to October. But he did not know the Isles well, and somehow both the *flota* of New Spain and the great East Indian carracks managed to evade him. The one rich prize he took, worth £100,000 and laden with hides, sugar and cochineal, was wrecked in Mount's Bay when nearly in port and became a total loss. In September, Frobisher was at sea taking his station off the coast of Portugal with the aim of intercepting what might elude Cumberland. Had the two joined forces they might have captured the *flota*; as it was, Frobisher got a couple of rich prizes which more than recompensed him for his pains. Spain was quite unable to get a fleet to sea this year to protect her trade. But the bulk of the treasure was not on this *flota* which got through the blockade; it was coming on the *flota* from the Mainland, whose sailing was delayed till next year. Philip had therefore to get through the winter without the precious means for the sustenance of his wide-flung forces throughout Europe.

Hawkins knew that the treasure had been delayed, and through the winter he pushed on the preparations to take the sea himself as early as possible. Suddenly the Council took fright at Bazan's preparations at Corunna and Ferrol: they supposed the new Spanish fleet could only mean another descent upon England. Hawkins's squadron was countermanded. In his laconic, repressed way he wrote with bitterness to Burghley: 'Being out of hope that ever I shall perform any royal thing, I do put on a mean mind and humbly pray your lordship to be a good lord to me.' [1] He might well be bitter: he had missed the chance of achieving the 'royal thing.' The second *flota*, trusting to the winter seas rather than the summer

[1] Williamson, 456.

or the autumn when they were alive with English ships on the look-out, crossed in the early months of 1590, arriving in port in March, with five million ducats on board.

Too late for this catch, the Council permitted both Hawkins and Frobisher, each with a squadron of six Queen's ships, to depart in May. Frobisher went to the Azores, with the *Revenge* as his flagship, while Hawkins lay off the coast of Spain to watch for the sailing of the Brittany expedition which had caused such trepidation in England, and for the homecoming trade. This time Frobisher was too late; a consignment of treasure in the new gallizabras had just passed through before his arrival and reached Portugal in August. However, his presence created alarm throughout the Islands and frightened Philip into countermanding the dispatch of any more treasure till 1591. When Frobisher's supplies were exhausted, Hawkins took his place in the Azores. But there was now nothing to intercept. At the end of September Bazan had collected sufficient forces to put to sea; with some forty ships, of which perhaps twenty were of any size or strength, he made for the Azores.[1] A battle might have taken place in less unequal conditions than came about next year: no doubt Hawkins would have considered six Queen's ships a match for twenty Spaniards. But when within ten leagues of the Islands, Bazan was driven back by bad weather; and at the end of October, Hawkins was recalled.

The alarm created in the Spanish world, in the colonies and in Spain no less than in the Islands, was intense. Linschoten, a Dutch merchant who was in the Azores at this time, wrote that the English 'are become lords and masters of the sea, and need care for no man,' and that the Spaniards themselves 'cursed those that had been the cause to provoke the Englishmen to fight.' The colonies in America had their own troubles to deal with, in addition to the King clamouring for treasure; but they were incapable of dealing with them. John Watts, lying in wait off Havana in the summer of 1590, had captured two ships of the New Spain fleet attempting to collect there. In the end it was decided to winter in the harbour, news which caused a panic in Seville. The governor of Havana declared that the

---

[1] Oppenheim, *Monson's Tracts*, I, 251.

Spaniards were bottled up, while the audacious Englishmen dared them at their very doors. The winter wore on, and the colony itself, under the inspiration of the governor, Texeda, constructed its own frigates for the transport of treasure. Four were finished and left Havana on 10 February 1591; three made Cascaes, at the mouth of the Tagus, on the night of 12 March, the fourth arrived at San Lucar on 19 March. The treasure was loaded on mule-trains and dispatched to Seville; and because money was desperately needed in Spain, the frigates were at once sent back to Carthagena for more.[1]

It was known in England that there was last year's *flota* in addition to the current year's to cross, but there was no knowledge at what time they were to be expected. Monson afterwards wrote that the King of Spain, 'being sensible how much the safety of that fleet concerned him, caused them to disembogue so late in the year that it endangered the shipwreck of them all.' He adds that there were two motives in bringing home the *flota* so late; one was to exhaust the supplies of the English squadron watching, the other to give him more time to prepare a strong fleet under Bazan to meet the *flota* at the Azores and convoy it home. In England it had not been realised what efforts Philip had put forth to reconstitute an ocean-going fleet, nor what measure of success Bazan had attained. The Government therefore went on with its policy of sending out small cruising squadrons, which in spite of the absence of any signal *coup* had been very promising of result, at a minimum of cost.

There was a good deal of discussion as to who should be sent out and what form the force should take. The first plan was for some twenty ships and pinnaces to be sent under the joint command of Lord Thomas Howard and Ralegh.[2] The latter, for some reason, perhaps because it was thought he would not agree with Howard, was not permitted to go. But he continued to participate in the expedition, for he victualled the *Revenge* and the *Crane*, while the *Defiance*, the flagship, was victualled by

---

[1] I am indebted for the information in this paragraph to the kindness of Miss I. A. Wright.

[2] Oppenheim, I, 257.

Lord Thomas Howard, and the *Bonaventure*, *Charles* and *Moon* by the Lord Admiral. Doubtless it was through Ralegh's influence, and in some sense as occupying his place, as happened before over the Voyage to Virginia in 1585, that Grenville was appointed Vice-Admiral of the squadron. He had had no part in these proceedings; he had simply received, as we saw, at the beginning of March, the command to come direct to Court and there the order to serve. Almost immediately, we hear from a letter to the Earl of Shrewsbury on 10 March, giving him news of the Court:

'My Lord Thomas Howard hath kissed her Majesty's hand, and is gone down to his ships, Sir Richard Grenville being his Viceadmiral, and they and their partners I assure your Lordship make a very goodly fleet. God send them good speed, and a safe return: My Lord of Cumberland is not yet ready.' [1]

The fleet with which Howard and Grenville were to put to sea consisted of the *Defiance*, Howard's flagship, the *Revenge*, in which Grenville sailed as Vice-Admiral, the *Bonaventure*, the *Nonpareil*, all of them medium-sized fighting ships of about 500 tons, the *Crane* of 250 tons, with the two smaller ships, the *Charles* and the *Moon* of 60 and 70 tons.[2] Later on, after some months at sea, there were changes: the *Moon* was sent home in July to hasten the supplies which had been promised, the *Nonpareil* followed because of 'the great infection of the ship'; and before the action off Flores, Howard was reinforced by two more Queen's ships, the *Golden Lion* of 500 tons and the *Foresight* of 300. Instructions sent later to Howard warned him that there was a Spanish fleet between Cape St. Mary and Cape St. Vincent, low down upon the south-west of the Spanish peninsula, and left it 'to my Lord Thomas's judgment by such intelligence as he shall learn, whether it be surer lying at the Islands for the Indian fleet, or at St. Mary's Cape, but it is thought by men of good judgment and experience that the Cape is the surer.' Howard was promised that victuals for two months would be sent after him. Cumberland, with a force of his own and backed

---

[1] Lodge, *Illustrations of British History* (ed. 1791), III, 28.
[2] Oppenheim, I, 256–9.

by Ralegh, Drake and others, was to take up a post off the coast of Spain.

In June, the Council made efforts to whip up reinforcements for the ships at sea; letters were written round to various ports to fit out ships for service in the Azores, for the most part eliciting despondent replies. Padstow replied that they had no ship exceeding 23 tons; Barnstaple and Bideford replied that of their ships of 100 tons burden, 'two are at the Newfoundland' and one, serving under a commission of reprisal, was already 'we verily think, before this time with one of her Majesty's fleets.' [1] But from their reply we obtain a last glimpse of Howard and Grenville making their final preparations at Plymouth:

'Also here are few mariners left at this time, because there are a great number forth in the said reprisal men, another company at the Newfoundland, and divers were pressed here hence by the Earl of Cumberland, Lord Thomas Howard and Sir Richard Grenville at their last being at Plymouth.'

It so happens that for what occurred on the expedition, particularly on board the *Revenge*, up to the time of their arrival in the Azores, we are more than usually well-informed. For there sailed in the *Revenge* with Grenville, a young gentleman-volunteer, Philip Gawdy, cadet of a Norfolk family, whose letters home – it is by singular good fortune that they have survived – give us a vivid picture of his time on board, and much useful information. His letters begin before their departure; they are very characteristic of a young man of the time, expressive, eager, elated with the chance of seeing action, full of a naïve pride at going to sea and at the attentions he receives at Grenville's hands, with quick changes of mood from the gay and whimsical to homesickness and a regret for the fields of Norfolk. The younger son of a younger son, Philip had no obvious prospects in the world; for some years, nominally attendant upon the Inns of Court, and having chambers at Clifford's Inn, he hung about the Court, was excited by the deeds of Drake and Frobisher and Howard, and longed for an opportunity for active

---

[1] *Hatfield MSS.*, IV, 119–20.

service. Once already, in 1588, he had been disappointed; now his chance had come.

'Sweet Brother,' he writes before leaving; 'over-charged with haste I will make me write with the shorter style, till it please God that I may write from Plymouth, when I will load you with news. How Sir Richard Grenville and my Lord Thomas have sought for me I will not tell you. Let Tom in his simplicity tell you whether he saw them make any reckoning of me or no. To be short, the news I know is thus much. The Queen hath commanded all possible speed to be made. Sir Richard and other captains will presently go to the court with whom I will go. And so away as fast as the ships will fall down [sc. the Thames]. I have already bought my arms and target, the very fellows to my Lord Thomas and Sir Richard. My apparel will be made to night, what is necessary else I do provide, besides the great kindness I find both at Sir Richard's hands and at Mr. Langhorne's [the captain of soldiers on board the *Revenge*].' [1]

Philip's next letter to his brother is written from on board the *Revenge*, 3 April. There seems to have been a strong affection between the two brothers, in spite of the excessive good fortune of the elder in marrying an heiress. Philip sends his sister-in-law his good wishes, 'And I trust she will ever love me, till I give her other cause. And that shall not be till the salt seas be dried up and then we shall come home for want of water.'

He sends friendly commendations to all the neighbourhood; and upon the margin of the letter, Sir Richard himself wrote a few words to the elder brother in testimony of Philip's conduct of himself, that 'no sickness, no danger, no fear . . . nor no extremities of weather, mutiny, hard[ship] or other peril or grief could provoke' him from his duty. From a postscript by Captain Langhorne, we gather that they had already experienced 'the extremest fury of the weather,' which drove Lord Thomas's ships to take shelter at Falmouth, while the *Revenge* rode out the gale at the mouth of the Channel. [2]

From his next letter, which is very long and informative, and, it is not too much to say, delightfully written, we have a com-

---

[1] *Letters of Philip Gawdy*, Roxburghe Club 1906, 53. [2] pp. 54–5.

plete journal of their proceedings from the time of leaving Plymouth, till midway between Cape St. Vincent and San Miguel in the Azores they captured a hulk which they sent home with their letters. This one was dated from the *Defiance*, 24 April, for Lord Thomas had sent for Philip that day; he was writing at it when he was sent for and completed it on board the flagship, to be despatched on the prize that night. He describes the storm that overtook them, and becomes ingenuously nautical about the *Revenge* which rode it out between Scilly and Ushant. 'We spent both our masts, but by God's grace, they were espied in good time, and strengthened with fishes, wolding and caulking, and now, thanks be to God, they be in very good plight.' The *Revenge*, being a fast ship, went on ahead of the rest, and off Finisterre met with four or five ships of Hamburg from which 'we borrowed some victual, for other good thing had they not any.'

Off the Burlings about 18 April, seven or eight sail were descried from the topmast, with one large ship which they took to be a carrack among them. The *Revenge* prepared for action; but the big ship proved to be a great hulk of Lübeck, of 1,000 tons, laden with masts and deal, which was being chased by some of Lord Thomas's ships. The Lübecker yielded herself to Grenville, who placed a crew in her; she turned out to be good prize, for her lading was bound for the King of Spain, and worth £10,000. Off Cape St. Vincent, Lord Thomas with five of his ships came up with them, and 'we made great joy to meet him.'

Howard and Grenville determined to send the prize home, and in her went someone who promised to deliver Philip's letter to his brother in Norfolk.

'Sweet brother, I am become a reasonable good mariner, and thanks be to God as strong at the sea as any in our company. I want nothing but thy sweet company. I do continually meditate upon thee, and verify the old proverb *"Celum non animum mutant, qui trans mare currunt."* Sweet brother, my lord sent for me this day to be with him, so that I am hasted by him wonderfully to dispatch my letter, for he sends away with all speed. I honour him much and have great cause to love him. I thank

God I am contented with this life which I have framed myself
to. We want the sweet flowers and herbs to breathe upon, for
here we find nothing but only *Celum undique, et undique mare.*
There is not a good ale-house within twenty leagues of us.'

He continues with innumerable commendations to 'the good
company of Harling' which 'maketh me long home. And when
I think of Norfolk and your sweet company, and someone besides of that country, I sigh and say the sea doth not content
me.' Then, with a touch of pride in such a home-bred country-
man, 'And hitherto I may justly say that I have travelled
further than any of my name.' He bids his brother look in his
map at home for the course they have so far followed, which
he describes for him in detail. 'These seas that we be now in
are almost as sweet as a river in the country'; yet again, 'the
southern seas cannot blow the remembrance of my friends out
of my mind.' The fleet had heard the news of the four treasure-
ships arriving at San Lucar, and was now immediately bound
for the Islands.

A little later, he adds a postscript with the information that
they had met the hulk again, being an unwieldy vessel, midway
between San Miguel and Cape St. Vincent.

'There hath not anything else happened worth the writing,
but only this: we sunk a carvel, where we only saved three score
jars of oil, the men and a bushel of letters which they carried of
intelligence to the Islands to meet with the fleet coming home,
whither we are now going. The most of us like lions that have
been almost famished for want of prey, or rather like a bear
robbed of her whelps. Sweet brother, I do this day wish myself
a-maying at Harling, with a sudden return. Once again farewell to thy sweet self, this first of May.' [1]

It is evident that so far the cruise had been singularly unpro-
ductive; apart from Grenville's capture of the great Lübecker,
only one hulk had been taken and a carvel sunk. On 18 May,
the Council wrote to Howard saying that they still could give
him no reliable information when the *flota* was to be expected,

[1] pp. 56–62.

but it was thought either in September or October.[1] A month later, Burghley and the Lord Admiral wrote that two months' victuals had been sent out, and that having learnt that the *flota* would be convoyed by twenty men-of-war and more, besides the fleet going out from Spain to meet it, they thought it advisable to reinforce him with two ships of the Queen, the *Lion* and the *Foresight*, and six armed merchantmen. The two Queen's ships sailed at the end of June or the beginning of July to join Howard without delay; but the armed merchantmen, powerful ships of their class, the *Susan*, the *Centurion*, the *Mayflower*, the *Cherubim*, all round about 300 tons, with the *Margaret and John* and the *Corselet* of 200—a very desirable reinforcement, were held up by bad weather at Plymouth and did not leave the Sound till 17 August.

For three months there is no news of Howard and Grenville's doings in the Islands, except that, as we gather from Philip Gawdy, they ran up to Flores to water. We are not told whether they came back again to the midst of the Islands, Flores being in the extreme north-west about 110 miles from Terceira in the centre, but that would be their likeliest course; the Spanish information was that they were cruising about. Gawdy wrote home again on 6 July by the pinnace which brought the Council's letters:

'We stay and pray every day heartily for the Spanish fleet's coming; and if they come not suddenly I thank God we are and shall be sufficiently provided to look for their longer coming. Since my last writing we have had some adventures. We watered at Flores. And I saw the dolphin course the flying fish, whereof I saw one fly as far as your young partridges will do at the first flight. I thank God we have good ships with us, both of her Majesty's and otherwise. I never had my health better in my life, thanks be to God; and the better for the good usage both of Sir Richard, and Captain Langhorne, whose commendations I willed to remember to you, and to my Uncle Anthony, also from his kinsman Sir Richard Grenville. I am bound to them both in many courtesies. I like the sea and the

[1] Oppenheim, I, 260.

sea life, and the company at sea, as well as any that ever I lived withal. The place is good and healthful to a willing mind.'

There follow the usual bantering commendations to his relations; his sister-in-law is bidden 'let her imagine that I am now so in love with the sea as I had rather be married to a mermaid, except only in Norfolk.' He concludes: 'I can appoint no certainty of my coming . . . Commend me lastly to thine own heart and most loving thoughts, and think sometimes of him that daily museth, and nightly dreameth of thy welldoing. From aboard her Majesty's good ship the *Revenge*.' [1]

It was the last letter which Philip Gawdy wrote, or at least dispatched from on board the *Revenge*. His next was to be written as a prisoner from the castle at Lisbon.

[1] Gawdy, pp. 62–3.

CHAPTER XVII

THE LAST FIGHT OF THE *REVENGE*

It was after this that their troubles began. From Gawdy's letter it is clear that sickness had not yet broken out in the squadron, or not to any serious extent, or he would have mentioned it. But by the end of the month, it had gained a terrible hold in the fleet; half the crews of the ships were down with it, and on 23 July, the *Nonpareil* had to be sent home because of the 'great infection' reigning in her.[1] Howard must have been anxiously awaiting by now the tight little squadron of armed merchant-men promised him. He had given them a rendezvous some sixty leagues west of the island of Fayal, 'spreading North and South betwixt $37\frac{1}{2}$ or $38\frac{1}{2}$ degrees.' If he were not to be found there, Captain Robert Flicke, who was in command of the merchantmen, was to run up to Flores or Corvo, where, if Howard had gone, a pinnace would be left to meet him until 31 August. After this date, the place of meeting was to be the coast of Portugal, west of Cape Roca. Since he was already so late, Flicke went first down to Cape Roca, and on 29 August bore away westwards for the Azores. On the 31st, when his presence might have made all the difference to Howard and enabled him to engage the Spaniards, he was only two days out in the Atlantic. Don Alonso de Bazan, with a strong force of some fifty-five ships, of which twenty were fighting vessels, and with 7,000 men on board, was already in the Azores.

The forces which were to make the name of Flores in the Azores so celebrated in maritime history, were converging upon the Island. The English knew that the *flota* from the West Indies might be expected any time now. But they were forced,

[1] Oppenheim, I, 256.

owing to the prevalence of the sickness and the foul condition of their ships after four months' cruising in southerly waters, to set their sick ashore and thoroughly 'rummage' and clean the ships. The operation meant clearing out the old ballast into which all the drippings and the waste of the ship had run, scrubbing out the interior and fumigating with vinegar, and finally taking on board new clean ballast from the shore. Doubtless they thought there was time, and kept a pinnace to warn them of the approach of the *flota* from the west. What they did not know was that Don Alonso was approaching from the east.

In the Indies, meanwhile, the Spanish *flotas* were collecting at Havana, losing individual vessels right and left to the English privateers. The fleet from New Spain [i.e. Mexico] left San Juan de Ulloa on 13 June with twenty-two sail ; two of these which straggled from the convoy were taken by John Watts, one of them carried plate. Watts lying off Havana had previously captured seven ships of the San Domingo fleet. The Governor of Havana described himself as sitting in rage upon a piece of ordnance Navarro brought him, surrounded by horse and foot, but unable to lay hand on the enemy who sailed by under his very nose. On 27 July, Ribera, commander of the mainland *flota*, set out for Spain from Havana with some seventy-three or more sail: the armada, the merchantmen who had wintered there, the New Spain fleet which Navarro had just brought in, and various oddments from the Honduras and other quarters. This was the quarry that Howard and Grenville were lying in wait for at Flores, with little suspicion that they themselves had now become the quarry for someone else.[1]

A Spanish Relation written from on board Bazan's flagship a day or two after the action, enables us for the first time to follow events from the Spanish side.[2] It is the only first-hand account of what happened at Flores. Hitherto we have had to rely for our knowledge of the engagement upon the English accounts, none of which was written by anyone present at it.

[1] For these details I am indebted to Miss I. A. Wright.
[2] Colección Sanz de Barutell (Madrid), Art 4, no. 1121.

If only Philip Gawdy had used his long and enforced leisure at Lisbon, or even in after years, to write as informative an account as some of his earlier letters: we may imagine that as the years went on, and he became old and garrulous, he often spoke of those last days of the *Revenge*. But nothing has come down to us, and he missed his one chance of being remembered by posterity.

Of the English authorities, the chief is Ralegh's famous pamphlet, *A Report of the Truth of the Fight about the Isles of Açores*, which was written that same autumn.[1] Ralegh's must rank almost as a first-hand account since it is based upon the examinations of survivors from the *Revenge*: 'two of the *Revenge's* own company, brought home in a ship of Lyme from the Islands, examined by some of the Lords, and others,' and an examination of four others of her company taken by Sir Francis Godolphin on their arrival in Cornwall. But Ralegh's pamphlet was written to serve a controversial purpose: to glorify his own nation and to vindicate his cousin Grenville's action. We have therefore to remember his bias in making a judgment upon disputed points. The other English authorities are Sir William Monson, in his *Naval Tracts*,[2] and Sir Richard Hawkins, in his *Observations*;[3] but these were written some twenty or thirty years later. There are lastly the recollections of the Dutchman, van Linschoten, who was resident in the Islands at the time of the action, and reported what was the current gossip about it there.[4]

But none of these is equal to the Spanish Relation, an official account, in giving the precise facts and movements of the ships, concretely and objectively. There has never been an adequate account of the battle so far, for want of information, though attempts have been made to reconstruct it.[5] In consequence it has given rise to a flood of controversy and supposition as to Grenville's motives. The latter can in any case never be any other than uncertain; but one can at least give an account which is consistent with his whole life and character, now that

---

[1] *Arber's English Reprints* (1871).
[2] Ed. Oppenheim.   [3] Ed. Williamson.   [4] Reprinted in Arber.
[5] Notably Professor Callender's 'The Battle of Flores,' *History* (1919), vol. IV.

it has been explored. And for the course of the action – though there still remain points which are doubtful, and others on which we are ignorant – we can now take both the English and the Spanish accounts, checking each by the other, and draw a fairly full picture of the whole.

Don Alonso de Bazan with his fleet, arrived at Terceira, the Spanish stronghold among the Islands on 30 August, by their reckoning.[1] Here he learned from a despatch-boat which was sent him that the English were at Flores and Corvo, the two extreme north-westerly isles of the group. But for a week he was kept beating about in the channel between San Jorge and Graciosa by bad weather. During this time he learned from a Franciscan friar and a pilot, who had been captured by the English on their way from Havana and were some days on board the English flagship, the exact strength of their forces: they were not more than twenty-two ships, and of these there were only six great galleons of the Queen and one small one. The English fleet was commanded by Lord Thomas Howard, second son of the Duke of Norfolk, 'hombre moço y no marinero' (an inexperienced man and not a sailor) and 'Almirante Ricardo de Campo Verde gran cossario y de mucha estimacion entrellos' (Admiral Richard Grenville a great corsair and of great estimation among them). From this we already learn something of the light in which Howard and Grenville respectively were regarded in the fleet.

On 7 September, the wind came fair from the east and Don Alonso went forward on his course to Flores. Next day in the evening they met their pilots fifteen leagues due east from Flores, and having such certain information of the English it was agreed to put on sail so as to arrive upon them at dawn next morning when the wind was fresh; and that they should enter the channel between the two islands in several squadrons and others on both sides of the islands, surrounding the enemy on all sides. After proceeding some way with this plan in mind, General Sancho Pardo sent to Don Alonso to tell him that he

---

[1] The following paragraphs follow the Spanish Relation – are virtually a translation of it; and here I retain their dating.

was carrying a broken bowsprit on his galleon – one of the Santander squadron – so that he could not put on much weight of sail. It was agreed to keep company and not to leave the ship on its own where the enemy was cruising about. Hence Don Alonso was unable to arrive upon the Islands at dawn, but about eight leagues from them with a fresh east wind. He at once sent a pinnace to the islands to report how things were and to order General Marcos de Aramburu with a squadron of eleven ships – seven galleons of Castille, the flagship of the despatch-boats and the *San Francisco* of the prizes, with two fly-boats, the *Leon Rojo* and the *Cavallero de la mar* – to enter the channel between the islands.

Don Alonso himself with the rest of the fleet was going round by the left side of the isle of Flores, so as to catch the enemy whom he understood to be watering there, in the midst. On the windward side there sailed Don Luis Cuitiño with the eight fly-boats in his charge, on the leeward there were Generals Martin de Bertendona, Sancho Pardo and Antonio Urquiola; the rear was brought up by Don Bartholome de Villavicencio. In this formation they were sailing when the pinnace Bazan had sent to reconnoitre, signalled that she had seen the enemies hoist and lower their main-topsail four times and fire two pieces at the same time. Simultaneously with this Aramburu signalled that he saw the enemy fleet coming out from the isle of Flores on the side of Corvo, and he fired two pieces to tell Bazan that he had seen it and to put on sail because he was going in the direction of it. Don Alonso at once sent to tell Cuitiño, who was in command of the fly-boats to windward, ordering him to leave the first course they were taking and to follow him, Don Alonso; so that Cuitiño's squadron, which before was going in front of the wind of all the fleet, now brought up the rear upon the new course.

'At Flores in the Azores Sir Richard Grenville lay,' says the poet very truly; but the difficulty has always been that nobody knows precisely where, in relation to the island. Mr. Oppenheim in his edition of *Monson's Tracts* quotes observations to the effect that the prevailing winds in the Azores in these months are from north-east and north-west, and suggests therefore that

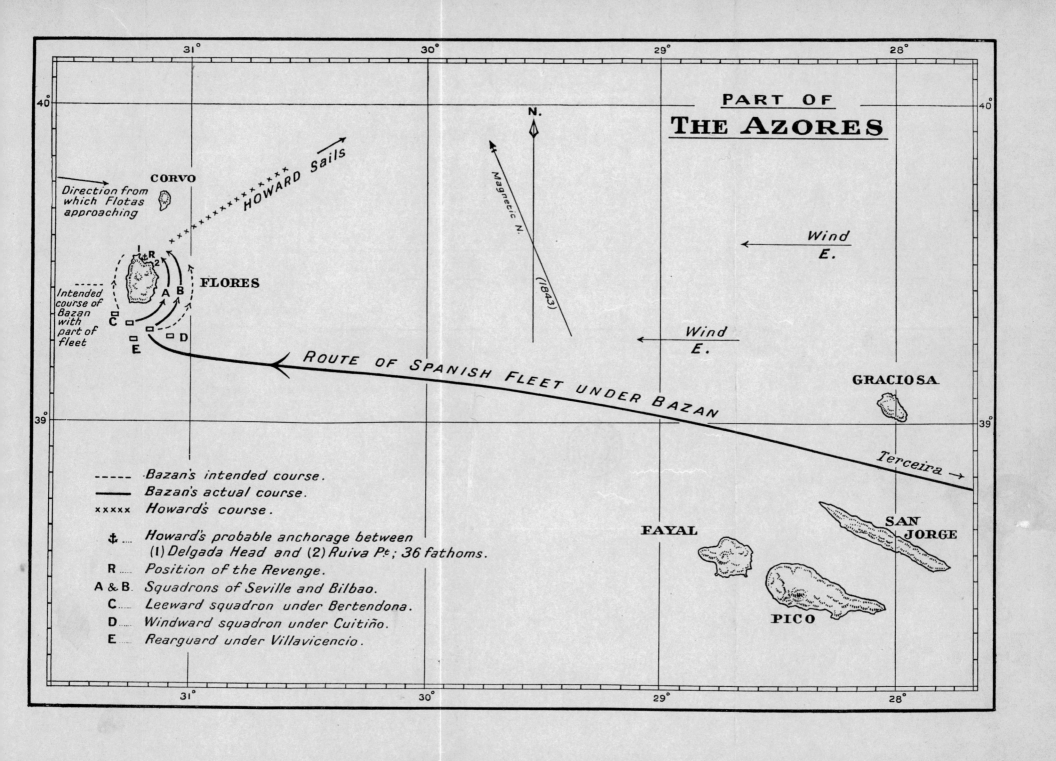

PART OF
THE AZORES

31°   30°   29°   28°

N.

Magnetic N.

(1843)

CORVO

HOWARD *Sails*

Direction from which Flotas approaching

Wind E.

I ⚓ R
2

FLORES

A B

Wind E.

Intended course of Bazan with part of fleet

C

E   D

ROUTE OF SPANISH FLEET UNDER BAZAN

GRACIOSA

Terceira →

39°

FAYAL

SAN JORGE

PICO

----- Bazan's intended course.
―――― Bazan's actual course.
xxxxx Howard's course.

⚓ .... Howard's probable anchorage between
    (1) Delgada Head and (2) Ruiva P.ᵗ; 36 fathoms.
R .... Position of the Revenge.
A & B. Squadrons of Seville and Bilbao.
  C .... Leeward squadron under Bertendona.
  D .... Windward squadron under Cuitiño.
  E .... Rearguard under Villavicencio.

FAYAL

BAZAN

PICO

St. JOHN

Wind
E

Wind
E

ASTOR PUBLIC LIBRARIES
ASTOR PUBLIC LIBRARIES
ASTOR PUBLIC LIBRARIES

the anchorage would be on the east of the island. But it is fairly clear from the Spanish Relation that the English were on its west side, probably to the north-west near the channel between it and Corvo; while the wind, we are informed, held from the east. That same morning – it was 31 August in the English reckoning – Howard received warning of the approach of the Spanish fleet. Bazan had been observed upon leaving Ferrol by some of Cumberland's squadron keeping watch there, and the Earl despatched a pinnace, the *Moonshine*, Captain Middleton, to warn Howard. Middleton kept company with Bazan's fleet by way of discovering their strength some three days prior, and then sped on to Flores with the news of their approach.

Time was very short, even if not quite so short as Ralegh says:

'He had no sooner delivered the news but the Fleet was in sight: many of our ships' companies were on shore in the Island; some providing ballast for their ships; others filling of water and refreshing themselves from the land with such things as they could either for money, or by force recover. By reason whereof our ships being all pestered and rummaging every thing out of order, very light for want of ballast. And that which was most to our disadvantage, the one half part of the men of every ship sick, and utterly unserviceable. For in the *Revenge* there were ninety diseased: in the *Bonaventure*, not so many in health as could handle her main-sail. For had not twenty men been taken out a bark of Sir George Cary's, his being commanded to be sunk, and those appointed to her, she had hardly ever recovered England. The rest for the most part, were in little better state.'

Besides this, the English were fairly taken by surprise, since they were expecting the *flota* from the west; and some odd-ments of the Spanish fleet, pinnaces or fly-boats, were taken to be the expected *flota*, which added confusion to surprise.

The English fleet consisted of the six ships of the Queen, the *Defiance*, the *Revenge*, the *Bonaventure*, the *Lion*, the *Foresight* and the *Crane*; the last two being small ships, the rest of middle size.

In addition there were six victuallers of London, the bark *Ralegh* and two or three pinnaces riding at anchor.

'The Spanish fleet,' says Ralegh, 'having shrouded their approach by reason of the Island: were now so soon at hand, as our ships had scarce time to weigh their anchors, but some of them were driven to let slip their cables and set sail. Sir Richard Grenville was the last weighed, to recover the men that were upon the Island, which otherwise had been lost. The Lord Thomas with the rest very hardly recovered the wind, which Sir Richard Grenville not being able to do, was persuaded by the master and others to cut his main-sail, and cast about, and to trust to the sailing of his ship: for the squadron of Seville were on his weather bow.[1] But Sir Richard utterly refused to turn from the enemy, alleging that he would rather choose to die, than to dishonour his self, his country, and her Majesty's ship, persuading his company that he would pass through two squadrons, in despite of them: and enforce those of Seville to give him way. Which he performed upon divers of the foremost, who as the mariners term it, sprang their luff, and fell under the lee of the *Revenge*. But the other course had been the better, and might right well have been answered in so great an impossibility of prevailing. Notwithstanding out of the greatness of his mind, he could not be persuaded.'

When Bazan first caught sight of the English ships they were coming out from Flores 'on the side of the island of Corvo, to the windward of it, giving their right side to our fleet whose aim was to grapple the first ships of the enemy.' [2] The English had only their main-topsails and foresails out, their great sails taken in. Howard's flagship was leading, the rest behind her. From this it appears that Howard was tacking up against the wind, so as to get the windward of the Spanish fleet: the very manœuvre which Drake and the Lord Admiral Howard had

---

[1] This shows that Grenville had the Spaniards on his right; and it would be the Seville squadron that would first come in contact with him, for after Bazan had given the order to change course, the Seville squadron, which had previously been on the right wing, became the van of the whole fleet.

[2] Spanish Relation.

successfully brought off under the lee of Mount Edgcumbe and along the Cornish coast when the Armada was off Plymouth Sound. It was a close thing then; it was still closer now. In fact, the *Revenge*, which was the last ship to weigh anchor, could not manage it; and her commander, who could almost certainly have run back before the wind, showing the Spaniards a clean pair of heels, refused to do so. It was not in his nature to run. Soon it would be too late, anyhow.

At five o'clock in the afternoon, Aramburu was sufficiently near to exchange shots with Howard. There was a good deal of firing on both sides as the Spaniards advanced in two squadrons into the Channel, broadsides from the guns, and arquebus and musketry fire; but he was unable to grapple with the English flagship, which was besides unrigged. Bazan followed with the rest of the fleet, putting on more sail; and the great galleon *San Phelipe* and the *San Barnabe* now coming level with Howard tried to board the English flagship, and not being able to, gave her a great broadside at close range. Then passing on with the wind filling her sails, the *San Phelipe* caught up with the *Revenge*, which, according to the Spaniards, putting its trust in being the best sailing-ship of the fleet, came swaggering up (*gallardeando*) – the word catches the very spirit of the ship and of the man. Now, Ralegh says,

'the great *San Philip* being in the wind of him, and coming towards him, becalmed his sails in such sort, as the ship could neither weigh nor feel the helm: so huge and high carged was the Spanish ship, being of a thousand and five hundred tons. Who after-laid the *Revenge* aboard.'

The *Revenge*, remember, was a ship rated at 500 tons, though actually more like 450. The Spanish account of this episode is that the *San Phelipe* boarded her, and at the first encounter threw nine or ten soldiers into her; but not having grappled with grappling irons, but with a rope, it could not stand the strain and broke, so that the ships parted.

In this interval, General Bertendona came up in the *San Barnabe*, which grappled to the *Revenge* so well that he could not disengage to throw the grappling-iron. Bertendona was the commander of the Biscayan galleons – son of the captain of the ship which conducted Philip to his marriage in England in 1554.[1] He had a score to pay off against the *Revenge*: he had been on duty at Corunna when Drake arrived there in her in 1589 and he had been forced to set his great galleon on fire to save it from falling into Drake's hands. So he held on, while the great *San Phelipe* sheered off; according to Ralegh, she 'having the lower tier of the *Revenge*, discharged with crossbar-shot, shifted herself with all diligence from her sides, utterly misliking her first entertainment.' The *San Phelipe* was the largest of Bazan's newly-built 'Apostles.'

It was now nightfall, and according to the Spaniards, the rest of the English ships hoisted their mainsails and took to flight. Don Alonso went in pursuit of them and if night had not come down at once, they said, he would have taken several ships, at the least Howard's flagship because it was the least good of sail; but through the obscurity of the night they were lost from sight and Bazan returned to collect his ships together. This was the end of Howard's part in the action. The *Revenge* received no more help; though Ralegh tells us that

'in the beginning of the fight, the *George Noble* of London, having received some shot through her by the Armados, fell under the lee of the *Revenge*, and asked Sir Richard what he would command him, being but one of the victuallers and of small force: Sir Richard bade him save himself, and leave him to his fortune.'

The *Revenge* meanwhile lay locked in the embrace of Bertendona's galleon; the English at the first shock of the encounter put themselves into the high works of the ship fore and aft, whence they fired their artillery and musketry, and threw grenades. Of the soldiers that the *San Phelipe* had thrown into her seven were killed, but the rest gave such a good account of themselves that when Bertendona came up they went aboard his ship, whence no more were thrown into her because of night falling. Bertendona's ship lay on the larboard of the *Revenge*. Now Aramburu came up to give aid and boarded her poop with

[1] C. F. Duro, *La Armada Invencible*, I, 211.

his prow, throwing some men on to her quarter-deck who captured the ship's ensign, killed some of her men and got as far as the mainmast. But Aramburu's ship was so badly damaged by the encounter, all her prow being destroyed down to the water, that she too had to sheer off, and burnt flares for Bazan and his ships to come to her aid. She was then succeeded by the galleon *Ascension*, under Don Antonio Manrique, who boarded by the *Revenge's* prow and Bertendona's. Next came up Don Luis Cuitiño who boarded by joining on to Manrique. So the firing continued at intervals all night long.[1]

Ralegh says:

'The Spanish ships were filled with companies of soldiers, in some two hundred besides the mariners; in some five, in others eight hundred. In ours there were none at all, beside the mariners, but the servants of the commanders and some few voluntary gentlemen only. After many interchanged volleys of great ordnance and small shot, the Spaniards deliberated to enter the *Revenge*, and made divers attempts, hoping to force her by the multitudes of their armed soldiers and musketeers, but were still repulsed again and again, and at all times beaten back, into their own ships, or into the seas.'

But as often as they attacked and were beaten off,

'so always others came in their places, she having never less than two mighty galleons by her sides, and aboard her. So that ere morning, from three of the clock the day before, there had fifteen several Armados assailed her; and all so ill approved their entertainment, as they were by the break of day, far more willing to hearken to a composition, than hastily to make any more assaults or entries.'

Don Alonso de Bazan cruised about all night collecting his ships, and ordered them to circle round this tangle of locked, splintered and sputtering ships that could no longer move on their own. Ralegh says that the *Revenge* was 'not able to move one way or other, but as she was moved with the waves and billow of the sea.' The Spanish account tells us that she was

[1] Spanish Relation.

unrigged and without her masts. But their own ships that had engaged her were in even worse case. The galleon *Ascension* and Cuitiño's ship, the flagship of the hulks, were so badly damaged by each other and by the *Revenge* that both went to the bottom. The *Ascension* went down that night, saving most of her mariners and soldiers in Bertendona's ship; Don Luis Cuitiño's ship next day, her men having been taken out.

Day broke:

'And the night went down, and the sun smiled out far over the
      summer sea,
And the Spanish fleet, with broken sides lay round us all in
      a ring':

'But,' Ralegh says, 'as the day encreased, so our men decreased: and as the light grew more and more, by so much more grew our discomforts. For none appeared in sight but enemies, saving one small ship called the *Pilgrim*, commanded by Jacob Whiddon [a Plymouth ship: a Plymouth man], who hovered all night to see the success; but in the morning bearing with the *Revenge*, was hunted like a hare amongst many ravenous hounds, but escaped.'

The total result of the night's fighting and of the evening before, was that the *Revenge* was still unbeaten: she had beaten off every assault, and the Spaniards were reluctant to push conclusions any further home. But her condition was desperate: Ralegh compares it to a slaughter-house, 'the ship being marvellous unsavery, filled with blood and bodies of dead and wounded men.' Sir Richard himself had remained on the upper deck till an hour before midnight, when he was wounded with a musket-shot in the body; then as he was being dressed, he was dangerously wounded in the head, his chirurgeon being killed beside him. The powder of the *Revenge* was spent by the morning, all her pikes broken, forty of her best men slain, and most of the remainder hurt. At the beginning of the fight she had but a hundred men free from sickness, and ninety sick laid in hold upon the ballast. She had no hope of supply either of ships, men or weapons, as against the large reserves of the

Spaniards: her 'masts all beaten over board, all her tackle cut asunder, her upper work altogether razed, and in effect evened she was with the water, but the very foundation or bottom of a ship, nothing being left over head either for flight or defence.'

It was in this desperate condition that Grenville's courage rose to heroic heights: a sort of fixed, dæmonic will, a gesture against the world and fate, by which a man is for ever remembered. Perhaps it was due to his being a dying man; but he was in full command of his senses and capable of still imposing his will upon the ship. One might have thought that there was no alternative but surrender. But no; there remained another, a more absolute way out, his deliberate and determined choice.

'Sir Richard finding himself in this distress,' says Ralegh, 'commanded the master gunner, whom he knew to be a most resolute man, to split and sink the ship' – there was evidently enough powder left for that – 'that thereby nothing might remain of glory or victory to the Spaniards . . . And persuaded the company, or as many as he could induce, to yield themselves unto God, and to the mercy of none else; but as they had like valiant resolute men, repulsed so many enemies, they should not now shorten the honour of their nation, by prolonging their own lives for a few hours or a few days. The master gunner readily condescended and divers others. But the Captain and the Master were of an other opinion, and besought Sir Richard to have care of them: alleging that the Spaniard would be as ready to entertain a composition, as they were willing to offer the same: and that there being divers sufficient and valiant men yet living, and whose wounds were not mortal, they might do their country and prince acceptable service hereafter. And (that where Sir Richard had alleged that the Spaniards should never glory to have taken one ship of her Majesty's, seeing that they had so long and so notably defended themselves) they answered, that the ship had six foot of water in hold, three shot under water which were so weakly stopped, as with the first working of the sea, she must need sink, and was besides so crushed and bruised, as she could never be removed out of the place.'

What an extraordinary scene it is! It is more like the dæmonic determination, the self-dedication to death of those early Norse seamen, whose blood, the Grenvilles boasted, ran in their veins, than it was like sixteenth-century warfare. No wonder the Islanders believed that Grenville's soul was possessed by devils. It may be that his resolve was due to the oncoming of death, as conversely it was an argument to those 'whose wounds' they pointed out 'were not mortal,' that they should live. Their case was a strong one: they had made one of the most heroic fights against odds in the annals of the sea: no-one could say that they were not 'valiant resolute men' as Grenville called them in persuading them to death. And they were right: the Spaniards would not long enjoy the glory of possessing the carcase of the *Revenge*; she was in a desperate state, and in the storm that followed was one of the first ships to go to the bottom. Nevertheless it is probable that if Grenville had not been mortally wounded, he would have had his way, and he and the master-gunner would have blown up the ship themselves.

The issue entered a new phase, a no less extraordinary scene.

'And as the matter was thus in dispute,' Ralegh wrote, 'and Sir Richard refusing to hearken to any of those reasons: the master of the *Revenge* (while the Captain won unto him the greater party) was conveyed aboard the General, Don Alfonso Bazan. Who finding none over-hasty to enter the *Revenge* again, doubting lest Sir Richard would have blown them up and himself, and perceiving by the report of the master of the *Revenge* his dangerous disposition: yielded that all their lives should be saved, the company sent for England, and the better sort to pay such reasonable ransom as their estate would bear, and in the mean season to be free from galley or imprisonment. To this he so much the rather condescended as well as I have said, for fear of further loss and mischief to themselves, as also for the desire he had to recover Sir Richard Grenville; whom for his notable valour he seemed greatly to honour and admire. When this answer was returned, and that safety of life was promised, the common sort being now at the end of their peril, the most drew back from Sir Richard and the master gunner, being no hard matter to dissuade men from death to life.

'The master gunner finding him self and Sir Richard thus prevented and mastered by the greater number, would have slain himself with a sword, had he not been by force witheld and locked into his cabin. Then the General [i.e. Bazan] sent many boats aboard the *Revenge*, and divers of our men fearing Sir Richard's disposition, stole away aboard the General and other ships. Sir Richard thus overmatched, was sent unto by Alonso Bazan to remove out of the *Revenge*, the ship being marvellous unsavoury, filled with blood and bodies of dead, and wounded men like a slaughter-house. Sir Richard answered that he might do with his body what he list, for he esteemed it not; and as he was carried out of the ship he swooned, and reviving again desired the company to pray for him. The General used Sir Richard with all humanity, and left nothing unattempted that tended to his recovery, highly commending his valour and worthiness, and greatly bewailed the danger wherein he was; being unto them a rare spectacle, and a resolution seldom approved.'

Thus much Ralegh says he derived from a Spanish captain in Bazan's fleet, who afterwards became separated in the storm and captured by a small English ship, the *Lyon*, was brought home prisoner to London. It is borne out also by the Spanish Relation, which says that Don Alonso had him brought aboard his flagship, where, because he was wounded, a head-wound from an arquebus-shot, he might be taken care of and refreshed, receiving good treatment and being consoled for his loss; *mas la herida era grande y murio otro dia* (but his wound was grievous and in a day or two he died). The Spaniards, as was to be expected, behaved like great gentlemen, and when he died, the Relation writes his epitaph: *el Almirante de los mayores marineros y cosarios de Inglaterra gran hereje y perseguidor de catholicos.* And Ralegh wrote, on his information:

'Sir Richard died as it is said, the second or third day aboard the General, and was by them greatly bewailed. What became of his body, whether it were buried in the sea or on the land we know not: the comfort that remaineth to his friends is, that he hath ended his life honourably in respect of the reputation won to his nation and country, and of the same to his posterity, and that being dead, he hath not outlived his own honour.'

There is some further evidence of Grenville's last hours, that of the Dutchman Linschoten, which is not to be neglected. It is true that it is not first-hand, and there are points in it which are doubtful. On the other hand, he was resident at Terceira at the time of the action, and when Bertendona's ship came in there, the very one which lay all the time of the fight beside the *Revenge*, he went on board and was received by Bertendona.

'He seeing us called us up into the gallery, where with great courtesy he received us, being as then set at dinner with the English Captain [i.e. Langhorne] that sat by him, and had on a suit of black velvet, but he could not tell us anything, for that he could speak no other language but English and Latin, which Bertendona also could a little speak. The English Captain got licence of the governor that he might come on land with his weapon by his side, and was in our lodging. The Governor of Terceira had him to dinner, and showed him great courtesy. The Master likewise with licence of Bertendona came on land, and was in our lodging, and had at the least ten or twelve wounds, as well in his head, as on his body, whereof after that being at sea, between Lisbon and the Islands he died.'

It may be seen that Linschoten was in a position to pick up information directly after the engagement; for the rest he is useful in that he records the gossip current in the Islands, the impression that these events made upon the Islanders. Linschoten tells us, quite correctly, the name of the Spanish flagship (the *San Pablo*) on board which Grenville was taken in a dying condition, and he says that his wounds were dressed; but he continues that

'Don Alonso himself would neither see him, nor speak with him: all the rest of the captains and gentlemen went to visit him, and to comfort him in his hard fortune, wondering at his courage, and stout heart, for that he showed not any sign of faintness nor changing of colour.'

Whether it be true or no that Bazan would not see Grenville, it is not incompatible with the otherwise good treatment that Grenville received from the Spaniards. After all, the action reflected little or no credit upon Bazan; what credit there was on the Spanish side was due to Bertendona, whose prize the *Revenge* became. Bazan may have been chagrined by the long resistance the *Revenge* put up, and when he arrived in Spain was much criticised for not having taken the rest of the English ships. On the other hand, there is no hint of this in the Spanish Relation which appears to come from the flagship itself. Linschoten goes on to report the gist of Grenville's last words on board the *San Pablo*.

'Feeling the hour of death to approach, he spake these words in Spanish, and said! "Here die I Richard Grenville, with a joyful and quiet mind, for that I have ended my life as a true soldier ought to do, that hath fought for his country, Queen, religion and honour, whereby my soul most joyful departeth out of this body, and shall always leave behind it an everlasting fame of a valiant and true soldier that hath done his duty, as he was bound to do. But the others of my company have done as traitors and dogs, for which they shall be reproached all their lives and leave a shameful name for ever." '

This last speech as reported by Linschoten is much disputed and has given rise to controversy. It may indeed be a Thucydidean speech, truer in drift and intention than as a report of Grenville's actual words. Then, too, when Linschoten's account was translated into English, the last sentence of scorn and reproach was omitted. But it is precisely this sentence which is so true in character to Grenville; he was not the man to spare the feelings of those who had crossed his will, in order to make a good, a more pious ending. It has usually been considered that the target of Grenville's contempt was Howard and the rest of the English ships that had got away. It would seem, however, that it is those of his own company, those on board the *Revenge* who had thwarted his will, who incurred his wrath; that his mind had become fixed in the determination to blow up his ship and that their crossing of his will was what possessed his dying thoughts.

The Spaniards were proud to have got possession of the *Revenge*, even in her present condition and upon terms. The Spanish Relation says of her:

'This Admiral-galleon was one of the best there were in England; they called her the *Revenge*. She was the flagship that carried Drake to Corunna . . . She carried 42 pieces of artillery of bronze without three which were given to another ship a few days before, the 20 on her lower-deck of 40 to 60 quintals, and the remaining 22 of 20 to 30 quintals, all good.'

She was rated among the Queen's ships as a second-rater; but she was the crack ship of her class, the middle-sized fighting galleon. She was laid down in 1575, and represented the new ideas of fast, but heavily-armed ocean-going galleons, which Hawkins introduced into the Navy Board. When built she was actually 441 tons, though rated at 500; she was 92 feet in length, 32 in beam, and 15 in depth, and was regarded by Drake as the perfect warship of her time.[1] Alas that no picture of her has survived! But there is her fighting record, most of it, though not all, accomplished under Drake's command. She was overhauled and made readier for the approaching war, in 1583; she was off the coast of Spain with Hawkins in 1586; in the triumphant year 1588 she was Drake's flagship and as such the glory of that year reflected her name; in 1590 she was in the Azores with Frobisher. It is another of the ironies of history that in the end, and to all posterity, her name should go down with another's name.

The younger Hawkins, Sir Richard, in his *Observations* describes her as 'ever the unfortunatest ship the late Queen's majesty had during her reign,' and he recounts the accidents that happened to her in her crowded life: how she was nearly cast away upon the Kentish coast, coming out of Ireland with Sir John Perrot; how she struck aground at Plymouth before

---

[1] Corbett, i, 371-2.

the voyage with Hawkins in 1586, and sprang a leak upon her return with Drake from Lisbon which nearly sank her; then coming into Plymouth ran upon the Winter stone, and at Portsmouth was twice aground; and now at last, 'the cost and loss she wrought, I have too good cause to remember, in her last voyage, in which she was lost, when she gave England and Spain just cause to remember her.' [1] Of the men in her, she carried 250, the Spanish Relation says; and only 100 remained, who were divided among all the ships of the Spanish fleet, 'not having among them any person of quality except for a young gentleman who is not a soldier nor a sailor, and another who was killed who was a sailor.' The former of these is evidently Philip Gawdy. One wonders with what party he had sided, with Grenville or with Captain Langhorne, when the ship might have been blown up on Grenville's orders? Perhaps those last hours on board were a nightmare to him, a sufficient reason for him never, so far as we know, to have written down the experience.

The Spaniards admitted to greater damage to their ships than actual loss of men: the Relation says only 100 men, including those drowned in the *Ascension* who were most in number. Two of their captains were killed: Luis de San Juan and Don Jorge Broano. They claimed that in the running fight Howard's flagship received a good deal of damage by the *San Christobal* and the *San Phelipe*. They say nothing about the *Foresight*, which Ralegh says

'performed a very great fight, and stayed two hours as near the *Revenge* as the weather would permit him, not forsaking the sight, till he was like to be encompassed by the squadrons, and with great difficulty cleared himself. The rest gave divers volleys of shot and entered as far as the place permitted and their own necessities, to keep the weather gauge of the enemy, until they were parted by night.'

The Spanish Relation states that they

'took to flight in disorder, some bearing west and others towards

[1] Hawkins, *Observations* (Hakluyt Society), p. 9.

the Isles [i.e. east] taking advantage of the obscurity of the night, and others by different ways; of whom up to now we do not know that they have collected together, nor seen them, except for one very far off plying to windward; though we have gone with the Fleet more than 40 leagues in the direction in which the flotas have to come, carrying light ships on the flanks separated some eight leagues from the Fleet so as to discover them, besides others sent still further ahead for that purpose.'

It had been a notable scattering of the English; but a still greater scattering of the Spaniards was to come. The autumn of that year was an exceptionally stormy one, and the commercial fleets in the Indies had been at sea in those tropical waters so long, that they could not withstand the gales that blew. Before ever they reached the Havana, the fleets of New Spain, the Mainland, San Domingo and Honduras had endured losses, from weather and by the depredations of the English, which reduced their number from 120 to something over 70. Further storms while they were on their way across the Atlantic weakened them still more. When Don Alonso met them off Flores and Corvo, having collected all his ships in the vicinity together, there were in all some 140 sail under his command, according to Linschoten.

Then when they were all proceeding under his convoy to Terceira, a storm far worse than all those preceding, one which reached the velocity of a cyclone, suddenly swept down upon them. It wrought tremendous havoc in Bazan's fleet but even more among the *flotas*. Ralegh says, and he is not exaggerating, that fifteen or sixteen of Bazan's ships of war were lost upon the Islands, and of the Indies fleets, what with those lost on the way and in the cyclone, more than seventy perished.

'The 4 of this month of November, we received letters from Tercera, affirming that there are 3,000 bodies of men in that Island, saved out of the perished ships: and that by the Spaniards own confession, there are 10,000 cast away in this storm, besides those that are perished between the Islands and the main.'

Linschoten bears this out. There had never been such a storm in the Azores in living memory, he says. It lasted not a day or two, but for seven or eight days continually. On Terceira where he was living, twelve ships were cast away, on every side there was nothing but crying and lamenting that here was a ship cast ashore, and here another and all the men drowned, so that for twenty days after the storm the drowned men came driving continually ashore. On San Jorge, two ships were cast away, on Pico two more, on Graciosa three, on San Miguel four, while between Terceira and San Miguel 'three more were sunk, which were seen and heard to cry out, whereof not one man was saved.'

Among those cast away in the storm, as the Captain and the Master had predicted, was the *Revenge* herself. It must have pleased them as it did Ralegh, who wrote of that great destruction and the last of the *Revenge* with a touching emotion: 'So it pleased them to honour the burial of that renowned ship the *Revenge*, not suffering her to perish alone, for the great honour she achieved in her life-time.' Linschoten tells us that she was

'cast away upon a cliff near to the Island of Tercera, where it brake in a hundred pieces and sunk to the ground, having in her 70 men gallegos [i.e. Galicians], Biscayans and others, with some of the captive Englishmen, whereof but one was saved that got up upon the cliffs alive, and had his body and head all wounded, and he being on shore brought us the news, desiring to be shriven, and thereupon presently died.'

Of all the ships of the Indies fleets that year, a double *flota*, only some twenty-five or thirty ever reached Spain. Fortunately for Philip the treasure was not on board; that was waiting for the fast frigates at Havana and did not reach Spain until next year. The losses suffered by Spain were enormous, and in that country people were forbidden under severe penalties to speak of them. But in the Azores they talked, and Linschoten reported what was said. They said that Spain lost even more this year than she had by the Armada;

'that, the taking of the *Revenge* was justly revenged upon them, and not by the might or force of man, but by the power of God, as some of them openly said in the Isle of Tercera, that they believed verily God would consume them, and that he took part with Lutherans and heretics: saying further that so soon as they had thrown the dead body of the Viceadmiral Sir Richard Grenville overboard, they verily thought that as he had a devilish faith and religion, and therefore the devils loved him, so he presently sunk into the bottom of the sea, and down into Hell, where he raised up all the devils to the revenge of his death.'

A credulous people: but then this was the sixteenth century. Grenville was an even greater torment to them in death than ever he had been in life. The *Revenge* had justified her name in a whirlwind of disaster.

CHAPTER XVIII

CHARACTER AND MYTH

Give me a spirit that on this life's rough sea
Loves to have his sails filled with a lusty wind,
Even till his sail-yards tremble, his masts crack,
And his rapt ship run on her side so low
That she drinks water, and her keel ploughs air.

There is no danger to a man who knows
What life and death is; there's not any law
Exceeds his knowledge: neither is it lawful
That he should stoop to any other law.
He goes before them and commands them all,
That to himself is a law rational.

CHAPMAN

The action in the Azores gave satisfaction neither in England nor in Spain. In Spain it was asked why the English squadron had not been totally destroyed; in England how it was that the *Revenge* should have been caught in that manner. This led to much public discussion, and the discussion, in a sense, has gone on ever since. With the aid of the Spanish Relation newly brought into light, we have been able to determine more clearly than ever before, what precisely happened off Flores. But still we do not reach certainty as to what it was that determined Grenville's action. All depends upon our interpretation of his character; and it is only now that all the facts regarding his life, such as they have survived the passage of time, have been brought together into a coherent whole. It is upon his life as a whole that we must base our reading of that action upon which rests his popular, his world-wide fame: one of the great myths of the English people.

We have shown in this book that there is a solid basis of

achievement for his name to have been remembered in the ordinary way, and to have come down to us as one of the most active of those who fashioned the Elizabethan triumph. There is his record of consistent and crowded service to Crown and country; there were his sea-enterprises, his development of the trade of Bideford, his great project for the South Seas, unaccomplished through no fault of his own; he was the first planter of Virginia, by far the most important step, for it was the first of all those by which, in the usual English method of trial and error, the mainland of North America was colonised by the English people. But it is not upon any of these achievements – few indeed have ever known of them – that his legendary fame rests: that is due simply to the heroic quality of his last action. Nevertheless, that final quality has nothing inconsistent with the general tenor of his life—now that the mystery of that has been lifted. Indeed, we may say, as frequently is the case with men who turn out to have genius, that the predisposing conditions were there: that his nature, from what we have seen of it in other actions of his life, and however little we may be attracted by its qualities – harsh, hard-hitting, as hard upon himself as upon others, with a strain of nervous over-balance in it – was just the nature to have accomplished such an end, the heroic gesture which sets the imagination of a people on flame.

So perhaps, in view of this consistency – that the end is of a piece with his life, that it was just to him of all the Elizabethan fighting-men that this thing would happen – we may not be so uncertain after all, even in the realm of character and motive.

I

The Spaniards could not but be expected to make the most of their capture of one of the Queen's great ships – the first, and the last, that was to be captured in the whole war. Monson, who had been himself taken in a small ship off the Burlings, tells us that he saw one of Bazan's twelve apostles coming into harbour at Lisbon all decked for the capture of the *Revenge*.

'It happened on St. Andrew's day following, that being upon the walls [i.e. of Lisbon Castle] at our usual hour, we beheld

322

a great galleon of the King's turning up the river in her fighting sails, being sumptuously decked with ancients [ensigns],
streamers and pendants, with all other ornaments to show her
bravery. She let fly all her ordnance in a triumphant manner
for the taking Sir Richard Grenville in the Revenge at the
island of Flores, she being one of that fleet and the first voyage
she ever made.' [1]

This ship was the *St. Andrew*; and whether we are to believe
him or no, Monson tells us that in his annoyance he wagered
the other Englishmen in his company ten to one that he would
live to see her taken yet. He did: in 1596 in the descent upon
Cadiz, it fell to Ralegh's good fortune to tackle the great *St.
Philip* and the *St. Andrew*, both ships which had boarded the
Revenge. It was a chance of war that Ralegh leaped at, 'being
resolved,' as he said, 'to be revenged for the *Revenge*, or to second
her with mine own life.' [2] The attack was so furious that the
Spaniards themselves set fire to the *St. Philip* to prevent her falling into English hands; the *St. Andrew* was captured and brought
back to England.

It was only natural that one of Bazan's fleet should have made
the most of the 'victory'; but in Spain itself, when the extent of
its losses became known, there was general murmuring against
Bazan for not having utterly destroyed Howard so that not a
ship escaped, since he had had such a large force under his
command. [3]

Similarly, in England, the first news of the loss of the *Revenge*
created much concern and a host of rumours. [4] She was already
such a famous ship, Drake's favourite, her name associated in
the public mind with the triumphs of 1588. As yet the public

---

[1] Monson, V, 171–2.　　　　　　[2] Edwards, *Ralegh*, II, 151.

[3] cf. Duro, *Armada Española*, III, 81: 'viendolas estampadas en España
contra D. Alonso de Bazan por no haber destruido a Howard sin que un solo
navio se escapase, teniendo tantos a sus órdenes.'

[4] cf. the evidence of Gonzalo Gonzales del Castillo, one of the prisoners of
1588, who was in England at the time: 'They were much grieved at the loss
of one of the Queen's galleons, called the *Revenge*. They say that she was the
best ship the Queen had, and the one upon which she relied the most.' *Cal.
S.P. Spanish 1587–1603*, 597.

did not know the circumstances of her last fight, nor whether she had gone to the bottom or not. At the end of October, Sir Henry Killigrew, writing from Dieppe to the Earl of Essex, had heard that she had been towed, a complete wreck without deck or mast, into Lisbon by two galleys.[1] This, as we know, was untrue.

On 31 October, a letter was written by Thomas Phillips the decipherer, to an English spy in Paris to be sent on to Charles Paget, from which we may learn something. He

'can write him no good news from hence,' the draft says, 'the loss of the *Revenge* with Sir R. Grenville being now stale, which you keep quiet, as they disguised it here with the sinking of so many ships of the King of Spain and loss of so many men, besides that she should be since sunk in the sea with so many Spaniards that were in her. Here they condemn the Lord Thomas infinitely for a coward and some say he is for the King of Spain. The quarrel and offer of combat between the Lord Admiral and Sir Walter Ralegh about the matter you are sure he hath heard of. Here be seven prizes brought in as they say parcel of the West India fleet by the merchants that went to second my Lord Thomas and they give out that the great part of the rest and the King's ships of war are drowned by tempest and but twenty-six arrived in Spain.'[2]

This takes us a good deal further on in the reception of the news by the English public. It is interesting to hear of a challenge between Lord Admiral Howard and Ralegh; later there was no love lost between Ralegh and the Howards, and the news may well be true. The rest of the information is substantially correct; by the end of October, people in London knew pretty well what had happened.

For the benefit of the public, which was a prey to all sorts of rumours, and as a statement of the English view of the action, as well as a defence of his cousin's conduct, Ralegh wrote his famous pamphlet, which was published anonymously that autumn. Its full title was: '*A Report of the truth of the fight about the Isles of Açores, this last summer, betwixt the "Revenge," one of her*

[1] *Hatfield MSS.*, IV, 155.   [2] S.P. Dom. Eliz. 240, no. 53.

Majesty's Ships, and an Armada of the King of Spain.' [1] It was his first prose-work to appear, the first proof he gave of that magnificent command of English prose which was to find full expression in his *History of the World.*

It was not so much European opinion that he had in mind, though he began his tract with a recital of Spanish expectations of the Armada and their grievous disillusionment in 1588. After all, the Spaniards had not been able to make much of their capture of the *Revenge*; the official Relation which was sent home from Bazan's fleet was singularly objective, unimpassioned, faithful reporting. It was the English who were more uncertain of themselves, new to power, and therefore more exaggerated, more Italianate in the sixteenth century; Ralegh more than any. What he set himself to do was to still the unfavourable rumours which questioned Grenville's conduct, to reconstruct the action in a manner that would convince and vindicate the memory of the man who was no longer there to speak for himself.

For there was a case against Grenville: why had he delayed so that his ship was caught by overwhelming numbers? Ralegh says that Grenville was the last to weigh anchor, 'to recover the men that were upon the Island, which otherwise had been lost.' That made it too late to follow Howard's course in tacking to windward of the Spaniards. It remained for him either to run away from them before the wind, or – what seemed incredible for anyone to attempt – to try and cut his way through the whole Spanish fleet. Dr. Williamson has constructed a defence of Grenville's action, mainly on the ground that we do not know what his conditions were.[2] But the evidence points to an explanation, not in technical but in psychological terms. Grenville *would* not 'cut his main sail, and cast about, and trust to the sailing of his ship,' as the ship's master and others tried to persuade him; he

'utterly refused to turn from the enemy, alleging that he would rather choose to die, than to dishonour himself, his country, and

---

[1] Printed for William Ponsonbie, London, 1591; reprinted under Ralegh's name in Hakluyt, *Principal Navigations.* Text in Arber's *English Reprints.*
[2] 'Sir Richard Grenville' in *The Great Tudors*, 445.

her Majesty's ship, persuading his company that he would pass through the two squadrons in despite of them: and enforce those of Seville to give him way.'

Thus much Ralegh admits, and he comments a little sadly – it is an adverse judgment: 'But the other course had been the better, and might right well have been answered in so great an impossibility of prevailing. Notwithstanding out of the greatness of his mind, he could not be persuaded.' There was perhaps one chance in a hundred, or, more exactly, in fifty, that he might get through; if he should not, he did not fear the consequences. In that act of will – it is not rational, nor perhaps even intelligent – lies the quality of the heroic.

The judgments of the experts, both those who were friendly and those who were unfavourable, seem to converge upon this explanation in terms of Grenville's character, rather than of technical conditions. Sir William Monson, writing his account of the action some years afterwards, strongly approved of Howard's 'wary and discreet' conduct in getting clear of the Spaniards.

'But Sir Richard Grenville, being astern, and imagining this fleet to come from the Indies, and not to be the Armada of which they were informed, would by no means be persuaded by his master or company to cut his cable to follow his Admiral, as all discipline of war did teach him, nay so headstrong, rash and unadvised he was that he offered violence to all that counselled him to the contrary.' [1]

This is rather exaggerated, and it is hardly likely that Grenville imagined Bazan's fleet to be the *flotas* from the Indies, after the warning that Captain Middleton had delivered the night before. Nevertheless, the substantial point remains, and it is borne out by the impression the Spaniards got that Grenville trusted in his ship being the best sailing ship of the fleet.[2]

Since Ralegh's pamphlet was virtually an official account of

[1] Oppenheim, I, 254.
[2] 'La Almiranta que fiada en ser el mejor Navio de vela de su Armada,' Spanish Relation.

the action, it fell to him at the same time to exonerate Howard's conduct. This he did very handsomely. If there had been a quarrel and a challenge between him and the Lord Admiral, there had evidently been a reconciliation, for Ralegh now wrote defending Lord Thomas:

'Notwithstanding it is very true, that the Lord Thomas would have entered between the squadrons, but the rest would not condescend; and the master of his own ship offered to leap into the sea, rather than to conduct that her Majesty's ship and the rest to be a prey to the enemy, where there was no hope nor possibility either of defence or victory. Which also in my opinion had it sorted or answered the discretion and trust of a General, to commit himself and his charge to an assured destruction, without hope or any likelihood of prevailing: thereby to diminish the strength of her Majesty's Navy, and to enrich the pride and glory of the enemy.'

Such was Ralegh's reconciliation of the conflicting points of view with regard to the action, the picture which he wished to impress upon the public mind. In this he was entirely successful; posterity came to view the last fight of the *Revenge* through his eyes – a proof, if any be needed, of the power of literary genius to impress its views upon men's minds. The growth of the pamphlet's influence can be traced in the literature of the time.

But first, to gather together the few remaining recorded facts, last floating spars of the wreckage of the *Revenge*. Philip Wyot's *Diary* lets us know how, towards the middle of October, the news came home to Barnstaple and Bideford: '12 October . . . report came that her Majesty's ship at sea, Sir Richard Grenville, Captain, was taken by the Spaniards after encountering the whole Spanish Fleet for two days.'[1] One can imagine the sensation the ill news caused through all that Grenville countryside; but of its reception at Stowe, now suddenly turned into a house of mourning, not a word remains. How much one regrets the destruction of its records at such a time!

The Government, to mark its sense of the exceptional services of the men who had fought in the *Revenge*, paid them, according

[1] f. 46 Diary, ed. Chanter.

327

to Hawkins, six months' wages; [1] or according to a more certain source of information, a gratuity of six months' pay to the widows of the men who had perished in her. [2] The Spaniards had been as good as their word, and allowed the men they had taken in the ship to come home free. That autumn and winter, the prisoners came dribbling back, most of them evidently belonging to the West Country. There is an examination of Thomas Meade of Topsham, preserved among the State Papers; he was taken in the *Revenge* and landed at Dartmouth, 15 December. [3] Among the business before the Privy Council in that month, there was an appeal from a woman

'pretending herself to be the wife of one John Carew, mariner, said to have served in her Majesty's ship the *Revenge*, doth inform us that her said husband hath been slain in the said ship and she, left poor, with child and without relief, doth desire such wages as was due unto him before his death.' [4]

A pathetic piece of the wreckage left; hers was a case of what not seldom happens when a sailor goes to sea and never returns.

Lastly there is Philip Gawdy, who after such ardours and expectations from a sea-life, found himself downcast and dejected in Lisbon Castle, with Captain Monson for company. He was lucky, indeed, to be alive. The Spaniards on this occasion had treated their captives handsomely, but since Philip was almost the only person of quality left on the ship, they kept him at Lisbon for ransom. [5] Whether Lord Thomas Howard intervened on Philip's behalf or no, we are not told; but almost certainly he did – were they not both Norfolk men? For next year, we find Philip once more in England, having 'now passed my long and wearisome troubles, and by the help of good friends I am now returned into mine own country.' With his return, we may say that the last account of the action in the Azores was liquidated.

Not so its fame: that went on mounting with the years. Nor was it so much due to Ralegh's pamphlet: action in itself was what

[1] *Observations* (ed. Williamson), 16.   [2] Oppenheim, I, 256.
[3] S.P. Dom. 240, no. 97.   [4] *A.P.C. 1591–2*, 121.   [5] Gawdy, 63–4.

appealed to the mind of the Elizabethan public, unusually susceptible as it was to the appeal of the heroic, the dare-devil, the bloody – witness their early drama just entering on its astonishing efflorescence. Such events as the fight of the *Revenge* have their importance for the development of mind which led to such creative activity. In 1595, there appeared a long poem, *The Most Honorable Tragedy of Sir Richard Grenville, Knight*, by Gervase Markham.[1] Tedious as it is, the poem is not without merit; indeed, one may doubt whether it has ever had justice done to it, so few can have got through it. To some extent it may have suffered from Markham's later reputation, as a hack-writer on every conceivable subject from the arts of love and war to those of farriery and husbandry. The Grenville poem is, however, a poem of his youth; he was only twenty when he wrote it: it has therefore something of the freshness as well as the naïveté and the *longueurs* of youth.

It is for the most part an exercise in verse, a sort of exhibition piece, taking the compact and moving prose of Ralegh and expanding it until all genuine emotion has gone out of the thing. Markham was something of a scholar and knew the classical languages. The result is that his poem cannot move for classical machinery, the action is made the consequence of a dispute between the goddesses of Good and Ill Fortune, and there is a good deal about Phoebus and Neptune, the loves of Jove and (of course) the shears of Atropos. The only tolerable way of regarding the poem is as a baroque piece, comparable to the furniture and the building of the age. One stanza has a fair baroque seascape:

> By this, the sun had spread his golden locks,
> Upon the pale green carpet of the sea,
> And opened wide the scarlet door which locks
> The easeful evening from the labouring day;
> Now Night began to leap from iron Rocks,
> And whip her rusty wagon through the way,
>   Whilst all the Spanish host stood maz'd in sight,
>   None daring to assail a second fight.

[1] Reprinted in Arber, *English Reprints*.

When all is said, it is but poor stuff. It is odd that it was not until three hundred years later, out of a far subtler and more sophisticated age, that there came the simple and direct 'Ballad of the *Revenge*' of Tennyson, a perfectly satisfying poem. The inspiration of that, even to verbal echoes, came direct and immediate from Ralegh's prose.

It was only natural that Carew, whose *Survey of Cornwall* appeared in 1602, should in his own quaint way, commemorate the dead hero: who

'made so glorious a conclusion in her Majesty's ship the *Revenge* . . . that it seemed thereby, when he found none other to compare withal in his life, he strived through a virtuous envy to exceed it in his death: a victorious loss for the realm; and of which the Spaniard may say with Pyrrhus, that many such conquests would beget his utter overthrow.' [1]

Sir Richard Hawkins's commemoration of Grenville in his *Observations*, is altogether warmer as befits a fellow seaman and one who went through a similar ordeal to Grenville, fighting an action against odds, though not such odds, in the Bay of Atacames off the coast of Peru. It is a complete vindication of Grenville's conduct at Flores; Hawkins belonged to the same school of thought, but he must have had plenty of opportunity of hearing the whole action thrashed out in discussion:

'In this point, at the Isle of Flores, Sir Richard Grenville got eternal honour and reputation of great valour, and of an experimented [i.e. experienced] soldier, choosing rather to sacrifice his life, and to pass all danger whatsoever than to fail in his obligation, by gathering together those which had remained ashore in that place, though with the hazard of his ship and company . . . and I account that he, and his country, got much honour in that occasion . . .' [2]

Such was the code of honour among the Elizabethan seamen, and such the view that prevailed.

Last of all comes the tribute of the noblest intellect, if not the noblest mind, of the age – all the more moving because in that

[1] Carew, 176.   [2] Hawkins, 16.

ERITH PUBLIC LIBRARIES

RIHARDVS GRENVILVS Mil. aur.

Neptuni proles. qui magni Martis alumnus
GRENVILIVS patrias sanguine tinxit aquas

SIR RICHARD GRENVILLE.

way at any rate after a lifetime of rivalry and mutual dislike, Bacon was at one with Ralegh: 'that memorable fight of an English ship called the *Revenge* . . . memorable (I say) even beyond credit, and to the height of some heroical fable.' [1]

II

The concentration of posterity upon this one episode, even though it is the last and most exciting in his life, meant that the sense of Grenville's career as a whole became submerged, and, when to this was added the destruction of Stowe and its archives, was forgotten. We have to attempt to assess his career as a whole, and to fix the character of the man in the light of that.

He was a man very representative of his time. His career was an embodiment of those tendencies which were characteristic of the age and made it what it was. We can see that he was neither the romantic and chivalrous survival from the Middle Ages such as Corbett imagined, nor the inhuman and ravening figure of the islanders' legend in the Azores. He was very typical of his age and class – that small class of captains and commanders by land and sea, which set the pace for the Elizabethan Age. Like them he was strenuous, hard-working, acquisitive, restless, devoted; more selfless than most: there was nothing of the egoist in him, as in so many of those others. He had the passion for action that was common to them all; indeed, he was solely the man of action; for though he was very capable of giving an opinion on public matters, for example the vexed question of the settlement of Munster, he was, unlike Ralegh, singularly unspeculative. We may be sure that such doubts as he had were not of an intellectual character.

Again, it is notable that when he was consulted on public matters, it was usually on technical affairs: matters relating to defence, or harbour-works, which were regarded in much the same light as fortification; or questions of detail relating to the administration of his county – musters, the supply of corn,

[1] Bacon, 'Considerations touching a war with Spain.' *Letters and Life*, ed. Spedding, VII, 491.

keeping the peace, bringing offenders to book. It is obvious that he would not be consulted on high policy; he had not the mind or temperament for that in an age when, the political system not being democratic, politics moved upon a higher intellectual plane. He was used upon committees in the House of Commons; that in itself was only another tribute to his local importance and the possession of average business ability. The field of action was his real sphere; he was a devoted public servant, the chosen instrument of the government in the West and of Ralegh in the wider fields of colonisation and plantation.

How wide that sphere of action was, we have seen in this book. The foundation of his career rested upon a long record of work in his county. Long before his career came to its premature end, he had come to occupy a pre-eminent place in Cornwall: in itself evidence of his competence, at a time when Godolphins and Carews and Hawkins', men of ability, were also content to spend themselves upon local affairs – critical as they were in the west in those years before and after 1588! Over and above this local work as Justice of the Peace, and serving at Westminster as member for the shire, there were his military qualifications which meant that further services and his advice were required relating to more general questions of defence. In addition there was his early interest in exploration and discovery; his very great services towards colonisation and planting in Virginia and in Ireland; and his fairly constant interest in privateering, a favourite avocation with west-country gentry on the sea-board, more professional in his case, as with the Hawkins' and Ralegh, since it grew naturally out of shipping interests.

Of his private virtues (or otherwise) we have no speaking evidence: not a letter of any intimate character, which might enable us to descry his emotional life, has survived. Perhaps that in itself is some evidence. It is clear that family pride was a strong instinct with him as with all Grenvilles: a sense of the family, the maintenance of its tradition and the constant purpose of advancing its interests, no less ardent than with Drake or Hawkins, though they had the spur of belonging to new families which had their name yet to make. Though his was one of the oldest in the land, Grenville was no less ambitious for it. That too was very Elizabethan: the elbowing struggle, the competitiveness, the vulgarity.

In this sphere, as in his public life, he displayed an equal and a passionate devotion to business and duty. He must have cared for his sons, at any rate for his second son, John, who was a lad after his own heart. In this region we really know nothing. It all appears rather hard and bleak; the passion of his nature was concentrated upon action. I do not suppose that he was a likeable man; what is more important, he lived a significant life. It may be that the hardness is in part due to the absence of information. Those all too brief glimpses of him at his cousin Roscarrock's with other friends among the Cornish gentry, playing bowls and 'idling and trifling the time away,' enable us to guess what a picture in the round would be like if the materials existed for it. We have had some glimpses of him as Justice of the Peace at his house, hot-tempered and rough-handed with obstreperous disturbers of the peace, hanging his dial up upon a pole and dispersing a mob of country-people with the gesture – we can imagine with what contempt. For the rest we are to suppose him like his fathers before him, taking his part in all the life of country and town: coursing the hare, flying his falcons, gathering in his wheat in the high corn-fields towards Kilkhampton where he went to church on Sundays, receiving his rents, or sitting over his accounts in the town house on the quay at Bideford, the ships passing in or out of the river beneath his eyes.

In religion also he was a man of his time, and moved with the times. We can be sure that the subject did not arouse his intellectual curiosity as it did Ralegh's very remarkably. In the early years of the Elizabethan settlement these issues were not so clear as they subsequently became; and it may be that he would have preferred then to remain attached to the ways of his fathers, *stare super antiquas vias*. But the movement of the time, like a tide, was too strong for that and with such a man, whose whole instinct was for action. He was no religious *dévot* like the Arundells or Tregian – indeed it is likely that their attitude inspired him with anger and contempt. He was anything but a mystic; he was essentially worldly, finding his satisfaction in the things of this world and judging by its standards.

So was the age – taking its cue from the extraordinary woman who stood at the apex of their society, and had led them to such success. Those who put themselves against that movement became defeatists, or if by instinct men of action, like Parsons, were driven into conspiracy. Grenville went with it, with an increasing conviction as the years went on and the struggle in Europe and upon the high seas developed, giving great outlet to men of action like him, so that in the end he was prepared to die for it. But there is no sign that the religious formula had any inner meaning for him. Of course he had God on his lips, like the rest of them as the years passed and times became more dangerous. But everthing points to this being but form, conventional acceptance of what society in general thought, a simple but sufficient faith. There is not the same personal conviction as Drake and Hawkins had; but they were bourgeois and Puritans. Grenville was an aristocrat: his attitude was more like the Queen's or the Howards'.

Deep down, however, at the root of the man, there was, surely, an element of unbalance, of overstrain. It comes out in his impulsive temper, terrifying to his subordinates, which made him unloved where Drake was adored. It is not without significance that his very first appearance upon the public scene was an act of manslaughter. No doubt it was an accident, and the Elizabethans thought little of an affray; but the rashness, the intemperateness were there, and the determination to see a thing through. One wonders if this overbalance, this nervous strain, may not have been due to the absence of the restraining influence of a father, acting upon a passionate temperament. A young heir, he must have been left a good deal to himself. We do not hear of his guardian concerning himself with him in any way. He must have had to learn to discipline himself by his own experience; the experience was a hard one and we cannot say that it was ever wholly learned. He remained to the end a man with whom passion and pride were the fundamental elements in his character: again, the Elizabethan man. Yet that he did try to subject himself to discipline is equally evident from his public career: the long laborious service to the State in so many fields, and on the whole, as was Elizabeth's way, so little rewarded. Yet there was no word of recrimination or complaint from him that greater reward did not come his way, a fuller share of the dazzling light from the throne so amply permitted to Ralegh, and even, so much more generously than to himself, to Drake. Perhaps he was unattractive to the Queen, a hard man, without gallantry; she may not have felt entire confidence in him, and, shrewd judge of men that she was, she would not have been wrong.

Over so much of his character, as we have analysed it, Grenville is not dissimilar from his fellow-men of action, Ralegh, Drake, Hawkins, Howard. Only in this case there was something added, this element of undependability, of strain: Essex had it too and we know where it led him. There burned in Grenville the same intemperate ardour for action, even though it was less romantic, a headlong taking to a course, and a fixity of will in persisting in it – evident in his pouncing upon Mayne and the Cornish Catholics in 1577, no less than in the end he brought upon himself. That he had the extreme of courage that goes with such a nature, this whole book is evidence of. We know of no occasion when he drew back: clearly he deliberately determined not to, off Flores; and the knowledge that he really intended to blow up his ship rather than surrender, shows what an intensity the flame of that courage had blown into.

Out of such a mixture of qualities is the quality of the heroic made. There *is* the element of the undependable about it, as with genius: some sport of nature. Grenville was not a genius like Ralegh, but he was a hero. In the end, it is by this dæmonic quality of the heroic that he survives to us. He would not have made the indelible impression he has upon the tradition of the English people without that; he would have been but one more Elizabethan commander. As it is, everybody knows the name of Grenville, however few know anything of his life beyond that one solitary action, lighting up the horizon with its dark glow. There is historic justice in that: the sense, the tradition of a nation is a better test of these values than any rational calculation of chances of survival.

335

For it was by this last action alone that Grenville emerged as the legendary hero of Elizabethan sea-warfare. The manner of his death won him that place which he could never have attained to in life. In life, he was disappointed of the opportunities and the good fortune which came to Drake, nor anyhow had he Drake's genius as a commander. It is the irony of fate that by his death, the chief legend in all that legendary time in our history should be his and not after all Drake's, who died quietly enough at sea a few years later and was buried off Portobello in the Spanish Main.

CHAPTER XIX

POSTERITY: EPILOGUE

A MAN's life does not begin, nor does it end with himself. His life is but a link, unless he wills it to be otherwise, between all the generations that went before and those that come after. We have traced with Grenville something of the tradition of his fathers that went to make him the man he was; we must not leave him without a word of what he handed on to the generations succeeding him.

We have to draw together the few threads that are left, concerning Grenville himself. There is no will of Grenville's remaining; he died intestate, yet not without having made certain settlements and arrangements regarding his property which he may have thought sufficient for any contingency. The usual Commission to inquire post-mortem was issued to Sir Richard Bevil and five others on 15 December 1591.[1] The return, which was made at Bodmin on 27 September in the next year, deals with certain properties about which there may have been some uncertainty, outside the main entailed estate at Kilkhampton and Bideford.[2] What is of more interest is that it refers to the settlement not now remaining, which Grenville made on 6 February 1591, for the marriage of his heir Bernard and for the jointure of Lady Mary Grenville his wife. For the latter's benefit, a number of trustees were appointed, including Sir William Bevil and William Langhorne, evidently the Captain of the soldiers on board the *Revenge*, to hold the manors of Kilkhampton, Wolston and Bideford to her use after Grenville's death, and so long as she remained unmarried.

[1] S.P. 38, vol. 2 (Docquet).

[2] Inq. post-mortem. Chancery Series II, vol. 233, no. 119; and for Devonshire property, vol. 237, no. 138.

Lady Mary did not marry again, but lived on to a ripe old age at Bideford where she died in 1623. There were other sorrows yet to come to her, so that it is not surprising that in her will, the only personal document that we have left of her – indeed the only glimpse of her it is possible to obtain – she should speak of her 'departure out of this vale of misery,' a phrase rare in the wills of that time.[1] She affixed her sign to the document, not her signature; so that it is probable she could not write and that may help too to account for the absence of personal letters between her and Grenville. A charitable soul, with the good nature of the St. Legers, she left small legacies to the poor of the parishes of Winkleigh, Broadwood Kelly, Monk Okehampton and Bideford; further small sums to her manservant and three women-servants; a ring to a godson; the rest of her property, houses, land and goods, she bequeathed to her daughters Katherine Abbot and Bridget Grenville. Bridget afterwards married Sir Christopher Harris of Radford, the friend and executor of Drake, through whom the sale of Buckland had been arranged. Their sister Ursula was left in the care and 'under the government and tuition' of Katherine and Bridget, who were to receive her yearly allowance from their brother for her maintenance. She may have been an invalid: victim of the over-nervous strain in the Grenvilles or of the weakness and debility of the St. Legers. She died at Bideford in the same year that Sir Bevil, her famous nephew, was killed at Lansdown.[2]

It is interesting to know that Grenville provided for his son Bernard's marriage, before he left on his last voyage. It was a very eligible match that he had arranged: Elizabeth Bevil of Brinn, in the parish of Withiel, was the sole heiress of her father and eventual heiress of her uncle, Sir William Bevil. The marriage, which took place at Withiel, that little granite church on the edge of the moor overlooking the Camel valley, on 10 July 1592, ten months after Sir Richard's death, brought both Brinn and Killigarth and other properties in mid- and south-Cornwall into the Grenville family.

At the time of his father's death, Bernard was twenty-four.

[1] Exeter Wills J.C. 24/934.   [2] Granville, 123.

His was an unexciting personality: it was as if the land, exhausted by so much energy, such restless spending of itself, lay fallow. He did his duty well enough; he too in his turn became the chief servant of the Crown in Cornwall, and his was a long record of service in a quiet way. In his earlier years, succeeding to his brother's interests in Ireland, he had some experience of Irish affairs and was knighted in 1608. Then, having had, no doubt, more than enough of the troubles and disappointments of Ireland, it was he who slipped the connection; and Sir Richard's Irish estates, upon which such efforts had been expended, came, like so much else in Munster, into the possession of the great Earl of Cork. In the West Country, Sir Bernard was a single-minded and devout supporter of Charles I in all his causes, particularly against Sir John Eliot's immense personal influence which carried over with it into the Opposition, Sir Bernard's own son Bevil. In the end, Sir Bernard's main *raison d'être* seems to have been the begetting of his two sons, Bevil and Richard, the one famous, the other infamous.

Much more exciting than Bernard's is the all too short career of John, Grenville's second son, who must have been a lad after his father's heart. Grenville took him with him in the contingent of ships that he brought round from Bideford to Plymouth to serve against the Armada; and John commanded the *Virgin God Save Her* in those anxious, glorious days. At the time of his father's death, he was serving in the Low Countries, taking hold, as Carew says, 'of every martial occasion that was ministered him.' [1] Next year, we find him in Ireland, whither he had gone to enter upon his patrimony; which makes it clear that Grenville's aim in his Irish ventures was to provide an estate for his second son. The difficulties there were as great as ever, the discouragements as sickening, the situation intractable.

Sir Warham St. Leger and John Grenville, who had succeeded his father in the partnership, were driven to appeal to Burghley to permit them to enjoy their seignory of Kirry whirry. [2] The Commissioners who were surveying the land settlement of Munster had granted away 39 ploughlands out of the 56 in their seignory. Out of the whole there remained to

[1] Carew, 176.   [2] S.P. Ireland Eliz. 167, no. 37.

them only some 15½. Yet the lands had been mortgaged by Desmond to St. Leger and Grenville, upon a statute of £7,000; and without regarding that, £8,000 had been spent within the last six years in bringing people over and settling them upon the land, besides the losses that they had sustained in the Fitz-maurice and Desmond rebellions. They ask Burghley to consider Sir Warham's old age and long service,

'and then to think on the sudden death of Sir Richard in her Majesty's service, whereby his youngest son, your poor suppliant, had not left him any other portion but this poor Irish patrimony to live on, being also at the time of his death in her Majesty's service, in the Low Countries, where he performed the part of a faithful soldier. Neither hath he any means to relieve himself if this be taken from him.'

Sir Warham added a postscript:

'I most humbly beseech you to consider of the estate of your poor suppliant, Sir Richard Grenville's son, whose father even to the end, carried a true testimony of his loyal mind towards his prince and country, as the world generally doth witness . . . and that you will vouchsafe to have that remorse of him as that he may be the better encouraged to good actions and be able to relieve himself as the son of him who lived and died her Majesty's most loyal and vowed soldier and servant; or otherwise he shall be driven to wander as a distressed soul to seek his relief, which were a case most lamentable.'

Nor was this the end of their troubles. It is a mistake to suppose that most people made anything out of the attempt to settle and civilise that unhappy country: far more frequently fortunes were swallowed up in its bogs, legal and political no less than physical. It is clear that Grenville had overspent himself on the Irish venture and made nothing but losses by it. He would have been better off if he had stayed at home. Later on we find Sir Bevil Grenville complaining against the burdens laid upon the estate by his 'wasteful predecessors.'

Is it any wonder that life in Ireland did not appeal to John Grenville? That same year, 1593, we find him at sea, serving as a captain in the fleet set out by Ralegh to watch off Spain and the Azores for the great East Indian carracks.[1] Two great ships of the Queen, the *Garland* and the *Foresight* were of the company. The fleet was divided into two squadrons; John Grenville being on board the *Garland* under Frobisher which was detailed to watch off the Spanish coast; the other squadron, under Sir John Borough, off the Azores captured the *Madre de Dios*, the richest carrack ever brought to these shores, and burned another, the *Santa Cruz*. Two years later the young Grenville joined Ralegh's great expedition for the discovery of Guiana: the first voyage of exploration which Ralegh was to lead himself, and the beginning of that life-long preoccupation with the idea of an English Empire in South America which brought him to his end.

In the superb account which Ralegh wrote of the voyage, we frequently hear of John Grenville in the forefront of adventure, exploring the numerous and intricate channels of those great rivers, going sometimes forward in the galley-boat with Ralegh himself ('my cousin John Grenville'), sometimes coasting along the fever-laden river-banks in the barge; but always with a gallant company of west-countrymen whom Ralegh's call had brought forth to the adventure: his cousin young Gilbert, Captain Thynne, or Captain Whiddon, Butshead Gorges or William Connock, or Captain Facey, his father's friend.[2] So that there were west-country faces around him to the last; for though Ralegh does not tell us how, upon this voyage he died, and, as Carew says, 'under the command of Sir Walter Ralegh, the ocean became his bed of honour.'

So much for the family which Grenville begot; his son and successor, Sir Bernard, had a long and peaceful reign, and did not die until well on in the reign of Charles I, in 1636. The specific qualities of the Grenville character remained latent with him; he was not at all venturesome, but rather a stay-at-home; so far from being passionate, he was inclined to be easy-going, good-tempered, pacific; something of an antiquarian. Only the devotion to duty was there. There was no doubt also the living influence of his father's heroic quality, of his life of

[1] Hakluyt VII, 108.   [2] Hakluyt X, 350, 396, 403, 417, 422.

service to the state, ever present with the family and increasing its hold on the mind of later generations. It is a thing in its nature intangible, impossible to calculate.

But we have something more striking, and more certain, in the family's heredity. It is remarkable how the Grenville qualities come out in the second generation, with Bevil and Richard, Grenville's grandchildren, and how they seem to bifurcate into these two. All the best qualities of Grenville, the adventurousness, the high mettle, the devotion to duty, with an added tenderness and charm which made him a figure so poetic and appealing, went into Bevil; and all the bad into Richard, intensified to such a degree that he becomes a caricature of his grandfather. His temper made him impossible to live with; he quarrelled with everybody; his acquisitiveness was such that in the Civil Wars he embarked on a career of high-handed plundering on the grand scale; the harshness and unbalance of the man came near to insanity. Yet he was a good soldier. He had courage, and, being a Grenville, could somehow carry off all the bravado and swagger. When he was deposed from his command by the Prince's Council in the west in 1645, Hyde was astonished to find that in spite of all his depredations and his consistent record of oppression, the country people besieged the Prince on his retreat through the west with petitions to pardon and release him. So high stood the name of the Grenvilles in the west country in the darkest days of defeat for their cause!

That their name stood so high in the land was due to Bevil Grenville, the 'most generally loved man' in the west. His was a nature singularly gallant and lovely. He had not always been on the King's side; as a young man, he had been Sir John Eliot's closest friend and supporter: Eliot, with that fascination he must have had, exercised an empire over his mind. As the years went on (Eliot now dead), and it became clearer that the ancient foundations of the monarchy were being challenged by the Parliamentarian party, Bevil Grenville, like many of the choicest spirits in the country, like Hyde and Falkland, came over to the King. They were the heart and soul of the King's cause, and not all the Endymion Porters, the Finches and

Windebanks. When the war with Scotland came, Bevil Grenville wrote:

'I cannot contain myself within my doors when the King of England's standard waves in the field upon so just occasion: the cause being such as must make all those that die in it little inferior to martyrs. And for mine own part, I desire to acquire an honest name or an honourable grave. I never loved my life or ease so much as to shun such an occasion, which if I should, I were unworthy of the profession I have held as to succeed those ancestors of mine who have so many of them sacrificed their life for their country.'

Such was the spirit in which Sir Bevil answered the call in the King's hour of still greater need with the outbreak of the Civil War. His services to the Royalist cause in the west were inestimable. He was the first to raise the King's standard there and to call his friends and tenantry to arms; his influence in the country was enormous. He it was who, with Hopton, organised the royalist forces and made such a wonderful fighting instrument of the Cornish foot. He led them to victory at Braddock Down, Stratton and Lansdown, where at the last he fell; on the battlefield his young son John was lifted on to his charger to lead his men. But with his death, the heart went out of the cause; and with the terrible decimations which the Cornish army suffered at Roundway Down and the siege of Bristol, even though victorious, they ceased to be the fighting force they had been. Bevil Grenville had not, as his brother Richard had done, received any training as a soldier. But he was a born leader of men, an instinctive soldier, all the fighting qualities of his race came out in him, pure and unadulterated with any selfish passion. As the historian of that splendid moment in the history of the Cornish people has said: 'his death, in the moment of victory for a cause in which he believed implicitly, was happy.' [1]

There were other qualities too, very endearing, in Bevil Grenville's nature: his affectionateness to his friends, the concern he felt for them in their troubles, the love that passed between him and his wife, so that they were never happy away from each

---

[1] M. Coate, *Cornwall in the Civil War*, 88.

other. A few years after they were married, about 1625, they went to live at Stowe, which Sir Bernard handed over to them, himself retiring for the last ten years of his life to one of his other Cornish houses, Killigarth or Brinn.[1] Bevil in these early years was much engaged in repairing and rebuilding at Stowe, making walls for sheltered closes, planting trees, buying pictures and carpets for the house. His wife writes to him while he was away in London attending Parliament: 'Your case of pictures was loose and almost open, before I had it, and the King's and Sir John Eliot's hath received some hurt in carriage, but none since it came hither. I pray you make haste and come home, so God keep you well and be not angry with me.' Or Bevil writes home: 'Your beds are amaking, and some Turkey work for stools and chairs I have seen, but not yet bargained for; it is very dear, but if money hold out I will have them'; with a post-script: 'Charge Postlett and Hooper that they keep out the pigs and all other things out of my new nursery and the other orchard too. Let them use any means to keep them safe, or my trees will be all spoiled if they come in, which I would not for a world.' Or he sends home a box of dried sweetmeats to his wife, the best that he can get, of all sorts saving only apricots: 'The note of particulars is herein enclosed, wanting only one box of the Quidiniock, which I have eaten.'

Then there are more important matters to worry him: money, Sir John Eliot's imprisonment, or his son Dick's wasting his time at Oxford. To the latter he writes recommending him to keep to his logic and his Aristotle, and to give over reading so much history and poetry:

'I am my self in this very point a woeful example; I pray God you be not such too. I was left to my own discretion when I was a youth in Oxford, and so fell upon the sweet delight of reading Poetry and History, in such sort as I troubled no other books, and do find my self so infinitely defective by it, when I come to manage any occasions of weight, as I would give a limb it were otherwise.'

But Dick went his own way, even as Bevil himself had gone his

[1] For following paragraphs cf. Granville, and *Dict. Nat. Biog.*

against his father; and we find him writing to his wife later: 'He shall stand or fall by his own judgment for mine is despised by him' – a frequent sentiment with fathers. Then, a year or two, and the lad was dead.

The Civil War sweeps down upon them all; Bevil is caught up into it from the first, every moment occupied, and yet has time to write to his wife of the progress of their arms. He sends her immediate news of the first Cavalier victory at Braddock Down; how the night before 'we could march no further than Boconnock Park where (upon my Lord Mohun's kind motion) we quartered all our Army by good fires under the hedge.' In the midst of these employments he thinks of his orchards at Stowe and remembers to send home graftings of fruit trees: 'I did send home some pear grafts from Truro about Michaelmas; let them be carefully grafted also, and note which is one and which the other.'

It is very fortunate that these letters, at least, have been preserved, giving us the details, intimate and trifling, by which we may reconstruct the picture of their daily life. Lady Grace's letters are no less charming than his, with her 'Sweet Mr. Grenville' answering his 'Dear Love.' It is only by these fragments that remain, and sometimes when one looks upon their memorials in the quiet Cornish churches, the seasons racing by outside the windows, that one has a sudden apprehension of these men and women long dead and of what they were when they were alive, going about the countryside on their concerns. In those moments, it is as if one were listening to the beating of their hearts, and they all the more intimate and moving, being dead.

All was very different with Sir Richard, Bevil's brother. His was the life of a turbulent soldier; we are back in an earlier Grenville atmosphere, earlier and coarser. Richard began life fighting in the Palatinate and the Netherlands: the Thirty Years' War is the background against which to see him. Then he served in the various unsuccessful expeditions of Buckingham, to Cadiz and the Isle of Rhé; he was knighted and appointed to command a regiment against Rochelle. Through Buckingham's influence, too, he was married to a rich Devonshire widow, the daughter of Sir John Fitz of Fitzford, widow of Sir Charles Howard. The pair were not unequally matched; the one was a brute, and the other a vixen, and no better than she should be into the bargain. Needless to say, their married life was one prolonged contest, in which, in the end the lady came off best. For by the Howard influence, Grenville was ruined at law by being fined large sums for insulting the family. He went abroad; but on the outbreak of the Irish Rebellion took service there. He fought energetically, bravely, savagely. In 1643 he returned.

Since he had not declared himself for either King or Parliament, the latter invited him to London, made much of him, thanked him for his services, paid his arrears in full and gave him command of a troop of horse. The plan for a surprise attack on Basing House was also confided to him. Equipped with this, with a troop of horse and £600, he drove out of London in coach and six – and straight to Oxford to place himself under the King's orders. Parliament was furious, not unnaturally; he was proclaimed 'traitor, rogue, villain and skellum' and a gibbet was set up for him in Palace Yard. Henceforth, he was always called Skellum Grenville in all their proclamations and excepted by name from those malignants who might be pardoned, in all negotiations set on foot by Parliament. It seems he had a pretty sense of humour. The Royalists were vastly amused: 'O credulous Parliament!' one of their newsletters wrote, 'If Sir Richard Grenville was indeed a Red Fox, what were the sagacious ones who hearkened to him?'

Within a few days of his arrival at Oxford, he was given a command in the West and was particularly charged with the siege of Plymouth. Operations around Plymouth lasted for the rest of the war and the town never capitulated. But one of the consequences of this charge was that Grenville took up his residence at Buckland Abbey; the Drakes were Parliamentarians and driven out of possession. So once more, for a brief period, a Grenville ruled at Buckland: a curious ghostly harking-back to an earlier period in its history. The King sequestrated the estate to him, and with it also the large estates of the Earl of Bedford and then Lord Robartes. Sir Richard now ruled with a high hand; during the last years of the Royalist cause in the West, he was the leading west-countryman on the spot and that gave him a popular hold in spite of all his misdeeds. He hanged the solicitor who had conducted his wife's case in the Star-Chamber: that was a good joke, to him. His quarrels with the other commanders were incessant; he was at daggers drawn with Hyde, the leading member of the Prince's Council, a sort of Royalist Prime Minister ('So fat a Hide ought to be well tanned,' he wrote); and when he was at length laid by the heels, the whole West Country rose up in protest. When the débacle came, he was permitted to get away from St. Michael's Mount, where he had been confined; he escaped to France and there died, after further recriminations with Hyde and being at length forbidden to come into the Prince's presence. This he took very seriously, became a misanthrope – of which he had the makings already; shut himself up and died two years before his Majesty's happy Restoration, which might have recovered him.

In bringing about the Restoration, the Grenvilles had a very significant, if necessarily backstairs part. Sir Bevil Grenville had left two sons, John and Bernard. John, though very young, fought on in the Civil War, his father's heir; he was severely wounded, in fact left for dead, at the second battle of Newbury, when only sixteen. On the execution of the King, he left the country for Jersey, whence he sailed to assume the command of the Scilly Islands, which were held in force for Charles. For two years he maintained himself here, building up a formidable force of privateers – again a harking back to an old family tradition – which preyed upon the shipping and trade of the Commonwealth. At last, the Islands had to be reduced; but it took a large force under Blake, with the help of the Dutch under van Tromp, to do it. By the articles of surrender, Grenville was permitted to visit Charles abroad and then to return. This he did, made his submission, lived on at Stowe helping Charles financially all he could and with his finger in every western conspiracy against the Protectorate.

It so happened that Grenville was on close terms of intimacy with the Monks – they were cousins of his, a Devonshire family; of whom one, George Monk, was a Cromwellian general, left in a dominating position at the head of the army by Cromwell's death. John Grenville established contact with the General in these uncertain decisive days, 1658–9, through Nicholas Monk, the General's brother, whom he had presented to the living of Kilkhampton. Grenville himself made the contacts with Charles II abroad; and after a long period of negotiation, Monk's going over to the King's side enabled the Restoration to be brought about.

This small group was, of course, richly rewarded by the King on his return, and remained in high favour and influence throughout his reign. Monk was given a dukedom: he became Duke of Albemarle. Charles I had intended to make Sir Bevil an Earl for his services; they were rewarded now in the person of his son, who became Earl of Bath, Viscount Lansdowne and Baron Grenville of Kilkhampton. This was the hey-day of the Grenvilles; it rained titles upon them. Now was the time when the great rococo legend was fabricated, of their descent from the Earls of Granville in Normandy: the inflated and bogus antiquarianism which so much appealed to later generations of Grenvilles, and so aroused the ire of the learned Dr. Round. Very ridiculously, they changed the spelling of their name to Granville. The new Earl of Bath was given permission to use the titles of Earl of Corbeil, Thorigny and Granville 'as his ancestors had done.' They had a good enough Norman descent without this absurdity. Bath maintained throughout Charles's life a position of very intimate friendship with the King. As first gentleman of the bedchamber and Groom of the Stole, he was constantly with the King; and when Charles on his death-bed was received into the Roman Church, Bath and Feversham were the only Protestants admitted into the room.[1]

In the west, the Earl's position was tremendous and beyond comparison; for the time, at any rate, the Grenvilles had outsoared all competitors. At the very beginning of the reign, he had been made Steward of the Duchy of Cornwall, of all the castles and other offices belonging to it, and Rider of Dartmoor Forest. A little later he was made Lord-Lieutenant of the county and Lord Warden of the Stannaries. Then, in addition to his offices at Court, he became Captain and Governor of

---

[1] cf. the vivid description of the scene in Bryant, *Charles II*, 368–9.

Plymouth, with the castle and fort. To this period belongs the building of the Citadel overlooking Plymouth Hoe, with the great gate which we still see with the Earl of Bath's arms over it, the famous (if obscure) Grenville clarions. Further promotions and appointments were still to come. Perhaps the most interesting in view of Sir Richard Grenville's part in first planting an English colony in Virginia, was the constitution of Carolina, all the country between Albemarle Sound and the river St. John, into a colony under eight Lords Proprietors, of whom Bath was one and Albemarle another. The Grenville connection with Carolina was maintained after Bath's death by his second son, John, who was created Baron Granville by Queen Anne and was also a Lord Proprietor. He died without issue in 1707, his title lapsing with him.

But there was a certain insecurity in the foundation of this too exalted position; the fact was that the Grenvilles were not a rich family, and their estates were not adequate to support such grandeur. Much of their wealth must have been drained generation after generation from the time of Sir Richard for their various enterprises and their costly services to the Crown. It was only right that the Crown should recoup them, and Charles did his best by making Bath a number of grants, various fees, the grant of deodands and felons' goods in certain Cornish manors, the agency for issuing wine-licences, a lease of the duties on the pre-emption and coinage of tin in Devon and Cornwall – some £3,000 a year which was later charged upon the revenue from tin and made a grant to him and his heirs in perpetuity. Fortified by these grants, Bath embarked upon pulling down the old medieval mansion at Stowe which had served so many generations of Grenvilles, and putting up a superb great classical building in the new style in brick. It was sumptuously furnished, wainscoted with cedar.

What all this ostentation ignored, was that the position depended so much upon royal favour. With James II, who resented Bath's stubborn Protestantism, it was withdrawn. Nor was the position ultimately made any better by the Revolution of 1688, though Bath after long hesitation threw in his lot with the Prince of Orange; for the Grenvilles were far too much bound up with the loyalist cause and with the exiled Stuarts, to feel happy under Dutch William. Moreover, the Earl received a bitter disappointment over the dukedom of Albemarle. It had always been understood that the dukedom should devolve upon the Grenvilles, on the failure of heirs to the Monks. Charles II had made a promise to that effect, but he was of course unable to commit his successors. It was the wish of the second and last Duke, who died in 1688, a hopeless drunkard and without children, that his cousins should succeed to his title and property. Bath spent the next seven years trying to make good his claim to the latter, upon which enormous sums were spent at law. Then in 1696 the Albemarle title was suddenly granted by William III to his friend Keppel.

The Grenvilles were bitterly mortified; the dream, or rather the confident expectation, of a dukedom was disappointed, their estate burdened, and in his last years Bath was made to resign his lord-lieutenancies and some of his other appointments. This was the position to which his heir, Lord Lansdowne, succeeded; it is said that when he learnt the full facts of the position, a fortnight after his father's death, he shot himself, and both were carried down to Cornwall and buried the same day at Kilkhampton. The only significant thing in the young Lansdowne's life was that he served, like his great ancestor before him, in the wars of Austria and Hungary against the Turk; he fought in the last siege of Vienna, among the foreign contingents under John Sobieski who delivered the city when it was at its last gasp in 1683. For his services he was created a Count of the Holy Roman Empire.

He left a young son, William Henry, who became third Earl. He also took to the profession of his family, and quite young, fought two campaigns in Flanders. While he was on one of these, his cousin George Granville, wrote a long letter of advice to the young head of the family, which, sententious though it is, like everything that George Granville wrote, is remarkably interesting as expressing the Grenvilles' conception of their family and of its place and duty in the west.

'You are placed at the head of a body of gentry entirely disposed in affection to you and your family . . . You are upon an uncommon foundation in that part of the world, your ancestors for at least five hundred years never made any alliance, male or female, out of Western Counties. Thus there is hardly a gentleman either in Cornwall or Devon but has some of your blood, or you some of theirs. I remember the first time I accompanied your grandfather into the West, upon holding his Parliament of Tinners as Warden of the Stannaries, when there was the most numerous appearance of gentry of both counties that had ever been remembered together. I observed there was hardly anyone but whom he called cousin, and I could not but observe at the same time how well they were pleased with it. Let this be a lesson for you when it comes to your turn to appear amongst them . . .

'There is another particular in my opinion of no small consequence to the support of your interest, which I would recommend to your imitation: and that is to make Stowe your principal residence. I have heard your grandfather say that, if ever he lived to be possessed of New Hall, he would pull it down that your father might have no temptation to withdraw from the ancient seat of his family. From the Conquest to the Restoration your Ancestors constantly resided amongst their country men, except when the public service called upon them to sacrifice their lives for it. Stowe in my grandfather's time till the Civil Wars broke out was a kind of academy for all young men of family in the country; he provided himself with the best masters of all kinds for education, and the children of his neighbours and friends shared the advantage of his own. Thus he in a manner became the father of his country, and not only engaged the affection of the present generation but laid a foundation of friendship for posterity, which is not worn out at this day.' [1]

Alas, that such good advice should have been of no effect, on either point! For it never came to the young Earl's turn to appear amongst the gentry of the west-country like his grandfather. The very next year he died on service in Flanders under

---

[1] Granville, 397–8.

Marlborough; and within ten years Stowe was pulled down and the materials all sold, the place made desolate. It is said – and it is quite credible – that a man of Stratton remembered the place where Bath built his great house, a little away from the old one, first a cornfield, and then a cornfield again forty years after. The egregious woman who was responsible for this was the Countess Granville, created so in her own right in 1714, daughter, and a coheiress, of the first Earl.

The male line continued for some time longer in the descendants of Bernard Granville, Sir Bevil's second surviving son, Bath's brother. Bernard's eldest son, another Bevil, served in the army in the Low Countries, there fought a duel in which he killed his man, the Marquis de Rada; was made Governor of the Barbadoes under Anne and died of fever at sea on his way home in 1706. His brother George, Lord Lansdowne, was one of the peers created by the Tories in 1711 to secure a majority in the House of Lords. He had a somewhat variegated, but dilettante, career in politics and literature. Like his uncle, Denis Granville, Dean of Durham, Lansdowne was a Jacobite; the Dean went into exile for the sake of the Stuarts, but had the satisfaction of living at Corbeil for the sake of his 'ancestors,' where he died. Lansdowne compromised, and led an active political career under Queen Anne; but this was ruined with the accession of the Hanoverians and he took to literature: an unattractive frigid figure, from whom all the Grenville fire had departed, an unpleasant mixture of the pompous and the frivolous. Indeed the male line, with such a fearful mortality in the early years of the century, what with deaths by fever and by their own hand, like the deaths on the field of battle or at sea in earlier generations, was becoming exhausted. A certain rigidity, a lack of the old *élan*, becomes noticeable with the men of the stock; the talent and the attractiveness come out only in the women.

There remained only Bernard Granville's third son, another Bernard, who had any boys to carry on the line. This second Bernard also served in the wars in Flanders and accompanied his eldest brother, the Governor of the Barbadoes, to the West Indies; on his return he became Lieut.-Governor of Hull. But his only significance was in his children; for he was the father of the vivacious and universally admired Mary Granville, subsequently Mrs. Delany. She was one of the most attractive of all the Grenville women, witty, clever, kind-hearted and of the most exquisite manner and breeding; rather a highbrow: the friend and correspondent of Wesley (she was Aspasia to his Cyrus), of Pope and of Swift in his later years. She was a counterpart among all the later Grenville women, the only one who is comparable in attractiveness and vitality to Lady Lisle among the earlier. When she was a very old woman, she became the close friend of George III and Queen Charlotte: their simple and unaffected kindness to her was one of the most charming features in their rather dreary domesticity.

There were two brothers of Mary Granville's; Bernard the third and Bevil. The latter was a clergyman, and died without progeny – at least without any legitimate progeny. The former, Bernard, was the last male heir of the Grenvilles. He began in the army, but on the death of his uncle, Lord Lansdowne, who seems to have had an affection for him and left him his heir, he retired. About the same time, he benefited considerably by the death, at last, of the old Duchess of Albemarle who had caused the Earl of Bath so much trouble a generation before; her property was divided between the Countess Granville, Lord Gower and Bernard Granville as the heirs of Lord Bath, though the old lady had lived till 1734 to spite them all.

With his considerable fortune, Bernard Granville bought an estate in Staffordshire, Calwich Abbey. His desertion of Cornwall after so many centuries of the Grenville connection has something peculiar in it; and it is said that a disappointment in love, while he was staying there with his sister Mary, then Mrs. Pendarves, turned him against the place and soured his disposition. Certainly he never married, and he was a queer character for the Grenvilles to come to an end with. He was accomplished and well-bred, a musician and a connoisseur of pictures. Among his few close friends were Jean Jacques Rousseau, while the latter lived in this country, and Handel who was a frequent visitor at Calwich, where an organ was built for him by Father Smith and where a magnificent collection of his original manuscripts accumulated, along with the rare antiquarian books, the choice pictures and family portraits.

But there was another side to his nature. He was stern and unbending, unloving and unlovable in character. He had all the family haughtiness and family pride; he never forgave his spirited and charming sister for her marriage to Dr. Delany. The old Countess Granville gave Mary and her husband a *mauvais quart d'heure* when they went to call on her; they literally stopped there no longer than a quarter of an hour. Bernard kept up his resentment throughout the rest of his life; and though he liked corresponding with his sister, he would not have her near him when he lay dying. Mary wrote of him that his unhappiness was due 'to a temper never properly subdued'; the last of the Granvilles was evidently a true Grenville.

Upon the death of the young William Henry, last Earl of Bath, his aunts, Lady Leveson-Gower and Lady Carteret (afterwards Countess Granville) laid claim to the estates. It would seem that Lord Lansdowne had a better claim, but as he was a prisoner in the Tower at the time, he was glad to accept a composition for £30,000. The estates in the West Country, instead of descending in the male line, thus descended in the female line; the Gowers and through them the Sutherlands, got the Devonshire property, and the Carterets the Cornish. It is through the latter that the Thynnes inherited what remains of the Grenville lands in Cornwall, mostly in the parish of Kilkhampton and including the site of Stowe. Through the various lines of female descent, the Grenville blood has disseminated itself through the peerage: the Sutherlands, Ellesmeres, Granvilles, Dysarts, Baths and Spencers. The last Bernard Granville, the last male branch, are represented by the Granvilles of Wellesbourne, who descend from Anne Granville, Mrs. Delany's younger sister, who married into the D'Ewes family which took the name of Granville. Last there are the far-flung relationships of the west-country gentry, among whom the Stucleys of Hartland represent the chief female Grenville descent.

But it should not be forgotten that in the numerous and fascinating clan of Cornish Grenfells – the spelling is an indication of how the Grenvilles pronounced their name in earlier centuries – the male stock in its junior line going back to the time of Sir Richard Grenville of the *Revenge*, though not to the hero himself, goes on. The Grenvilles were a very prolific family in the fifteenth and early sixteenth century; and it is from that time that the numerous Grenfells scattered over Cornwall, and to be met with beyond, descend. It is astonishing how faithfully too they reproduce the family characteristics, for they have been mostly fighters, adventurers, explorers. And in the last generation, their exploits in capturing peerages – three of them, the Grenfell, Desborough and St. Just peerages – almost equal those of the Granvilles at the Restoration. But the dominant note has been that of fighting and adventuring. A family which has produced in short space Admiral Grenfell of the Brazilian exploits, Grenfell of the Congo, explorer and missionary, Field-Marshal Lord Grenfell, and Grenfell of Labrador, remains true to type.

And never was it truer than in producing those fighting men, the soldier-sons of Lord Desborough, Julian and Billy Grenfell, both killed in the War. Julian Grenfell was the incarnation of the fighting-man, as much as Sir Richard Grenville himself.

'I *adore* War,' he wrote home from the Front. 'I have never felt so well, or so happy, or enjoyed anything so much. It just suits my stolid health, and stolid nerves, and barbaric disposition. The fighting-excitement vitalizes everything, every sight and word and action. One loves one's fellow-man so much more when one is bent on killing him.' [1]

It is what so many generations of Grenvilles felt, though they could not have put it in words: Sir Richard, Marshal of Calais, Roger drowned in the *Mary Rose*, his son Richard killed in the Azores, John who died at sea upon Ralegh's expedition to Guiana, Sir Bevil killed at Lansdown in the Civil War, the young Earl who died in Flanders fighting under Marlborough and his cousin who died at sea on his way home from the Barbadoes. It is curious to reflect that so many centuries should have passed and then the spirit of the family achieve belated expression in Julian Grenfell's poem:

[1] *War Letters of Fallen Englishmen*, 117–18.

The fighting man shall from the sun
  Take warmth, and life from the glowing earth;
Speed with the light-foot winds to run,
  And with the trees to newer birth;
And find when fighting shall be done,
  Great rest, and fullness after dearth . . .

And when the burning moment breaks,
  And all things else are out of mind,
And only joy of battle takes
  Him by the throat, and makes him blind,

Through joy and blindness he shall know,
  Not caring much to know, that still
Nor lead nor steel shall reach him, so
  That it be not the Destined Will.

The thundering line of battle stands,
  And in the air death moans and sings;
But Day shall clasp him with strong hands,
  And Night shall fold him in soft wings.

On the day on which his poem was published, his death in
France was announced, leaving, as so often before in the history
of the Grenvilles, a place desolate and empty. What does it all
mean? one asks, reading his poem and his letters glorying in war,
or casting back over all that history; to what purpose?

In the end, one comes to rest upon the place they all sprang
from, no less empty and desolate. There are the *emplacements*
where the last house stood, there are even portions of its brick
foundations, the levelled spaces beneath the grass where the
terraces were. But beyond those empty spaces through which
passed so much crowded life for so long a time, the country has
not much changed. There it is, just as Sir Richard surely saw
it in his mind's eye in those last hours in the Azores: the corn-
fields are still there and something of the orchards; below are
the woods of Coombe, in the east the tower of Kilkhampton
church putting a term to the horizon, and in the west, the sea.

INDEX

INDEX